Ronald O. Moore

—Mar '??

W9-ABJ-446

EARLY MODERN
EUROPE

AN OXFORD HISTORY

EDITED BY

EUAN CAMERON

OXFORD
UNIVERSITY PRESS

Oxford University Press, Great Clarendon Street, Oxford OX2 6DP

Oxford New York

Athens Auckland Bangkok Bogotá Buenos Aires Calcutta
Cape Town Chennai Dar es Salaam Delhi Florence Hong Kong Istanbul
Karachi Kuala Lumpur Madras Madrid Melbourne Mexico City Mumbai
Nairobi Paris São Paulo Singapore Taipei Tokyo Toronto Warsaw

and associated companies in
Berlin Ibadan

Oxford is a trade mark of Oxford University Press

Published in the United States
by Oxford University Press Inc., New York

© Oxford University Press 1999

British Library Cataloguing in Publication Data
Data available

Library of Congress Cataloging in Publication Data
Early Modern Europe
Edited by Euan Cameron   p. cm.
Includes bibliographical references and index.
ISBN 0-19-820528-7
1. Europe—History—1492–1648.   2. Europe—History—17th century.
3. Europe—History—18th century.   I. Cameron, Euan.
D228.E187 1999
940.2—dc21 98-26115 CIP

1 3 5 7 9 10 8 6 4 2

Typeset by Hope Services (Abingdon) Ltd.
Printed in the United States

CONTENTS

LIST OF ILLUSTRATIONS

LIST OF CONTRIBUTORS

JEREMY BLACK is Professor of History in the University of Exeter, and has published widely on seventeenth- and eighteenth-century history. His recent books include *A Military Revolution? Military Change and European Society, 1550–1800* (1991) and *European Warfare, 1660–1815* (1994). He has also edited *The Origins of War in Early Modern Europe* (1987).

T. C. W. BLANNING is Professor of Modern European History in the University of Cambridge. His books on the French revolutionary period include *The Origins of the French Revolutionary Wars* (1986), *The French Revolution: Class War or Culture Clash?* (1997), and *The French Revolutionary Wars 1787–1802* (1996). He is also the editor of *The Oxford Illustrated History of Modern Europe* (1996).

ROBIN BRIGGS is Senior Research Fellow at All Souls College, Oxford, and has published on both science and religion in the seventeenth century. His recent publications include *Communities of Belief: Cultural and Social Tensions in Early Modern France* (1989), and *Witches and Neighbours* (1996).

EUAN CAMERON is Professor of Early Modern History in the University of Newcastle upon Tyne. His publications include *The Reformation of the Heretics: The Waldenses of the Alps 1480–1580* (1984) and *The European Reformation* (1991).

STEVEN GUNN is Fellow and Tutor in Modern History at Merton College, Oxford. He is the author of *Charles Brandon, Duke of Suffolk, c.1484–1545* (1988), and *Early Tudor Government, 1485–1558* (1995), and the editor, with P. G. Lindley, of *Cardinal Wolsey: Church, State, and Art* (1991).

NORMAN HAMPSON is Emeritus Professor of History in the University of York. His many books on the eighteenth century include *The Enlightenment* (1968), *The First European Revolution, 1776–1815* (1969), *Danton* (1978), *Prelude to Terror: The Constituent Assembly and the Failure of Consensus, 1789–1791* (1988), and *Saint-Just* (1991).

R. A. HOUSTON is Professor of Early Modern History in the University of St Andrews. His publications include *Scottish Literacy and the Scottish Identity: Illiteracy and Society in Scotland and Northern England, 1600–1800* (1985), *Literacy in Early Modern Europe: Culture and Education, 1500–1800* (1988), *The Population History of Britain and Ireland 1500–1750* (1992), and *Social Change in the Age of Enlightenment: Edinburgh, 1660–1760* (1994).

ANTHONY PAGDEN is Harry C. Black Professor of History at Johns Hopkins University. His recent books include *Spanish Imperialism and the Political Imagination, 1513–1830* (1990), *European Encounters with the New World: From*

Renaissance to Romanticism (1993), and *Lords of all the Worlds: Ideologies of Empire in Spain, Britain and France c.1500–c.1850* (1995).

JAMES C. RILEY is Professor of History at Indiana University, Bloomington. His publications include *The Seven Years War and the Old Regime in France: The Economic and Financial Toll* (1986), *The Eighteenth-Century Campaign to avoid Disease* (1987), and *Sickness, Recovery, and Death: A History and Forecast of Ill Health* (1989).

ALISON ROWLANDS is Lecturer in History in the University of Essex. She specializes in the social history of sixteenth- and seventeenth-century Germany. Her publications include 'Witchcraft and Popular Religion in Early Modern Rothenburg ob der Tauber', in R. W. Scribner and T. Johnson (eds.), *Popular Religion in Germany and Central Europe, 1400–1800* (1996), and ' "In Great Secrecy": The Crime of Infanticide in Rothenburg ob der Tauber, 1501–1618', in *German History* (1997).

H. M. SCOTT is Senior Lecturer in History in the University of St Andrews. He is the author of *British Foreign Policy in the Age of the American Revolution* (1990), and, with Derek Mckay, of *The Rise of the Great Powers, 1648–1815* (1983). He is editor of *Enlightened Absolutism: Reform and Reformers in Later Eighteenth-Century Europe* (1989), and of *The European Nobilities in the Seventeenth and Eighteenth Centuries* (1995).

EDITOR'S ACKNOWLEDGEMENTS

The suggestion for an illustrated history of early modern Europe originated with the Oxford University Press; I thank the Delegates and successive History Editors, Tony Morris and Ruth Parr, for their constant support and encouragement. The preparation of an illustrated book requires considerable collective effort from the publisher's production staff: thanks are due to all at Oxford, but especially to Anne Gelling, and the picture researcher, Anne Lyons. The matrix around which the book is organized is, however, my own, and responsibility for whatever limitations this has imposed on the themes covered rests with me alone. Any attempt to write the history of three centuries of a crucial phase in Europe's history will involve an unusually large measure of selection and compression. My hopes for this book are that the selection process may be at least clear and transparent, and that the whole text may offer a coherent vision, filtered through the insights of eleven diverse historians.

My ten fellow-authors have made the composition of this book into a true journey of intellectual discovery. All have responded to the challenge to write in this format with verve and commitment. They have handled my editorial interventions with unfailing courtesy and infinite patience, and have been in every sense collaborators rather than contributors. It is a pleasure to record my thanks to them here. The owners of copyright material used in illustrations are acknowledged elsewhere; here I add only my general thanks for their cooperation and assistance.

E.C.

Gosforth
July 1997

EDITOR'S INTRODUCTION

EUAN CAMERON

Historians use the term 'early modern', without thinking and without ambiguity, to describe the period which falls roughly between the end of the Middle Ages and the start of the nineteenth century. Yet to those who are not historians, the term may seem paradoxical or even contradictory. 'Early modern' is a description born of hindsight. It assumes that European culture was travelling towards something called 'modernity', but had not yet reached its goal: that the journey was begun, but not finished. One does not need to be a historian to see the dangers in reading events from their outcome back to their source in this way. The people of the sixteenth to eighteenth centuries did not think that they were living in an 'early modern' period. The more optimistic intellectuals among them at times thought that they were living in an age of restored culture, an 'age of gold', or an 'age of reason'. The more dourly religious feared that they were living in the last age of the world, the era of Antichrist, under the shadow of the coming Last Judgement. Some believed, or claimed to believe, that all history went round in perpetually repeating cycles. Those who stood nearest to our own ways of thought considered themselves to be simply 'modern', as opposed to the 'ancients' or the people of the 'Middle Ages'.

Some 'modern' assumptions

'Early modern' is, then, a quite artificial term. Nevertheless, historians use it for valid reasons. Certain features of 'modern' European culture are so much a part of the furniture of our lives that they largely pass unnoticed. Yet all of these originated at specific periods in the past. In the economic sphere, we live in a developed system. Most Europeans work in fairly specialized activities in which they trade their skills in the community, rather than labouring for their own immediate household needs. Average incomes provide significantly more than is needed for a life of basic subsistence; the latter is classed as 'poverty' and a social evil. The land, and the economy in general, have surplus capacity beyond what is required to feed, clothe, and house the population. In consequence, much economic activity is devoted to producing luxuries, and to the providing of services. A relatively free traffic in goods across international and continental frontiers is taken for granted.

In the sphere of thought and beliefs, the developed world asserts the right to a similarly free traffic in ideas and literature. Such traffic is constrained by decency and respect for human rights, rather than by the duty to conform to any prescribed ideology. This free exchange of ideas was not, of course, allowed over much of eastern Europe between the Second World War and 1989. Yet the subsequent recovery of those freedoms may in due course show up the Communist period for the bizarre anomaly in European history that it was. Those people in modern Europe who remain religious practise their religion through conscious choice rather than because of the dictates of state or community. However strong their personal beliefs, they generally regard the civil toleration of diverse beliefs as morally right. Systems of belief are as likely to challenge the social and political conventions of their country as they are to reinforce them. More importantly still, thinking people regard statements of faith in the ultimate meaning of the human predicament as 'true' in a quite different sense from the 'truths' learned through scientific investigation. The physical universe, it is generally agreed by religious and non-religious alike, needs to be investigated and understood as an organic system. It may—but need not—have any ultimate purpose behind it, other than keeping itself going. Its workings can be analysed quite apart from any assumptions about its ultimate meaning.

In political life, modern society has largely adopted the assumption that individuals stand as equals before a more or less monolithic state government. Concepts of rank, class, or hierarchy, in which the 'inferior' related to government mostly through their 'betters', have yielded to a pragmatic attitude to government, whose officials command no particular personal respect. The notion of inherited political superiority has been relegated to the ceremonial margins of ruling, even in that most traditional and evolutionary of states, the United Kingdom. 'Privilege' in its alternative passive sense, meaning the right of certain regions, communities, classes, or professions to special treatment or partial immunity before the law and their governors, has given way to general ideals of political accountability owed to all citizens.

The result of this unitary attitude to national government is that when modern states need to call on the resources of their countries for defence, they do so absolutely and largely without contradiction. To a lesser degree, a government with sufficient legal and constitutional mandate calls on the resources of its people to provide state welfare, health provision, and education. It takes chief, though not sole responsibility for the management of economic affairs, and is often judged by its electorate by whether or not it is seen to have handled the economy to the general benefit.

None of these assumptions held for Europe in 1500, as may be seen in Chapters 1–3. At the start of this period the economy largely revolved around the subsistence needs of the masses. Religion and philosophy belonged to one integrated system where physical and metaphysical principles were deliberately intermingled. Political life was a matter of feudal and dynastic superiority, and the interplay of corporate and individual privileges, more than of 'reason of state' (even though that slogan was known and used). Yet by the era of the Enlightenment and the French Revolution, many of these 'modern' ways of thinking were already discernible. They had not attained the status of unquestioned principles which they have since become; yet they were quite visibly on the way to becoming such principles. A consumer economy, a free exchange of ideas, toleration, and the rational, unitary state were *beginning* to emerge: it is in this sense that the centuries between 1500 and 1800 formed the 'early modern' period of Europe's history.

The contributors to this volume were given no specific brief to hunt out those themes which give the term 'early modern' its meaning and reference. Yet one may follow such themes through each of the sets of three chapters per approximate 'century', devoted respectively to society and the economy, to ideas and beliefs, and to political and diplomatic affairs. These sets of chapters form the matrix around which this book has been written. The themes of emerging 'modernity' are always present, even when—as necessarily happens—the authors show that developments were neither uniform nor one-sided, or that older assumptions persisted long and changed only gradually and imperfectly.

'Europe'

One ought to pause a little, however, over the term 'Europe'. Europe is neither a land mass, nor a single people, still less is it a single political entity, at least not yet. Yet as Anthony Pagden's prologue shows, 'Europe' means something despite the fact that it is very difficult to define it precisely. Europe was, from many centuries past, a cultural space. European culture, which combined constituents inherited from various peoples in the ancient Mediterranean world, gave its educated people a sense of belonging more closely to each other than to the rest of humanity. The Greeks bequeathed to Europe a philosophical outlook, and a belief in the value of city life for developing the human personality to the full. The Roman Empire gave a universal language and a legal system. Christianity gave a shared faith, but a Church divided into eastern and western. Ancient learning somehow instilled the belief that free Europeans possessed the skill, the craft, the quest for understanding to master the world through ingenuity and technology. This belief gave early modern Europeans the confidence that they were thus destined to dominate the rest of the world.

Modern political correctness may be understandably embarrassed by these sentiments. One may detect a sorry contrast between the literature which proclaimed a shared destiny for Europeans in the wider world, and the often savage rivalry with which individual countries actually competed for real colonies and trading-posts. However, it is an inescapable fact of history, whatever one's response to it, that European culture and government did extend itself over much of the world, in a way that Asian cultures, say, did not. It is also clear that the rival countries of Europe set about the enterprise at approximately the same time; that they were conscious of each other's activities; and that they brought similar assumptions about their place in the world to bear upon it.

Towards the end of his Prologue, Anthony Pagden shows how towards the end of this period, European writers were beginning to think of themselves as belonging in a wider humanity and bearing responsibility for the race as a whole. He also shows how aspirations towards a supranational unity of the whole 'continent' had been expressed even as early as the sixteenth century. In these senses the drift towards 'modern' Europe forms a story which is still far from complete.

Society and the Economy

Chapters 1 and 4 depict, in part, a traditional economy and society. Survival was determined by access to the fruits of the land, and by the fruitfulness of that land. Crop yields were in the main poor and inflexible, and left little leeway for bad harvests or the exactions of state and Church. Family structures were shaped by the customs and conventions inherited by different regions of Europe: nuclear households in the north, larger extended units in the south. The overwhelming majority of people who lived close to the soil coped with their predicament as best they could. They used ingenious systems of borrowing to tide them over bad times, and scarcely less complex forms of divination and magic to bring good luck and guard against misfortune. This was what is sometimes called the 'old world' or 'pre-industrial' society, where change appears slight, continuity overwhelming, and the life of the majority always precarious and often miserable.

However, the appearance of unchanging permanence is deceptive. The sixteenth century saw profound changes in the life of the masses, even though these were understood very little, and controlled not at all. More people were born than died across Europe. The increased numbers of mouths to feed put pressure on basic foodstuffs and on the land which produced them. Among the labouring classes, most found that rents increased and wages fell in real terms. A minority of wealthy tenant farmers exploited the rise in food prices to become peasant aristocracies, while their neighbours sank into wage-labouring poverty. The economy, as a whole, 'expanded' in the sense that more was bought and sold at higher prices: but this expansion only made the majority more wretched.

In the seventeenth century, as Chapter 4 shows, this pattern changed. A slowing of the pace of population growth, combined with the continued effort to grow food, stabilized basic food prices. Crop yields increased very slightly in certain areas, particularly the Netherlands and England, to the point where the agricultural economy produced more than was needed for subsistence. In this instance an economic slowdown actually improved the lot of some of the labouring population. However, the tailing-off of the increase in population owed something to the harsh effects of earlier crop failures on human fertility, and something to a series of devastating outbreaks of plague. Life was a little better, but only if one survived. Moreover, economic factors did not determine people's lives absolutely, but interacted with the social and political structures of the particular region. The better-fed and relatively free bourgeois of the Low Countries were fed with grain grown by unfree, in some cases newly 'enserfed' peasants on the vast estates of the eastern European nobility.

Chapter 7 charts even more significant change in the relationship between people and food. In the eighteenth century the population, and therefore the economy, expanded once again, with increasing speed from c.1750. Yet this time expansion did not bring increased misery. Bubonic plague ceased to be a major killer. Food supplies, although under pressure, kept up with demand. Crop yields were consistently improved across western Europe by new schemes for crop rotation to increase soil fertility. Ironically, however, it was the sheer volume of the grains produced by the unreformed and relatively inefficient agriculture of the sprawling estates of Poland which placed bread on many of the tables of western Europe.

From the middle of the seventeenth century, more of those tables began to have more than just the necessities of life placed upon them. Both Chapters 4 and 7 chart the gradual rise and spread of the 'consumer' market in at least two major areas: non-essential foods and drinks, including tea, coffee, and sugar, and secondly 'consumer durable' items such as clocks, glassware, and china. Items which individuals had bought as necessities in small quantities, such as clothing, they now bought in multiples. Europe's economic and material life was not transformed overnight; the new products trickled slowly down through the social strata. Nevertheless, the physical appearance of everyday life was quite different in 1800 from what it had been in 1500. As Chapter 7 shows, this enhancement of the material conditions of life had its cost: it may have meant a harder and longer working week, for more members of each family, in the decades just before the industrial revolution. It is an intriguing puzzle that the increase in consumption of goods occurred before, not after, the rise of mechanized prod uction methods.

Europe was spreading its economic tentacles into the rest of the world; yet as Chapter 4 shows, it was not operating a 'colonial' system in the sense of exploiting the labour or the raw materials of subject lands and peoples. Europe generated its own wealth; it was with the surplus wealth which they produced that European countries paid their merchants to trade over the immense distances of the oceans to buy luxury spices and textiles for domestic consumption. Most merchants made only a modest proportion of their investments in transoceanic trade. Yet the implications of commerce for peoples and their governments were very radical indeed. England played only a marginal role in the European conflicts of the sixteenth century, because its monarchy drew insufficient direct taxes from its small population to compete with France and Spain. By the 1700s it was a major European power, largely on the proceeds of indirect taxation of foreign trade.

By the end of the eighteenth century 'liberalism' and laissez-faire were beginning to take over from 'mercantilism' and 'cameralism' (two economic doctrines which justified restricting trade in the national interest) in the management of the economy. The call to strip away regulations and allow the free flow of goods rested on the recognition that the wealth of nations was not fixed, to be hoarded and coveted; but that diligence and cooperation could make the total cake larger for all to share. The fear of the mortal sin of greed and its consequences, which had governed price-fixing and market-rigging for several centuries, was replaced by the optimistic belief that everything would work out if left to itself.

Ideas and Beliefs

One technology is not discussed extensively in the economic sections, because its place more properly belongs with the ideas which it helped to spread, namely printing. The early modern period coincides almost precisely with the age of the hand press, where cast pieces of soft metal were arranged manually in print-formes, inked, and squeezed into contact with a sheet of paper by the physical force of the printer. Before *c*.1450, literature circulated in manuscript, and short fly-sheets were copied as woodblocks. From the early nineteenth century onwards, the machine-press mechanized and industrialized the process.

The press was primarily a tool, and none of the contributors to this volume would argue that it was inevitably associated with one body of ideas rather than another. However, the ambience which the printing press created changed the context in which ideas were discussed. Writers and scholars, however traditional their views, seized on the new technology with the same pragmatic haste that those of our own generation have adopted the personal computer. They then conducted their debates with dozens or hundreds of readers at a time, rather than a few; and over great distances at once. Impoverished young students in printing centres eked out their incomes as proof-readers; while so occupied they might meet authors, and read material in production, outside the constraints of the schools. Once the potentialities of the new medium were exploited—which did not happen at once—the way was open for ideas to be rethought and recast at far greater speed, and more comprehensively, than had been the case in the past.

With hindsight, the most important motif in the history of European thought in the sixteenth and seventeenth centuries is that of disintegration: of the breakdown of old certainties, and the appearance of new, rival, and opposed bodies of ideas which replaced them. The four elements, the four bodily humours and temperaments, the earth at the centre of a cosmos which became more perfect as one went out towards its outer limits: all these intuitive, philosophical ways of looking at the universe would gradually break down. The dominance of Aristotle was challenged by numerous other thinkers and other means of explaining the world. Yet this disintegration of old ideas, so obvious to us, was probably not nearly so obvious even to the most intelligent people at the time. As Chapters 2 and 5, and indeed Chapter 8 argue, the old frameworks were not discarded overnight. Some of the new ideas seemed just as fanciful and obscure as the medieval lore which they challenged. The old schemes proved quite elastic, and even exponents of the new science felt more secure if they clung to some of the earlier assumptions.

The critical change, as it appears in retrospect, occurred when the evidence of observation came to be accepted as more compelling and credible than inherited wisdom and authority: when natural philosophers quite literally insisted on believing in the evidence of their own eyes. That is why the most impressive attainments of sixteenth- and seventeenth-century 'science' are often descriptive, like the anatomical drawings of Vesalius, the zoological and botanical illustrations of Gesner, the analytical geographies of seventeenth-century writers like Petty, or van Leeuwenhoek's drawings of micro-organisms seen through the microscope.

Yet mere description does not of itself bring understanding, though it may be useful to show the deficiencies of earlier accounts. Often it was precisely the *lack* of a clear explanation for the observed evidence which made contemporaries sceptical and dissatisfied with the new science. The descriptive botanical herbalist Paracelsus discredited some of his discoveries by an aggressive refusal to distinguish between healing remedies which might be natural, and those which might be the work of demons. Kepler's essentially accurate description of planetary movement languished for lack of a credible theory as to *why* the planets were pulled round in their courses, until Newton provided one in the shape of gravity. Propagandists for descriptive science like Francis Bacon might linger too long over 'prodigies' and 'marvels', in the belief, usually mistaken, that reports of the extreme abnormalities of nature would be especially helpful for revealing natural laws.

Nevertheless, by the middle of the eighteenth century informed and thinking people in western Europe were increasingly ready to accept the moral lesson of the new astronomy and some of the new sciences of terrestrial life: namely that the universe was much larger, much older, and much more complex than ideas based on the Book of Genesis in the Old Testament had allowed. One of the most striking lessons of Norman Hampson's presentation of Enlightenment thinking in Chapter 8 concerns the early history of evolutionary theory. Philosophers of the eighteenth century speculated that species originated from vastly remote times and from common ancestors; they did so many decades before Darwin and Wallace would independently explain the mechanisms by which this had occurred.

Evolution placed humankind squarely within the created order. Though alone of all creatures in being given free will and intelligence, the human race had grown out of the soil, rather than being placed on the earth as in a sort of moral gymnasium where it must struggle to keep laws fixed by God. People 'belonged' in the world, and what was natural was either ordained by an essentially benign and wise Providence or worked out through some form of natural selection. The Enlightenment, then, largely replaced the idea of *sin*, of moral wrongdoing as the main threat to humanity, with the belief that ignorance and superstition were the great enemies to be overcome.

Here one confronts perhaps the most disturbing paradox of the 'early modern'. In the sixteenth century, not only was religious belief vitally important; dogma actually played a larger role in people's lives than ever before. Yet by the end of the eighteenth, the reverse process had occurred. The philosophers of the Enlightenment moved dogma to the sidelines, and the French revolutionaries effectively disestablished Roman Catholicism in France. Nevertheless, with patience, this paradox can be explained. In 1500 Europe's Christianity was not so much a single system of belief, as an organic way of life. Within it different types of religious activity, from the extraordinary intellectual dexterity of scholastic theologians to the crude polytheism of those who mingled charms and spells with prayers and holy water, existed side by side. These were in conflict no doubt, but within a shared framework. The power of heaven discharged itself through all sorts of terminals on earth, whether these were the pardoning power of the papacy, the spiritual grace of the sacraments, holy relics, special shrines, or just specially powerful holy words. The Reformation took place when a theological challenge to part of this system was mishandled by the hierarchy. It ran out of control among the thinking religious people of northern Europe, until it dragged down the entire organic system of late medieval Christianity.

Protestant Christianity confronted the believer directly with God. It offered him or her the infinite power of the sacrifice of Christ, undeserved and unearned, to cover all sins. It did not claim to represent or channel the power of God through reliable rites or authoritative institutions; it simply proclaimed and taught what was immediately available to all. Although it is not inevitable that Protestantism should become intellectualist and individualist, that has been the route which it has tended to take since the sixteenth century. To know, understand, and accept something as true, inwardly and by oneself, became the test of a true Christian. To live a devout and morally upright life, rather than to attend a large number of purificatory ceremonies, became the best evidence that one was headed in the right direction.

In due course this intellectualism and individualism would provoke a reaction. In the short term, Roman Catholicism (as one may now call that part of western Christianity which remained loyal to the papacy) tended to borrow some of the intellectual traits of the Reformation, and use them to defend its own, unitary approach to godly life and authoritative Church. Catholic preachers became as dogmatic, as argumentative, as preoccupied with written formulas and educational techniques as their Protestant adversaries. In the early seventeenth century, both fought doctrinaire battles against deviants within their own camps, as well as against each other.

This individualist stress on personal belief provoked antagonism and splintering within Christianity, as England in the 1650s found to its cost. It has proved impossible to reintegrate the various fractured traditions. The more one tried to define the contents of faith in technical language, the more disagreements arose, and the worse the fragmentation became. Thus by the end of the seventeenth century the idea that any particular set of dogmas could be utterly 'right' was, itself, on the way to being discredited. The reaction came in the form of a renewed appeal to the emotions, which arose earlier in baroque Catholicism than in Lutheran Pietism or English Methodism, no doubt, but for similar reasons. That broad-thinking undogmatic churchmen in the eighteenth century embraced many of the ideas of the Enlightenment, testifies to the sheer implausibility of the claim made by any one of the competing schemes of religious belief that it was entirely correct, and that all the others were dangerously wrong. Simply to live according to human decency and the dictates of reason seemed far more 'godly', according to the eighteenth-century view of the divinity. The rise of arbitrary and competing dogmas had contained the seeds of their own decline.

Politics, the State, and Warfare

General histories of Europe usually begin with politics, and take political life as the 'spine' around which the rest of the exposition is organized. This book quite deliberately takes the contrary course. It begins each century with the life of the majority, on whom great events and great personalities impinged only erratically, through war and taxation. This is not to suggest that political life was not vitally important. The point is rather that the long-term shifts in statecraft and political life which tended towards 'modernity' are best understood against the background of the life and values of the people whose efforts sustained them—and paid for them.

There is a very, very long trend in European political development according to which power has tended to coalesce in the central governments of a relatively small and easily identifiable number of nation states. This trend is neither complete nor confined to the early modern period. Some countries, such as England, had become fairly centralized before 1000. Others, like Germany or Italy, only acquired a central government in the latter half of the nineteenth century. However, the prevailing tone of the years around 1500 was one of aggregation rather than disintegration. France had seized back the lands held by the English and reabsorbed most of the duke of Burgundy's French possessions in the fifteenth century. The whole of the Iberian peninsula would acknowledge one sovereign between 1580 and 1640. German Emperors tried fitfully and unsuccessfully to make the limited central institutions of the Holy Roman Empire work better.

More important in real terms, as Chapter 3 shows, was the triumphalist propaganda which created an illusion of superhuman dignity around the crowned heads and princes of Europe. Royal courts, where state business alternated with ceremonial and symbolism, bridged the gap between the household-based ruling institutions of the Middle Ages and modern, institutionalized government. Courts worked through favour and petition, and allowed courtiers to carve out careers for themselves by cultivating patrons and showing their worth in service which was part personal, part political. It has been said that one of the last 'courts' in this sense was the ruling clique around Adolf Hitler.

However, even if the aggregation of power and the glorification of the ruler seemed to be the trend, it is striking that both in Chapter 3 and in Chapter 9 we read how many of the most majestic monarchies were really composite states. They had grown up through the bundling together of separate political units with often diverse traditions, and the differences between them remained both durable and significant. The primary instance of this phenomenon was the monarchies of the Habsburg dynasty. Just before our period, the archdukes of Austria had become conventionally accepted as the usual heirs to the elective crown of the Holy Roman Empire. Convenient deaths and tactical marriages brought them within a few generations the Netherlands, Franche-Comté, Castile and Aragon (with its claims in Italy), and the crowns of Bohemia and part of Hungary. The attempt to hold all these lands under one person eventually broke Charles V's spirit and deranged his mind. The effort to keep the Spanish-Dutch monarchy together drove his son to repeated bankruptcies. After the extinction of the Spanish Habsburg line in 1700 the dynasty focused on its lands in what would become Austria-Hungary. Yet rarely was the structure of this monarchy regulated by conscious design; custom, convention, and dynastic accident played far greater roles.

From the perspective of the 'Habsburg issue', the rise of centralized states may be nothing more than a red herring. As several of the authors insist, the prime mover behind state growth in early modern Europe was not centralization but the need to fight ever more expensive and demanding wars. From one point of view, fighting defensive wars was a matter of mere survival for early modern governments. Whatever other areas of governing it might abdicate or leave to others, a European regime could not fail to defend its status and territory without ceasing to exist. From another standpoint, warfare was, at the start of this period, still the *raison d'être* of the aristocracy and royalty: in the three-part order of society described by Alison Rowlands, the nobility were defined as those who fought. Finally, even a ruler who had no chivalric aspirations of his own, such as Philip II of Spain, would still regard it as a matter of honour to hold on to all the 'estate' which he had inherited from his father.

Yet these traditional values, important though they were, do not account for the dramatic rise in the cost to governments of early modern warfare. Waging wars grew vastly more expensive, because it became necessary to keep larger and larger numbers of massed infantrymen in the field for longer campaigns, and at least in the period before *c*.1650, for longer-drawn-out sieges. From an effective maximum of 50,000 soldiers at any one time in a given nation's army in the sixteenth century, numbers rose through the later seventeenth century until in the 1690s the French army perhaps numbered 300,000, and the total number of soldiers in the continent approached one million. A century later the French revolutionary army alone was made up of some 800,000 men. Some of the reasons for this increased size of armies were technological: the pike, and then the musket, required large blocs of massed foot-soldiers grouped in sufficiently large amounts to survive the attrition of battlefield artillery. Fortifications perfected in Italy in the early sixteenth century spread northwards: these made walled fortresses almost impregnable to bombardment and forced armies to sit out sieges in sufficient numbers to last the course. However, the primary reason for the increase was political will. Governments became sufficiently organized and resolute to require of their people to maintain larger armies than their neighbours, and so the process escalated, as the major players in the diplomatic game outbid each other. By the end of the eighteenth century, the Napoleonic war machine dedicated the entire human resources of France to the maintenance of the national war effort, in the 'levée en masse', the first such 'modern' military mobilization.

In consequence the machinery of government grew more sophisticated, and in some respects more professional. More money was raised in taxes; this required more elaborate official structures to administer them. Since taxes were usually levied in the form of arbitrary exactions from the agricultural economy (by far the largest sector of the economy at this period) the peasants bore the bulk of the load. Nevertheless, the nobility, and sometimes also the bourgeoisie, had surplus wealth which governments needed to tap; yet these had often secured partial exemption from direct taxes as a price for their consent to the growth in state power. These classes usually made most of their contributions to government in the form of loans. More and more cumbersome systems of funded state debt were developed to maintain the edifice of government borrowing in some sort of balance. Despite these efforts, sometimes, as in the case of eighteenth-century France, the structure eventually collapsed under its own weight.

Money was not enough. As armies grew, they outstripped the capacity of the land around them to support them, at least when they were stationary. States which wished to maintain large forces on a permanent basis had to devise sophisticated schemes for logistical support, supply lines, commissariats, eventually barracks, and a system of discipline. Without such devices these huge armies would soon have impoverished and devastated the countries which they were created to defend. As H. M. Scott's discussion shows, states did not all respond to these pressures in the same way: political will and the economic and agricultural realities of different countries combined to produce different systems. France, and its imitators, taxed, controlled, and borrowed on the basis of a growing central machine and a more or less permanent army. Sweden, and her imitators in northern and eastern Europe, operated a system of legally enforced conscription of a certain number of soldiers paid directly by each agricultural district.

The early modern period is sometimes described as the age in which a 'bureaucracy' emerged. The term can be used either loosely, to mean whatever kinds of officials are employed to keep such administrative routines as exist turning; or it can be used in a more precise fashion, to mean a professionalized cadre of properly trained and qualified administrators, chosen on merit and loyal to the ethos of administration before any external or sectional interest. In this latter, more precise sense, there were probably no 'bureaucrats' in early modern Europe. Yet, with the passing of time and the increasing complexity of governmental tasks, offices of state grew towards the critical mass within which a 'bureaucratic' ethos could develop. Nevertheless, all contributors show how personal connections and clientage continued to suffuse even the most professionalized of government machines. 'Early modern' in this instance clearly meant 'pre-modern'.

It is probably futile, in the light of the great political upheavals of the past century, to speculate whether there is, or ever was, a 'natural' system of nation states within Europe. Powers always rise or fall in importance with the interplay of economic, political, diplomatic, dynastic, and other forces. During the period *c.*1520–1660 European diplomatic issues revolved around the power and connections of the lands ruled by the Habsburg dynasty. From 1660 onwards the focus of other powers' worries shifted to the growing assertiveness and demands of France. France and its claims on other states dominated the years covered by the 'Epilogue' chapter: but as

H. M. Scott notes, by 1815 something like a system of five major powers, Great Britain, France, Russia, Austria, and Prussia, had come into being. In the intervening period other powers, notably the Ottoman Empire, Sweden, and the Dutch Republic rose to prominence and then declined in influence once again. As T. C. W. Blanning's epilogue shows, Napoleonic Europe witnessed a transition. It ended the era when the power and problems of France were the major issue in European diplomacy, and began one in which the power and structure of the German peoples and their states became the key issue. In the age of 'early modern' Europe, Germany was dominated by the complex, unplanned checks and balances of the Holy Roman Empire, which conspired to restrain the potential strength of its people. Post-Napoleonic Europe marked the end of that phase, with whose consequences Europe is still coming to terms.

The End of Old Europe

'The *ancien régime* of kings, nobles, and priests was sailing in serene unawareness towards its doom, as industrial society gradually emerged to replace its agrarian predecessor. This long-term process was only possible through a vast intellectual revolution . . .' This comment, from the conclusion to Chapter 5, very largely sums up the message of the entire book. It claims that the huge upheaval which created the first industrialized society in Europe depended on the intellectual changes which made it possible, and then transformed the political structures which sheltered it. The three themes of the forthcoming analysis, then—society, ideas, and politics—are inextricably intertwined. However, Robin Briggs's summary also points out that these mighty transformations were neither obvious nor foreseeable at the time. On the contrary, they corroded the intellectual and political structure of Europe so gently, so subtly beneath the shell of apparent continuity, that the collapse, when it came, appeared far more sudden and shocking than with hindsight it is seen to be.

That collapse came in the form of the French Revolution, and the thrust towards a more rational ordering of society which was ultimately to prove irresistible. 'Early modern' Europeans had for three centuries overwhelmingly endorsed the idea of 'authority', in the sense that some ideas, some people, some ways of doing things were inherently superior to others. They continued to do so in parts of their lives, even as they were busy dismantling the arguments for 'authority' in some other area. Early modern man unpicked the seams which held the fabric of the 'old world' together, but continued to wear the garment until it suddenly fell from his shoulders.

In revolutionary France, and the wholesale military mobilization of resources to which it led, the subtle discriminations which marked off some people from others, or which protected 'privilege' from the insistent demands of the totality, abruptly lost their credibility and their justification. Society became more rational, but also less restrained. The way was cleared for both the great liberalizations, and the horrendous acts of totalitarian brutality which have characterized modern society.

Prologue:
Europe and the World Around

ANTHONY PAGDEN

Europe: The Myths of Europe

It begins with a story, the story of an abduction. And a metamorphosis. Europa was the daughter of Agenor, king of the city of Tyre on the coast of Sidon. One fine day she was carried off by Zeus, who was transformed for the occasion into a white bull, to bear their offspring on the continent which would also bear her name. This is the myth. There is, however, as with all myths, another more mundane version, which was suggested by the Greek writer Herodotus and seized upon by the early Christian theologian, Lactantius, eager to debunk and demystify such unsettling erotic fantasies from the ancient world. In this version it is Cretan merchants who abduct Europa in a ship shaped like a bull as a bride for their king Asterius. Since the Cretans are Europeans, and Europa herself an Asian woman, her abduction was taken by all Asians to be an affront. Later the Trojans, also a people of what we now call Asia Minor, seize a (not wholly unwilling) Helen, wife of Menelaus, in revenge. In turn, Menelaus' brother Agamemnon raises an army, crosses the sea and begins the most celebrated war in European history. The Persians, Herodotus tells us—and 'Persians' is his shorthand for all the peoples of Asia—found this tale of abduction puzzling. 'We in Asia', they say, 'regarded the rape of our women not at all' (thus establishing an enduring Asian cultural stereotype) 'but the Greeks all for the sake of a Lacedaemonian woman mustered a great host, came to Asia and destroyed the power of Priam. Ever since then we have regarded the Greeks as our enemies.' What in myth had been a divine appropriation, becomes in mythopoeic history a story of the hatred between two continents, a hatred which would burn steadily down the centuries, as the Ottoman Turks replaced the Phoenicians and the Russians replaced the Ottomans.

But no myth is as simple as that. Most myths are tales of metamorphoses where everything is not merely not what it seems, but is also frequently its very opposite. For fleeing from the ruins of Troy, with his father Anchises on his back, and leading his son Ascanius by his hand, comes Aeneas, who, years later, will land on the shores of Latium, and found the city and the state of Rome. And it is Rome which will be the true creator of 'Europe'. Europe, which will fashion itself for generations in opposition to Asia, thus owes to Asia its historical origins. This sense of double ambiguity, further-more, survives even the collapse of the political structures of the Graeco-Roman world and the dominance of Graeco-Roman origin myths. For Christianity, which was to provide Europe with much of its subsequent sense of both internal cohesion and its relationship with the rest of the world, was also in its beginnings an Asian religion. In an attempt to secure the glory of Christ's apostolate, and of the overseas mission, exclusively for Europe, the English propagandist for the settlement of America, Samuel Purchas, wrote in 1625: 'Jesus Christ, who is the way the truth and the life, has long since given the Bill of Divorce to ingrateful Asia where he was born and of Africa the place of his flight and refuge, and has become almost wholly European.' 'Almost wholly', however, for not even Purchas could entirely discount the continuing existence of the Greek and Russian churches, who refused either fully to submit to the authority of the papacy or, as the English fitfully hoped, convert to Protestantism. The fact that the undeniably Christian adherents of Greek orthodoxy had for long been under Ottoman rule, and thus fully absorbed into Asia, remained an addi-tional reminder of the alien origin of Christianity. Thus an abducted Asian woman gave Europe her name; a vagrant Asian exile gave Europe its politi-cal and finally its cultural identity; and an Asian prophet gave Europe its religion.

Christianity also brought in its train the need to adopt a Judaic account of the creation, and in particular a Judaic account of the origins of the vari-ous races of man. If the biblical narrative was to be believed, then all mankind had to have a common ancestor first in Adam, then in Noah. And in the era after the flood all the world had to have been repeopled by one of Noah's sons. Ever since St Jerome translated the Bible into Latin in the fourth century CE, Japhet has been taken to be the progenitor of the races of Europe, Shem those of Asia, and Ham of Africa. Jerome's rendering of Genesis 9: 27, God 'shall enlarge Japhet and he shall dwell in the tents of Shem', was taken to mean that Japhet would produce more offspring than

The 'Mappa Mundi', drawn in the late thirteenth century and now in the library of Hereford Cathedral, offers an example of the earliest style of world map. The land-mass is drawn as a circle surrounded by the ocean. Asia lies towards the top of the map, with Europe below to the left and Africa to the right. Jerusalem is therefore placed at the centre, where three continents meet.

his brothers and that, one day, his progeny would come to conquer Asia, just as they would inherit from the Hebrews the mantle of the true religion. As Hegel was later to observe, Europe was 'the centre and end' of History, but History had begun in Asia: 'characteristically the *Orient* quarter of the globe—the region of origination'. The course of civilization, like that of empire and the sun itself, moves inexorably from east to west.

In the beginning, however, the world had been divided not into two, but three. These were Europe, Asia, and 'Libya', as Africa was generally called: although as Herodotus, the first to travel well beyond the limits of his own home and who revelled in the oddities of the behaviour of those he found there, complained with characteristic Greek misogyny, he could not conceive 'why three names, and women's names at that, should have been given to a tract which is in reality one'. For most Greeks the difference between what they called Europe—by which they meant frequently if not consistently Hellas, the lands around the Aegean sea—and Asia or Africa would remain, as it had been for Aeschylus, one not only of climate and disposition, but also of race (*ethnos*). Herodotus, however, had understood that 'Europe' had no natural frontiers, and that, as most subsequent cosmopolitans came to realize through experience, cultures are never so incommensurable as their members often like to suppose. If 'Europe' had, or came to acquire, an identity as a place, it was always one which lived in the uneasy realization that not only were Europe's origins non-European, but that no one could establish with any precision where Europe stopped and Asia and Africa began.

These predominantly conceptual divisions between the continents are perhaps best understood in visual terms. The first surviving maps are very late: they date from the eleventh century. But they still show the world very firmly divided into three segments, with Asia as progenitor, on the top, Europe and Africa beneath. These so-called 'TO' maps (named from the stylized T-form of the waters separating the continents and the ocean surrounding the entire world) are depictions of lineage as much as they are of space. Here each segment of the globe is ascribed to its founding father with no regard to size or relative position. What matters is not where, but who we are. Until the sixteenth century maps served this, rather than any other function. They showed not so much our place upon the surface of the planet, as our relationship as races to one another. It was only with the advent of oceanic navigation that cartography was transformed from the representation of mythic into real geographic space. Europe, however, could never be located at the centre of the world as China was for so many Chinese geographers. Its origins in Asia, and the fact that no educated person since the Greeks had seriously doubted that the world was a sphere, made that impossible.

A Continent and its Peoples

But if Europe the land mass could not be said to be at the centre of the world, and if, as Herodotus had noticed, its borders with Asia and Africa are at best indistinct, it could still be placed at the centre of some other conceptualization of the environment. For the Greeks and their Roman heirs the means of establishing a relationship between them and the rest of humanity rested upon a complex theory of climate and physical environment. This claimed that the northern parts of the world were inhabited by peoples whose inhospitable climates had made them brave and warlike, but also uncouth, unthinking, and—to use the Latinized term which will become central to all modes of European self-fashioning—'uncivilized'. Those who lived in the south—the Asians—were, by contrast, quick-witted, intelligent; but also, lethargic, slow to act, and ultimately corrupt—a claim which, in time, was to become another enduring stereotype of the 'Oriental'. Europeans, which at this time meant only the peoples of the Mediterranean, living as they do midway between these extremes, are the mean. This conception of Europe, much modified it is true, but still insistent on the radical distinction between north and south, retained its imaginative force until the nineteenth century. Even Hegel, writing in the 1830s, and writing very much from the viewpoint of an intellectually and culturally emergent north, could still speak confidently of the Mediterranean as the 'uniting element' of the 'three quarters of the globe' and 'the centre of World-History'. (He had already relegated America firmly to the domain of the future, 'where in the ages that lie before us, the burden of the World's History shall reveal itself'.)

'Europe', wrote the first-century Greek geographer Strabo, in the earliest surviving attempt to demonstrate and explain the continent's perception of its superiority over all others, 'is both varied in form and admirably adapted by nature for the development of excellence in men and governments.' The two instincts in man, the peaceable (which Strabo significantly called the agricultural) and the warlike, live in Europe side by side, and 'the one that is peace-loving is more numerous and thus keeps control over the whole body'. In Strabo's account the Greek dialectic between the world of nature (*physis*) and that of men (*nomos*, a term which relates to law, but which we would translate 'culture') has been resolved in Europe, and only in Europe. Because of this harmony Europe becomes, in another image which has survived unbroken to this day, the home of liberty and of true government. The Greeks, Herodotus tells us, are the most free of peoples, because, unlike the Asians, they are subject not to the will of an individual, but only to the law. European society might have had many forms of government, some of them decidedly less liberal than others; but, centuries later, Voltaire was echoing an enduring commonplace when he claimed that the continent constituted a 'kind of great republic divided into several states', all of which were united in having 'the same principle of public law and politics, unknown in other parts of the world'. Most of Europe, as Montesquieu had remarked (he was a little uncertain about Spain), is ruled by 'custom', *les mœurs*. Asia, and still darker regions of Africa and America, is ruled by despots. The rule of law, restraint through custom, rather than will, was responsible for the fashioning of societies which provided a space for individual human action, while at the same time ensuring that that action was rarely capable of reducing society to a state of simple anarchy. From this we will see the descent of the notion that all human improvement depends upon conflict; that human beings are, by their nature, competitive creatures; and that only those societies which know how to harness what the German philosopher Immanuel Kant in the late eighteenth century called man's 'unsocial sociability', instead of attempting to suppress it, will flourish. As Machiavelli noted, the power of the Roman Republic had derived not (as so many had supposed) from the exercise of a common will, but precisely from the opposition between the Senate and the plebeians. And, like Herodotus, Machiavelli also believed that the excellence of Europeans in war was due to the fact that, whereas the peoples of Asia and Africa lived largely under princely rule, in Europe 'although there have been some kingdoms, there have been many republics'. There was, too, from the beginning the conviction, which the modern democratic societies of the West have inherited, that this vision of the world was, in the long run—if not always in the short—suitable for all peoples everywhere, and that its cultural power was irresistible.

How it should have come about that the highly chauvinist Greeks should have been able to speak of themselves as members of a larger grouping of peoples, which must have included non-Greek speakers and thus, in the Greek understanding of the term 'barbarians', it is probably impossible to determine. The answer may lie, as Strabo suggests, in the fact that Europe could provide for itself all the food, the metals, and the human resources for its defence: but only *Europe* as a continent, criss-crossed by trade routes from east to west, could do this, and never one alone of the many disparate peoples of the Mediterranean. Because life was so difficult for each of them individually, they could only survive, in particular when confronted by the menace of 'Asia', together. Europeans were therefore forced into political unions, the *symmachiai*, and *sympoliteiai*—such as the Achaean League which dominated the Mediterranean world in the second and first centuries BCE and on which James Madison was to model the future United States of America—and compelled to develop the great commercial networks which were to become the basis of their future expansion far beyond the limits of

Europe itself. This combination of strength and dependency made the recognition of a shared political culture difficult to withhold.

The Cultural Inheritance

This political culture was also centred upon a unique form of life: the city. Of course, as in most other civilizations, the vast majority of the populations of Europe actually lived and worked in the countryside until well into the nineteenth century. It is also true that for most of the rural peoples of Europe, and the illiterate majority in the cities themselves, identity was a question of attachment to micro-communities: the parish, the village, the guild, sometimes the county, the *pays*, or what the Castilians aptly called the *patria chica*, the 'small homeland', only rarely the nation, and never, one suspects, such an abstract cultural grouping as 'Europe'. But for the literate, intellectual élites who had far more in common with their similar groups from other nations than they did with their own peasantry, the spaces beyond the city walls were largely invisible, until they became sentimentalized in the mid-eighteenth century. What Voltaire mockingly called 'the supposed savages of America' were in his view indistinguishable from those savages one met every day in the countryside, 'living in huts with their mates and a few animals ceaselessly exposed to all the intemperance of the seasons'.

Despite its dependence upon agriculture, despite the real distribution of its populations, Europe, as a collection of social and political groups with a shared and historically determined culture, was conceived as overwhelmingly urban. Our entire political and social vocabulary derives from this fact. 'Politics' and 'polity' have their root in the Greek term *polis*. Similarly 'civil', 'civility', 'civilization' have their origins in the Latin word— *civitas*—for the same spatial, political, and cultural entity. Both *polis* and *civitas* became, in time, abstract nouns, sometimes translatable as 'the state', or the 'commonwealth', and definable in abstract terms. Originally, however, they had described the urban space itself, and a close association between urban ways of life and true 'civility' persist to this day. Cities were, of course, by no means unique to Europe. Like all else that defines European culture, these, too, had originated in Asia. But only with the rise of Athens after the sixth century did the association between an urban environment and a particular way of life begin to emerge. Man—and in this respect Greek thought was dismally, cruelly sexist—man, said Aristotle, was *zoon politikon*—quite literally an animal 'made for life in the polis'. For civility was not merely the best attainable existence. It was what the Greeks called 'the good life', the only life in which it was possible for man to achieve his ends *as* a man, to achieve that elusive goal which Aristotle termed *eudaimonia*, his Latin, Christian translators, 'blessedness' (*beatitudo*), and later writers rendered as 'happiness' or by the clumsy term employed by many modern philosophers, 'human flourishing'.

True *politeiai* were, furthermore, like the persons who inhabited them, autonomous entities. They were places of *autarkeia*, or self-sufficiency, which for the Stoics was the first among the virtues. This is also the moral force behind Strabo's claim that Europe was, unlike Asia, 'self-sufficient', for the ability to provide for one's own material needs suggests a high degree of personal autonomy also. Little wonder then, that for Aristotle, there could be no life beyond the limits of the city, but that of 'beasts and Gods'. Because humans were distinct from both beasts and Gods in being guided by rules, by laws and customs, the city was also the source of law. Those who lived within it had to abide by its rules. Beyond there was the wilderness which later writers would describe as 'the state of nature'. All humans began in this condition and all humans are constantly threatened by it. In the Greek world-view, and in the conceptions of generations of Europeans, to live in the state of nature, to live like a 'barbarian', or a 'savage' meant living as something less than human.

The *polis* was, in this way a bounded space. But it was also conceived as a community which had the power to transform all those who entered it. (Aristotle, to whom we owe much of what we now know about the place of the *polis* in Greek life, although he celebrated the city of Athens and wrote her political history, was himself an outsider by birth.) So long as you were outside you were a barbarian. Once inside, however, you would in time become, 'civilized'. Once inside you became that most precious of things, a 'citizen', that is, a member of the *civitas*.

This identification of a distinctive European communal life with a specific environment reached its peak with the effective domination of the whole of what we now call Europe, and much of Asia also, by the greatest city of them all: Rome. Like the Greek cities to which it was heir, Rome too was the source of law, the place of custom, *mores*, which in the poet Virgil's punning vision was now encircled and protected by its massive walls (*moenia*). And, even more than the Greek city-states, Rome welcomed outsiders within its walls. This, at a time when this particular *civitas* offered stability, security, and the access to world power, proved to be enormously attractive. As James Wilson observed in 1790, as he mused, prophetically upon the possible future of the United States as the new Rome in the West, 'it might be said, not that the Romans extended themselves over the whole globe, but that the inhabitants of the globe poured themselves upon the Romans'.

It is, therefore, unsurprising that by the first century CE this 'Roman Empire' which was merely an extension in space of the city of Rome itself, the poet Horace's 'Prince among Cities' (*Princeps urbium*), had come to be identified simply with 'the world', the *orbis terrarum*. The Roman historian Livy makes Romulus express the wish, on founding the city of Rome, that 'my Rome shall be the head of the world' and after the establishment of the Emperor Augustus' new regime in 27 BCE these imperial longings became formally expansionist to the point where Rome was transformed into a 'world state', bounded in Virgil's words only by *Oceanus*. This did not mean that the Romans ignored the actual existence of the rest of the globe. Indeed they possessed a lively and sophisticated ethnographical curiosity in the peoples who inhabited the lands beyond the frontiers of the empire. It was that these other worlds, the Syrians, for instance or the Chinese, had no separate identity as communities—much less as political powers—and that, in the nature of things, they would one day be absorbed into *the* world itself as the Romans conceived it. When in the second century, the Emperor Antoninus Pius assumed the title 'Lord of all the World', *dominus totius orbis*, he was merely giving legal expression to a long-held Roman belief, that, whether those who lived beyond their borders recognized it or not, the political realm of Rome and the human genus had been made one. 'The Roman people, or rather, I say, the human race', declared the Emperor Caligula with characteristic directness.

But crucially, Rome was not only a political realm, it was also the embodiment of the Stoic belief in the possibility of a single law for all humanity. If the Greeks had given to Europe the philosophy and the mathematics which had made its subsequent scientific development possible, it was the Romans who gave it its legislative habits. And although, as we have seen, the concept of Europeans as law-governed peoples originated in Greece, it was the Romans who elevated the law to the place it still holds today, as the sole guarantor of the continuity of 'civilization', however we choose to define that emotive term. Much of this was swept away during the Gothic invasions which followed the collapse of the Roman Empire, and, in the outer fringes of the empire Germanic customary law came to replace Roman law. But this law remained, and remains, the single most unifying feature of the continent. Edmund Burke, good European that he was, offered an image of a world of independent states united as a common culture, based upon 'the old Gothic customary [law] . . . digested into system and disciplined by the Roman law', in every part of which it would be possible for a European to feel at home. For this reason the creation of a single legislative order for the whole of Europe remained an ambition of the most powerful of Europe's rulers from the Emperor Justinian in the sixth century, through Philip II of Spain and Louis XIV to Napoleon and, in somewhat muted form, the European Court of Justice.

After the triumph of Christianity, ancient Greek and Roman notions of exclusivity were further enforced by the Christian insistence upon the uniqueness both of the Gospels and of the Church as a source of moral and scientific authority. Custom now, in Lactantius' words had been 'made congruent with religion'. Christianity was thought of as spatially coextensive with the Roman Empire. The world, the *orbis terrarum*, thus became, in terms of the translation effected by Pope Leo the Great in the fifth century the *orbis Christianus*, or, as it would be called in the European vernaculars, simply 'Christendom'. As late as 1761, such a relatively hostile witness as Jean-Jacques Rousseau conceded that 'Europe, even now, is indebted more to Christianity than to any other influence for the union . . . which survives among her members'. It was a union he abhorred, but from which he could never quite escape.

The scattered, diverse, and plural cultures which had grown up in the ancient world and constituted what we now call Europe, shared, therefore a single identity as so many places of 'human flourishing', bound together by a common system of law. When they gradually converted to Christianity they acquired a common religion and a common cult. They also shared a common language: Latin. Although, after the fourth century, Roman institutions, Roman architecture, Roman literature all gradually lost their power to unite Europe in a common culture, and the concept of a single body of citizens vanished altogether, Latin remained both as the language of the Church—it still does—and of the learned élites of Europe well into the eighteenth century. As the Italian Republican Carlo Cattaneo noted in 1835, Europe possessed four unifying features: the power of the former imperial authority, the Roman Law, Christianity, and the Latin language.

Latin, however, was almost wholly a written language, and even then it was largely confined to the clergy and the lay intelligentsia. Few could, or did, actually speak it. Even the professorate, who were bound by statute in most European universities to deliver their lectures in Latin, in fact spoke for the most part in a curious hybrid version of the language and when excited frequently lapsed for long periods into the vernacular. Diplomatic Latin also became restricted after the 1520s to polite formulas, and writers on the increasingly important science of diplomacy such as Ottaviano Maggi stressed the importance of living languages—although in his *De*

Legato of 1566 he did so in Latin. Most of educated Europe before the eighteenth century was multilingual. Rulers, such as the Holy Roman Emperors
ruled over peoples speaking a bewildering number of languages. Some of
these—Breton, Provençal, Aragonese, Wallon, Piedmontese—are now
only minority tongues for long made subservient to a national vernacular.
But throughout most of the early modern period these were the dominant,
and in some cases, even the official languages of the regions in which they
were spoken. Making oneself understood as one passed from one territory
to another was of crucial importance. The Emperor Maximilian, who
claimed to command no less than seven languages, had himself depicted in
the act of mediating between rebellious factions among his multilingual
troops. Since, however, few could hope to speak all the major languages of
Europe, most educated Europeans shared the conviction that there should
exist a spoken tongue which, if not as universal as Latin had once been,
should also be widely understood. In the sixteenth century this became Italian, the language in which Dante two centuries before had, in a self-conscious break with tradition, decided to write his great poem. Italian was the
language of literature and as such as familiar to the learned élite as English
is today. Montaigne learned Italian—although his father had brought him
up in an entirely Latin-speaking household—and when he crossed the Alps,
he changed the language of his journal from French to Italian. On returning through the Mont Cenis pass he noted—in French—'here French is
spoken, so I leave this foreign language in which I feel competent but ill-
grounded'. By the late seventeenth century, because of Louis XIV's effective political domination of mainland Europe, French had become the
language of diplomacy and the courts, and the language in which educated
Germans, such as Leibniz, wrote when they were not still writing in Latin,
or, in Leibniz's case struggling to devise a 'universal system of characters'
capable of 'expressing all our thoughts be we Frenchmen or Assyrians'.
French remained dominant until the end of the eighteenth century.

Frontiers and Boundaries

Despite the religious, cultural, and linguistic unity which they had given to
the continent, neither the Roman Empire nor Christendom were, of
course, identical with 'Europe'. Much of the Roman Empire lay in Asia and
in North Africa. Not only had Christianity begun as an Asian religion, but
some of the first Christian churches had been established on the North
African littoral. After the fall of Rome, however, and the attempt under
Charlemagne to rebuild the empire in the west, the notion of 'the world'

shrank until it covered little more than what is today continental Europe. Charlemagne, although frequently claiming some kind of world sovereignty, also called himself *pater europae*—'the father of the Europeans'—and the Emperor Charles V who in the early sixteenth century came closer than any ruler before or since to uniting Europe under one sovereign, was addressed as *totius europae dominus*—'lord of all Europe', an obvious allusion to Antoninus Pius' claim to be *dominus totius orbis*.

The shrinking of the frontiers in this way gradually forced upon the European consciousness a greater sense of the boundaries which lay between them and the rest of the world. Europe was the place of civility, of free men living in secure urban communities under the rule of law. The rest served out their day under tyrannies governed according to the caprice of individual rulers, or in nomadic or semi-nomadic groups never far from the primordial 'state of nature'. By the late seventeenth century this sense of exceptionality had found expression in a theory of stages in human development. In this universal narrative, all human societies begin as hunter-gatherers. They then become pastoralists, less mobile than their predecessors but still, as Montesquieu phrased it 'unable to unite'. Finally they invent agriculture and this, in time, transforms them into city dwellers and traders, into modern, civilized, social beings. All the peoples on the globe were bound to pass through each of these stages in succession. Only the Europeans had reached the final stage, that of 'commercial society', although it was generally recognized that some others, such as the Turks and the Chinese, were clearly not far behind.

For all this self-confidence, however, 'Europe' was, and always had been, a highly unstable term. Until the sixteenth and seventeenth centuries the boundaries between its various nations were at best indistinct. Its northern and southern limits were vague. Only the Atlantic and the Mediterranean provided obvious frontiers. For the Greeks, Europe had sometimes been only the area in which the Greeks lived, a vaguely defined region which shaded into what was once Yugoslavia in the north and is still Turkey in the east. For most, however, it had a larger, more indeterminate geographical significance, being seen as the lands in the West, whose outer limit, the point at which they met the all-encircling *Oceanos*, were still unknown. Beyond Europe lay Asia and Africa. Africa south of the Atlas mountains was dark and unimaginable; it remained so, despite the Portuguese exploration and settlement of large areas of the western shores, until the nineteenth century. Only the north coast, which had once been part of the Roman Empire and from the fifteenth century was the home of 'barbary' pirates and the focus of disastrous crusading ambitions by the

Portuguese and the Spaniards, was *terra cognita*. North Africa, however, was a frontier region where Berber states and Ottoman client rulers posed a constant threat to the settled places of Christendom until the extinction of Turkish hegemony in the Mediterranean in the late seventeenth century. All along the southern coast of Italy and Spain were strings of fortifications to guard local populations against the continual threat of Islamic incursions. These might be brief, but they could also be deadly. When in 1544 François I allowed the Turkish fleet to winter at Toulon, he was not merely giving assistance to the enemies of Christ (and, more to the point, of the Emperor Charles V) he was dissolving a centuries old antagonism. He was allowing Asia into Europe.

And if Europe's southern frontiers were in this way indeterminate, her eastern ones were forever undecided. For poised between eastern Europe and the recognizable Orient was the unsettling presence of Russia. Russia, sometimes friend, more frequently foe, threw into occasionally stark relief the fact that Europe was a culture, a shared way of life, rather than a place. Russia had many of the features of a European society, and it was undeniably Christian. Yet in its vast size, in the fact that so much of it had, for so long, been ruled by nomadic peoples who were clearly not European, it also lay beyond the formal limits of Romanized 'civilization'. While it thus remained stubbornly an oriental despotism, Russia remained firmly within Asia, the backward barbaric empire of the steppes. But once, in the eighteenth century, its rulers took to wearing silk brocade and conversing in French it became inescapably Europeanized. In their ambition to subjugate Europe, as Rousseau observed, the Russians had themselves been subjugated. Peter the Great, the first of the tsars to 'modernize' (which meant 'Europeanize') the Russian Empire was described by Montesquieu as 'having given the manners of Europe to a European power'. His successor the Empress Catherine the Great declared at the beginning of the reforming constitutional code she had devised—the *Nakaz*—'Russia is a European Power'. (Catherine herself, however, was German born and French educated and Russian only by marriage.) But if the Russia of Peter and Catherine was 'in', as far as the rest of Europe was concerned, it was only ever partially so. Frederick the Great of Prussia was not alone in denying the empire of the tsars any lasting place among what he described significantly as 'the civilized nations of Europe'. When seen in this way from the heartlands of Europe, Russia could appear distinctly 'other'. When set, however, against the image of the true Orient, she appeared, if only fleetingly, European. Edmund Burke's angry response to William Pitt's proposal during the Ochakov crisis of 1791 to send British troops to help the Sultan resist the

Tsar was: 'What have these worse than savages to do with the powers of Europe, but to spread war, devastation and pestilence among them?' Russia, if only briefly, had thus joined the 'powers of Europe'. Because it reached deep into Asia, Russia could only ever be in this way half civilized, half barbarian. As Napoleon, who should perhaps have been more cautious, declared in November 1815, Russia had 'the rare advantage', from the point of view of a world conqueror, of having 'a civilized government and barbarian peoples'.

Because of this ambivalence, which survives to this day, the 'official' frontier to the east, always in any case a faintly absurd notion, was forever on the move. It advanced steadily from the Don, where it had been fixed for a thousand years, to the banks of the Volga at the end of the fifteenth century, to the Ob in the sixteenth, to the Ural river and the Ural mountains in the nineteenth, and finally to the river Emba and the Kerch straits in the twentieth. Despite this juggling with geography, and the literalness with which geographers from Fra Mauro in the 1450s to the All-Union Geographical Society in the 1950s had treated what was in fact a cultural frontier, despite Catherine's efforts, and the absorption in the nineteenth century of the Romanovs into the families of the crowned heads of Europe, Russia has only ever been incorporated into Europe imperfectly.

Russia's relationship with the rest of Europe, however, was determined not only by language, codes of dress, and religion, crucial though these have always been in establishing who might, and who might not, count as European. It was determined, too, by a powerful European sense of exceptionality. This made recognition of those who, like the Russians, seemed to share some but not all the features of European culture, highly unstable. For to be exceptional, a culture has also to be whole. No people can be permitted to acquire part of its trappings without also acquiring the laws and customs, the political structures, and the social organization which give meaning to those things. This is why the spectacle of outsiders, be they Russians or later Africans and Indians wearing European clothes and conversing in their own forms of Portuguese or English, was made to seem so risible to so many metropolitan Europeans.

Technologies and their Impact

The European sense that Europe was distinct from, and by implication superior to, all the other cultures of the world derived, as we have seen, from the Graeco-Roman sense of the uniqueness of the political cultures of the *polis* and the *civitas*. It derived, too, from another ancient conception which was to have lasting consequences for the future history of the continent. In the physics of Aristotle, which was to remain dominant in Europe until the early seventeenth century, nature existed in a state of potentiality, whose *actuality* could only be realized through purposeful action. This action was in part nature's own. Acorns, as Aristotle said, were potential trees. But trees were also potentially, but not actually, chairs. It required man's art, his *techne*, to release from the tree its essential 'chairness'. *Techne*—or as we would say technology—and what in Latin, the other dominant language in our cognitive vocabulary, was called *scientia*—is the human capacity to transform the world according to human needs. This, for the Greeks, was a form of knowledge (*logos*). *Techne* is the abstract from *tikto*, which means to 'generate' or 'engender'; humans are the *teknotes*, the genitors; and the *tekna* are their offspring. *Techne* was the power to set in motion, a power which none besides humankind and the gods themselves possessed. This power could also be conceived as that exercised by one human group over another. As Michel Foucault once pointed out, what in the Greek Church was called *techne technon*, and in the Latin *ars artium*, was the direction of the conscience, and ultimately the government of men. The development of humankind with the *polis* was in this way a process of fulfilment analogous to the human manipulation of the natural world.

Men were thus encouraged to see in the natural world a design of which they were the final beneficiaries. 'Art itself', as the eighteenth-century Scottish social theorist Adam Ferguson was later to observe, 'is natural to man ... he is destined from the first age of his being to invent and to contrive'. But not precisely all men. For the European sense of superiority, of having been singled out, first by nature, then by God, to play a special role in the history of creation, derived from the conviction that only those who dwelt in the kind of law-governed free urban communities of which 'Europe' was constituted would ever be likely to possess the capacity to harness nature to their purposes. The others, the 'barbarians', ground down by the demands of their rulers, and thwarted in every attempt to express their individual selves, remained forever in unenlightened herds. In Europe the arts were, in the full sense of the term, 'liberal'. And if these, too, had begun in Asia, in Babylon and Egypt, it was only in Europe that their potential had been realized. 'The liberal arts', wrote a complacent Samuel Purchas, 'are more liberal to us, having long since forsaken their seminaries in Asia and Africa'.

It is this, too, which led to the assumption that science would always be superior to simple force. It had, claimed Herodotus, been their skills—their *techne*—which had permitted the vastly outnumbered Spartans ultimately to defeat the Persians. An enslaved people, such as the Turks—archetypal

Asians—were not merely denied freedom of action by their rulers, they were also denied all access to knowledge. Their military success, like those of the Persians before them, had been due in part to their ferocity, in part to the weakness and intellectual poverty of their opponents. Throughout the sixteenth century when successive Christian intellectuals called upon their rulers to bury their differences and mount a crusade against the Turk, the claim was always that European, Christian, science could never fail against Asian ignorance. As the sixteenth-century Spanish humanist Juan Luis Vives phrased it, 'never, in effect, has Asia been able to resist the most mediocre forces in Europe'. And when, beginning in the thirteenth century, Europeans set out to persuade the world of the truth of their religion, they assumed a self-evident association between knowledge and belief. The European capacity to span an open space using an arch was said to have instantly persuaded one Peruvian chieftain of the truth of Christianity. The Jesuits who travelled to China in the late sixteenth century took with them clocks, astrolabes, telescopes, clavichords, Venetian prisms, and suction pumps. If, the argument went, the European God had taught the Europeans how to devise such ingenious things, it followed that the European God must be the true one. The Chinese, however, had other conceptions of the necessary relationship between technology and religious belief, and while grateful for the clocks declined the offer of the gospel. This refusal to accept the obvious led the most famous of the Jesuits, Matteo Ricci, to declare that 'they have no logic' and the Chinese to accuse the missionaries of indulging in 'countless incomprehensible lines of reasoning'.

After Columbus' discovery of America, and the rounding of the Cape of Good Hope—famously declared by Adam Smith to be 'the two greatest and most important events recorded in the history of mankind'—the European belief in the capacity of European science to dominate the world became even more assertive. For both these oceanic journeys had been made possible through the use of the compass and the skill of European navigators and cartographers. Only those whom Purchas described as 'we in the West' had been able to achieve such triumphs. Asians and Africans had been capable of limited navigational feats. But only the Europeans had managed to cross oceans, to settle, and to colonize. Only the Europeans— as Amerigo Vespucci in Johannes Stradanus' engraving of 1589 is just about to do—have civilized peoples from other inferior worlds. It was Europe, here embodied by Vespucci, which had literally drawn back the curtains upon a new world of which neither Africa nor Spain, nor even Europe's own, now sometimes dubious, ancient ancestors had had any knowledge. In Stradanus' fanciful depiction of the first moment of encounter between a

This symbolic representation of Amerigo Vespucci discovering America, from Johannes Stradanus' 1589 engraving, contrasts the technologically empowered European with the passive and unadorned figure who represents the peoples of America.

European and a Native American, he, Vespucci, is shown with an astrolabe, the emblem of his empowering knowledge, in his hand. She, in recumbent allusion to Vespucci's own image of the continent as an ever available female, is raising herself naked from the long sleep of her ignorance.

From the early sixteenth to the late eighteenth century images of the four continents appeared in the most unlikely places as a reminder both of the newly acquired vision of a vastly enlarged world, and of Europe's triumph over so much of it, a triumph which only the sciences and the arts had made possible. Take one striking, but representative example. On the ceiling of the stairway hall, the *Treppenhaus*, in the residence built between 1719 and 1744 by the prince-bishops of Würzburg (then members of a princely family in no way associated with transoceanic navigation) the great eighteenth-century Venetian artist Giambattista Tiepolo depicted in lavish detail each of the four continents. These are so arranged that no matter where the viewer stands, Asia, Africa, and America can only be seen in relation to Europe. Here, too, Asia is marked by the exotic (the elephant) and the languorous, Africa and America by the barbarous. Europe—the only one of

the allegorical female figures to be seated on a throne instead of an animal—is given the attributes of the arts, of music and painting, of science, and of the technology of warfare. Technology had given Europe the domination of the world. Cesare Ripa's *Iconologia* of 1603, a work which provided artists with an easy set of iconographic rules, instructs its readers to depict Europe wearing a crown, 'to show that Europe has always been the leader and queen of the whole world' . Thus an abducted Asian princess had become, as she appears in the 1588 edition of Sebastian Münster's *Cosmographia*, a queen.

Europeans believed that they had discovered and subdued the world through science. The stories of the conquest of Mexico and Peru, where vast numbers of men had been vanquished by a handful of adversaries armed with canon, horses, and steel swords, or of the subjugation by Portuguese shipboard cannon of the peoples of the West African coast and southern India, served to further enhance this sense of superiority through

Giovanni Battista
Tiepolo (1696–1770)
painted this fresco in
1753 as part of a com-
mission to decorate the
sumptuous Baroque
Residenz designed by
Balthasar Neumann for
the prince-bishop of
Würzburg. The allegor-
ical figures who
represent the continents
illustrate the conven-
tional contrast between
creative, accomplished
Europe and the rest of
the world.

technology. 'Natives', so the British fondly imagined, fell down in awe
before European firearms, and mistook their owners for gods. H. Rider
Haggard's Allan Quartermain—and later Tintin—is able to escape from
the clutches of crazed indigenes by predicting, with the help of an almanac,
the solar eclipse. The realities of these encounters were certainly otherwise, but even the great critics of the whole European colonial venture in
the eighteenth century could not quite shake off their pride in the success of
their science. If only, as Diderot lamented, it had not fallen into such criminal hands.

The Sense of Being European

The ability, whether the consequence of environment or divine will, to
control the resources of the natural world, to make them work for the
greater good of humankind, had given Europe its assumed superiority

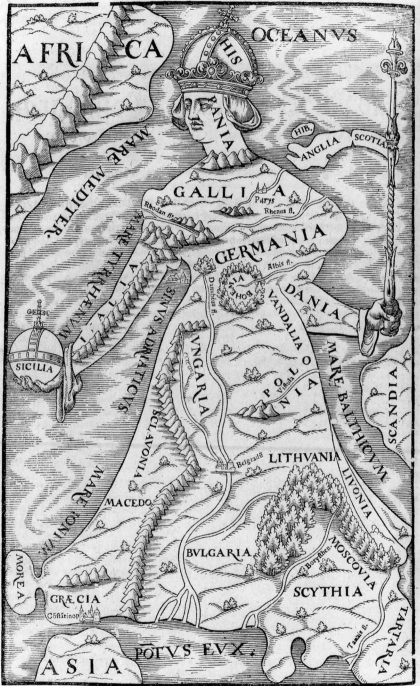

AFRI CA

OCEANVS

HIS

DANIA

HIB.
ANGLIA   SCOTIA

MARE MEDITER.

GALLIA
Rhodan fl.   Parys   Rhenus fl.

GERMANIA
Albis fl.
BOHE MIA

MARE TYRRHENVM

ITALIA

SICILIA

SINVS ADRIATICVS

SCLAVONIA

DANIA

VANDALIA

VNGARIA

P   O   L
O
Vistula   N
I   A

MARE BALTHICVM

SCANDIA

Belgradu   LITHVANIA   LIVONIA

MACEDO.

MARE IONIV.

MOREA

GRÆCIA
Cõstatinop.

BVLGARIA

Borysthe.   MOSCOVIA

SCYTHIA

Tanais fl.

TARTARIA

POTVS EVX.

ASIA

among the peoples of the world. This is the origin of the belief, which is still shared by many, that Europe, or 'The West' is exceptional. That the subsequent history of western imperialism has meant that much of the world was, until recently, and the world's economies still are, governed according to rules of European origin, has only helped to reinforce that belief. There can be little doubt, however much we all may now regret the fact, that the West has, for long periods of its recent history, exercised technological and political mastery over much of the rest of the world. It is also likely that the power of European technology derives from the ancient conviction, strengthened by the radical transformation of science in the seventeenth century, that the ability to harness nature is part of what it is to be human. But it should be stressed that the early modern Europeans' sense of their own distinctiveness has its origins in a period when those who thought of themselves as 'European' were still a small group of semi-nomadic peoples clinging to the lands around the Mediterranean basin.

European confidence in the exceptionality of the continent also served to reinforce the sense of being European, at least among the élites, even after the rise of the nation state as the accepted, and enduring, political unit within the continent in the sixteenth and seventeenth centuries. In 1623, Francis Bacon could speak confidently—although he did so in Latin—of 'we Europeans'. Cosmopolitanism was predominantly, however, an eighteenth-century objective which linked seventeenth-century ecumenism to the vision of a secularized world of wise men, bound by their common identity as rational beings. 'No citizen of Europe' claimed Burke—ever scathing about England's 'inclination to shrink into her narrow self'— 'could be altogether an exile in any part of it . . . When a man travelled or resided for health, pleasure, business, or necessity from his country, he never felt himself quite abroad'.

Transnational politics came also to occupy a literary space. The 'republic of letters' existed on paper, in a network of correspondence, and in that great unifying enterprise, Diderot and Jean d'Alembert's *Encyclopédie*, a work which drew its authors from across the whole map of Europe. Leibniz proposed the creation of a 'European academy', and a 'European tribunal'. Countless journals sprang up with 'Europe' in their titles—*Gran Giornale*

Sebastian Münster (1489–1552), professor of Hebrew at Basle, produced in his *Cosmographia*, first published in 1544, the standard and most frequently re-published textbook of geography and cosmography. Some forty editions were printed in Germany alone. In this illustration from the 1588 edition, the outlines of the European land-masses are turned with the west uppermost, to create the figure of a crowned queen composed of the different nations of Europe.

de Europa, *L'Europe savante*, *Correo general histórico literario y económico de Europa*. There was even 'Cosmopolis' itself, an imaginary city from which a large number of books were printed during the eighteenth century. Rousseau's lament—he hated all forms of cosmopolitanism which he attributed to a 'passion for gold' and the 'lust for women'—that 'today there are no longer any Frenchmen, Germans, Spaniards, even Englishmen, whatever one might say, today there are only Europeans' may have been overstated, but it was true enough of the intellectual circles in which he moved.

Eighteenth-century century cosmopolitanism, however, was linked both back to a recognition of the very real differences which existed between nations, and forward to a more generous notion of 'humanity', a humanity which embraced the peoples not only of Europe, but of the entire globe. 'The highest purpose of nature', wrote Kant in 1784, 'is a universal *cosmopolitan existence*', which was to be the 'matrix within which all the original capacities of the human race may develop'. Kant's vision, it is true, was loftier than many, but most enlightened Europeans had come to perceive unity in terms of a scale which ran from the nation at one end to the whole of humanity at the other. European success, as Europeans understood it, had brought untold benefits, but it was that very success, and in particular the commercial networks which now sustained it, which made the former isolation of the continent unsustainable. Europeans might still believe that they possessed the key to all human understanding and the technologies that flowed from it, but in so doing they had also acquired an obligation, something few Greeks or Romans had ever recognized, to employ that for the greater good of the larger world. As David Hume once remarked: with regard to Britain he was a citizen of Europe, but with regard to Europe, he was a citizen of the world. The belief that any human group could maintain itself 'disjointed from the community of mankind' was, said Burke, 'an opinion [that] does not deserve refutation as absurd, but pity as insane'. Burke's cosmopolitanism was, of course, based upon a belief in the enduring force of a stable form of government, namely monarchy, a stable religion, and stable laws and customs. He abhorred revolution. But his objectives, and those of the founders of the two great revolutions of the eighteenth century, the American and the French, converged in their conclusions that 'the rights of man' which had been proclaimed in 1776 and 1789, were not merely the rights of the Americans or the French; they were the rights of humanity at large. By the end of the eighteenth century, as European technology and European trade appeared to have encircled the world, it might seem that Cicero's vision of Rome as the 'republic of all the world' had been realized in ways Cicero could never have imagined. Instead of reducing the world to Rome, Rome had gone out to the world.

It is here, too, that we can find the origins of that capacity for collective self-scrutiny which could, at times, collapse into a bleak self-hatred which is a feature of so much modern European culture, and underpins much of Europe's relationship with the wider world. Recognition that one could belong to something called 'Europe' only as a subgroup of something immeasurably greater which might include peoples and cultures not merely difficult to understand but as yet unknown had already by the second half of the eighteenth century begun to compel a re-evaluation of all that had been done in Europe's name. It is this which allowed Johann Gottfried Herder, for long regarded as the father of German nationalism, to speak at the very end of the eighteenth century for 'the genius of humanity' against 'all those writings which feed the arrogance of the Europeans—already sufficiently overbearing—with claims which are unproven, and manifestly unprovable'.

The Quest for Peace and Union

European cosmopolitanism, and the nationalism which, paradoxically, was to emerge from it after the conclusion of the Napoleonic wars, must also be seen as perhaps the final phase in the centuries long search for peace through unity. The reason Strabo had given for the excellence of Europe was that there, unlike Asia or Africa, the interests of peace had succeeded in keeping 'control over the whole body'. For if one part of the European identity derived from the recognition and exploitation of human competitiveness, and its control though the rule of law, another was the belief that Europeans held peace to be a greater good than war. In view of the succession of European empires which have followed that of Athens, then of Rome, and of the language of militarism which sustained and sustains most European states, this must seem at best a crazed delusion. But militarism has never had it all its own way. Even the Romans, at least in theory, looked upon war as a means of last resort whose objective was to acquire, not cultural and religious transformation, much less territory, but peace and justice. 'War', as St Augustine told the Roman general Bonifatius in about 417, 'should be waged only as a necessity . . . For peace is not sought in order to kindle war, but war waged in order that peace may be secured.'

The Roman Empire itself, and the Christian 'republic' which succeeded it had, in their ways, been conceived as instruments for acquiring peace. What Rome had sought to export had been precisely a way of life which would be guaranteed at all times and all places by the *Pax Romana*. After the collapse of the Roman Empire, and the progressive enfeeblement of the medieval empires which had grown up out of its remains, Europe relapsed into long periods of internal warfare. In the sixteenth century these struggles, whose origins had been largely dynastic, were fuelled by ideological conflict as Catholics fought Protestants within the same national communities. Prolonged confessional hostilities which were to culminate in the Thirty Years War between 1618 and 1648, and which left most of central Europe in ruins, together with the threat from another Asian empire, the Ottoman Turks, gave rise to a number of more or less improbable schemes for what at the time was known as 'Universal Monarchy'. Although some of these, for instance that of the Neapolitan magus, Tommaso Campanella, were genuinely universal—Campanella was confident that China, Japan, and India would all succumb to European arms as Mexico and Peru had done—most were confined to Europe. All of these projects argued that if Christendom was to be made safe the princes of Europe had to abandon the pursuit of their individual interests to make way for a single world monarchy. The various unions of arms which had, throughout the sixteenth century, been proposed and, on occasions fitfully achieved, had had no lasting success. The princes of Christendom were too many and their interests too diverse. But a universal monarchy ruled by a single prince might. 'I believe', wrote the Piedmontese failed Jesuit Giovanni Botero in 1607, 'that the human race would live most happily if it were all brought under a single prince.' Such a world where one might travel 'with the same language and the same money' would constitute a common *patria*. It would eliminate the risk, and hence also the crippling cost, of internal war and consequently, by comparison with any existing monarchy, be able to reduce drastically the fiscal burden on its subjects. It would, Botero believed, be a safer, richer, and hence happier, place. None of these imperial ambitions came to anything. But they remained a more serious possibility than many have supposed, serious enough to trouble the sleep of a deeply sceptical David Hume as late as the second half of the eighteenth century.

The 'universal monarchy' projects of the sixteenth and seventeenth century had aroused only fear and hostility, even among those who were their supposed beneficiaries. They had done so because they all involved the triumph of one European state, first Spain and then France, over another. And whereas Rome had exported a common body of law, the conception of a single trans-ethic community—that of citizenship—and had offered to its conquered provinces a common culture, it had always remained a loose federation of quasi-independent societies, which for long periods of time had been governed by emperors and administrators who were themselves neither Roman nor even Italian. The possibility of establishing such a pan-European monarchy perished with Charles V, the last European ruler to possess no obvious national allegiances, who was born in the Low Countries but chose to die in Spain, a man who was said to have spoken Spanish to God, French to his mistress, and German to his horse. After Charles's abdication in 1556 the Habsburg Empire divided into two: the empire of Philip II, which until the early eighteenth century was to remain the Spanish monarchy; and the remains of the Holy Roman Empire, the lands of Germany and east-central Europe. Neither could offer the basis for a truly pan-European state in which no one nation would predominate over another.

After the devastation of much of central Europe during the Thirty Years War and the demise of both the Catholic Church and the Holy Roman Empire as international agencies with any real authority, there emerged a succession of more or less improbable and impractical projects which sought not to rebuild the old imperial systems but to devise something far closer to the leagues of Ancient Greece. Of these, the so-called 'Grand Design' devised in the 1620 by the duc de Sully, Henri IV of France's first minister, was probably the earliest and the most grandiose. This involved altering the boundaries of Europe to create fifteen nation states, ruled collectively by a senate composed of sixty members, four from each state, with seats in Nantes, Metz, and Cologne. It was also intended to have a standing army and a fleet.

Sully's 'Grand Design' was never more than a dream. A realist and an experienced statesman, he knew full well that the short-term objectives of princes, not to mention the growing sense of national identity among the peoples of all the European states, would prevent any such strategy from ever becoming a reality. Moreover, even Sully, cosmopolitan though he was, could not resist suggesting that any future European meta-state would have to have its centre in, or at least very near, France. In his plan southern and northern Europe were relegated to the political periphery, which was hardly a realistic view to take of the balance of power within Europe in the early seventeenth century. But as a dream it remained a powerful reminder that there existed the possibility, and there had once existed the reality, of an alternative to the persistent antagonism between nation states. In the nineteenth century, when there was a widespread revaluation of Europe's Gothic past, a number of German Romantics—Novalis, the Schlegel brothers, Adam Muller, even fitfully Madame de Staël—attempted to revive the idea of an old Germanic Reich as the instrument of European unification. But few Europeans, who were not also 'Goths', were any more eager to see a European federalism, in Muller's words, 'wearing German colours' than they had been to see it in Spanish or French ones.

Such projects can best be understood in the context of a series of designs for 'perpetual peace' which ranged from Emeric Cruce's *Le Nouveau Cynée* of 1623, through the Abbé de St-Pierre's *Projet pour rendre la paix per- petuelle en Europe* of 1712—which Voltaire complained could no more exist among princes 'than it could among elephants and rhinoceroses, or between wolves and dogs'—to perhaps the most influential, and certainly the most compelling, Immanuel Kant's *Perpetual Peace* of 1795. All of these operated with the notion that peace could only be secured in Europe, and ultimately the world, through some kind of *con*federacy, as the Ancient Greek Amphictyonic council had been, of independent states, each of which, in the words used by James Madison to urge a similar proposal upon the United States of America, 'retained the character of independent and sovereign states and had equal votes in the federal council'.

In the modern world, commercial and politically and culturally pluralist, only a confederated system of this kind, divided by climate, culture, and language, but united in its economic and political objectives, could be the ground upon which, in Kant's words, 'that of every distinct society depends'. 'In an unregulated world-system', argued Kant, each state must 'expect from any other precisely the same evils which formerly oppressed individual men [in the State of Nature] and forced them into a law-gov- erned civil state.' The only escape from a world where the large, technically skilled, and militarily powerful states were empowered to absorb all others would be a federation of peoples in which every state, even the smallest, could expect to derive its security and its rights not from its own power or its own legal judgement, 'but solely from this great federation from a united power and the law-governed decisions of a united will'.

Europeans are, I suspect, unusual in sharing in this way a sense that it might be possible to belong to something larger than the family, the tribe, the community, or the nation, yet smaller, and more culturally specific, than 'humanity'. The claim that all Chinese maps placed China at the centre of the world is false. There are Chinese maps which, for political and cultural as well as geographical reasons, place Japan at the centre. But there are no Chinese maps or Chinese histories which suggest that Japan and China belong to a single continental grouping. If the Chinese, the Japanese, the Koreans, the Thais now sometimes choose to identify themselves as Asians this is because European notions of ethnicity and the domination of the world economy by European concepts of exchange have compelled them to do so. Similarly the peoples of, say, Uganda and Nigeria—themselves the products of European impositions—are highly conscious of belonging to a continent called 'Africa' largely if not wholly because European colonization, and the marks of European racism, have made it impossible for them to think otherwise. Being African in Africa, or Asian in Asia provides only the loosest cultural or political cohesion, and, at most levels, no cohesion at all.

This is not, of course, to endorse any kind of European exceptionalism. All the peoples of the world are the outcome of the combination, dispersal, and recombination, through warfare and the pursuit of subsistence, of myriad diverse groups of peoples. China, which is larger than Europe, was not inhabited by one ethnic group either. Nor was Assyria, Elam, Urartu, Persia, ancient Mexico, or Inca Peru. But these were ethnic states. They invited (or compelled) the outsiders whom they conquered into their homelands and absorbed them into the dominant ethnic community. What is unusual about 'Europe' is that it possesses an identity as a cultural space, within which there have been and continue to be, frequent political unions, but which has never constituted a single state, much less a single ethnic group.

By the end of the eighteenth century that identity had been firmly established for centuries. But it had never achieved, nor has it yet achieved, lasting political expression. Napoleon, in pursuit of the first European-wide empire to be established since Roman times, would dream consistently of a single continental federation, one which would transform identity into lasting political union, one in which it would be possible to apply to 'the great European family, the American Congress or the Amphictyonic Council of Greece, and what a vision that opens of power, grandeur, happiness and prosperity'. He added, however, that in order to do that one had first to create a Europe of nations. The foundations of European nationalism lie outside the scope of this volume. But it remains something of a paradox that the conditions for unity, which were so heavily dependent upon Europe's evolving relationship with the worlds beyond Europe, should have been in place before each of its individual communities had developed the resources to create states which would be coextensive with the nations of which the continent was composed. Kant's ecumenical vision furthermore could easily be reclaimed by those who found, after the Congress of Vienna, that the new Europe of nations had created a world which was potentially far more perilous than the one which had preceded it. Even Nietzsche, who had no time for Kant, looked forward to the 'destruction of nations'. Modern life, he believed, and the speed of modern communications would soon dissolve the artifical boundaries between the European peoples. It was Nietzsche's 'Good European' and Kant's cosmopolitan citizen—unlikely companions though they may be—who inspired Jean Monnet and Altiero Spinelli and who, however dimly perceived, still drive the search for greater European union. We—we in Europe that is—still await the day when the conflicting forces of nationalism will resolve themselves into a fully integrated federation of states. But if the United States of Europe—a phrase, and the proposals to match it, which begin to crop up from the 1840s—ever comes into being it will be the embodiment of a vision which reaches back nearly three millennia.

I

THE SIXTEENTH CENTURY

*c.*1500–*c.*1618

The Conditions of Life for the Masses

ALISON ROWLANDS

Who Were the Masses?

Late fifteenth-century Europeans often thought about their society in terms of the traditional tripartite image they had inherited from their medieval forebears. According to this image people were divided into three distinct orders, each defined by its own God-ordained function and accorded different privileges and status. The clergy occupied pride of place as those who prayed for their fellow Christians. They were closely followed in prestige by the nobility as those who fought and provided military protection for the wider Christian community. The rest of the population—the commonalty, or in German *das gemeine Volk* (literally 'the common people')—constituted the largest and lowliest group. They made up the broad social base on which the two privileged orders reposed and they laboured as peasants and artisans 'to pourveye for the clerkes and knyghtes suche thinges as were nedeful for them to lyve by', as William Caxton wrote in 1480.

Always more of an ideal than a guide to historical reality, this image of the masses becomes increasingly inadequate when compared to their experience between the late fifteenth and early seventeenth centuries. It is too general: it takes no account of the fact that the common people of sixteenth-century Europe were not a homogeneous mass but individuals whose experience of life was influenced by many factors: their gender, wealth, age, marital and social status, and especially the type of community (rural or urban) and region in which they lived. It is also too static an image: it fails to reflect the fact that the sixteenth century was a time of significant change, notably in demographic and economic terms. This change had particularly adverse effects on the common people, exacerbating processes of social polarization and reducing many of those who were ideally supposed to work to the status of paupers. This chapter will delineate some of this finer detail by discussing the material and mental world of peasants, the processes and effects of sixteenth-century change, and the urban experience of the lower orders.

The Peasant Household

The landscape of sixteenth-century Europe was overwhelmingly rural, its economy predominantly agrarian. Most of its common people, totalling 85–90 per cent of the entire population, lived in the countryside and were involved in agricultural production. While the word 'peasant' does little justice to the great regional diversity in size of holdings, types of tenure, and farming methods of the period, it can usefully be deployed to denote a rural cultivator farming a plot of land with the labour resources provided by his or her household, with the aim of subsistence rather than profit. In about 1450 rural Europe was dominated by a middle peasantry possessing holdings of adequate and similar size; as a result of changes which will be described later, the next 150 years saw this peasantry polarize into a minority of wealthy yeoman farmers and a majority of land-poor and landless labourers.

Peasant life was organized around the household and the landholding. Everyone who lived under the same roof belonged to the household even if—as was the case with resident servants—they were unrelated by blood or marriage. Generally speaking the nuclear household, centred on a single married couple and their children, dominated in north-western Europe, while in southern France, Italy, and parts of Austria households were extended, and more likely to contain more than one married couple. There was much variation in these arrangements, however. In addition to the core family nuclear households might also contain an aged grandparent, an orphaned niece or nephew, or resident servants if the couple's children were too young to work, while extended households were often nuclear at some stage in the life-cycle of their inhabitants and could only survive in the long term on larger farms. Regardless of geographic location, the poorer peasants were, the more likely they were to live in small and simple households. Peasant households also incorporated livestock in addition—and often in close and malodorous proximity—to its human inhabitants. The economic importance of livestock (particularly oxen or horse plough-teams and cattle) was such that peasants resorted to all man-

Albrecht Dürer's late fifteenth-century print of the Prodigal Son sets a biblical story in the surroundings of rural Germany *c*.1500, complete with livestock and dung-heap.

ner of herbal and magical remedies to protect them against disease and witchcraft.

The peasant household's locus of authority was its male head. He controlled the disposition of household resources, was owed obedience by his wife, children, and servants (and could physically chastise them if it were not forthcoming), and represented the household in communal politics. However, patriarchal authority was more absolute in theory than practice. Sixteenth-century court records show that peasant women had the power to disrupt household harmony and to make their husbands' lives miserable by scolding them or by cooking them inadequate or irregular meals, while praise for their talents as keepers of house and livestock suggests that their contribution to the household economy was so vital that the day-to-day marital relationship was more of a partnership (albeit an unequal one) than a hierarchy. Moreover, a man whose domestic behaviour was thought to contravene expected norms also risked interference in his household's affairs from kinsfolk, neighbours, and even the authorities. For example, an official investigation was carried out in the German village of Detwang in 1540 after Hans Kuelwein's wife died of a strange illness and rumour spread that Kuelwein's violence towards her had been the real cause of her demise. The question of patriarchal authority was also complicated by age, in households where there was more than one married couple. It was rendered virtually irrelevant in the smallest, most poverty-stricken households, many of which, especially in towns, were in any case headed by widows.

The house inhabited by the peasant household was more than just a structure which provided living space and shelter from the elements. It also offered its inhabitants legal refuge. In Germany, for example, the legal principle of *Hausfrieden*, or 'house peace', guaranteed the house and everyone in it special protection within a boundary formed symbolically by the line of drops which fell from the eaves on to the ground when it rained. Anyone breaking this peace incurred particularly harsh penalties; this was why German peasant men tried to lure their neighbours across their thresholds when they wanted to fight or insult them. House-boundaries also figured in beliefs about supernatural safeguards. For example, people and animals were thought to be protected against witchcraft if bundles of special herbs were placed in the lintels of doors through which they left the house.

Attached to the peasant house was land. The size of a peasant family's landholding depended on local population density and inheritance customs. The latter varied widely throughout Europe. A general distinction, however, can be drawn between areas of impartible and partible inheritance. In the former, land was bequeathed intact to a single heir, usually the eldest son in many English counties, although elsewhere it could be the youngest son, a son-in-law, or, more rarely, a daughter. In the latter, land was divided between all heirs, often the sons, as in Normandy, but sometimes all children. Partible inheritance was practised in certain parts of England, western France, and south-western Germany, where the principle of equal division was based on the local dictum 'as many mouths, so many pounds' (that is, an equal share in the value of the property to all those with claims on it). In some areas of sixteenth-century Europe the line between impartible and partible inheritance blurred as the heir was made responsible for providing for siblings from the profits of the main holding. This reflects the tension between the two chief and often conflicting aims of the peasant: to keep the family land as intact and viable as possible and to make provision for all offspring.

Different inheritance customs had different social and economic effects. Impartible inheritance could cause bitter rivalries between the privileged heir and less privileged siblings who had to leave the family home to find work or stay on, unmarried, as the equivalent of resident servants. Partible inheritance risked the division of holdings into economically unviable units; it worked best where the soil was most fertile and where peasants could draw on common resources of pasture, woodland, and water as well as their own land. Not all peasants adhered slavishly to local inheritance custom when this became impractical, however. In the face of increasing population pressure some peasants in the English Midlands and the south-west German county of Hohenlohe reverted from partible inheritance to impartible to keep their holdings intact and maintain familial wealth.

Hard physical work was the lot of the members of the sixteenth-century peasant household. Some contemporary sources stressed the Christian virtue of labour by likening peasants to their original forefather, Adam, but this was probably of little consolation to peasants in their struggle to produce enough food to subsist with very little technological aid and at the mercy of the vagaries of climate and disease. Good health and physical fitness were of paramount importance to peasants; old age to them meant bodily frailty and inability to work, while men in their prime bemoaned physical injuries sustained in fights (and could bring civil suits for compensation against whoever had inflicted them) because they fundamentally affected the ability to toil. It was this thinking which prompted German peasant Hans Sturm to ask his opponent 'What have you done to me and my small children?' during a fight in 1545 in which Sturm's hand was badly damaged.

Plebs aret, ædificet, fodiat, metat, otia vitet, Nec Regum aut Cleri munia folicitet.

An engraving showing the seasonal labours of peasant men. Women's overall economic contribution to the peasant household's economy is marginalized by its focus on field-work; the engraving shows only one woman, binding sheaves at harvest-time.

Although there were parts of sixteenth-century Europe which specialized in livestock (cattle in parts of Hungary and Denmark, for example, and sheep in regions of Spain and England) arable farming was on the increase as the population grew. Arable farming always necessitated the keeping of some livestock for manure (the only fertilizer available in the period) and a large and prominently displayed dung-heap was an important indicator of peasant wealth and status. Hugh Latimer listed the seasonal tasks undertaken by men on arable farms in his 1548 sermon *Of the Plough*. Using his knowledge of agrarian practices as the son of a Leicestershire yeoman, Latimer noted that 'the ploughman first setteth forth his plough, and then tilleth his land, and breaketh it in furrows, and sometime ridgeth it up again; and at another time harroweth it and clotteth it, and sometime dungeth it and hedgeth it, diggeth it and weedeth it, purgeth it and maketh it clean'. Men then sowed the grain (usually rye, oats, barley, wheat, or millet, which went to make the bread and gruel which were the staples of the peasant diet) and later reaped and threshed it. Men also fetched wood (the main source of fuel), made and repaired tools and farming implements, mended shoes, and wove.

As they were largely responsible for childcare, peasant women's work centred more on the house and its vicinity. They did the household's cooking, cleaning, and washing, fetched water, took care of poultry and the small livestock, made bread, dairy products, cloth and beer, and tended the garden. They also took rural produce to market and worked in the fields at harvest time, either reaping with a sickle, or binding the sheaves and gleaning. This gender division of labour meant that a peasant household could only hope to survive with two healthy adults at its core; and helps to explain why rates of remarriage after the death of a spouse were faster in rural than urban areas. Peasant children were involved in work processes by their parents as soon as they were able and often began their working lives as goose or swineherds.

The Peasant Life-Cycle

The formation and re-formation of peasant households in sixteenth-century Europe revolved around the life-cycle events of birth, marriage, and death. Although there were some areas where more than one married couple lived under the same roof, marriage was synonymous with social adulthood and independence for most peasants. This meant that they tended to marry late (in their mid to late twenties in western Europe) after receiving an inheritance or working to amass sufficient capital to establish an independent household (however small), and that a significant proportion of the population (perhaps a tenth in total, and usually more women than men) never married at all. It also made marriage very desirable for men and women alike. Husbands and wives enjoyed higher status than bachelors and spinsters and marriage legitimized sexual relations between them.

Peasant marriage was preceded by courtship. Individuals were freer to choose their own spouses if their father or both their parents were already dead, or if they were not tied to parental wishes by inheritance expectations. Even then most peasant youngsters shared in communal mores which advised that a good marriage partner was one who would bring some property to the marriage and work hard thereafter. They tended to marry locally (although ecclesiastical rules regarding marriage within certain degrees of consanguinity and affinity encouraged them to look for partners beyond the confines of their own village) and within their own wealth and status bracket. Opportunities to meet potential spouses were offered by village dances and by the gatherings of women to spin, knit, and sew (the *Spinnstube* in Germany and *veillée* in France) which were visited with enthusiasm by the village youths. A more intimate custom was bundling, in which a courting couple spent the night together in the woman's bed. Sexual petting occurred but full intercourse was rare; the village community frowned on illegitimacy as strongly as the Church, though for economic rather than moral reasons.

For a peasant couple a marriage was made once betrothal vows had been exchanged and the property transfer between their two families irrevocably sealed by an act of intercourse. Women's dowries (which excluded them from any further claim on their birth-family's inheritance) usually consisted of money or valuable movable goods rather than land: a marriage bed, household utensils and bed linens, and perhaps a cow or two. A church wedding ceremony often followed only when a woman became pregnant. The peasant emphasis on betrothal rather than church wedding as the real start of a marriage was attacked in the sixteenth century by Protestant (and to a lesser extent Counter-Reformation) authorities in their attempts to

A drawing from the German town of Volkach from 1504, showing a peasant, Hans Hemp, and his wife bringing their produce to sell at the town market. Intended to illustrate a point about the taxation practices of the town, it also shows the economic partnership of the married peasant couple.

stamp out the perceived evils of clandestine marriage and premarital sex and to make marriage more subject to parental and communal control. They met with only limited success by the early seventeenth century. For the peasant the church wedding was anyway but a prelude to the wedding feast, where unrestrained enjoyment of food, drink, and dancing was high on the agenda. Wedding feasts varied in scale according to resources, but many families were willing to incur debts in order to uphold their honour by entertaining their kin and neighbours in suitably lavish style.

Once they were married a peasant couple expected to have children. Church teaching (that the procreation of children was one of the main purposes of marriage) and the more prosaic desire for heirs concurred here, and infertility (always the wife's fault) was regarded as a problem to be solved by means of prayer in Protestant areas, the intercession of saints in Catholic areas, and all manner of herbal remedies and magical rituals generally. Due to the late age at which they married, their often spartan diet, their life of hard physical work, and the fact that they breastfed their babies, peasant women usually had only six or seven children, although high rates of infant mortality ensured that only two to four of them would survive.

A woman knew definitely that she was pregnant only when her child quickened, or moved inside her. From then until she gave birth the mother was thought able to affect the child by what she did; outbursts of anger, for example, were thought to risk miscarriage, while women who craved rabbit during pregnancy were thought likely to bear hare-lipped children. Pregnant women were also accorded certain privileges; examples of customary laws from rural Franconia show that they were allowed special fishing rights in order to supplement their diets. As well as being a time of responsibility and privilege, however, pregnancy was also a time of anxiety for most sixteenth-century women, who ran a 6–7 per cent risk of dying giving birth in the course of their reproductive lives. A host of remedies (including saints' relics, such as the belt of Saint Elizabeth, charms such as eagle stones, prayers, and herbal concoctions) were employed during birth to help procure the mother a safe and speedy delivery.

Childbirth was an event exclusively connected with women. A mother gave birth in the presence of women she had specially invited to assist and support her: neighbours, relatives (if they lived close enough), and the midwife. After giving birth she would lie in for about six weeks during which time female guests attended her childbed feast, where they ate, drank, and gossiped. The child's father and godparents attended its christening but again women dominated, with the midwife carrying the child to the church and women guests at the ceremony (and subsequent festivities) in the majority. The mother returned to work and communal involvement at the end of her lying-in period after she had been churched. Rather than regarding the lying-in period as a negative reinforcement of Old Testament ideas about the impurity of childbirth, sixteenth-century women probably saw it in more positive terms, as a time to recover from the birth, to rest from work and sex, and to socialize with female friends. The poorer women were, the more likely they were to lie in for only a short time or not at all and the less likely they were to hold childbed feasts.

Death was the greatest disrupter of sixteenth-century peasant households. Average life expectancy was around thirty years, a figure largely accounted for by rates of infant and child mortality which saw 40–50 per cent of children die before they reached the age of 10. Parents could expect to lose half or more of their children and spouses to lose their partners after only relatively short lives together; even in Protestant areas the number of marriages ended by divorce compared with death was infinitesimal. This led to frequent remarriages (although men found it easier to find new partners than women did, and rural women found it easier than their urban counterparts) and meant that families often included step-parents and half-siblings.

Most people (and especially children) died of disease in sixteenth-century Europe—of plague, smallpox, dysentery, and the more vaguely designated fevers, fluxes, dropsies, and wasting diseases. Normal levels of mortality were also maintained by accidents (often drowning), death in childbed (for women), and as the result of fights (for men). Mortality was periodically exacerbated to crisis levels by epidemics, war, and dearth. Epidemics, especially of the plague, had particularly devastating effects on the common people in crowded urban quarters: Venice lost 27 per cent of its population to the plague in 1575–6. War and dearth hit peasants harder. Town walls offered a modicum of protection against armies which ruined crops, slaughtered livestock, and spread disease, while town-dwellers were closer to stores of grain and the élites from whom they might beg food in times of scarcity.

The harvest failures which caused food shortages and lowered resistance to disease were usually the result of bad weather. In Franconia 1570 saw an extremely wet summer and autumn ruin both the grain and wine harvests and herald four years of scant supplies and high prices, while the bad harvests of the late 1590s throughout Europe were due to unusually wet weather. For peasants, occasional years of dearth punctuated their everyday struggle to subsist. As a result of limited technology and supplies of manure agrarian productivity was low, with average yields of only four to six grains for every one sown. This meant that a peasant household needed an average minimum of 5 hectares of land for subsistence, a great deal more if the land were less fertile and the weather poor.

Ways of Coping

Peasants were not passive in the face of threats to their survival. In times of war and dearth they might flee the land, usually to the nearest town, for succour, and petition their lords for help in rebuilding their communities thereafter. A mortality crisis also occasioned a rapid spate of remarriages and first-time marriages (often at younger ages) to make good population loss. Of far greater significance to peasants, however, was the wide range of resources and techniques on which they drew to help them foresee and cope with the everyday problems of inclement weather, inexplicable illness, infertility, and failure to thrive in humans, animals, and agricultural processes. Peasants believed that the world around them was full of 'signs', or events which could be interpreted as portents: sunshine on St Vincent's day, for example, meant a good wine harvest, while the birth of a monstrously deformed child was usually an omen of disaster. At the same time peasants believed that they could ward off ill fortune by various means. The wearing or carrying of amulets or herbs (which might first have been blessed in a special way) and the recitation of quasi-religious formulas were preventative and protective measures which were extremely common throughout Europe. Once misfortune had occurred, and the peasants' own stock of supernatural remedies had been exhausted, they would turn for aid to any or all of the local purveyors of more powerful (and hopefully more efficacious) magic: the saint's shrine, parish priest, or folk-healer. Folk-healers were often blacksmiths or shepherds who offered (for a fee) to cure sickness, lift spells, and find lost or stolen objects for their owners. Georg Kissling, the smith of a south-west German village called Ergersheim, was renowned in 1582 for healing people with salves, finding stolen goods with the help of a crystal, and protecting livestock against witches with special herbs. Evidence suggests that folk-healers were very common in sixteenth-century rural Europe: contemporary English writers thought they probably equalled, and perhaps even exceeded, the parish clergy in numbers.

Sixteenth-century ecclesiastical visitation records show that peasants had no sense of any meaningful division between religion and magic in their strategies for coping with the vagaries of life. To them, the idea that a cure for toothache consisted of the saying of five Our Fathers and five creeds, or that a crumbled mass wafer and the intercession of saints were seen as guarantors of the fertility of the local soil, was eminently logical: the end result justified any means employed to obtain it. This world-view was attacked after the Reformation and, to a lesser extent, the Catholic Counter-Reformation. Protestant reformers taught that misfortune was a punishment from God for sin and that the only theologically valid response was repentance and prayer. John Calvin told women in childbed to call no more to the Virgin Mary and St Margaret for help but instead to offer their groans to God, while German Lutherans ordered such women to send their midwives away if they started muttering 'superstitious' blessings. Given the impracticality of such suggestions in peasant eyes, sixteenth- and early seventeenth-century attempts to extirpate the magical from popular religion were largely dismal failures.

Ironically, at the same time as they were trying to stamp out popular 'superstition' and misuse of church resources by peasants, many Protestant and Catholic authorities offered their rural subjects a deadly tool in their fight against one of the most feared instigators of misfortune—the witch. Peasants saw many misfortunes as the result of ill-will, asking when mishap occurred not *how* it had happened but *who* had made it happen. The answer was often a particular village woman who had long had a reputation for being able to cause harm by magical means, often by cursing or simply glancing at her victim. Peasants may long have associated women with witchcraft because they were traditionally in charge of many life-giving and nurturing processes, such as childbirth, cooking, and caring for the sick. These processes were at once mysterious and hence powerful, but also ambiguous because they could have negative as well as positive outcomes.

Once a witch was identified peasants might scratch her and draw blood to nullify the spell, or counter it with white magic of their own or a folk-healer's devising. From the late fifteenth century and increasingly from about 1560, however, élites who had come to believe that witchcraft was the renunciation of Christianity in favour of an alliance with the Devil gave peasants the opportunity of ridding their communities of witches through legal channels. As a result an estimated 60,000 people, four-fifths of whom were women, were executed for witchcraft during the early modern period. The intensity of witch-hunts varied greatly from region to region, however. The worst hunts occurred in places where a popular fear of witchcraft was taken seriously by local judicial authorities which had enough autonomy to bend legal procedures explicitly to the extirpation of witches: parts of south-western Germany, the Swiss Vaud, and the French Pyrenees, for example; or small ecclesiastical principalities like Trier.

Popular beliefs were more than simply mechanisms for dealing with the exigencies of everyday existence, however; they also enabled peasants to cope with life's only certainty—death. Various popular customs (such as the opening of all windows following a death in the house) were implemented with the express aim of seeing a deceased person's soul safely out of this world, while the merriment incorporated into funeral rites was a way of coping psychologically with the ubiquity of death by asserting the liveliness of the living. Peasants also periodically expressed great (and to their social superiors, often alarming) outbursts of eagerness for their own salvation. In 1476 many hundreds flocked to the call of Hans Behem, the so-called Drummer of Niklashausen, when he claimed that the Virgin Mary had told him to make the small south German town a place of pilgrimage, while spiritual enthusiasm was inextricably bound up with desires for greater social justice in the German Peasants' War of 1524–5.

Wider Links: Village, Lordship, Market

The peasant household was integrated into various wider social and economic networks. Arguably the most important of these, given the strong sense of localism prevalent in sixteenth-century Europe, was the network offered by the village. Villages ranged from tiny hamlets of five or six households to large settlements with sixty or seventy. Not all inhabitants were rural cultivators; large villages in particular might include rural artisans (usually blacksmiths and millers, but perhaps also tailors, bakers, or cobblers) and a parish priest. Living in a village benefited a peasant household in many ways. It offered some degree of protection against marauders, especially if the village boasted a sturdy church which could double as a defensive refuge in times of attack, and a focus of communal sociability in the village alehouse and annual festivities (particularly the celebrations connected with the local patron saint's day). It also often offered a share in the use of communal resources (such as common arable and pasture land and woods), communal farming implements and the services of village herdsman, and a communal ordering of life aimed at mediating social conflict.

Village assemblies still played an important part in the everyday running of communal life in many parts of sixteenth-century Europe: in France, Spain, and especially Switzerland and southern Germany, where rights of overlordship were particularly fragmentary. Consisting of all household heads with sufficient land to qualify them for a full right in the community, the village assembly met regularly to make decisions relating to the use of communal resources and regulation of agrarian work and to fine any vil-

lagers who had violated communal custom (these fines were then usually converted into alcohol and drunk by the village assembly). In the early sixteenth century village assemblies in certain areas could also act as channels for peasant rebellion: in the countryside around the city of Rothenburg ob der Tauber the decision to join the German Peasants' War in 1525 was made by village assemblies. Widows with communal rights could participate in decisions relating to the economic life of the village but were debarred from full political membership of the village assembly because they were not allowed to fulfil personally the duties of arm-bearing and physical work on communal labour projects which were expected of men.

Less formal aspects of village life, particularly relating to festivities and control over marriage, were also the preserve of men. In much of rural Europe single men formed groups (youth-abbeys or kingdoms) which had jurisdiction over women of marriageable age and often repulsed or fined outsiders who came to court them. They were also often the instigators of charivari, the public and very noisy ritual humiliation of a married couple who had offended communal norms, either because their difference in age was too great, or because the husband was hen-pecked or had been cuckolded. Legal records show that married women also participated informally in communal politics, primarily in the creation of rumours relating to individuals (an activity of significance in a society which placed great emphasis on a person's honour and in which the gaining of a bad reputation could be a prelude to communal or legal sanction for deviant behaviour), and possibly also via their influence on their husbands in assembly affairs.

Villages in sixteenth-century Europe were not bucolic utopias. Most village ordinances contained clauses forbidding household heads to fight with or insult each other at assembly meetings. Women, the unmarried, and the propertyless were excluded from formal political life. Surveillance of every aspect of household life by neighbours was the norm and the fate of those who were perceived to threaten village life could be unpleasant; for example, special village assemblies were established in the 1580s in the German Saarland to take the initiative in local witch-hunts. Belonging to a village with all its shortcomings, however, was infinitely preferable to being unsettled, and the subordination of individuals to communal norms was generally accepted as necessary for the survival of all. The annual ceremony of the beating of the village boundaries physically reaffirmed the limits of the community and the principle of exclusivity on which it was based.

A meeting under the linden tree in the Swiss village of Schüpfheim. The village linden tree marked one of the communal spaces at which village assemblies might meet in the late medieval and early modern periods.

Peasants were also bound into vertical social relationships with seigneurs, the noble lords who owned most of the land in sixteenth-century Europe. In return for obedient fulfilment of tenurial obligations lords were supposed to respect their tenants' customary rights, protect them in times of military threat, maintain justice and order, and show them mercy in times of dearth or other disaster. How closely lords adhered to this ideal had always depended on the individual concerned and the degree to which peasants were able to participate in and influence the power dynamics of their own domination. The sixteenth-century saw a general shift towards more exploitative lord–peasant relationships which was particularly marked in eastern Europe.

The vast majority of peasants rented their land from lords, although they were often able to bequeath it as they wished. The vast range of highly complex and localized tenurial arrangements which existed can be reduced to a general scheme of three. A simple annual payment of rent was the rarest (and more common in England). Sharecropping was an arrangement common in southern France and Italy in which the lord gave his tenant a half or third of the seed or livestock to farm and the tenant returned a half or third of the produce. Elsewhere in western and central Europe tenants were obliged to pay an annual rent with an additional bundle of dues (most commonly a transfer tax when a new tenant took over the land, either through death or sale), and to fulfil certain labour services (such as performing a certain number of days' work per year on the lord's demesne). Rents were paid in cash and, more commonly, in kind, and labour services became rarer in the sixteenth century.

With a good-sized plot of land, bountiful harvests, low rents, and a secure long-term lease a peasant would be in a relatively good position as a tenant. However, for most peasants overlordship involved burdensome economic obligations, especially as they also had to pay tithes to the Church and, increasingly, taxes to the state, as well as save enough of their grain for the next year's seed-corn from every harvest. These combined outgoings might leave a peasant household with less than half of what it had originally produced. The scales were further weighted against peasants as the demands of seigneurial dues often took little account of poor harvests and because lords and Church tended to choose the best quality produce for their share. The most oppressive form of lord–peasant relationship—serfdom, characterized by a predominance of labour services and by legal prohibitions on peasant freedom of movement—was relatively rare in western Europe by the sixteenth century (although some pockets survived in Burgundy and Franche-Comté, for example). East of the Elbe, however, formerly free peasants were increasingly bound to their lords' soil and had their dues in kind and cash commuted into labour services for reasons which will be discussed later.

Although generally geared towards production for subsistence rather than profit, peasant households were rarely totally self-sufficient. Most had economic links to other villages and nearby market towns. Artigat, the village below the Pyrenees which was the scene of the famous imposture chronicled in *The Return of Martin Guerre*, had economic links (such as agreements about the hiring of horses and the rearing of sheep and the sale of their fleeces) with neighbouring towns and villages, including Saint-Ybars and Pailhes. Peasant housewives, like the one portrayed by Hans Sachs in his comedy *The Strange Goose*, could often be seen carrying produce to market (milk, eggs, butter, cheese, fruit, and small animals, especially fowl) in order to earn enough to buy their households the wares made by local craftsmen or available from itinerant pedlars.

The degree of rural involvement in the all-important grain market depended on how good the harvest was (in times of plenty, many households might have a surplus to sell, while in times of dearth, most would be forced to buy) and, more importantly, on how much land the household farmed. Households with large holdings might regularly have a marketable surplus of grain. Those with little or no land would have to buy their grain on the market, generating the necessary income either by hiring out their labour or by selling what little they could produce, perhaps in a cottage garden or by small-scale viticulture. Many market transactions in the sixteenth century were made in kind or non-monetary forms of credit, although monetary exchange was gaining in importance, particularly in areas where rents and taxes were demanded in cash.

The Processes of Change

The traditional material world, economic status, and social relationships of peasants were put under increasing pressure in the sixteenth century by various interrelated processes of change. Most of these processes of change began before 1500, but the significance of their—usually adverse—impact on peasant life became clearest from the middle of the sixteenth century onwards.

Demographic expansion was the most important of these processes of change. Despite some regional variation in rates and timing of growth and periodic instances of crisis mortality, the population of Europe grew rapidly from the mid-fifteenth century until about 1600. By the 1580s most

areas had regained or surpassed the population density they had boasted
before the devastating Europe-wide bubonic plague epidemic of 1347–50.
In France, for example, the population increased from 7 or 8 million in 1450
to about 16 million a century later, while evidence suggests average annual
growth rates of about half a per cent for Germany and Norway
(1520–1600) and England (1570–1600). This demographic expansion was
the result of a decline in crisis mortality for the period *c*.1440–1540 (with
comparatively fewer outbreaks of plague and war and fewer harvest failures) combined with an increase in fertility (as the availability of land and
high wages after the mid-fourteenth-century Black Death encouraged
more people to marry). Contemporary writers commented on the growing
population and made suggestions on how to cope with it. In his *German
Chronicle* of 1538, for example, Sebastian Franck noted that 'there are so
many people everywhere, no one can move . . . if God does not inflict a war
in which many die, we shall be forced—chosen by lot or some such way—
to travel like the gypsies in search of a new land'.

Population growth put pressure on the agrarian economy's most valuable commodity, land. The price of land rose steeply during the sixteenth
century and in certain areas population density forced peasants to cultivate
once again land which had returned to waste in the wake of the Black Death
and to put under the plough land which was poorly suited to arable farming, either because it was too wooded, too hilly, or too wet. Overall agrarian productivity was increased by the expansion of arable farming, but not
sufficiently to keep pace with the rising population. This discrepancy
between the amount of food available and the number of mouths to feed
caused a rapid inflation of grain prices which was probably exacerbated by
an increase in the European money supply (due to the conversion into
coinage of silver from central European and South American mines) and
which has earned the sixteenth century its reputation as the age of the 'price
revolution'. Over the course of the century grain prices went up throughout Europe by an average of about 400 per cent, increasing particularly
sharply from 1550 and rising more rapidly than the price of manufactured
goods. Wages increased only about half as quickly as the price of grain as
demographic expansion meant that the supply of labour vastly exceeded
demand for it. The inflation of grain prices and deflation in the purchasing
power of wages had particularly adverse effects on those who had to buy
grain on the market and on those who were partially or wholly reliant on
waged labour for their income.

The second process of sixteenth-century change which affected peasant
life was a proliferation of market networks and the integration of increasing

DIE SPRICH SALOMO DAS XI CAPITEL
WER KORN INHELT DEM FLVCHEN DIE LEIT
ABER SEGEN KOMPT VBER DEN SO ES VERKAFFT
M D XXXIIII

A sixteenth-century broadsheet against the hoarding of grain, showing that those who hoard grain are cursed, whereas those who sell it are blessed. The image emphasizes the central importance of grain to the early modern economy and diet, as well as perhaps suggesting that the underlying demographic causes of spiralling grain prices were poorly understood.

numbers of peasants into market relationships. This change was caused by urbanization, closely linked to the expansion of trade, population increase, and rising grain prices. While certain parts of Europe were already comparatively highly urbanized in the fourteenth century (Flanders and northern Italy, for instance), the sixteenth century saw a marked increase in urbanization, with the number of cities containing over 100,000 inhabitants increasing from four to about ten. Towns grew because they were royal capitals or centres of administration, or because they were ports which gained in importance as the extent and volume of seaborne trade expanded following the late fifteenth-century voyages of discovery. Italian cities (notably Venice) dominated European trade in 1500, and Seville, Lisbon, and Antwerp rose to join them in trading prominence in the first two-thirds of the sixteenth century. By the early seventeenth century, however, Amsterdam and London achieved European pre-eminence in trade as a result of the Revolt of the Netherlands, the devastating impact of the 1590–4 famines in the

Mediterranean and Iberian peninsula, and the more flexible social and economic structures of England and the Dutch Republic. Sixteenth-century urbanization was also closely linked to demographic increase: towns grew rapidly as a result of immigration from overpopulated rural areas.

Urban concentrations of population stimulated demand for agricultural produce and encouraged commercial farming and crop-specialization (peasants traditionally tried to spread the risk of crops failing by planting several varieties). In some areas (around Paris and other northern French towns, for example) the opportunities offered by large urban settlements encouraged the expropriation of peasant smallholders by wealthier landowners wishing to consolidate their holdings for more commercial farming. Elsewhere specialization (the proliferation of market gardening around London, or the intensification of dairy-farming along the German North Sea coast to supply Dutch and Flemish towns, for example) gave peasants the chance to make profits. However, it also made them more reliant on markets for other produce, particularly grain, which was potentially hazardous in the short term if the lines of supply and distribution were unstable or interrupted, or if the price of grain rose to nullify any profits made. Ultimately even the poorest peasants played an—albeit unwitting—part in the proliferation of markets. Market expansion at the level of the smallest towns was encouraged by the fact that, by the second half of the sixteenth century, there were more peasants who had insufficient land for subsistence and who therefore had to buy grain. These peasants took whatever produce they had to local markets to generate sufficient income to meet this new and pressing need.

Sixteenth-century peasants also suffered seigneurial pressures as their lords attempted to maximize profits (in order to maintain status in an age of inflation) from the two commodities which population pressure and new market opportunities were rendering increasingly valuable—land and grain. In eastern Europe there was a general trend towards the re-enserfment of peasants, who were deprived of any land rights they may once have possessed and of their freedom of movement from their lords' estates, and who were burdened with increasingly heavy labour services by noble landowners who sought to consolidate their farms in order to produce as much grain as possible for west European markets. Danzig and Amsterdam were the centres of the lively Baltic grain trade. By 1600 Amsterdam imported over 100,000 tons of rye from Danzig, keeping some for domestic consumption and shipping the rest on to cities along the Atlantic and even Mediterranean seaboards.

In western Europe landowners sought to maximize income at peasants' expense in various ways. Some tried the trick that their eastern European counterparts were soon to perfect and tried to impose new (or reimpose old) labour services; German peasants protested against this practice in their Twelve Articles during the Peasants' War in 1525. Other lords shortened the leases of their peasant tenants (making the payment of entry fines and the possibility of rent increases more frequent) and increased entry fines and rents, which rose in the course of the century by as much as three to eight fold. Lords also attacked peasant rights to commons, either by depriving them of access to firewood, game and fish (in order to protect their own supplies and maintain their hunting grounds) or by expropriating peasants' common fields at a time when land shortages made any extra resources especially valuable. Enclosure of commons to raise sheep for the lucrative Antwerp wool trade was a bitterly resented feature of agrarian life in England in the first half of the sixteenth century, while there was a steady encroachment on communal village property by lords in France and Germany, largely as a result of indebtedness.

How effectively peasants could resist seigneurial pressure depended on various factors: how long and legally secure their leases were, whether or not they had developed the political culture and organization which enabled them to protest against seigneurial encroachment, and whether or not the powers beyond their lords (princes or churchmen) would listen to such protests. The odds were stacked against peasants, however, as ultimately they did not own the land they cultivated and because in the short term they had little control over the unseen forces of demographic expansion which tipped the market balance in favour of lords. Many sixteenth-century peasants also bore increasingly heavy fiscal burdens imposed by the state (England and the Netherlands were the exceptions here, with France the fiscal state par excellence); they also encountered assaults on their religion (in Protestant areas) and culture (in both Protestant and Catholic areas) in the wake of the Reformation and Counter-Reformation. This combination of attacks on what peasants regarded as their right to subsistence and on their traditional way of life made popular revolt—against seigneurial exploitation, high taxes, religious change, and food shortages—a frequent feature of life between the late fifteenth and early seventeenth centuries.

The Effects of Change

Some peasants benefited greatly from the rising grain prices and market opportunities of the sixteenth century. Those with enough land to generate surpluses for sale began to make profits, enabling them to consolidate their holdings and strengthen their economic position. The yeomen in England, *coqs de village* in France, and *Vollbauer,* or wealthy tenant farmers with full rights in communal resources in Germany, were all emerging as rural élites by the mid-sixteenth century. Two factors explained their success: their families had already been in possession of good-sized landholdings in the late fifteenth century, and since then they had held on to and often enlarged their holdings at the expense of their poorer neighbours. They managed this by refusing to subdivide their properties (even where partible inheritance was the local custom) and by keeping strict control over their children's marriages. By the later sixteenth century their increased wealth was obvious. They boasted the largest, most richly decorated houses, the most servants, oxen, barns, grain, wine, and silver. Their dominant economic and social status meant that they were entrusted with seigneurial tasks (like collection of dues and taxes, or acting as local administrative officials) and often acted as creditors within their local community.

Such rural élites were only ever a tiny minority of the peasant population, however. For the vast majority of peasants the demographic and economic changes of the sixteenth century significantly worsened their situation. The re-enserfment of east European peasants has already been discussed. In the west the story was one of progressive economic depression rather than legal servitude. Population growth and pressure on land led to an increase in the number of peasants who possessed holdings too small for subsistence. For example, village ordinances in the German south-west began in the course of the sixteenth century to list 'half' peasants (to distinguish them from those with enough land to qualify for full communal rights), followed by cottagers with 'poor little pieces of land' and cottagers possessing 'only a little house, with no land'. Such households were forced to buy grain and sell their labour at a time when the former was increasingly expensive and the latter increasingly cheap, subject to seasonal variation, and often simply unwanted. This, coupled with loss of common resources and the financial burdens imposed by lords, church, and state, pulled many peasants down into a spiral of debt, poverty, and possibly ultimate sale of whatever land they still possessed to land-hungry yeomen, nobles, and wealthy townsmen. The general trend was negative despite regional variations. French and German peasants were more likely to hold on to a scrap of land and to have their tenurial rights protected by their territorial ruler than their counterparts in England (where the trend was towards large commercial farms worked by day labourers) or Spain (where peasant expropriation was exacerbated by the system of rural *cen-*

sos, or annuities), although partible inheritance and—in France—share-cropping and high royal taxation left them vulnerable in other ways.

The process of peasant impoverishment had begun as a result of population increase around 1450, but was to accelerate markedly in the sixteenth century, particularly in the wake of sharper grain price rises from the mid-sixteenth century. By the late sixteenth century most villages had sizeable numbers—and often a majority—of land-poor and landless households. For example, the proportion of cottagers possessing only a garden within the English rural population rose from 11 per cent before 1560 to 40 per cent after 1640; in New Castile by the 1570s over half the rural population consisted of landless day labourers; while in Languedoc the number of peasants unable to feed their households without additional income had almost doubled between the late fifteenth and early seventeenth centuries.

Poverty brought a relentless decline in living standards for the rural poor as subsistence became an increasingly unattainable ideal. Their diet suffered as more of their income went towards buying grain; by 1550 Heinrich Müller already lamented of Swabian peasants that 'in the past they ate differently . . . then there was meat and food in profusion every day; tables at village fairs and feasts sank under their load'. As meat disappeared from peasant boards the only sources of protein were occasional small quantities of dairy produce, scraps of fat pork, and cheap fish; peas and beans (formerly regarded as livestock feed) became increasingly important supplements. Constant malnutrition was interrupted by times when starvation became a real possibility; during the famine years of 1570–4 many were reduced to eating bread made with bran, acorns, sawdust, and even grass, mixed with milk or animal blood. Given such dietary inadequacies it is hardly surprising that the poor were more susceptible to disease and that many early modern popular fantasies—like those of the witches' Sabbath or the Land of Cockaigne—centred on excessive feasting. Living in one-roomed cottages with few possessions and wearing old and patched clothing, the want of the rural poor was as visually obvious as their wealthier neighbours' plenty.

Villagers who found themselves sinking into poverty were reduced to an economy of makeshifts to make ends meet. They spent less and less on non-essentials, begged from their neighbours, borrowed money from whoever would lend to them, and worked as day labourers whenever possible, often moving as the rhythm of seasonal agrarian employment dictated. In some areas rural industry—primarily in mining, metallurgy, and textiles—offered the poor more opportunities for waged labour. The textile industry in particular expanded from the late fifteenth century as merchants took

A sixteenth-century woodcut showing the sparse diet (bread, onions, turnips, and porridge) of a poor woodcutter.

advantage of surplus rural population (especially in areas of traditionally low labour-intensive agriculture) by putting out textile processes to cottagers in order to escape the restrictive craft monopolies of urban guilds and to benefit from the market opportunities offered by expanding trade networks. Ultimately many of the poor simply left their villages and went elsewhere in their desperate search for work and, in times of dearth, food. Mobility, especially of the young, intensified markedly in the sixteenth century and urban populations, with their high mortality rates, were maintained and increased by a continual influx of rural poor. Lack of work and high rents continued to be problems for the rural poor in their new urban environment and, while they were closer to sources of food and wealth from which to beg, they were more likely to succumb to the diseases which were especially virulent in crowded urban quarters.

Social polarization, nascent in rural communities in the late fifteenth and early sixteenth centuries, was firmly entrenched a century later. The gulf between the wealthy few and the many poor was expressed and exacerbated along many lines. It was all too apparent in the differences in their respective standards of diet, clothing, and housing, and in their differing abilities to maintain family honour and social status by celebrating and offering hospitality in style when occasion demanded. Economic differences also affected the exercise of politics, as village assemblies and the decision-making powers they possessed increasingly came under the control of the wealthy village élite. Religious and cultural change further accentuated emerging economic and social disparities. The wealthy minority tended to adopt, and even to help enforce, the values of good order, industry, and sobriety which were espoused by post-Reformation and Counter-Reformation urban and state authorities. Such values helped rural élites protect their properties and confirm their social distance from their neighbours, whose poverty seemed to mock and threaten them and for whom the alehouse remained one of the few affordable social diversions. The wealthy were also more likely to be literate and therefore, especially in Protestant areas, more committed to the new Bible-based faith. These processes of social differentiation meant that villagers gradually began to feel that they belonged to a social group within the village rather than to the village commune itself. Early seventeenth-century payers of the parish poor-rate in Suffolk, for example, began to see their impoverished neighbours as 'a matter of heavy burden and a sore discommodity', while in late sixteenth-century Germany peasants started to call themselves 'the tenant farmers' or 'the poor' of a certain village in petitions to their lords and to see their interests as increasingly divergent. This was a far cry from the heady days of communal solidarity during the Peasants' War of 1524–5.

The Urban Experience of the Lower Orders

The same process of social polarization occurred in many west European urban communities between the late fifteenth and early seventeenth centuries. Ten to fifteen per cent of Europe's population lived in towns of greatly varying size. Most of Germany's towns, for example, had only 1,000–3,000 inhabitants, although a few were very large: Cologne, Nuremberg, and Augsburg had populations of over 30,000 in the early sixteenth century. Urban and rural communities shared certain similarities. In both the household was the core economic and social unit, life was shaped by the ubiquity of death, women and the propertyless were excluded from formal political participation, and communal government was obsessed with the regulation and maintenance of social order. Even the largest towns were not devoid of agrarian activity and ambience. Many citizens kept cottage gardens, pigs, and poultry; day labourers worked the vineyards and fields which lay just beyond town walls; and a few cities (notably Nuremberg, Rothenburg ob der Tauber, and Ulm in Germany) had annexed substantial rural hinterlands by the late fifteenth century. Moreover, although sixteenth-century townspeople were generally more educated and literate than peasants (and often constituted the earliest and most enthusiastic supporters of Protestantism), they still hunted witches and resorted to white magic: a notable example was the famous Ausgburg merchant-banker Anton Fugger, who employed a village cunning woman, Anna Megerler, to survey his trading empire through her crystal ball.

Other characteristics distinguished the urban community from its rural counterpart. Its greater size made for a more complex and stratified social structure; it contained a greater variety of communal buildings (often a town hall, municipal mills, fountains, granaries, commercial warehouses, and gaols as well as churches); and it offered inhabitants and visitors the benefit of a greater range of resources. Peasants from Rothenburg ob der Tauber's rural environs, for example, took legal cases before the city courts, sold their produce at its markets, attended municipal festivities and executions, and frequented the town brothel and taverns. The greatest difference, however, lay in the urban community's economic life. From their earliest days most European towns had boasted a high proportion of inhabitants who were craftsmen involved in the manufacture of finished wares, and the right to hold markets at which to sell these wares and the farm produce which was brought into towns to feed their predominantly non-agrarian populations or to be exported elsewhere was an urban community's earliest-won and most fiercely defended privilege. By the sixteenth century these markets had became the focal points of local, regional, or long-distance trade, ensuring that commercial exchange was a town's defining feature.

Many of the common people living in sixteenth-century towns belonged to craft households: over a third of all male taxpayers in Dijon and over a half in Frankfurt were craftsmen. Most were involved in the production of foodstuffs, textiles, leather goods, tools, and household utensils, and in construction trades, although the range of crafts practised in a town depended on its size and geographic location. Nuremberg, known by the early sixteenth century as 'the German Venice' in recognition of its status as a major European commercial centre, had at least 141 different crafts (including makers of the still-famous Nuremberg gingerbread) and specialized in highly diversified metal-ware manufacture. Different crafts were accorded different prestige. Goldsmiths ranked highest, as their work with that illustrious substance was clean, highly skilled, and profitable; tanners and knackers, whose work was dirty and, in Germanic areas, dishonourable, ranked lowest. Urban production was based on the household workshop, where a married master craftsman lived and worked with the help of resident apprentices and paid journeymen. His wife made a significant contribution to the household economy. Her dowry helped with the capital investment needed to start the workshop, she sold wares from the workshop or at the local market, she might supplement family income by retail or service activities (many municipal midwives, for example, were the wives of artisans), and she did all the household's cooking and cleaning, perhaps with the help of a maidservant. On the whole, however, women were excluded from the skilled procedures of manufacture by male-dominated guilds.

Guilds were the fraternities of master craftsmen which organized and oversaw all aspects of craft production and communal craft life. Their detailed ordinances stipulated the period of training apprentices had to undergo before they could become itinerant journeymen and the exact requirements of the piece of work journeymen had to submit to qualify as masters. They also inspected wares offered for sale by their members; shoddy goods from one workshop could jeopardize the standing of an entire guild. All guilds aimed to protect their production monopolies by minimizing competition (particularly from unregulated rural artisans) and by controlling entrance into apprenticeship and, ultimately, the status of master. Guild exclusivity was based on the idea of the maintenance of collective honour. Any master who failed to adhere to high standards of economic and sexual probity (or to ensure that his wife and household members did so) risked expulsion from his guild, while only young men who could prove that they were neither sons of serfs, nor members of ethnic or religious minorities, nor illegitimate, would be taken on as apprentices. To make this easier, many towns recorded 'testimonies of legitimate birth', in which witnesses swore that they had seen a prospective apprentice's parents process to church on their wedding day at least nine months before his birth. Guilds and their members were essentially conservative; even the enthusiasm of craftsmen for the Reformation has been attributed to the fact that they valued Protestantism's emphasis on patriarchal domestic authority as an added ideological prop to the traditional structure of the craft workshop. However, this conservatism stemmed from their belief that the good of their community was best maintained by a broad group of craft households striving not to make profits but simply enough money to maintain themselves and their honour.

Journeymen, apprentices, domestic servants, hired hands, and day labourers came below the master craftsmen and their wives in the social hierarchy of the sixteenth-century town. The first three groups were of lower status because they were single. They all hoped to earn enough money (and, in the case of apprentices and journeymen, to qualify as masters) to enable them to marry and establish independent households. It was harder for single women to achieve this aim because they were largely excluded from the skilled, regulated (and better paid) crafts, and because their wages were lower than men's. A long career as a maidservant often provided a dowerless woman with her only means of accumulating a marriage portion. Hired hands and day labourers might well be married but they lacked skills and capital. They had to rely on work which was subject to seasonal variation and market fluctuation; often they just stood in the town market place hoping to be hired by anyone with a few days' or weeks' wages to offer. Agricultural labourers and vine-dressers were in especially parlous positions. As a result, the latter emerged as vociferous spokesmen for greater social equality in certain south-western and south-central German towns during the Peasants' War of 1524–5. At the foot of the urban social ladder were the poor: beggars, vagabonds, and the settled poor, including those too young, old, or ill to make a living, and households unable for various reasons to support themselves. This group could constitute anything from 10 to over 50 per cent of a town's population, depending on its location and economic infrastructure, how its authorities defined poverty, and whether or not the area was affected by unusual circumstances, such as war or dearth. Rural migrants found positions as day labourers and servants if they were lucky or joined the ranks of the urban poor if they were not.

Sixteenth-century processes of change (notably demographic increase, exacerbated by rural in-migration, and the expansion of trade networks) affected western Europe's urban social groups in two main ways: they rendered the economic situation and social status of certain master craftsmen and journeymen less secure, and generally expanded the ranks of the urban poor and those reliant solely on waged labour. Eastern European towns were less affected by these changes because re-enserfment limited peasants' ability to migrate to towns and because a long-standing alliance between monarchs and noble landowners (in Poland and Prussia, for example) had severely attenuated the political and economic autonomy of all but the largest cities.

West European master craftsmen who produced either goods for local markets or luxury goods with stable markets managed to weather economic storms reasonably well. However, those engaged in non-luxury crafts (particularly textiles, certain types of metalwork, and construction) in cities involved in long-distance trade might fall foul of merchant-entrepreneurs. Most master crafts lacked the capital to enable them to cope with a sudden reduction or cessation in demand for their goods on distant markets. To then sell at a loss and buy raw materials on credit led many into debt, and ultimately into economic dependence as waged labourers on wealthy merchants who had the capital to secure raw materials cheaply and to survive market fluctuations. For example, most of Frankfurt's lacemakers worked on this putting-out basis for a few rich silk merchants by 1587; the same thing happened in Antwerp's silk and construction industries, Lyons's silk industry, Nuremberg's weapons and metalworking industry, and Hondschoote's textile industry. Where guild influence successfully resisted such developments (often with the support of city councils) merchants could look to rural areas beyond guild control for cheap labour for their enterprises.

Guilds traditionally limited the number of masters allowed to settle in a particular town to protect the livelihoods of existing craft workshops. Sixteenth-century population growth increased the number of journeymen who had learned a craft or trade but who were able to marry and establish independent households only after long periods working as itinerant waged labourers or not at all because an oversupply of labour limited their opportunities. Whether or not this reduced them to an economically precarious position depended on various factors: their skill level, the type of craft they did, and what sort of city they lived in. For as long as they were unmarried, however, they could attain neither full social adulthood nor the political rights which accompanied it. In reaction to their situation Swiss and German journeymen developed a distinctive culture which emphasized the virtues of being single and which revolved round the all-male environment of journeymen's hostels. This culture was peculiarly misogynistic, partly because a workshop's honour was thought to suffer if women worked there and partly because female labour was seen as an economic threat to journeymen's insecure situation. Guilds supported this view and from the late fifteenth century increasingly limited or ended women's economic opportunities within their crafts to protect men's livings.

European townspeople were particularly disadvantaged by the price of grain between 1450 and 1600 because it rose more rapidly than the price of the commodities which they made and sold and the wages which they were paid, and because they had to buy all their grain and most of their other foodstuffs on the market. By the second half of the sixteenth century only the most highly skilled, independent craftsmen who were assured of regular employment could manage adequately to feed their families: resident apprentices and servants who were fed by their masters were also spared the worst effects of spiralling consumer costs. Craftsmen who were less skilled or irregularly employed were more likely to suffer hardship, as were the day labourers and hired hands whose ranks were swelled and whose wages were depressed still further by the influx of the rural poor. In Lyons, for example, the wages of casual labourers fell below the poverty line (reached when at least 70 per cent of income had to be spent on bread, leaving virtually nothing to spend on other staples, rent, or fuel) almost every year from 1550 to 1600. These poverty-stricken households saw their living

A sixteenth-century woodcut showing the itinerant poor—crippled, pregnant, and burdened with children—entering a city in search of alms.

standards decline drastically and they had to rely on municipal charity with greater regularity.

The numbers of resident poor increased steadily from the late fifteenth century in towns experiencing the same process of social polarization between a wealthy minority and an economically insecure majority as villages. The problem of urban poverty was exacerbated, particularly in years of dearth, by the great multitude of itinerant and often rural poor who flocked to towns in search of any means of eking out a living (whether by working, begging, borrowing, or stealing). It was therefore hardly surprising that the earliest attempts to organize more efficient systems of poor relief occurred in the larger European cities such as Nuremberg, Lyons, Ypres, Strasbourg, and Lille during the period c.1520–1540 in response to the problems caused by several consecutive harvest failures (1527–34) and to the fears raised by frequent and often widespread eruptions of both urban and rural popular unrest, epitomized by the German Peasants' War of 1524–5. The reorganization of poor relief in Protestant cities was also associated with the expropriation by municipal authorities of the resources of the religious foundations which had hitherto provided a variety of social services, but there were striking similarities between urban poor relief schemes in Catholic and Protestant areas. Most prohibited unlicensed public begging, attempted to identify the deserving, indigenous poor, and centralized the collection of alms in poor-boxes; schemes were extended in times of dearth to prohibit grain-hoarding and to provide grain and bread at low or no cost to worthy paupers.

Most sixteenth-century élites acknowledged an obligation to provide relief for the settled poor of their communities, even if they often failed to comprehend fully that many paupers were simply unable to find work, or unable to subsist on what wages they did earn. Their attitude towards the mobile poor, or vagrants, was very different, however. Vagrants appeared to be deliberately idle, subject to the oversight of neither overlord nor community, likely to indulge in immoral or criminal habits, and thus to pose a serious threat to good social order. They were commonly thought to do 'nothing but walk the streets' and to be 'the rascals and very sink and dunghill knaves of all towns and cities', and were subject to especially punitive measures if apprehended by the authorities. The 1597 English Act for the Punishment of Rogues, Vagabonds, and Sturdy Beggars, for example, ordered the vagrant to be stripped half-naked and whipped bloody before being returned to his or her birthplace 'to put him or her self to labour as a true subject ought to do', while German towns regularly banished vagrants, often after subjecting them to a flogging or a spell in the pillory.

Conclusion

The period from the late fifteenth to the early seventeenth centuries is sometimes seen by economic historians and historical sociologists to have been an age of progress, during which economic growth in the spheres of trade and commercial capitalism brought Europe a stage closer to modernity. For the common people who lived through it, however, this period was anything but progressive. Re-enserfment, declining living standards, and, in particular, a huge increase in structural poverty and the emergence of a social and economic gulf between the few wealthy and the many poor were the lot of the vast mass of the population of sixteenth-century Europe. These adverse developments resulted from unseen and poorly understood demographic and economic forces, and from the policies implemented in reaction to those forces by the minority of people who possessed economic, social, and political power within sixteenth-century European society. The outcome of these developments was that, by the early seventeenth century, the idea of earning a living sufficient for untroubled subsistence within an independent peasant household or craft workshop had became as much a fantasy for many of Europe's common people as the fabled plenty of the Land of Cockaigne.

The Power of the Word: Renaissance and Reformation

EUAN CAMERON

The Renaissance and the Word

In 1500 the culture of the high Renaissance, which had already captivated Italy for several generations, was poised to dominate the cultural and intellectual life of the rest of Europe. During the previous half-century, little knots of scholars in France, Germany, the Low Countries, or England had begun to write classical poetry and rhetorical speeches, to collect classical axioms, and even to try to learn Greek. Less definably, the taste for balance and proportion in the visual arts had begun to make some impact on painting and building north of the Alps, not least among those artists who had visited Italy. There is an irony in all of this. Without doubt, Renaissance culture has helped to shape the thought-world of modern Europe: it belongs to the modern age. Yet the scholars and critics who defined its values claimed to look backwards to antiquity, at least in the humanities. They intended to revive literary skills which the Middle Ages had forgotten. '[In my youth] the times were still dark, and mankind was perpetually reminded of the miseries and disasters wrought by those Goths who had destroyed all sound scholarship. But, thanks be to God, learning has been restored in my age to its former dignity and enlightenment,' wrote François Rabelais's fictitious giant Gargantua to his son in 1532. Their claim to retrieve one golden age so as to inaugurate another was neither wholly insincere nor mere propaganda. Taken too literally, however, it can conceal what they took from the Middle Ages, and what they achieved for themselves.

The Word Written and Printed

The power and use of the word, spoken, written, and above all printed, ties together many of the themes of sixteenth-century intellectual history. One ought therefore to begin with its most basic component, the alphabet itself. From the Atlantic to the frontiers of Lithuania and the borders of the Turkish Empire in the Balkans, the Roman alphabet was the common currency of western Europe as in the days of the empire. However, medieval scribes had cluttered their alphabet with a host of additional ligatures, contractions, circumflexes, and other devices to speed writing and save precious parchment. Italian manuscript-collectors of the early fifteenth century such as Leonardo Bruni (1370–1444) and Poggio Bracciolini (1380–1459) discovered in the libraries of Switzerland and elsewhere what they took to be manuscript volumes from antiquity. Charmed by the open, rounded shapes of the letters, and the relative lack of abbreviations and contractions, Poggio and his friends began to copy this form of 'Roman' writing for their own compositions. As the fifteenth century progressed, writing masters taught this style of clear, open letters as a form of art. Having revived 'Roman' characters, scribes like Bartolomeo di San Vito and Pier Antonio Sallando then innovated: they compressed the open hand of the old manuscripts slightly, and sloped it to the right, creating what they called the *cancellaresca* or chancery hand, and we call simply 'italic'. The italic hand inspired style-books such as Sigismondo Fanti's *Theorica et Pratica* (1514) or Ludovico Vicentino degli Arrighi's *La Operina* (1522). A little later, in a short treatise of 1540 Gerardus Mercator would show scribes how to cut the quill, the correct pen-travel, and the proper position of hand and arm.

Ironically, the 'Roman' hand linked the writers of the Renaissance not to the ancient world which they revered, but to earlier European 'Renaissances'. The manuscripts which they collected and copied were not antique: they derived from ninth-century scholars in Charlemagne's Francia, based in centres like the abbey of St Martin at Tours. The 'Carolingian minuscule' hand of these books had been used up to the eleventh and twelfth centuries, from northern Italy to the scriptorium of Christ Church, Canterbury. In the sixteenth century the Roman hand tended to be used chiefly for writing in the languages of the Mediterranean. German and English were still written and printed in vertical Gothic characters for some time: French vernacular texts usually appeared in the rounded gothic styles known to typographers as 'bastarda' and 'civilité'. Yet wherever the common language of learning was read, Latin text appeared more and more often vested in Roman characters. By the middle of the seventeenth century, Roman letters became standard for French and English, too. The alphabet used by the book-collectors and scribes of the Renaissance became the norm for all western languages today.

Although one begins with the written word, by 1500 the word printed from movable type was already nearly fifty years old. The printing press evolved as a practical solution to a practical problem. In the fifteenth century the number of universities, schools, and colleges, and the demand for books among the clergy had grown prodigiously. Though some stationers' shops had adapted by 'farming out' portions of a text to out-workers to speed the copying process, still they could not cope. By the early 1450s, after some little-known experimenters, Johannes Gensfleisch zum Gutenberg (d. 1468) had devised, and perfected, a mechanical technique to replicate a manuscript book by other means. None of the machinery involved was complex or even particularly new. A screw-press squeezed paper on to a forme of pre-inked metal type between a solid platen above and a solid press-stone below. The key to the 'print revolution' was the combination of accuracy and flexibility. The type-founder could make from durable master punches large numbers of identical pieces of soft metal, each containing one character, the piece of 'type'. These were gathered together by the compositor line by line and wedged together in pairs or groups of pages in the forme, from which the impression was made. The text could thus be replicated identically until the type wore out; but more importantly, it could also be partly dismantled, and revisions or corrections made, before the process resumed. The same type could be separated and reused for later sections of a long work, or for a quite different task. Movable type allowed one to print long books with modest amounts of type; to check proofs and make corrections before the print-run; and at the other extreme to issue ephemeral material cheaply. All these developments were to liberate the communication and thought processes of the sixteenth century to sensational effect.

In the early experimental period printers had set up in all kinds of tiny centres; but tying up capital in presses and paper for months or years was a risk. So, towards 1500 printeries concentrated in those places where venture capital could be found, patrons sought, and contracts negotiated: places like Mainz, Strasbourg, Nuremberg, Augsburg, Basle, Venice, Rome, Paris, or Lyons. The commercial risks ensured that early publishing had very little to do with the Renaissance. To sell books in bulk, one stuck religiously—one might say—to conventional books printed in conventional gothic characters on conventional subjects. Bibles, mass-books, breviaries, encyclopedias, manuals for clergy and confessors provided the staple diet of early printing-houses. Religious works are estimated to account for three-quar-

ue maria
gra plena
dominus
tecū bene
dicta tu in mulierib'
et benedictus fruct'
uentris tui : ihesus
christus amen.

Gloria laudis resonet in ore
omniū Patri genitoqz proli
spiritui sancto pariter Resul
tet laude perhenni Labori
bus dei vendunt nobis om
nia bona. laus:honor:virtus
potētia: z gratiaz actio tibi
christe. Amen.

Uiue deū sic z vines per secula cun
cta. Prouidet z tribuit deus omnia
nobis. Proficit absque deo null' in
orbe labor. Illa placet tell' in qua
res parua beatū. Ose facit z tenues
luxuriantur opes.

Nemo suę laudis nimium lętetur honore
Ne uilis factus post sua fata gemat.
Nemo nimis cupide sibi res desiderat ullas
Ne dum plus cupiat perdat & id quod habet.
Ne ue cito uerbis cuiusquam credito blandis
Sed si sint fidei respice quid moneant
Qui bene proloquitur coram sed postea praue
Hic erit inuisus bina cp ora gerat

Pax plenam uirtutis opus pax summa laborum
pax belli exacti precium est precuumque pericli
Sidera pace urgent consistunt terrea pace
Nil placitum sine pace deo non munus ad aram
Fortuna arbitrius tempus dispensat ubi
Illa rapit iuuenes illa ferit senes

κλιω Τευτερπη τε θαλεια τε μελπομενη τε
Περψιχορη τεράτω τε πολυμνεια τουρανιη
τε καλλιοπη θεΔη προφερεςατη εξιυατα
σαωψ ιεουα Χριςουα μαρια τελοσ.

Indicis characteʒ diuersaʒ mane
rieru impressioni paratarū. Finis.

Erhardi Ratdolt Augustensis viri
solertissimi:preclaro ingenio z miri
fica arte:qua olim Denetijs excelluit
celebratissimus. In imperiali nunc
vrbe Auguste vindelicoʒ laudatissi
me impressioni dedit. Annoqz salu
tis. M.CCCC.LXXXVI.Kale.
Aprilis Sidere felici compleuit.

---

ters of all books published before 1520: sixteen editions of the Latin Vulgate Bible
appeared at Paris alone between 1475 and
1517, while translations into the various vernaculars numbered at least sixty editions
across Europe before 1520. Yet gradually
and on a smaller scale, the taste of the
Renaissance began to interact with the world
of the publisher-printer. In 1465 Konrad
Sweynheym and Arnold Pannartz, two German printers working at the abbey of Subi-
aco outside Rome, issued Cicero's *Orator* in
Renaissance roman type, and Augustine's
City of God in the same type two years later.
About the same time humanist letter-forms
were being used in Strasbourg and Paris. A
Frenchman, Nicolas Jenson, produced editions of Eusebius, Cicero, and Virgil
between 1470 and 1475 at Venice in one of
the most beautiful of early Roman types. By
1501 the Venetian printer Aldus Manutius
and his type-carver Francesco Griffo had
not only adopted a version of the roman
type; they achieved the technically difficult
feat of converting the *cancellaresca*, the
'italic', into a printing-type as well. Aldus
succeeded where other printers had so far
failed, in turning the publishing of Renaissance classical literature into a successful
commercial proposition. For the first few
decades of the sixteenth century Aldus and

The printer-publisher Erhardt Ratdolt produced this
specimen page of his printing types after he transferred his printery from Venice to Augsburg in 1486.
The large Gothic types are used for liturgical and
theological texts. The Roman types, based on
Nicholas Jenson's design, carry Renaissance poems
on virtue, honour, and fortune. The Greek types list
the nine Muses.

his heirs issued huge numbers of classical and Renaissance texts, Greek, Latin, and Italian, many of them in the relatively small format made possible by the compressed, economical quality of the italic type.

The cultural change brought about by the availability of the printed word must not be oversimplified, and it is difficult to pin down specifically. Medieval libraries and book-owners had owned popular texts in large numbers of copies; they had shrunk books into small format for convenience; they had varied the sumptuousness of the manuscript according to its intended use. Apart from the manuscripts which survive intact, innumerable fragments of lost books turn up dismembered and shredded to provide covers or spines for early printed books, to suggest how much has been lost. Nonetheless, the first decades of printing did generate a quantitative difference in the ease of access to the printed text. An early print-run produced between 200 and 1,000 copies, for labour (and expense) not many times greater than that required for a single manuscript copy of the same text. Collecting a library was not cheap, but it became feasible. A French royal official, Jehan Grolier, could amass one of the most wonderful of private libraries, wide in range and exquisite in bindings. At the opposite extreme, books could be left lying around, bound disdainfully in loose parchment or even paper covers. By the end of the sixteenth century there was a thriving industry in cheap broadsheets, ballads, and 'chapbooks' for the masses. If one were one of the growing minority which was literate, *or knew someone else who was*, one could hope to read, or hear read, a text which was at hand in print. By the mid-seventeenth century an English village parson, Ralph Josselin, could write in his diary: 'Whereas a supply of bookes is necessary for mee, and my meanes but small to purchase them, I have layd downe a resolucion, to buy but few, and those of choice and special concernment . . . and to purchase them at the second hand, out of libraries that are to bee sold.' Buying a book had become a normal part of life.

The Ancient Word and the Ancient Tongue

There is a persistent misconception that the Renaissance 'rediscovered' the literature and the arts of the ancient world. This belief owes something to the propaganda of the Renaissance literary men themselves, just as the Protestant reformers, a century or so later, would claim to have 'rediscovered' the text and message of the Bible. In truth, the ancient world and its literature had no more been lost to the Middle Ages than the Bible had been. Yet scholars of the high and late Middle Ages had used antique literature in

various distinctive—and to our eyes alien—ways. The ancient world provided them with a source of pearls of wisdom, quotations, examples,
instances known as 'authorities' (*auctoritates*, the 'auctoritees' of Chaucer).
Classical wisdom was not meant to be seen in its ancient context, whether
literary or cultural: it offered insights to apply immediately to current
problems and questions. Classical scholarship, in the Middle Ages, did not
flow backwards to its most ancient sources: it built upon texts, wrote commentaries over them, distilled them into extracts, and compiled these as
encyclopedias. It was no accident, for example, that the masters of the Latin
language most used, copied, and discussed in medieval Europe were Aelius
Donatus, the tutor of St Jerome (4th century), Martianus Capella (early 5th
century), the compiler of clichés on the liberal arts and cosmology, or
Priscianus of Caesarea (early 6th century), the last and most compendious
ancient grammarian. The latest and most considered version, for medieval
scholars, was usually best.

     This preference for viewing antiquity through the eyes of later com-
mentators coloured the way in which Greek classics, and above all Aristotle, the master philosopher, were studied. By the end of the thirteenth
century most of Aristotle's writings had become available in Latin translations: however, these were in many instances retranslations from earlier
Arabic versions of the Greek originals. With the medieval Aristotle had
come the essential baggage of his Muslim commentators, Ibn Sina ('Avi-
cenna', 980–1037), Ibn Rushd ('Averroes', 1126–98), Al-Zahravi, among
others. The Arab philosophers leaned more towards the scientific, practical
aspects of Aristotle's thought. His metaphysics were mediated for the
medieval West through the great synthesists of the movement—or movements—known as medieval scholasticism. For medieval culture, ancient
learning and literature formed part of a continuous web of knowledge,
formed by the search for practical, logically demonstrable truths about
physical and metaphysical being. By 1500 the classics of antique-Arab-
medieval philosophy were multiplying through the printing presses. This
system must have appeared a towering monument to the continuity of
human knowledge, to the endless process of lecture, dispute, commentary,
gloss on commentary, and synthesis.

     What we call the 'Renaissance' (accepting its bellicose self-advertise-
ment at face value) should perhaps rather be termed a revaluation, or
regrading, of the heritage of classical literature by the learned of early
modern Europe. It began modestly, with the needs and tastes of scholar-
bureaucrats in Florence and Rome around 1400. Style-conscious civic
administrators like Coluccio Salutati (1331–1406), or papal secretaries like

Poggio Bracciolini, sought to take further the art of elegant letter- and speech-writing, beyond the limits of the medieval specimen-books. In their chosen work, writing fine letters was a sign of professional skill as well as a passion. They wished to write Latin prose which would follow the rhetorical standards and values of the masters of classical Latin rhetoric, Cicero (106–43 BCE) and Quintilian (*c.*35 CE–*c.*96). This aim required more than excerpts and glosses: so began the characteristic early Renaissance hunt through the disused lumber of medieval libraries for old texts. The search was not for just any texts: it was for whole, complete, texts; texts bare and unadorned (or unadulterated) by later commentary; therefore the most ancient texts, the well-springs of literature. For these men, the oldest was the best.

It was not that such ancient texts had been, literally, lost or destroyed; but rather that they had been so irrelevant to the intellectual needs of the Middle Ages that they had, in Francis Bacon's words, 'long time slept in libraries'. Vespasiano da Bisticci reported how Poggio claimed to have found 'six orations of Cicero . . . in a heap of waste paper among the rubbish'. The earliest humanists' efforts were directed above all to the Latin language. As a by-product of this approach, some Italian scholars began to recognize, however dimly, that the classical languages were separated by a gulf of time and linguistic evolution from their own. Leon Battista Alberti (1404–72), in his manuscript grammar of the Italian language, proved that Italian was, and had long been, a language of its own; it derived from Latin, not from some mythical vulgar language supposedly spoken by the masses in ancient Rome. Once one recognized that the Latin tongue belonged to a past culture, one could begin, tentatively, to acquire historical sense and to come to terms with the discontinuities of time. The sense that there had been a 'middle age' between the ancient and modern periods derived from the militant propaganda of Renaissance historians such as Flavio Biondo; but in the longer term, it ultimately begat a more detached sense of historical distance and period. In much the same way, Protestant historians would later interpose a 'middle age' of anti-Christian corruption, between the pure Church of the Apostles and Fathers and their own reformed era.

Just to return to purer Latin sources was not enough. Roman culture was saturated with Greek ideas and Greek philosophy; so what was true for the sources of Latin literature had also to be true of Greek. From around 1400 expatriate Greeks, sometimes from Latin colonies in the Levant overrun by Turkish advance, found employment as tutors to aspiring European Hellenists, first in Italy and later in France as well. Manuel Chrysoloras taught the first generation of Italian humanists; by the end of the fifteenth century

Georgius Hermonymos was doing something similar in France. A cardinal of Greek extraction, John Bessarion, left a wonderful library including much Greek literature to the city of Venice (not that the city fathers appreciated it). Rabelais's Gargantua was no doubt guilty of colourful exaggeration when he claimed that 'the study of languages has been revived: of Greek, without which it is disgraceful for a man to call himself a scholar, and of Hebrew, Chaldaean, and Latin'. Few northern Europeans could write fluently in Greek like the touchy French scholar Guillaume Budé. Yet many could read it; and a basic awareness of its alphabet, its vocabulary, and its rules, sufficient to read a parallel-column text in Greek and Latin, must have been common among the educated by the mid-sixteenth century.

With the Greek languages came the Greek authors, vested in their own words rather than borrowed Latin. The preparing of a new translation of Aristotle based on the original Greek was a vast enterprise. Leonardo Bruni began the work in the early fifteenth century, and it reached a climax in the two great folio volumes of Greek and Latin parallel text published by Isaac Casaubon at Lyons in 1590. Meanwhile Aristotle—about whom one might have thought that every teaching aid imaginable had already been written during the Middle Ages—received a fresh Latin paraphrase from Jacques Lefèvre d'Étaples from 1492 onwards. Yet the philosopher of philosophers was repaired and revarnished only to have his ascendancy challenged by his ancient contemporaries and rivals. The works of Plato were Latinized by Marsilio Ficino in the 1480s; those of the later antique Neoplatonists, Plotinus, Porphyry, Iamblichus, or Proclus, were translated and published in due course. Writings of the 'Hermetic corpus', sub-Neoplatonist texts dating from the 1st–3rd centuries CE but attributed to the mythical figure 'Hermes Trismegistus', were also printed, often in association with those of the authentic Neoplatonists. Linguistic virtuosity, by a sort of domino effect, opened up a world of little-used writers and helped to dismantle, at least partly, the self-supporting Aristotelian approach. Western thought was more diverse and more fragmented by 1500 than it had been a century or two earlier. As with language, so with philosophers, to place a text in its literary and historical context was to pare away its medieval, Christian associations. Francesco Vimercati in 1543 poured scorn on the idea that one could 'Christianize' pagan philosophers: 'I think our faith is much more imperilled when we try to confirm and protect it with the testimonies of Aristotle, Plato, or other outsiders which are inappropriate, unsuitable, and not written by them for that purpose.'

For the 'humanists', of course, knowledge was far more than philosophy. Rhetoricians, letter-writers, and indeed poets found themselves elevated from the elementary schoolroom to become oracles of wisdom. From such writers one could distil images, similes, sayings, proverbs to make one's own prose richer, and to convey the insights of the antique past. Erasmus of Rotterdam (*c.*1467–1536), who embodied in his own career the poet, the educator, the textual critic, the satirist, and the theologian, provided from 1500 onwards a series of spectacularly successful printed collections of sayings, the *Adages*. This book allowed aspiring humanist writers to short-circuit the business of reading the entire corpus of ancient literature by simply leafing through his index of proverbs. Some of these were mere images, such as 'to cast the die' or 'to speak from the heart'; some were even single words, like 'inexorable', 'adamantine', or 'syncretism'. Others, like 'War is sweet to those who have not known it', provided the starting point for an extended moral essay, in this case a vehement attack on the evils of war. This collection of sayings continued to be republished through the sixteenth and into the seventeenth centuries, in ever more comprehensively cross-referenced collections drawn

from the work both of Erasmus himself and his imitators and followers. When the Catholic Church banned Erasmus' works, the printer-publisher Paolo Manuzio issued a purged version of the *Adages* for Catholic use. 'Paroemiography', the art of collecting sayings cultivated by the sophists and rhetoricians of late antiquity, was thus revived to become the hallmark of Renaissance ornamental writing. This was not the medieval collection of 'authorities': it was a quest for rich, abundant imagery, persuasive force, elegance of form and style.

The portrait medallion, which imitated the medals and coins of the Roman empire, was a characteristic form of Renaissance portraiture. This relief of Erasmus is by Quentin Matsys, who also painted conventional portraits of Erasmus. Matsys's medallion conveys something of the fastidious refinement and sensitivity which made Erasmus an exquisite stylist and an awkward friend.

The Word of Exhortation

The intention behind the elegance, however, was thoroughly moral. Erasmus, and other humanists to some degree, believed passionately that the educated person would be a morally good person, and that only such education as made a person more upright was worthy of the name. 'If anyone carefully and thoroughly peruses this Pythagorean maxim, 'things are in common among friends', he will find the sum of human happiness contained within such a short saying. . . . For if one could persuade mortals of this, at once they would dispose of war, envy, and deceit; in short the whole mass of evils would at once be abolished.' So wrote Erasmus without a trace of irony. The humanists had an almost infinite faith in the liberalizing and improving power of a classical education. The very word 'humanity' (*humanitas*) they interpreted as meaning a combination of instruction (*paideia*) and generosity of spirit (*philanthropia*). Much of their writing and some of their careers were devoted to the founding and running of schools, such as Vittorino da Feltre's or Guarino da Verona's in fifteenth-century Italy, or John Colet's St Paul's School in London. That peculiar combination of intellectual and literary disciplines combined with artistic, physical, and musical training which used to be called 'liberal' education owes its origins to the Renaissance. François Rabelais's ideal tutor, Ponocrates, taught the young Gargantua in a daily cycle of Bible-reading, study, discussion, and recitation: the student was to listen to and study classical wisdom about food while eating, about botany while walking in the fields, and even about farming while holidaying in the countryside. He was also to vary study with a range of military and gymnastic exercises. The astonishingly comprehensive curriculum was doubtless exaggerated (like everything else in this satire disguised as a tale of giants) but the ideal of an education 'so sweet, easy, and enjoyable, that it seemed more like a king's recreation than a scholar's studies' shows no signs of irony.

   To educate was one goal; to persuade was another. The whole thrust of Renaissance writing was so to frame an argument that it won support by elegant expression, by well-chosen quotation, by appeal to the tastes, and even the emotions (rather than by formal logic, as in the scholastic art of dialectic). The art of rhetoric was both the original starting point and the archetypal activity of literary humanists. Speeches and letters, the latter often written with publication in mind, celebrated virtue, originality, learning, artistic excellence, and (less agreeably) the dubious merits of rich or powerful patrons. Sometimes an author would celebrate his patron for the virtues which it was hoped he might in future possess (say, peaceful government, or generosity to scholars) rather than those he actually displayed. Thus the *Panegyrics* directed by Erasmus to Philip of Burgundy, or by the Scots humanist Archibald Hay (d. *c.*1547) to Cardinal David Beaton, set out a programme while appearing to flatter an ego. In this game of oratorical fireworks the entertaining and the earnest could be combined and even confused. In the most celebrated and most pyrotechnic of all the 'mock encomiums', Erasmus' *Praise of Folly*, Folly, personified, tries to convince her audience with dazzling classical erudition and acute observation of human behaviour that silliness—self-love, self-delusion, fondness—are indispensable if life is to be lived and endured. Yet after indulging in mock praise of real silliness for most of the book, the final version of the work ends with a passionate paean in sincere praise of that ecstatic indifference to the real world, the divine madness, which belongs to the true Christian.

High medieval culture had integrated, brilliantly, classical wisdom on earthly matters with the Christian heritage on questions of divinity. Only on certain boundaries, for instance on the nature of the relations between soul and body, had it been difficult to make the grafts heal up satisfactorily. In contrast, the Renaissance with its disintegration of medieval thought-patterns and methods, its rediscovery of the untidy, religiously unhelpful diversity of classical thought, held a potential threat for the certainties of faith. Yet on the whole, the Renaissance did not damage Christian convictions among the learned of Europe. The reasons why it did not do so are complex and manifold. Among some, no doubt, there were not many Christian convictions to damage: late medieval worship so stressed ritual acts that faith was allowed to be implicit rather than conscious. Others were indifferent to outward forms: Conrad Celtis, the German poet, prayed inwardly among the beauties of nature, not with audible mumblings in church. A few, like Machiavelli, looked on religion as a mere social cement by which the plebs could be kept in awe of their rulers. For yet others, more serious in their beliefs, the abstract monotheism of the Neoplatonists may have seemed so close to Christianity—at least the Christianity of St John's Gospel or St Augustine's *Confessions*—that the two could merge easily enough.

Yet the most corrosive impact on medieval Christianity came from the Renaissance thinker who was as devoutly, intelligently, and consciously committed to Christian faith as could be. Erasmus took the humanists' textual criticism, moral values, and belief in education and applied them uncompromisingly to theology. First, this implied that the New Testament text could be purged and revised according to the principles of the oldest manuscript, the best reading found in ancient commentaries, and so forth, exactly as if it were the text of Catullus or Lucretius. Theologians like Maarten Dorp of Louvain objected that the grammarians and philologists (toilers at the very bottom of the medieval academic hierarchy) were presuming to revise the source-texts of the theologians (who worked at its apex). Erasmus replied, unanswerably, that no Church could possibly have decreed, in effect, 'we set the seal of our approval on any error or corruption, any addition or omission which may subsequently arise by any means whatsoever through ignorance or presumption of scribes or through their incompetence, drunkenness or negligence'. The incorporation of a Greek text in Erasmus' New Testament edition of 1516 may have been an afterthought, and the text not a very good Greek edition at that: but as propaganda for the role of the linguist in religion, it was invincible.

Erasmus' application of the classical heritage to Christianity did not stop there. He felt instinctively that ancient moral wisdom and Christian ethics could and should coincide. This meant, in practice, that he sought for Christian moral messages among the maxims of the Greeks and Romans. One of the longest essays in the *Adages*, 'The Silenus-figures of Alcibiades', told the tale of some statues of an ugly, deformed figure, which could be opened up to reveal a beautiful god inside. By a bold analogy, Erasmus likened to one of these Silenus figures Jesus Christ, who was to outward appearances the poor son of obscure parents followed by fishermen, and yet to the eyes of faith was the eternal God himself. These, and many other, imaginative parallels allowed Erasmus to create a moral theology of great power and attractiveness. However, ethics so dominated this system that its implications for doctrine, the role of an authoritative Church, or even for communal worship, were not really explored. He was clearly confident that educated, humane people could live good Christian lives, and that with trust in divine mercy that would be sufficient.

Time in due course separated out the enduring legacy of the early modern Renaissance from what one might call its froth—the affected aping of Ciceronian periods or classical medallions, the florid 'copious style', or the excessive optimism about the improving power of letters. By the end of the sixteenth century serious scholars accepted the need to purge the texts of ancient authors to recover their original meaning. They inaugurated methods of textual criticism which have continued and evolved to this day, not least among biblical scholars. The idea that classical literature and muscular exercise should form the core of secondary education endured in the public schools of England until about a generation ago. An easy, accessible written style became the ideal, if not always the norm, for academic authors: the tortuous and schematic propositions, contradictions, conclusions, and objections of a Thomas Aquinas were abandoned. Yet the literary Renaissance did not provide all the answers to early modern questions, nor were the answers which it did provide uniformly satisfactory. In natural philosophy—what would become known as the sciences—the cult of the antique followed a rather different course. In religion, sixteenth-century people were to insist on clear answers to questions which the Renaissance had left obscure.

Describing the World and the Universe

The new media for communicating and preserving knowledge had their impact first and foremost on literature; but they were almost immediately applied to other forms of learning. If the printed book was a catalyst for developments in the realm of pure ideas, the *illustrated* printed book had an equally liberating effect upon the descriptive sciences. Medieval scholars had combined and distilled ancient and later lore on plants, animals, and the human body with the same reverence for authority and sense of the continuity of knowledge that they showed in theology. This did not mean that their system was closed: the curious animals featured in medieval bestiaries testify to a ready appetite for the unusual. Where they had difficulty, it seems, was in discarding knowledge rather than accumulating it. The classic text in this field, the *Natural History* of Pliny the Elder (*c*.23–79 CE) was a vast compendium on cosmology, geography, physiology, zoology, botany, and geology. Works in this tradition collected all available information, regardless of reliability, and presented it in a diffuse, disorganized manner.

Renaissance natural philosophy progressed because it learned to discard the old knowledge as well as accumulating the new. By publishing the results of new, empirically acquired information in a form which was for practical purposes imperishable, the new anatomists, zoologists, and botanists made a decisive new departure in describing the world around them. The most heroic feat in this phase was performed by the physician and anatomist Andreas Vesalius of Brussels (1515–64). Vesalius worked in the tradition of classical-cum-Arab medicine until 1540, when he began, while teaching at Padua and Bologna, to carry out his own dissections. He realized that the anatomical views of the greatest classical authority, Galen of Pergamum (129–*c*.199 CE) had been based not on human dissection but on analogies drawn from work on pigs, dogs, and apes. With startling speed he prepared a comprehensive new anatomical textbook, the *Seven Books on the Fabric of the Human Body* (Basle, 1543), illustrated with a sequence of magnificent woodblock diagrams. The diagrams themselves arrived at a

SECVNDA
MVSCVLO,
RVMTA
BVLA.

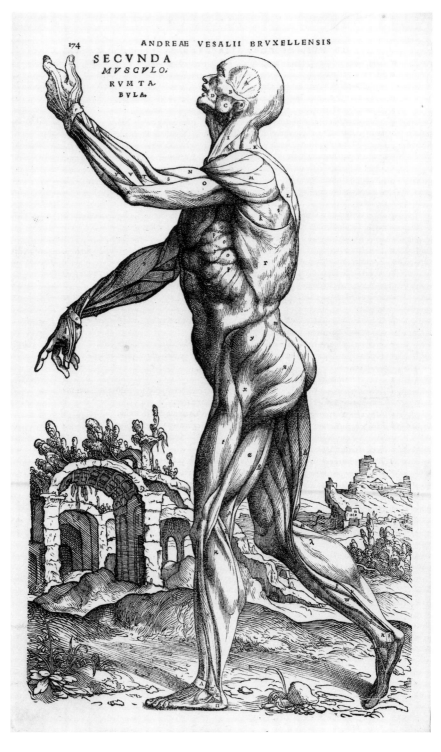

time when Renaissance techniques in figure-drawing had developed to the point where truly realistic depiction was possible. Equally impressive was the speed with which these new insights were taken to a wide readership. Vesalius himself prepared a summary, the *Epitome*, which appeared in the same year as the *Fabric*; a German translation soon followed.

Descriptive anatomy was transformed. Still, the implications for medical understanding of the human body were modest; the emancipation from classical authorities was only partial. Vesalius, and most of his contemporaries, remained locked into Galen's theory of the 'humours' (four body fluids supposed to correspond to four universal elements and four psychological temperaments), which had all the vices of a closed, self-sufficient intellectual system. The *Fabric*, however, helped to inaugurate the textbook written in good, clear humanist prose accompanied by reliable illustrations. At almost exactly the same time, Renaissance botanists were achieving something similar. Just as the needs of surgeons inspired and provided a market for Vesalius' anatomy, so the needs of medical herbalists prompted improvements in descriptive botany. Otto Brunfels, Hieronymus Bock, and Leonhart Fuchs issued their pioneering botanical textbooks from 1530, 1539, and 1542 respectively. Once again, vernacular translations soon followed. Classical authorities continued to be cited: Brunfels's text was largely derivative, while Fuchs routinely included extracts from the *Materia Medica* of Dioscorides (*c.*60 CE) in his own articles. A handful of empirical investigators of medical herbalism like Theophrastus Paracelsus (1493–1541) made only slight inroads into the embedded notions inherited from antiquity. It was in the accuracy of the depictions, and their reliable reproduction through woodblocks, that the novelty of these works lay. The Zürich scholar Konrad Gesner (1516–65), though better known subsequently as a bibliographer and zoologist, prepared many high-quality botanical woodblocks which later authors used. Gesner, moreover, published his *History of Animals* in four volumes between 1551 and 1558, covering respectively viviparous quadrupeds, egg-laying quadrupeds, birds, and fish; a fifth volume on snakes appeared posthumously in 1587. Once again, some selectivity in the use of sources, and conscientious effort to depict animals accurately with woodblock illustrations, marked the demise of the bestiary and the start of a descriptive system.

A diagram from Andreas Vesalius' *De Humani Corporis Fabrica Libri VII* of 1543. One can easily imagine the impact which Vesalius's highly accurate anatomical diagrams must have made on their first appearance. However, it was to be several centuries before the body's workings would be understood enough to make aggressive medical intervention anything other than highly dangerous.

Genuine discoveries in early modern natural philosophy were often made in the course of trying to further an entirely spurious system of belief. Herbalism was hit-and-miss; the theory of humours was entirely misguided (and perniciously so, since it justified the practices of bleeding and purging). Yet the most spectacular achievement of the period before 1618, the discovery of the arrangement of the solar system and the course of the planets' orbits, arose as much out of Neoplatonist magical theories and the needs of judicial astrology as from higher mathematics. More remarkable still is the slow, gradual way in which the theories of planetary motion were perfected; and the even more protracted process by which they won general recognition and acceptance.

The standard astronomical theory of the Middle Ages was based on the major work of the second century CE astronomer Ptolemy, known (by the Arabic version of its title) as the *Almagest*. This work established in great detail a cosmology in which the celestial bodies revolved around the earth in circular motion: the planets travelled on small circular 'epicycles' around a central point, which itself described a circular orbit round the earth. The farther stars were believed to orbit on a fixed sphere. It is easy to ridicule Ptolemy's elaborate system with its epicycles and equants, its intricate devices to reconcile motion in the perfect form of a circle with the erratic observable course of the planets. Yet it offered the most mathematically meticulous and the most successful system of predictive astronomy in late antiquity. It survived not because the Arabs or the medieval astronomers were hidebound or ignorant, but because it worked better than any other system, within the limits of available techniques of observation. Moreover, its medieval form had a persuasive moral content. The earth was both the centre of the cosmos and the lowpoint of creation, where all was change, decay, and fragility. As one moved out past the changeable moon to the more predictable sun, and to the fixed stars, things became more fixed, more reliable, more perfect. Beyond the firmament and the outer spheres was the ultimate unchangeable, the heaven itself.

The 'revolutionary' discoverer of the Earth's orbit round the sun, Nico-laus Copernicus of Toruń (1473–1543) arrived at his working hypothesis in characteristically Renaissance fashion. At Cracow and Padua in the 1490s and 1500s, he began to make astronomical observations while sharing in humanist rediscovery of earlier classical authors, whose fragmentary ideas had been obscured by the success of the later *Almagest*. Measurement and observation confirmed that Ptolemy's system was producing larger and larger discrepancies, partly through accumulated error and partly through procession—slow changes in the arrangement of the fixed stars for which the theory did not allow. Meanwhile, study of antique sources revealed that Heraclides Ponticus (fourth century BCE) and Aristarchus of Samos (third century BCE) had both theorized that some planets orbited the sun; the latter had also proposed that the earth revolved on its axis. Aristotle himself reported that the even more obscure Philolaus, pupil of Pythagoras (fifth century BCE) claimed that the earth, planets, and the sun orbited around a central cosmic fire.

Copernicus began in the 1510s to develop a mathematical model according to which he correctly identified the known planets as orbiting around the sun in their true order, while the moon orbited the earth; he also recognized the earth's daily rotation around its axis. This theory remained in manuscript and the theme of private discussions for nearly all the rest of Copernicus' life. Eventually he was persuaded to release *On the Revolutions of the Heavenly Spheres* for printing, in the edition which appeared in 1543.

NICOLAI COPERNICI

net, in quo terram cum orbe lunari tanquam epicyclo contineri diximus . Quinto loco Venus nono mense reducitur. Sextum deniqʒ locum Mercurius tenet, octuaginta dierum spacio circū currens, In medio uero omnium residet Sol. Quis enim in hoc

The crucial page of Nicolaus Copernicus' *De Revolutionibus Orbium Coelestium* of 1543, which showed for the first time the correct relationship between the sun and the known planets.

pulcherimo templo lampadem hanc in alio uel meliori loco po neret, quàm unde totum simul possit illuminare: Siquidem non inepte quidam lucernam mundi, alij mentem, alij rectorem uo- cant. Trimegistus uisibilem Deum, Sophoclis Electra intuentē omnia. Ita profecto tanquam in folio regali Sol residens circum agentem gubernat Astrorum familiam. Tellus quoqʒ minime fraudatur lunari ministerio, sed ut Aristoteles de animalibus

Yet *On the Revolutions* reads only partly as a modern work. The famous page which contains Copernicus' diagram of the solar system is surrounded by a Neoplatonic paean to the sun, 'which [Hermes] Trismegistus calls the visible God, and Sophocles's Electra calls the all-seeing'. The system still insisted on circular orbits for the moon and planets, although this created small mathematical errors which forced Copernicus (ironically) to locate his central point for the orbits slightly away from the sun.

From even before the publication of *On the Revolutions* there was some uncertainty, deliberately fostered by various astronomers, as to whether the Copernican system was a true representation of the facts, or a mere mathematical model used to make more accurate predictions of planetary positions. This distinction, absurd as it may seem to us, was a vital issue as late as the trial of Galileo. It was not yet taken for granted that the universe worked according to mathematical or mechanical laws, rather than by the motion of conscious spirits. Astronomy progressed slowly, because of a further problem, experimental rather than theological. In the age before the telescope, the only people who would wish to refine astronomical theories still further were those fanatically obsessed with minute discrepancies in the position of the planets. The mathematical principles needed merely to perceive the problem were accessible only to a handful of adepts. The next critical discovery arose through the collaboration of an observer of extraordinary precision and meticulousness, Tycho Brahe (1564–1601), and a mathematician of exceptional ingenuity, Johann Kepler (1571–1630). In his observations made in Denmark and later in Bohemia, Brahe had dramatically revised the tables of planetary motion. When in 1600 Kepler joined Brahe at his observatory at Benátky near Prague, he witnessed Brahe's care in measurement, but could not reconcile the orbit of Mars with any model based on circular motion. In his *New Astronomy* of 1609 Kepler demonstrated that the true shape of planetary motion was an ellipse, not a circle, and that the sun stood at one of the two foci. Within a further ten years he had arrived at the mathematical relationships governing the variations in the orbital speed of planets and between their distance from the sun and orbital period.

These insights were epoch-making, and nothing can detract from their significance. Yet to grasp the atmosphere in which they were made, one must also note the occultist, Neoplatonist theory in which Kepler (for instance) worked, and the selective way in which each theorist chose which new ideas to accept or reject. Kepler's first major astronomical work, the *Cosmographic Mystery* of 1596, tried to prove that the number and distances of the planets were determined by a series of imaginary perfect

Pythagorean solid shapes inserted between each of their orbits. Brahe's solar system placed the earth back at the centre, with other planets orbiting the sun on an epicycle of its terrestrial orbit. Galileo Galilei (1564–1642) did more than anyone to publicize the Copernican theory beyond the circle of mathematicians, and his discovery of sunspots and a nova showed the changeability of the heavens. Yet he still insisted, despite Kepler's calculations, that the motion of bodies around the earth and the sun had to be circular.

Eventually, the European scientific community would devise explanations and theories which would turn the heavens into a mechanical system subject to mechanical laws no different from those obtaining on earth. The stars and planets would be seen to be both changeable, and infinitely vaster and more complex than any intuitive classical theory had allowed. The skies, and the planets, would cease to be full of spirits. With such insights, the notion that the heavens were literally a visible, perfect embodiment of the divine handiwork would suffer a fatal blow. Galileo's judges were right, in retrospect. Nevertheless, this evolution in western thought occupies the entire period covered by this volume; no one generation brought it about.

The Word of Faith: The Old Faith

Secular historians sometimes look back on the early modern period as the one in which western Europe gradually emancipated itself, however incompletely, from the superstition of organized religion. Religious historians, whatever their personal beliefs, tend to see a transformation rather than a rejection: from a religion based on ritual purification to something more thoughtful, rational, and ethical. That change implied that religion would become more personal and less communal. Regardless of viewpoint, all acknowledge that something changed in the sixteenth century, faster and more profoundly than anything seen in the previous five centuries.

At the end of the Middle Ages, western Europe's Christianity was Catholic. That term means far more than the simple fact of acknowledging the authority of the Roman papacy, though nearly all in the western Church did so. Of the churches of the East, the Greeks were subsumed in the Ottoman Empire by this period; those of Russia and Lithuania rarely impinged on the western European mind. 'Catholicism' is defined as that form of Christianity which locates the saving power of God in the work and rites of an authoritative Church, descended by a reliable and continuous tradition from the time of the Apostles. The guarantee of the Church's spiritual power was the continuity and permanence of its ministry. 'There is indeed one universal Church of the faithful, outside of which nobody at all is saved,' proclaimed the first constitution of the Fourth Lateran Council of 1215, in one of the defining statements of late medieval religion. In this sense, almost all western Christians save a few thousand Lollard heretics in England and a similarly modest number of Waldensian heretics in the south-western Alps were 'Catholic' on the eve of the Reformation.

To believe in an authoritative Church meant placing the means of salvation in notoriously unreliable and often unworthy hands, as the late Middle Ages showed. That people did believe in it, therefore, shows just how much value they set on a reliable source of spiritual reassurance. Medieval people had a great deal to be reassured about. From dangerous and little understood childbirth through appalling infant and child mortality to an adulthood regularly haunted by the illness and death of one's spouse or children, uncertain harvests, or the devastating impact of armies, life was full of threats against which practical wisdom offered little security. As though to draw people's minds away from one source of anxiety to another, religious art dwelt heavily upon the threats which hung over the soul in the next world. The 'Four Last Things', Death, Judgement, Hell, and Heaven, provided a standard theme for such painters as Hieronymus Bosch. The copious literature on the 'Art of Dying' stressed the need to make a full and complete confession of all one's sins, with restitution to anyone whom one had wronged, before one's death; it warned of the diabolical temptations to despair which lay in wait for the dying.

Underlying all this was a fear quite specific to the later Middle Ages. Far greater emphasis had come to be placed than in earlier times on the doctrine of 'purgatory'. To purgatory the souls of those destined for eventual salvation were sent, so that they might complete, through sufferings like those of the damned in Hell, the purification and atonement for sin which they had failed to perform in their lives on earth. This belief accompanied the practice whereby Christians were obliged from 1215 to make individual private confession of every serious sin at least once a year to a priest, and after absolution to complete the 'penance' which he imposed. Those who made a final confession at death would probably have no time to finish their penances. If deathbed confessions lacked a penance in this world, they must, it was reasoned, entail a penance in the next. Purgatorial penance was assumed to be enormously long compared to the penances carried out on earth. A rumour circulated in the late fifteenth century to the effect that since 1295 no soul had entered Paradise. In the light of this fear and expectation, the most dreadful risk to medieval people was that they might die suddenly, unprepared and without the spiritual insurance for their journey into eternity. A range of rituals were practised to guard against that one risk of sudden death, from daily attendance at mass to a seven-year cycle of 'Lady Fasts' in honour of the Virgin.

Yet it would be misleading to dwell, as some historians do, on a late medieval religion dominated by fear and anxiety over natural and supernatural threats. We cannot tell just how seriously, on average, medieval lay people took the warnings of religious artists and writers. We can be sure, however, that most of them participated enthusiastically and generously in the shared religious culture. This culture was designed to allay anxiety, to reassure people by dispensing that quantifiable, negotiable unit of spiritual currency called 'grace'. 'Grace' was a measurable quantity of worth or goodness before God and the Church. The supremely accessible and reliable way to acquire grace, for lay people and clergy alike, was to take part in religious rites; supreme above those, in the late Middle Ages, was the mass, or Eucharist, in which the priest consecrated the unleavened wafer and the mixed water and wine in the chalice, so that they became, according to orthodox theology, essentially the body and blood of Christ. So consecrated, the mass was 'offered up' as a sacrifice akin to and participating in the sacrifice of Christ on the cross: its value for the souls of the living and the dead, of those present and of those named in the accompanying prayers, was believed to be certain and trustworthy. The mass achieved its miracle and acquired its grace irrespective of whether any congregation partook of the wafer or indeed was present at all. As Archbishop John Pecham of Canterbury declared in the late thirteenth century, it was unthinkable that one mass for a soul could achieve as much, other things being equal, as a thousand masses for the same soul. The value of Christ's sacrifice was thought to be 'distributed' into units corresponding to each mass said. So towards 1500 it became common to provide for ever-increasing numbers of masses for the souls of the dead, and to attend larger numbers of masses in life. Particular celebrations were thought specially helpful, like the 'Trental of St Gregory', a series of thirty masses celebrated at specified times and in a particular order (which varied according to the region where it was celebrated).

One cannot overemphasize the importance which was attached to the real, bodily presence of the risen Christ in the wafer and in the chalice on the altar. When the priest raised the consecrated body of Christ above his head after the consecration prayer, all eyes in the church turned towards it, to acquire the grace assuredly offered to those who saw their creator, including freedom from sudden death for the day. Even in sophisticated Florence, the elevation was the moment chosen by the Pazzi conspirators to try to murder Lorenzo the Magnificent on 26 April 1478, while all eyes were averted. As an English verse guide to the mass, *The Lay Folk's Mass Book*, said:

> And so the elevation thou behold,
> for that is he that Judas sold,
> and then was scourged and done on rood [*cross*],
> And for mankind there shed his blood,
> And died and rose and went to heaven,
> And yet shall come to deem [*judge*] us . . .

The legend that Pope Gregory the Great had a vision of the crucified Christ on the altar as he consecrated mass is, apparently, entirely a late medieval invention: the persistence of the legend and its many artistic representations serve to show how graphic, how physical was the sense of Christ's presence in this rite.

If the mass was the 'core' ceremony of late medieval religion, there was a range of other ritual acts available. Although this religion placed great stress on the spiritual powers vested in a ceremonially ordained clergy, that did not mean that the lay majority were excluded or alienated. Religious processions and festivals enlivened and varied the seasons of the year. The celebration of Holy Week and Easter was conducted in a highly theatrical manner. In Germany it began with the Palm Sunday procession where a 'Palm-ass', an often exquisitely carved figure of Christ on the donkey, was dragged through the streets on a trolley. After the bleak ordeal of worship before the crucifix on Good Friday, the Christ-figure would be buried in a sepulchre, to be raised (with pulleys) triumphantly in the Easter resurrection scene. Religion was not confined solely to the framework of the parish community: lay men and women could belong to a range of religious brotherhoods, within and beyond the parish, which worshipped in common and carried out a range of ritual and charitable acts. From the early fourteenth century the Eucharist acquired a particular cult and a festival of its own across Europe, the Corpus Christi celebration and procession on the Thursday after Trinity, in which the sign became almost as celebrated as the one whom it signified.

If ritual brought help, so did the company of heaven. For many centuries

The 'Mass of St Gregory' depicts a late medieval legend according to which Pope Gregory I (590–604) had a vision of the crucified Christ on the altar as he celebrated mass. It expressed the intense sense of Christ's presence in the Eucharist typical of the age. Christ is shown surrounded by the instruments of his passion, themselves objects of devotion at the time.

it had been taught that heaven was a hierarchy, as was earthly society. On earth, patrons looked after their clients, lords looked after their supporters. One approached the ruler not directly and unaided, but surrounded by those who knew him and could guarantee access. Something similar, it was assumed, must take place in the heavenly hierarchy. It was argued that the supremely holy Christians who had died before, the saints, would undoubtedly feel the same charitable warmth towards their followers as they had done to their brother Christians while in life: so how could they fail to help those who approached them? Such arguments would be used in all seriousness to rebut the sixteenth-century reformers. Saints, therefore, were vested with enormous patronage networks, which extended to particular nations, regions, or peoples, to trades and crafts, or to activities such as travelling or childbearing. Alternatively, they were given particular duties in helping and healing particular ailments. Later reformers would amuse themselves ridiculing the belief that one saint healed plague, another fevers, another toothache, and so on. Yet paintings such as those of the Fourteen Holy Helpers, or Auxiliary Saints, testify to the seriousness with which such beliefs were held.

One saint towered above the rest, so much that she significantly distorted the traditional role of Christ in redeeming humanity. The late Middle Ages was the great age of the cult of the Virgin Mary. Orthodox theology portrayed her as the greatest and most generous of mediators on behalf of humanity with the Godhead. The pious literature written in celebration of her cult went rather further. She became the 'co-redeemer', the shelter and protection of vulnerable humankind. She was portrayed as the Virgin of Mercy, covering with her vast cloak all sorts and conditions of humanity from the terrors of divine judgement. 'If the sinner flees to her with trust and good intention, in repentance and sorrow and horror for his sins, with firm and strong faith, she receives him mercifully and covers him under her mantle of grace and mercy,' as a late medieval German tract on the Virgin assured its readers. In the eyes of the Franciscan Order and of many laypeople, she uniquely had been conceived free from the original sin which tainted the rest of humankind: consequently, her own birth and her own mother, St Anne (mentioned nowhere in the canonical scriptures, a creation of post-biblical tradition) acquired their own distinct cults and festivals.

One final shift in religious thought and practice on the eve of the Reformation deserves notice. When a penance was imposed after the confession and absolution of sins, it had to be performed by the penitent, unless it was commuted into some other good work, or 'indulged', that is, remitted by the authority which imposed it. Towards the end of the Middle Ages the Church became increasingly confident of its power to remit penances. Comprehensive remissions of penance, 'plenary indulgences', had been offered to crusaders from the end of the eleventh century; by the fifteenth they could be acquired by those who visited Rome in a Jubilee year, or contributed to the building of a church, or bought a 'confessional letter'. It was taught that Christ and the saints had acquired a 'treasure' of so much superabundant merit that the Church could, at will, assign it to make up the deficiencies of ordinary Christians. From the 1470s onwards the Church took the dubious step of offering similar indulgences for those who had already died and were presumed to be working off their debts in purgatory. This claim marked the high water mark of 'Catholic' assumptions of the visible Church's ties to the celestial hierarchy. In 1500 bogus papal bulls circulated among the pilgrims dying of the plague in the north Italian plain, in which the Pope apparently commanded the angels in heaven to transport the souls of dead pilgrims straight to paradise. Wishful thinking had gone where the Church's claims stopped short: the earthly Church's claim to control admission to heaven was becoming perilously oversold.

The Reformation Challenge

The more seriously one takes late medieval Catholicism, the harder it becomes to explain why belief in so many of its central principles abruptly collapsed across much of western Europe in the four decades or so after 1520. Historians no longer pronounce in Olympian fashion that the old Church was uniformly 'corrupt' or 'decayed'. The often ingenious attempts to demonstrate that the European Reformation was 'really' about class conflict, socio-economic stresses and strains, or the emergence of a new bourgeoisie, largely died at around the same time as the Marxist regimes which helped to sponsor them.

We are a little clearer about how this profound religious upheaval took place. It began, undoubtedly, with some of the guardians of the religious order, the theologians, preachers, and pastors of Germany and Switzerland. Inspired by Martin Luther (1483–1546), though not all personally bound to him, a generation of religious teachers, mostly under the age of 40, refused to tolerate the Roman court's negative and patronizing response to Luther's critiques of current practice. They took their protests to the literate laity of the towns, who responded with interest, and in many cases with fervent enthusiasm. The urban communes not only refused to silence their preachers when told to do so: they embodied the preachers' ideas in wide-ranging edicts of reform. These transformed the Church in the affected areas from a branch of the international hierarchy, into a self-regulating spiritual department of the local political community. A reformed Church was effectively the city, the town, sometimes even the village, and eventually the principality or kingdom at prayer. In varying degrees, the prayer and worshipping life of the community was simplified and purged. The flamboyant excesses of late medieval spirituality were toned down or suppressed. More profoundly, a new system of belief emerged. 'Reformed' Christianity assigned to the visible Church the role of teaching the people the Word of God's favour, rather than dispensing according to a set formula the rations of his grace. The preaching of the gospel and the signs of God's promises made a true Church, not the possession of traditional, inherited authority.

One entirely valid way to explain the appeal of the Reformation is to consider the sequence of impressions with which it presented the thinking people of Europe. The crisis took its origin when Dr Martin Luther issued his ninety-five theses for disputation concerning the power of papal indulgences, especially those issued for souls in purgatory, on 31 October 1517. We need not worry about when, or indeed whether, he pinned his theses to the door of the Castle church in his university town of Wittenberg. What mattered was that he sent them respectfully to Albrecht of Mainz, the archbishop responsible for the indulgence-sale, and then to his friends, who in due course had them printed as a single-leaf poster. The precise argument of the theses cannot have meant much to most people. Written in theological school-Latin, they were by turns technical and lyrical: the meaning of some of them remains obscure to this day. What people saw was that a teacher, preacher, and pastor stood up against the Roman hierarchy's notorious habit of squeezing money out of the gullible and pious on doubtful pretexts. In so doing, Luther appeared to take the side of sincere German laypeople against cynical clerics of his own caste. The earliest portrayals of Luther point out the paradox: he was celebrated as a member of the Augustinian order and as a Doctor of Theology, though he was to overthrow the principles of monasticism and transform theology out of recognition.

As Luther resisted repeated attempts to browbeat him into submission to religious authority, other intellectual clergy joined his standard, or examined his books and approved or reinvented his ideas. So the pattern repeated itself: preachers who had been used to preaching down to the people from the inaccessible heights of theological authority, now aired their disagreements in public and asked the ordinary townspeople to discuss their views and adapt them. When Huldrych Zwingli (1484–1531), the

Martin Luther, as depicted by Lukas Cranach the Elder in 1521. Luther became a celebrated icon in the German Protestant tradition which he helped to establish. This portrait shows the thirty-eight-year-old Luther's tenacity and spiritual defiance with particular clarity. On its appearance it was quickly superseded by images which represented its subject more conventionally as a devout friar.

LVCAE ⬧ OPVS ⬧ EFFIGIES ⬧ HAEC ⬧ EST ⬧ MORITVRA ⬧ LVTHERI ⬧
AETHERNAM ⬧ MENTIS ⬧ EXPRIMIT ⬧ IPSE ⬧ SVAE ⬧
⬧ M · D · X · X · I ·

'people's preacher' of the Swiss town of Zürich, presented some theses for discussion in front of the city fathers in 1523, his argument could not have been better calculated to please the self-esteem of burghers increasingly conscious of their religious responsibilities:

> The Vicar-General [*representing the local bishop*] . . . says that things of this sort ought to be dealt with in some national synod, or in a general council of bishops. But I believe that in this very hall we have a Christian assembly gathered together. For I hope that by far the greatest part of us have come here out of love for God's will and zeal for the truth . . . Since, therefore, in this our assembly there are great numbers of true faithful people both from our own district and from beyond, and these are just like so many pious and learned bishops, . . . I see no reason whatever to prevent us here and now from lawfully disputing the Vicar's opinion on these matters, and discerning what the truth teaches us.

In at least sixteen German and Swiss towns the city fathers found themselves drawn into managing strife between their clergy: they issued edicts requiring preachers to 'stick to the Scriptures' and avoid contentious debates. By the inexorable logic of that decision, the burghers discovered that they had become the arbiters of what Scripture really meant. What fragmented the clergy flattered the sensibilities of the laity.

The superficial appeal of an enticing preacher, however, would have lasted a pitifully short time if his ideas had seemed repellent, self-evidently wrong, or to place souls in mortal danger of damnation. In fact, the message of the early reformed preachers, like their manner, enjoyed a honeymoon period of several years despite the challenge which it posed to a belief system hitherto shared by most western Christians. The Reformation message appeared, to an uncautious observer, to be merely a more emphatic and bolder restatement of a series of familiar criticisms. First of all, in his *To the Christian Nobility of the German Nation* in 1520 Luther thundered against the 'deceit and hypocrisy' that made of the clergy a separate legal estate, who alone could regulate their own affairs without reference to the rest of society. The Imperial assembly, the Reichstag, had complained for sixty years about Roman control of church posts and Roman taxation of German clergy; many cities had tried for as long to persuade priests to accept the same tax burdens and legal duties as other citizens. Luther echoed both these complaints, denouncing papal bureaucracy and clerical exclusiveness alike.

Secondly, Luther attracted forward-thinking laymen and priests by several entirely specious similarities between his thought and the religious ideas of Erasmus' Christian humanism. Erasmus had made fun of people who pursued a superstitious quest for pardons or indulgences, 'measuring their time in purgatory as though by water-clock': Luther did so too, though for different reasons. Erasmus had no time for a school-theology which had bored him at Paris in the 1490s: one of Luther's earlier statements was a *Disputation against Scholastic Theology*. Erasmus wrote scathingly of the shrines scattered across Europe where bogus relics attracted pilgrims and pulled in money: Luther recommended that the field-shrines of Germany with their bleeding Eucharistic wafers or miraculous images of the Virgin should be razed to the ground. Erasmus urged that the Bible be made accessible to everyone: Luther based his beliefs on Scripture and translated it for the German people. In 1518 Martin Bucer, a Dominican and humanist who was later to teach the Reformation in Strasbourg and Cambridge, wrote of Luther 'he agrees with Erasmus in everything, except on one point he seems to excel him, for what Erasmus merely insinuates, Luther teaches openly and freely'.

Yet there was much more to the essential Reformation than these apparent extensions and applications of the Christian Renaissance. At its heart, the Reformation held a new view of how God intervened to save human souls from their predicament. For medieval theologians, God intervened to save mankind, usually, by the simple fact of instituting the means of grace through Holy Church. The reformers saw things differently. Their God did not purify sinners in order to accept them: he accepted sinners, and forgave their sins, in spite of their continuing state of sin. The righteous, the 'elect', were righteous only in the sense that God had chosen them for his favour. Divine 'grace' or 'favour' (the terms were synonymous for the reformers) meant just that, the unearned and non-transferable favour of God. The righteousness of the saints was a garment, a cloak draped over their continuing faults and imperfections. The draping of this cloak over human nature was what saved the soul; and the immensity of that gift was understood through faith—a trusting belief in God's mercy which was itself a divine gift.

In the light of this unearned and unearnable forgiveness offered for Christ's sake, any good that the Christian might do in life was a result, not a cause, of being forgiven by God. 'Good works' could not even help to purify, to undo the consequences of sin: that was what Christ had done on the cross. This epoch-making religious insight, discovered first of all by Luther and then rediscovered and reformulated by Huldrych Zwingli and later by John Calvin (1509–64) among others, changed forever the style of religion in reformed Christianity. If voluntary actions could not make a person better, then ritual acts of piety, ceremonial actions to purify the soul or earn merit, were at best futile and at worst a blasphemy. Therefore, there remained no place in reformed teaching for the cycle of sin, sacramental confession, priestly absolution, and ritual penance which had defined the lives of the faithful since the thirteenth century. If there was no penance, there was no purgatory: the souls of the saved 'paid all their debts by their death', as Luther said. If the sacrifice of Christ was complete and all-sufficient, the sacrificial mass, especially the private mass performed for the benefit of a named soul, was an abomination. If the elect of God were saved despite their sins, not because of their virtues, then there could not be a communion of superabundantly holy 'saints' to intercede: prayer should only be addressed to God. Not only that: the idea that there was surplus 'merit' available to the papacy to dispense at will via indulgences was a grotesque fiction. By a feat of theological reasoning, all the most distinctive and popular rites of late medieval religion were simply blown away.

So what was left to the Christian? The only response to the promises of the gospel, thus understood, was to learn of them, to understand them, and to let one's gratitude overflow in actions of neighbourly goodness, in care for one's community, which in no way contributed to salvation. The psychological control which the old Church had held over believers, to confess this sin for fear of judgement, to pay for that mass for fear of purgatory, was lost. Reformed congregations soon took full advantage of this freedom from ritual constraints. Worship became simpler, briefer, and much more cerebral. On the other hand, a formidable campaign of mass religious education began, which was soon to give the 'liberated' people of Protestant Europe a rude shock. From the 1520s onwards reformers issued dialogue 'catechisms', rigmaroles of stereotyped questions and answers, to establish a set form of doctrine in the minds of their congregations. Not for nothing did John Calvin entitle the greatest textbook of reformed theology, first published in 1536, *Instruction in the Christian Religion* (which translates *Christianae Religionis Institutio* better than the more familiar *Institutes*). The Church became, whether people liked it or not, a 'house of learning', where reading the word of Scripture and hearing the word of moral exhortation was the highest duty of all and every Christian.

Reformed Churches and Reformed People

The Reformation thus brought about profound changes in the culture and social life of large areas of early modern Europe. Broadly speaking, northern and eastern Germany and Scandinavia fell under the sway of a conservative, traditionalist Lutheran creed. England and Scotland, parts of the Netherlands and Rhineland, northern and western Switzerland, and regions of southern and south-western France adopted the more sweeping, rationalist form of Protestantism known (not quite accurately) as 'Calvinism'. The visual differences between churches of the two creeds were considerable. Lutheran worship tended to preserve whatever of the old styles of ritual and church ornament was not clearly offensive to the new faith. So, many of the vestments and rites of late medieval religion lasted a long time after the Reformation. Religious paintings, sculptures, and above all many of the wonderful carved altarpieces of the German Renaissance were at least partially preserved. Organs survived; hymns and religious music remained quite elaborate even before reaching their creative zenith in the age of J. S. Bach.

In the 'Calvinist' or reformed tradition of the Swiss and south German theologians, however, only what was clearly necessary, by severely rational criteria, was allowed to remain. Pictures and statues disappeared more or less completely from the churches (for which ample compensation would be made by the great flowering of secular landscape and marine painting in the seventeenth-century Netherlands). Church music was simplified: ultimately, and in the most extreme puritanical forms, only the human voice (helped, on sufferance, by a tuning-fork) was supposed to sing psalms or Scripture paraphrases. In the most developed form of high Calvinist worship, virtually the only set forms of words acceptable were those taken from the Bible: everything else was to be extemporized. Not every Church went quite so far. In the Low Countries and even more in England, the austerity of the reformed settlement was moderated first of all by traditionalist resistance or inertia, and in the seventeenth century by revisionist liturgical movements which revived some of the beauty of worship and rediscovered the traditional language of the ancient Church.

There were important common factors between all Protestant churches as well, though. All reformed churches, and no Catholic ones, renounced the use of Latin in common worship (save in schools and universities where ancient languages were taught). All reformed clergymen, and no Catholic ones, had the right to marry, and the duty to live as citizens. Vowed, celibate monastic communities dwindled and died in the lands of the Reformation, only to be revived centuries later in some English and German churches. All reformed churches came in some way under the ultimate control of secular government; usually this entailed a simplification or abolition of the old hierarchy, though the Church of England, for no very good reason beyond political stalemate, retained its old bishops, chapters, and administrative system. The people's dealings with the old church courts—over marriage and moral regulation, wills and inheritance, and church tithes—were reconstructed, again with the illogical exception of England.

The new ideas did not grow of themselves: they found adherents among particular sorts and conditions of people, who then tried to have them adopted by the whole community. The pattern of sectional support for Protestantism varied from the extremes of monarchical diktat, in Denmark or some of the German principalities, to a collective decision by vote of the village commune, in parts of rural Switzerland. In between was a vast range of individual and group choices, whose diversity makes nonsense of any simple theories of bourgeois or proletarian protest, of Reformation 'from above' or 'from below'. In the larger cities of central Europe, the cause of Reformation was espoused sometimes by respectable civic worthies, like the lawyer Christoph Scheurl or the municipal secretary Lazarus Spengler at Nuremberg, sometimes by political radicals from the artisanate like Jürgen Wullenwever of Lübeck. More common were the regions where great nobles and aristocrats guided—or forced—their estates and

tenantry to follow them, such as the German princes of Saxony, Brandenburg, Hesse, or Württemberg, whose power was like that of small monarchies; or in more conventional kingdoms, feudatories like the earls of
Leicester or Huntingdon in England, the Montmorency-Châtillon brothers
in France, or the Leszczynskis or Radziwills in Poland-Lithuania.

Spiritual zeal led in due course to religious strife and violence. Some of
this violence expressed in an almost ritual way people's disillusionment
with the images, the 'idols' in which so much faith (and cash) had been
invested. Luther's uncontrollable colleague Andreas Karlstadt at Wittenberg urged the utter removal and destruction, as soon as possible, of the
relics of the old cult in the first 'image-breaking' of the Reformation in
1521–2. When a procession of the burghers of St-Gallen broke open the
shrines of two local saints in 1528, they found a skull, a large tooth, and a
snail-shell. In these early stages, the 'pollution' of wrong teaching was
located in the material objects of the old cult, whether an image, a relic, or
the 'pastry god' of the mass. However, as time went on and it became clear
that some communities would not renounce their 'idols', the pollutants
ceased to be inanimate things and became one's neighbours. Catholic
regimes tried to purge 'heresy' among their subjects with fire, in Flanders
up to the 1550s, in France from 1534 and 1547, in England between 1555 and
1558. In Switzerland and Germany neighbouring provinces of diverse
faiths kept the peace only by armed truces, like that established after a short
war in northern Switzerland in 1531 or the fragile treaty agreed in Germany
in 1555, after the Emperor Charles V had won a war against his Lutheran
subjects only to make a disastrous mess of the ensuing peace.

Worst affected of all were those countries where Protestant nobles and
bourgeois gained just enough power to destabilize the legitimate monarch,
but not enough to establish their civil rights for the reformed faith in
durable form. This dilemma afflicted France after 1562 and the Netherlands
after 1566. In each case, of course, complex internal politics were at work.
However, for European ideas, the importance of these conflicts was that
Protestantism provided a binding ideology which led all sorts of Calvinists,
and even some radical Lutherans, to make common cause with one of the
parties in another country's civil conflict. Ideology, a faith to die and to kill
for, not sectional self-interest, led English volunteers to fight at Zutphen

The interior of Calvin's church, St-Pierre, at Geneva. In the 'reformed' as opposed to the
'Lutheran' tradition, churches were rigorously stripped of all their medieval ornaments.
Nothing was to detract from communication of the Gospel through the word written and
spoken. Note how the pulpit is located almost centrally, with a large sounding-board above
it.

against the king of Spain, Brandenburger clergy to call for intervention in the French civil wars, or the English Protectorate to lobby the duke of Savoy about the treatment of his Protestant subjects in the 1650s. The age of the international 'cause', with its selfless nobility and its boundless capacity to bring misery, had arrived.

The Old Church Responds

The central organization of the Catholic Church in the west had not been idle or complacent while large segments of its membership defected from its allegiance and transformed its teachings. Several factors had made it exceptionally difficult to respond effectively to a northern European crisis from central Italy in the early sixteenth century. The type of problem was quite new: the popes' previous political antagonists had always wanted to be part of the universal Church and believed in its power, whatever they thought of its leader's policies. That will, that need to reunite with Rome was now gone: so the old tactics of excommunication and interdict, which blackmailed the Pope's enemies with exclusion from the Church, no longer worked. Secondly, since the French invasion of Italy in 1494 the peninsula had become a cockpit where armies from France, Spain, and Germany competed over the prizes of Milan and Naples. The popes were drawn into these wars by their possession of the Papal State across the middle of the country. The sack of Rome by German troops in 1527 forced the Pope temporarily to become a client of the Emperor. Sensitive times needed politically adept popes like Alexander VI or Julius II, who were manipulators and managers of people. In such days a spiritual leader was a luxury. The two most important popes of the period, Clement VII (1523–34) and Paul III (1534–49), respectively of the Medici and Farnese dynasties, had their own political agendas to follow; despite this Paul III, at least, made some real efforts in the spiritual sphere. Even when the will to repair or reinvigorate the Church's central organs was there, Rome was still locked in by squabbles within the College of Cardinals and by its finances, which had become heavily dependent on the sale of offices.

The Church could not respond decisively to the Reformation challenge for another, more fundamental reason. It could not answer a challenge based on religious belief, when its own stance on the disputed questions had not yet been defined. All Catholics agreed that Luther's views on the mass, monastic vows, or papal authority were wrong. To convince wavering lay people that they were, one had to show just how the mainspring of his ideas, the doctrine of salvation, was erroneous: since it was from that moving force that every other 'error' was derived. Yet there was no agreed Catholic doctrine on this issue.

Worse still from the point of view of orthodoxy, there were many in prominent positions at Rome whose beliefs differed from Luther's by barely a hair's breadth. A circle of sensitive souls brought up in the states of Venice under the aegis of Gasparo Contarini (1483–1542, cardinal from 1535) tried during the 1530s to come to terms with the spiritual message of the Reformation, but at the same time to ignore its destructive implications for the ordering of the Church. 'Heretics be not in all things heretics,' wrote one of the group, Reginald Pole, the future archbishop of Canterbury, with unconscious irony. In 1541 a like-minded team of moderate German Catholic theologians tried, with Contarini's assistance, to reach doctrinal agreement with moderate Protestants at the last of a series of conferences, held at Regensburg; on justification they nearly succeeded.

The way of concession and accommodation was only finally discredited after the death of Contarini and the sensational defection of two of his followers to Protestant Switzerland in 1542. Sterner and more unbending temperaments took over, above all Gian Pietro Caraffa (1476–1559, cardinal from 1536, Pope as Paul IV from 1555). He even procured the establishment of a central office of the Inquisition for Rome and Italy, the 'Holy Office', whose archive remained stubbornly closed to all but a tiny handful of favoured scholars until January 1998.

Clarification of beliefs—which meant, in effect, selecting one of the many available interpretations as the official one—was now urgent. The General Council of the Church, long projected and much delayed, met on 13 December 1545 at Trent, an episcopal city in the foothills of the Alps, on the margins of Italy and Austria. The location, more or less equidistant from the influence of the Pope and the Emperor, was symbolic as well as expedient. Charles V, during the first session of the council, fought a successful campaign against the armies of the Lutheran league: but to accomplish his ambition of reuniting Germany in one faith, he needed a moderate and accommodating attitude from the Council. The papacy, in contrast, needed clear, simple, effective pronouncements to come from Trent.

In the end, the Council fathers seem to have acquired a momentum of their own as they debated complex issues of belief and discipline: the needs of German politics were forgotten. The cathedral at Trent witnessed a curious spectacle, where the most profound questions regarding the understanding of the relationship between humanity and its creator were resolved by a process of haggling, proposal, counter-proposal, and resolution between a group of mostly Italian bishops and theologians. The decree on 'justification', the core issue, was complex, subtle, and carefully phrased, but it left no room for the distinctive Protestant view. Reginald Pole, one of those who had held to a theology of salvation not very different from the reformers', left in apparent displeasure when the result was decided. Having resolved that issue on 13 January 1547, the Council passed a series of decrees reaffirming Catholic positions on a range of other issues with the specific and obvious intent of arming its preachers to repel Protestantism. The place of tradition alongside Scripture was vindicated; the need for specific confession of sins reasserted; the primacy of the Latin Vulgate Bible reaffirmed. Each decree on doctrine was accompanied by a series of 'anathemas', which condemned a sometimes distorted or burlesque version of reformed teaching. Dogmatic militancy had triumphed.

Yet as with the Renaissance, it would be quite wrong to read the Counter-Reformation simply as a reaffirmation of the old. The very act of reaffirmation, 'clarification', or selection of doctrine entailed a tremendous change of style in Roman Catholicism, which cannot be summarized by such one-dimensional moral terms as 'restoration' or 'reinvigoration'. The same Council which issued the decrees on doctrine and discipline also issued the first uniform mass-order for western Christendom, and the first catechism to be imposed from the centre. Worship and teaching were to be harmonized; the message was to be taken to the people with the same streamlined, humanist-inspired eloquence and persuasiveness that the reformers had given to their beliefs. The Church embarked on a long but ultimately successful campaign to educate its priesthood, in specialized theological seminaries rather than via the diffuse medieval academic curriculum. Little by little secular priests were persuaded to adapt a distinctive garb when not conducting services (something entirely absent in the Middle Ages, when complaints about furred short coats, bright colours, or extravagantly pointed shoes had been repeated ineffectually). Orders of priests regular, above all the Society of Jesus (founded in 1540), led both the missionary effort in regions like Austria, Poland, and England where reconversions were thought possible, and the educational enterprise in Spain, Germany, Rome, and elsewhere. This missionary effort ensured doctrinal uniformity and a thoroughly professional, at times seductive presentation of the renovated Catholic creed. It also contained the risk that

The religious art of the Counter-Reformation used all the available artistic techniques of dramatic angles of view, foreshortening, and perspective to evoke an emotional response in the viewer. Here the Virgin Mary is shown attended by the semi-mythical Saints Cosmas and Damian, two healing saints and patrons of physicians, who were invoked in the Canon of the Mass and in much popular piety.

all intellectual effort would be focused on confessional goals: the validity of scientific thought, or political thought, or philosophy, could be judged by whether or not it helped to spread and support the faith.

There is another side to the spiritual life of the Roman Catholic Church after the Council of Trent. The growing professionalism of the Church's personnel caused a significant change in relations between the Church and its people. In the Middle Ages 'mass-priests' or confessors had sometimes been treated almost as the employees of the individuals, brotherhoods, or parishes whom they served. Lay people had exercised much choice and even some collective control over their religious life. The reformed Catholic clergy assumed a more authoritative and directing role: often they related as much to individuals as to communities, or more so. This was the first age of the confessional box, the booth where anonymous penitents could confess their sins to an anonymous priest, devised in the hope of encouraging more regular lay confessions. Private confessors sought to ease the consciences of the great and noble; coincidentally, they lured some Protestants away from the embarrassingly public discipline of Calvinism, at least in France. Religious art appealed to the emotions and the senses. Where late medieval religious painting had been hierarchical and some-times static, baroque art exuded spiritual energy; it drew the observer into the rapture of an encounter between the individual soul and the divine. From the sculptures of Bernini to the little engraved motifs in a pocket Bible, Roman Catholicism now appealed unashamedly to the sympathetic devotion of its faithful.

Conclusion

In 1516, not long after the opening of the sixteenth century, Erasmus had looked forward to:

> an age of gold, if such a thing there ever were. For in this age, . . . I foresee that three of its greatest blessings will be restored to the human race: that true Christian piety which in so many ways is now decayed, the study of the humanities in part neglected hitherto and in part corrupted, and that public and perpetual harmony of the Christian world which is the fountain and the parent of religion and learning.

That vision, in the form in which Erasmus saw it, was in fragments by 1550 if not before. However, the fragments of the total Renaissance vision remained, to form part of a greater mosaic of early modern culture. Such things as textual criticism, educational techniques, or a better understand-ing of the laws, architecture, or coinage of the ancient world may seem like the cold, dry embers of a much more far-reaching vision. Yet from another point of view, the 'critical Renaissance' of the end of the century, with its improved understanding of classical literary culture epitomized by scholars such as J. J. Scaliger and Isaac Casaubon, represented real achievement where the earlier heroic concept had only been promise and potential, not to say propaganda. The slow disintegration of the Renaissance vision allowed literary studies, after several decades of intense vogue, to fall back into their proper proportion alongside all other forms of knowledge. Moreover, the Renaissance contribution to written style and typography ensured that the new scientific and other discoveries would be transmitted in as clear and lucid a form as the subject-matter and the writer's talent allowed.

Religion in 1600 presents a grim face. The various dogmatic systems abandoned the Renaissance elegance in which they had first clothed themselves in favour of a revived scholasticism. Prickly, defensive, gladiatorial debates were conducted endlessly between theologians who seldom if ever met and who wrote in prose intelligible only to their own kind. Lutheran, Calvinist, and Catholic armies were poised within a few decades to lacerate each other on the battlefields of central Europe. If the later seventeenth and eighteenth centuries saw a rise in religious scepticism, it was at least partly in response to the terrible conviction of the professional clergy.

One cannot say with certainty whether, given time, Christendom could have turned away from its obsession with purifying rituals without such a fearful rupture as the Reformation. There was, however, little sign that the religious humanists of c.1500 had been about to reshape the religion of the masses as the reformers did. While trying to make ordinary believers better Catholics or better Protestants, most of the new clergy did try rather harder and more consistently than the old to wean people away from the charms, spells, and vulgar magic which had lived parasitically on Christian practice for many centuries. By turning away from both the low and the high Catholicism of the past, Europe set itself on the long road towards modern critical Christianity, with all its questionings and hesitations. There was still a very long way to go.

3

War, Religion, and the State

STEVEN GUNN

States and Borders

To the modern eye, the political map of sixteenth-century Europe looks more familiar in some parts than in others. France, Spain, and Portugal are recognizable; so are England and Scotland, though not yet united; so are the Benelux countries, though ruled as seventeen provinces by a single prince. In the centre of the continent, Germany and Italy are strangely parcellated, though the authority of the Holy Roman Emperor stretches tenuously over the first. To the north and east the impression is rather one of unlikely agglomeration, of rambling empires and multiple monarchies. These might prove unstable: the election of Gustav Vasa as king of an independent Sweden in 1523 broke the union more than a century old between the Danes, the Norwegians, and the Swedes. Or they might prove surprisingly stable, even when they combined very dissimilar peoples. The Greeks, Turks, Albanians, Bulgars, and Serbs were for the moment successfully blended in the expanding Ottoman Empire. The Catholic Poles, the Orthodox Ukrainians, the Ashkenazi Jews, the lately pagan Lithuanians, and the Lutheran German burghers of Danzig, Posen, and Thorn rubbed along together as denizens of the vast Polish-Lithuanian commonwealth.

Even in the west, the appearance of familiarity is in part an illusion. International borders were vaguer than today, as islands of one ruler's jurisdiction or military control could be found well within the area ruled by a neighbour. The first map of Europe to attempt to show state borders was not printed until 1602. The kings of France had gained or regained control over Normandy, Gascony, Picardy, Burgundy, Brittany, and Provence only in the sixty years before 1500, and to the north and east much of modern France lay beyond their control. The Spanish kingdoms of Castile, Aragon, Catalonia, and Valencia were united under joint rulers by marriage only in 1479; Moorish Granada and francophile Navarre were added by conquest in 1492 and 1512. Amidst complex family politics Castile was briefly separated from the Aragonese realms in 1504–6 and might have been so again. In 1543 the unfulfilled treaty of Greenwich, providing for a marriage between Mary Queen of Scots and the future Edward VI, promised to unite England and Scotland sixty years before they were eventually joined under James VI and I. Everywhere political boundaries and political alignments were in flux, reshaped by the strategies of war and marriage, by the accidents of royal fertility and untimely death.

The trend over the long term was for the larger states to consume the smaller and digest them in a slow process of internal consolidation. Thus the empire-building republic of Venice chewed her way across the north Italian mainland, absorbing smaller city states and despotisms until all the major western powers combined to halt her expansion in the war of 1509. Thus Sweden, Denmark, Muscovy, and Poland fought for the spoils of the ailing Livonian Order of Teutonic Knights from 1558 to 1582 in Latvia and Estonia. Thus provinces were tacked on to the Netherlands one by one from the 1520s to the 1540s: Tournai, Friesland, Groningen, Overijssel, Utrecht, Gelderland. Yet the duchy of Gelderland had resisted assimilation in war after war ever since the 1470s.

Other well-organized smaller powers could hold their own against the greatest rulers in Europe. The best example was the Swiss confederation of townsmen and free peasants. Victors over the ambitiously expansionist Duke Charles the Bold of Burgundy in the 1470s, they went on to beat the Holy Roman Emperor Maximilian I in the Swabian War of 1499 and force a humiliating peace on Louis XII of France in 1513. At length they met their match in his successor François I, who checked them in a bloody two-day battle at Marignano in 1515. In Germany and Italy the economic power of city states such as Augsburg, Nuremberg, and Genoa enabled them to steer a perilous course through the envies of their larger neighbours, generally by making themselves financially useful to such great protectors as the Holy Roman Emperors or the kings of Spain. And in the corners of Europe there prospered communities and rulers still further removed from the world of consolidating national states: the free peasants of Dithmarschen, the Cossack bands of the Polish and Muscovite frontiers on the steppe, the

Gaelic lords of Ireland beyond the English Pale, and the Uzkok pirates of the Dalmatian coast.

Even in the stronger monarchies, the power of the state could look fragile when rural or urban communities combined in protest. The *Comuneros* of Castile in 1520–1, the Pilgrims of Grace in northern England in 1536–7, the burghers of Ghent in 1538–40, the peasants of Småland in southern Sweden in 1542–3, the inhabitants of Guyenne in south-west France in 1548, and many others rebelled against heavy taxation, enforced religious change, or other unpopular impositions from above. Yet each revolt was at length pacified. The upper orders tended to rally round the monarch when the social order seemed threatened. Local particularism enabled rulers to draw on the military and financial resources of other provinces or kingdoms to confront the rebels in force. Most importantly, such rebels nearly always conceived of themselves as loyal petitioners rather than enemies of their prince: they would rather submit once their grievances were acknowledged than wage all-out civil war.

Only once in the century did the entire social and political order seem to totter under pressure from below, in the German Peasants' War of 1524–6. As the teaching of Luther and more radical reformers swept across Germany, villages, towns, and whole regions began to agitate for local control of a reformed church and wider communal self-government. The participants' aims were vague and disparate. Some were responding to the social disruption of population expansion, economic change and seigneurial exploitation of serfdom. Others resented the varying pressures of government by dukes and counts, archbishops and abbots, imperial cities and imperial knights. Social and political grievances might each become entangled with Luther's slogans about the freedom of the true Christian. Whatever their motives, the rebels were sufficiently numerous and well organized to cause lordly authority to cave in across large areas of Germany. In time the movement was systematically suppressed by the few princes able to raise reliable armed forces, but its lessons were not lost on German rulers. Political protest was criminalized by the immediate tightening of treason law. Religious reform was harnessed to the purposes of the state: as the margraves of Brandenburg told their preachers in August 1525, Christian freedom really consisted in 'keeping God's commandments . . . and being obedient to authority'. The Anabaptist movement was the legatee in religion and politics of the more radical end of the reforming coalition of 1524-6. In most of Europe it was assiduously persecuted for the remainder of the century, above all when some of its Dutch adherents took over the city of Münster and proclaimed the kingdom of

God—complete with polygamy and community of goods—in 1534–5, only to face siege and destruction. After this disastrous experiment in building the new Jerusalem most Anabaptists retreated from government and the state altogether; they found precarious refuges in the Netherlands and in Moravia.

When German princes were not worrying about the aspirations of their peasants, they could be forgiven for worrying about the Ottoman Turks. The Turkish peril had been evident since before the fall of Byzantium in 1453, and by the 1470s the Sultan's borderers were raiding into Styria, Carinthia, and the Friuli, lighting fires that could be seen from the tops of the towers of Venice. Sultan Selim the Grim (1512–20) focused the energies of an empire tuned for expansion away from Europe, to conquer Syria, Arabia, and Egypt. But his son Suleiman the Magnificent (1520–66) returned to the traditional holy war against Christendom, and in his first dozen years took Belgrade and Rhodes, smashed Hungary and killed its king in battle, and besieged Vienna twice. The end of the Jagiellon line of kings in Hungary added Bohemia and a slice of Hungary to the Habsburgs' hereditary lands in Austria. But it left this complex as the bulwark of Europe, one heavily and expensively fortified as the century went on. The Ottomans were at times distracted by their Shi'ite enemy to the East, the Iranian Safavid dynasty; they were led by uninspiring rulers from Selim the Sot (1566–74) to Mustafa I (1617–18, deposed for incompetence); they were weakened by social upheaval in Asia Minor. Yet the Ottomans remained strong. In a dogged war from 1593 to 1606 they fought the Habsburgs to a draw despite the Austrians' success in seducing the Ottoman client rulers of Transylvania, Moldavia, and Wallachia into a grand Christian alliance.

Ottoman advances in the Mediterranean followed a roughly similar pattern to those in central Europe: they prospered mightily under Suleiman but stalled later on. Here official campaigns—Suleiman's capture of Rhodes in 1522 and failed siege of Malta in 1565, the conquest of Cyprus in 1571 and regular sweeps by the Ottoman fleet—were combined with raiding on the Christian coasts by the corsairs of Algiers and the extension of the Sultan's patronage over the independent kingdoms of North Africa. Venice and Spain were the Ottomans' rivals, and when they allied they were capable of victory, most spectacularly so at Lepanto in 1571. But more often each fought the exhausting struggle alone, achieving at best a stalemate parallel to that in Hungary. Thus what had been Europe's most fluid border of all, the frontier between Christendom and Islam, roughly stabilized for a century or more.

The Habsburgs and their Rivals

Spanish and Austrian resources could never be fully focused on the struggle against the Turks. This might seem all the more curious in that Spain and Austria were ruled by members of the same dynasty, the Habsburgs. Between 1506 and 1526 Charles of Habsburg and his brother Ferdinand assembled an empire larger than any in Europe since Charlemagne's. Well-planned marriages and well-managed elections brought Charles the Burgundian Netherlands (1506), then the Spanish kingdoms (1516), then the Austrian lands and the imperial crown as Charles V (1519). Ferdinand, to whom his brother delegated control of Austria in 1520–1, gained Bohemia and the rump of Hungary in 1526. Charles's son Philip married Mary Tudor, to rule as king of England from 1554 to 1558, and Ferdinand's son Charles came as near as anyone to marrying Queen Elizabeth. Meanwhile the Spanish conquistadores spread their monarch's sway steadily across the New World, and sent back growing quantities of gold and silver to fund Spanish enterprises in Europe. In 1580 Spanish troops marched into Portugal, claiming the crown for Philip by descent through his mother. With it came the Portuguese trading empire from Brazil and West Africa to Goa and the Moluccas. Charles and Philip saw these remarkable accumulations of territory and resources as the God-given means to fulfil the crusading ambitions of their Burgundian ancestors, whether against the Turks or against Protestant heresy. The other rulers of Europe saw things differently: for them the astonishing power of Charles and his family raised the spectre of Habsburg universal monarchy. In the reign of Charles's lacklustre great-grandfather, the Emperor Frederick III, the Habsburgs' Latin acrostic device AEIOU (the rule of the whole world is Austria's) must have seemed an absurdity. Under Charles it seemed to his friends the token of an impending golden age, one redolent of the *Pax Romana* to which the Renaissance of classical learning and classicizing art was turning attention. To his rivals it seemed an apocalyptic threat and a cause for desperate resistance.

The Habsburgs' most powerful and consistent enemy was France, the strongest single European state under a succession of forcefully ambitious kings: Charles VIII (1483–98), Louis XII (1498–1515), François I (1515–47), and Henri II (1547–59). The 'most Christian' kings of France laid claim to the moral leadership of Christendom as the true heirs of Charlemagne the Frank. They asserted their rights as overlords to parts of the Burgundian inheritance within the ancient borders of France, some of which (Burgundy and Picardy) had been taken in 1477, others of which

(Artois and Flanders) had not. They aspired at times to extend their possessions eastwards into territory under imperial overlordship, in Lorraine and the Franche-Comté. They wielded inherited rights of succession to Milan and Naples; Milan was a fief of the Holy Roman Empire, Naples long claimed by the kings of Aragon. Moreover, they had the standing army of noble cavalry, the companies of Swiss and German mercenary infantry, the state-of-the-art artillery train and the heavy regular taxation to assert these claims with vigour.

To his admirers, Charles V surpassed both the emperors of Rome and his own crusading ancestors. On this ceremonial shield, which may have been presented to him at Milan in 1541, he rides an ancient warship to conquer his enemies and liberate their captives, amidst the plaudits of Victory and Fame. Beside him Hercules carries his pillars, the limits of the ancient world, beyond which Charles's empire stretched across the Atlantic.

Thus there were plenty of grounds for conflict between Habsburgs and Valois. Charles V's councillor Granvelle told an English ambassador 'that he hadde his sleve full of querelles against the Frenche whenne ever th'empereur list [liked] to breake with them'. War broke out between François I and Charles V in 1521 and outlasted both their reigns. Each time a treaty was made only to be broken, the recriminations became sharper, most obviously when François was captured in battle at Pavia in 1525, signed away many of the disputed lands at Madrid in 1526 and repudiated these concessions as soon as he got home to France. Between him and Charles, the war became increasingly a test of personal honour, to the extent that they spent the later

Hans Schäufelein's woodcut of the battle of Pavia in 1525 shows the combination of forces needed on the sixteenth-century battlefield. Cannon and arquebuses or muskets were becoming ever more important, but heavily armed noble cavalry and well-drilled squares of mercenary pikemen were still vital as shock troops.

1520s exchanging ever more insulting challenges to personal combat. But what drove the conflict on through four wars across four decades and threatened to restart it early in the next century was the compelling fear of Habsburg hegemony.

That fear gave the French allies. In Christendom and in Italy the Habsburgs were too powerful for the liking of most popes, and the sack of Rome by Charles's mutinous troops in 1527 did not improve relations. In Italy the Habsburgs threatened to be too powerful for the liking of the Venetians and other, smaller, states, with the ironic effect that the French, who had begun the rape of Italy by foreign powers with Charles VIII's march on Naples in 1494, became the hope of those who yearned to free Italy from Spanish domination. By military might and the painstaking construction of a network of client rulers, Charles tightened his control of Italy from the 1530s. Yet in the face of defeat the system could always crumble, as it was to do briefly in the 1550s.

In Germany Charles's task was more delicate still. The Emperor's power over a large, variegated, and highly decentralized polity rested more than that of neighbouring rulers on negotiation, leadership, and mystique. Charles's predecessor Maximilian had tried to establish a firmer fiscal, military, and institutional basis for his power across Germany but had largely failed. Like previous emperors he had to govern by combining his *Hausmacht*—the money and men provided by his inherited Austrian estates—with the influence he derived from alliances with individual princes and cities within Germany, and with whatever wider loyalty he could stir up as the self-appointed knightly hero of a nascent German national sentiment. Charles and Ferdinand, then, did not inherit a strong machinery of government in Germany. Yet, wielding the resources of Spain, the Netherlands, and Bohemia, they looked likely to invest the emperor's power with more steel than the princes and cities would stomach.

The problem was rendered critical by the spread of Lutheranism against Charles's will, first in the cities, then amongst the princes, half-a-dozen of them by 1526 and nearly two dozen by 1546. By 1531 there was a political alliance of Protestant princes and cities, the League of Schmalkalden. Its members were ready to use their agreement to German financial and military support to save Vienna from Ottoman siege, in order to bargain for toleration. They were ready to assert themselves more directly against imperial authority if needs be. They were more than happy to accept pensions from France. Meanwhile in England Henry VIII's divorce from Charles's aunt Catherine of Aragon threw him for a time into the French camp *faute de mieux*. And if one were desperate enough, there were always the Turks. François I expanded his commercial and political cooperation with the Sultan through the 1530s, until in 1544, to the scandal of neutral Europeans, the Ottoman fleet set up base at Toulon.

This hydra-headed resistance to his leadership of Europe, or indeed to the solution of any one of his problems in international politics, since they all became so intertwined, drove Charles V eventually into despair. His final tragedy began in 1544–5, as he made peace with François and truce with Suleiman to concentrate on Germany. Spanish money and troops and, for once, papal support, enabled him to crush the League of Schmalkalden in 1546–7 and dictate a religious settlement accommodating the more pliant among the Lutherans. But fears of 'Spanish tyranny' soon combined with Protestant dissatisfaction and French prompting to stimulate a new princely revolt in 1551–2. This was coordinated with a French thrust into Lorraine and war on the borders of the Netherlands, with a French-backed revolt in Siena, and French-induced corsair raids on Naples. It even co-incided with renewed war in Hungary. In Germany, Charles left Ferdinand to negotiate the Religious Peace of Augsburg (1555), guaranteeing the princes, and to a lesser extent the free cities, qualified self-determination in religion. In Italy, Lorraine, and the Netherlands he tried and failed to recover Metz and then left matters to his subordinates and his son. They fought on until 1559, finally agreeing a relatively advantageous peace with an exhausted France at Cateau-Cambrésis. By then, worn out by his trials and nagged by his bickering relations, Charles had abdicated all his thrones and retired to die in a Spanish monastery.

Charles's retirement brought partition to his empire. His brother Ferdinand succeeded to the imperial title and the Austrian lands were settled in his line, to form with Hungary and Bohemia the basis of the Habsburg monarchy on the Danube. Philip received the Spanish kingdoms with their New World dependencies and their Italian satellites. He also received the Netherlands, in a misalliance pregnant with strategic, political, and religious difficulties. It was there, in the decade following Charles's abdication, that the next great challenge to the Habsburgs would begin, in a revolt which was to offer endless opportunities to the rivals of the house of Austria and spread the complication of international religious enmity far beyond Germany.

War and the State

The reign of Charles V suggests both the central importance and the curious indecisiveness of sixteenth-century warfare. Armies grew steadily in size as the number of campaigns multiplied. The French invaded Italy in 1494 with 28,000 men, but Charles may have had 150,000 men in his pay in 1552, even though the largest force one could usefully deploy for a single campaign was a third of that size at most. Fleets expanded too. The northern maritime powers competed to deploy the new gunned sailing ships in ever larger numbers: the tonnage of the Danish fleet nearly doubled between 1560 and 1565, while that of the Swedish navy increased by a factor of two-and-a-half. By the 1570s Elizabeth was maintaining the English fleet in peacetime at the maximum size it had reached in wartime under her father. In the Mediterranean the three great powers multiplied galleys between the 1530s, when Spain ran perhaps 40, Venice about 100, and the Ottomans 140 or more, and the 1570s when they maintained 146, 159, and nearly 300 respectively.

The increasing use of firearms, the rising price of food and the new

The Fortezza da Basso at Florence was built by the Medici from 1534 to overawe the citizens of the once fiercely republican city over which they ruled as princes from 1530. Its sloping walls and angled bastions were typical of the new *trace italienne* fortifications, which resisted artillery bombardment and harnessed defensive firepower much better than medieval castle or town walls.

sophistication of defensive fortifications, as the *trace italienne* spread north-wards from the 1530s, all made the cost of war rise even faster than its scale. Mercenaries were indispensable for serious warfare because of their mastery of the new weapons and of the drill necessary to coordinate pikes and arquebuses against hostile cavalry. Yet they cost dear, and had little compunction about striking for pay or simply leaving the army if financial difficulties arose. Many commanders might have echoed the weary verdict of the French general Montmorency on his Swiss soldiers of fortune: 'These people ask for so much money and are so unreasonable that it is almost impossible to satisfy them.' In encampments with populations the size of that of early sixteenth-century London, disease was a perennial problem, and whole armies could dissolve under the impact of an epidemic, as the French besieging Naples did in 1528. When combined with desertion, sickness meant that, as the English captain Sir John Norris put it in 1591, 'three months being in the field is enough to ruin the greatest army'.

Lastly, if one did win some great victory, it was rarely decisive unless the opposing ruler was killed or captured. Most larger countries disposed of reserve defence forces for emergencies—more than a million men in the English militia in 1588, of whom 111,000 were trained—and would take desperate measures if foreign conquest seemed imminent. They resorted to scorched-earth tactics like those used in Provence against Charles's invasion in 1536, the razing of suburbs to make walled towns defensible, or the opening of the dykes to flood the land around Leiden in the Spanish siege of 1574. Naval victories might look more final, as the enemy fleet sank or was boarded and captured wholesale. But the vagaries of wind and current made them equally hard to follow up, and rapid rebuilding or the commandeering of merchant ships could resurrect a navy, as the Turks did after Lepanto or the Spaniards after the defeat of the Armada in 1588.

What war did achieve was a drastic increase in taxation. Larger states with old-established systems of direct and indirect taxation struggled to make their taxes tap developing commercial and agricultural wealth. This was no easy task, since by and large it was the social élites whose political influence was needed to secure the collection of taxation who held most of the wealth and were understandably reluctant to pay it over in taxes. Even in the wide areas where nobles enjoyed total or partial exemptions from taxation, they did not want to see their peasants taxed so hard that they could not pay the rent. In France, England, Spain, and the Netherlands, the century to 1560 saw dramatic increases in the sums raised in cash terms and real terms alike. Regular direct taxes in France yielded 1.5 million *livres tournois* at most in the 1450s, 8 or 9 million by 1549. When measured in wheat (to dis-

Taxpayers stand with bared heads and empty purses before a smugly fur-collared official and his earnest clerk in Marinus van Reymerswaele's *The Tax Collectors* (1542). Archives all over Europe are full of the paperwork generated by the growing bureaucracy and fiscalism of sixteenth-century states.

count for inflation), taxes in rural Walloon Flanders tripled from 1450 to 1553. Yet these increases were insufficient to fund warfare on the scale of that in the 1550s, and kings had to borrow at terrifying interest rates: these reached 54 per cent per annum on some of the loans Philip II took out in 1557. State debts grew until bankruptcy forced both France and Spain into the peace of 1559. England avoided bankruptcy, but only because Henry VIII and his son Edward VI found two-thirds of their war funds in the 1540s from the sale of confiscated church lands and the debasement of the coinage, and because the crown had no permanent tax income against which to borrow on a continuous basis.

In western Europe, the mid-century seems to represent a significant plateau in the level of taxation that could be extracted with the available political and administrative means. From there, some states limped along with the same basic system, producing real yields to the mid-seventeenth century no higher than those of the mid-sixteenth, as in England and France. One, the rebel Dutch republic with its booming trading economy, built on strong local traditions to use indirect taxes and a funded state debt in the sort of 'financial revolution' others would imitate in the later seventeenth century. But elsewhere tying tax revenues to the payment of debt manacled rather than liberated state expenditure. In Naples, heavily pressed from the 1530s to pay for Habsburg wars in Germany and the Netherlands as well as Italy and the Mediterranean, the proportion of revenue spent directly on warfare fell from 45 per cent in 1550 to 23 per cent in 1626, while the proportion spent servicing the debt rose from 31 per cent to 56 per cent.

Everywhere smaller or less developed states were dragged through this fiscal expansion by the threat from their larger neighbours. Demesne states, in which most revenue came from the ruler's landholdings and other rights, were converted into tax states, partly because sales of demesne land were a quick way to raise cash in a crisis. Those untroubled by major war kept their medieval financial system longest. Denmark, where in 1600 half of net crown income came from crown lands and one-third from the tolls on Baltic trade passing through the Sound, is a good example. But if rivals remodelled their finances first, the results could be severe. Sweden modernized before Denmark, to enjoy double the revenues by the 1620s: Danish victory in the war of 1611–13 was succeeded by four successive defeats later in the century, and consequent losses of territory and resources. For the smallest states, such reform might in any case be to no avail. The last native duke of Gelderland so upset his subjects by the levies necessary to save himself from the Habsburgs that they were not sorry to lose him in 1538. The republic of Siena bankrupted itself in the attempt to fortify the city against the Spaniards and the Medici princes in 1552–5 and was absorbed into the Medici's duchy of Florence.

The larger states avoided such fates, though resistance to tax increases and the billeting of soldiers often enough troubled them with popular unrest, as in France in the 1540s and 1590s. But where they intensified taxation too successfully, they could depopulate the countryside and cripple the rural economy, as peasants, incapable of making enough money to pay their taxes, simply gave up and left. In Castile they left for the towns, Seville with its rich Atlantic trade and Madrid with its court and bureaucracy to govern half the world. In Muscovy they fled to the southern borderlands—

often to join the Cossacks—as cash taxes rose thirty times over between the 1500s and the 1590s, largely to pay for the wars of expansion against the Tartars and in Livonia of Tsar Ivan the Terrible (1533–84). Tax registers of the 1580s suggest that between 40 and 90 per cent of agricultural land around Moscow and Novgorod had been left uncultivated as a result. The drastic effects of Ivan's exactions paved the way for the social and political chaos of Muscovy's 'Time of Troubles' early in the next century. Meanwhile funded state debts could bring economic dangers of a different kind: they drew investment capital out of agriculture, manufacturing and trade, as they seem to have done in Naples and Castile.

Despite such disastrous effects, fiscal expansion was in general a sign of growing state power. More officials were appointed to administer taxation. Subjects had to be reminded of their obligations to the ruler and of the benefits of his or her rule to encourage them to pay. Representative assemblies had to be wooed, manipulated, or bypassed to secure consent to tax increases. Service in expanding fiscal and judicial bureaucracies drew urban élites into closer affinity with and dependence upon princely government, and thereby undermined the autonomy of towns.

Warfare also spread the tentacles of government through society by drawing the nobility into state service. Where standing armies were set up, their core consisted of heavy cavalry recruited from amongst the lesser nobility into companies commanded by the greater nobility. Here noblemen could pursue the military traditions of their ancestors and seek in the wages of war the means to compete with the prospering mercantile and office-holding élites of the towns in income, conspicuous consumption, and the purchase of land. Here too the greater nobles could consolidate their political followings amongst the lesser nobles of their regions of landed influence. France and the southern Netherlands presented the purest examples of this trend, but variations on it were evident far and wide. In Germany, princes were drawn more closely into the political orbit of the emperors by their commissions to raise mercenary forces or command expeditions at the Habsburgs' expense. In Italy, mercenary commanders were converted into loyal noblemen by the granting of fiefs held from the governments they served, as in the Venetian mainland empire. In Muscovy, noblemen who found their lands confiscated in the frequent political purges of Ivan the Terrible's reign were resettled in border regions to hold estates by tenure conditional on permanent military service. Yet such holdings gradually evolved back into hereditary noble estates more like those of the West, just as the *timar* estates granted out to support the heavy cavalry of the expanding Ottoman Empire began to do from the later sixteenth century. Such relations between government and élites were a matter of complex social negotiation, not of princely diktat.

Courts and Government

Princely courts, like armies, grew apace in the sixteenth century. The personnel of the French royal household, for instance, more than doubled in number between 1480 and 1523. The provision of posts for the nobility at court, as in standing armies, helped secure their loyalty. More generally, large and splendid courts aimed to overawe subjects and foreign rivals alike with a ruler's magnificence and power. Even Philip II of Spain, whose personal taste was for sombre withdrawal, had to force himself into splendid court rituals in the last years of his reign to bolster his political control, for courts were centres for the justification of power as well as for its advertisement and practical exercise. Philip was certainly not short of ammunition in this area, as legatee of centuries of intricate myth-making by his Habsburg ancestors and their predecessors on the imperial throne. Maximilian and Charles V proclaimed themselves blood relations of Priam of Troy and the emperors of Rome and Byzantium, of the Old Testament patriarchs and indeed of Christ. Charles and Philip combined with this mythology strong doses of the crusading tradition of the Burgundian dukes, and the apocalyptic expectations aroused by their rule of a New World beyond the pillars of Hercules, the bounds of the ancient world. Philip adopted in 1555 a personal device identifying himself with the sun-god Apollo, ruler of a reborn world, and in the last year of his reign the Italian utopian writer Tommaso Campanella explicitly hailed him as the Last World Emperor long prophesied to usher in the millenial golden age. Such themes were expressed in very concrete ways. The galley *Argo*, the Spanish flagship at Lepanto, was decorated with images and inscriptions linking Troy, Jason and the Argonauts, Constantinople, crusading, and Columbus. Philip's combined palace and monastery, the Escorial, enshrined the Habsburgs' family devotions to the cross and the Eucharist, and Philip's attachment to St Lawrence on whose feast he had beaten the French at Saint-Quentin in 1557, while hinting at the temple of Solomon, the temple-palace of Augustus, and the new temple of the heavenly Jerusalem.

Similar though more modest confections of princely imagery could be found at most courts. Elizabeth I was the empress Gloriana, Astraea the nymph of the golden age, a vestal virgin and so on; François I was a new Constantine, Charlemagne, and Julius Caesar. Rulers without the military and political might and genuinely distinguished ancestry of a Habsburg or a Valois had a still greater need to create the illusion of unchallengeable power. The Medici, dukes of Florence, then from 1569 grand dukes of Tuscany, had a good deal to erase from the memories of their subjects. The banking family who had been Florence's most influential citizens for sixty years until their expulsion in 1494 managed to have themselves restored to power in the city by Charles V when he crushed the republican regime in 1530, thanks to the influence of Clement VII, the Medici pope. They proceeded to secure their power by many means: judicious Spanish, Austrian, and French marriages, the construction of a bastioned fortress to cow the city and an imposing block of government offices from which to administer the state, the creation of an international entrepôt at Livorno, and lavish patronage of the arts. Fresco cycles, equestrian statues, triumphal arches, public spectacles, and proto-operas with amazing stage machinery all rewrote Florentine history to show its progression towards the perfection of Medicean princely rule. Spectators were awed into submission.

Yet how far such effects really spread beyond the fevered contrivers of princely propaganda is very hard to know. The favoured reading of the intellectual élites best placed to observe these spectacles, from Erasmus' *Praise of Folly* and More's *Utopia* at the start of the century to the cool Tacitean histories of authors such as Jacques-Auguste de Thou at its end, must have encouraged a healthy scepticism about princes, their fawning entourages, and the public images they conspired to project. By the later sixteenth century several European languages had developed a genre of anti-court literature, often admittedly penned by courtiers themselves. 'Say to the court it glows | And shines like rotten wood', wrote Sir Walter Ralegh. Meanwhile amongst a largely illiterate population away from the courts and the capital cities, the impact of princely propaganda can have been muffled at best.

The political centralization which accompanied the growth of courts was also a rather ambivalent means to the advance of princely power. The more influence rulers could exercise over local affairs, the more their subjects came to court to sway the deployment of that influence in their own interests: to ask for posts in the administration, the army or the Church, to ask for princely intervention in a lawsuit or local quarrel, to deflect a tax demand, to seek fame and fortune as the prince's trusted servant. As a result competition for patronage and influence intensified around the ruler; networks of clientage centred on the great men of the court became more elaborate, whether these were leading noblemen, senior ministers, or the prince's intimate attendants who could judge the best moment to ask him for some favour.

Niccolò Bellin's miniature of François I depicts him with the attributes of a pantheon of classical deities, from the helmet of wise Minerva to the winged boots of eloquent Mercury, from the sword of valiant Mars to the horn of huntress Diana and the graceful skirts of Venus the perfect lover. Did such erudite but faintly ridiculous confections really make convincing propaganda?

Such networks assisted the ruler, in that they provided informal means to manage local affairs more effective than the primitive chains of bureaucratic command. Yet when they competed to influence him, they threatened to destabilize the whole exercise of government or deprive him of effective control. Some rulers succumbed to the pressures and became the playthings of faction. Ladislas II of Bohemia (1471–1516) and Hungary (1490–1516) was colloquially known as *kral dobrʒe* (King Okay) because he would agree to anything. Some rulers managed to maintain a rough-and-ready balance between competing groups. Some put their confidence in a single chief minister and hoped he would remain both loyal and competent; if needs be, he could always be disposed of, as Henry VIII cast off Cardinal Wolsey and Thomas Cromwell.

Some attempted to preserve themselves against the dangers of all these styles of rule by conducting all important business by themselves in as much secrecy as possible and systematically distrusting their senior subordinates. Philip II of Spain typified the last approach. 'I do not want these matters to be dealt with so exclusively by one person', he directed in one early letter. From his desk, he later claimed, he could 'govern half the world with two inches of paper'. Yet his secretaries—eight were needed to keep the papers flowing past him—were less sanguine about the effects of Philip's style. 'His Majesty loses track of many things' wrote one of them in 1566 '. . . and thus it is not surprising that different orders go out, even contradictory orders'. In the 1580s and 1590s Philip had to compromise his natural inclinations and institute a privy council of ministers in all but name, the initially furtive *junta de la noche* and its successor the *junta grande*. Such conciliar bodies, made up of half-a-dozen or a dozen expert ministers and a few leading nobles and endowed collectively with executive as well as advisory functions, seem to have been the best available solution to the problem of exercising royal control over increasingly complex governmental machines. Henri IV of France (1589–1610) and Elizabeth I in England (1558–1603) used them to particularly good effect. But they were potentially as susceptible to factional rivalry as any other body, and they demanded careful management if they were to work at their best.

Philip's paperwork was an extreme illustration of the growing bureaucracy evident in sixteenth-century government. By mid-century most of the major rulers maintained resident ambassadors at each other's courts. Their regular reports were read and then filed away in growing state paper archives, where they joined reports from local officials, memoranda of advice from councillors, and financial statements and budgets from the fiscal experts. Even in countries such as England where the central law courts, financial institutions, and chancery issuing royal grants had been generating bulky records for centuries, the sixteenth century saw a proliferation of records in many areas of government. Such records were also physically different from their predecessors, as paper tended to replace parchment and arabic numerals replaced roman. Print also came into play as a means of communication between ruler and ruled. New laws and regulations, declarations of war and denunciations of heresy, all were printed and circulated for public proclamation and display. More extended works recounting royal marriages or victories in battle met the public demand for news while inculcating admiration for the ruler's feats. Homilies on obedience and prayers for the powers ordained by God rolled off the presses, as religion was turned to the consolidation of political loyalties.

Society, Justice, and Sovereignty

One practical use for the widening powers of the state was in the management of the economy. From the early part of the century, the pressures of dearth, disease, and poverty, intensified by population growth, invited remedial action by urban or national governments. Humanist or religious idealism combined with the fear of disorder to stimulate the introduction of quarantines, control of food supplies, restraints on vagrancy, and poor-relief schemes. Rulers of trading centres also tried not to kill the goose that laid the golden eggs: 'These lands are rooted above all in commerce,' wrote Charles V of the Netherlands in 1534, 'we must not lose sight of this.' But by the years around 1600 some regimes looked to stimulate economic strength more generally, by securing supplies of armaments and food without the danger of enemy interruption, replacing imports which drained the nation's wealth with the products of domestic industries to employ the poor, or inviting international traders to wealth-generating entrepôts on the model of Venice, Antwerp, or Seville. Monopoly rights to market new products were granted to inventors and entrepreneurs, communications by road and canal were improved to facilitate trade, and refugees from religious persecution—French and Flemish Protestants in Germany and England, Portuguese Jews in Amsterdam—were welcomed, or at least not persecuted, in order to benefit from their skills and connections. In France Henri IV even established a council of commerce, which considered over 200 projects for industrial enterprises between 1602 and 1604. Overall, the positive impact of government on the economy was not large, and some schemes misfired disastrously; but such ventures manifested the growing ambition and interventionism of the state to ever more of its subjects.

Older ideals were also drawn into the process of state growth. One of the most fundamental tenets of medieval kingship was the ruler's duty to provide justice. It justified his power in theoretical terms, elevating him above all his subjects and making him the agent of God's justice on earth. It also extended his power in practical terms, tightening his control over local society as litigants turned to his courts and obeyed their judgements. Many causes combined to increase the recourse to central justice, as opposed to lordly tribunals or local community courts, in the sixteenth century. On the demand side worked economic growth, advancing commercial integration, the spread of literacy, social mobility, and the political domestication of noble élites, which discouraged them from solving their quarrels by simple violence. On the supply side worked the rising numbers of graduate lawyers in the service of the state, keen to supplant local customary justice with the standardized procedures and written, rational, usually Roman, law taught in the universities and applied in the ruler's courts. Judicial institutions multiplied: every significant German territorial prince set up a *Hofgericht*, or superior appeal court, in the late fifteenth or early sixteenth century. Judicial work-rates rose: the average councillor in the Council of Flanders sat for 92.5 days in 1518, 127.5 days in 1528, and 171 days in 1555. Comprehensive new or reformed law-codes were issued: for the empire in 1532, for Milan in 1541, for Württemberg in 1555, for Savoy in 1561–5, for Castile in 1569, for Saxony in 1572, and so on. The number of lawsuits exploded: they nearly tripled in the *Chancillería* of Valladolid between 1500 and 1580, and rose at double that rate in the English courts of King's Bench and Common Pleas over the same period.

State justice was far from perfect. Effective courts clogged up as they became popular, such that only 12 per cent of completed cases at Valladolid took a year or less in 1620, whereas 21 per cent had finished in that time in 1540. Corruption, political favouritism, and the danger that those with enough money to hire the cleverest lawyers would always win, were ever-present dangers. The temptation for rulers to make money by selling judicial offices, as the French kings did wholesale, posed the risk that judges would escape royal control and even at times oppose royal policy. Moreover, though customary laws were often codified—as in a major campaign in France in 1506–15—rather than merely swept aside, opposition to the reception of Roman law could mobilize considerable public opinion, as it did in many parts of Germany. Nobles saw it as an assault on their privileges, peasants as an attack on their communal freedoms, and nobles, burghers, and peasants alike endlessly complained about it at meetings of territorial estates. Yet the reception, and the judicial and governmental centralization of which it was a part, ran onwards inexorably. In the end even those who resisted it seem to have done so with an air of fatalism, like the spokesman of the Bavarian estates who apologized to Duke Wilhelm IV for opposing him, by explaining that 'even a little worm curls up and defends itself, when it is about to be stepped on by a large animal.'

The expanding effectiveness of government was matched by the later sixteenth century by the development of a stronger ideological base for state power. Political thinkers in the middle decades of the century, German, English, Scottish, French, and Dutch, had elaborated theories justifying resistance to tyrannical monarchs, but by 1600 the tide was flowing in

the opposite direction. In France Jean Bodin reacted to the Wars of Religion by formulating a comprehensive theory of royal sovereignty in his *Six Books of the Republic* (1576). From the Netherlands Justus Lipsius, the correspondent of 700 leading intellectuals across the continent, outsold Bodin with his *Six Books of Politics* (1589), which went through fifteen Latin editions by 1599 and had been translated into seven other languages by 1604. Lipsius deployed the teaching of the ancients, above all Tacitus and Seneca, to advocate a strong government run by active, self-disciplined statesmen, constant amidst the troubles of the world. He was all the more influential because he did so without straying into the amorality of Machiavelli or the uncomfortably unfettered absolutism of Bodin. Everywhere the Italian term 'reason of state' took hold as the justification for action to strengthen the powers that maintained stability. As Maximilian of Bavaria wrote to his father Duke Wilhelm V in 1596, 'Among the spiritual as among the secular, what counts nowadays is *ragion di stato*.'

State growth, however, was not as linear a process as it may have appeared, whether to its proponents or its enemies. Social and economic disruption could undermine the most superficially impressive judicial and administrative systems. By the late sixteenth century the vendettas and banditry, which troubled Spanish Milan, Naples and Sicily, and the Papal States, were also running out of control in the traditionally better-governed Venetian territories. When added to such underlying economic difficulties, the strains of war could drive whole patterns of state development into reverse. Spain's burden as the leading defender of European Catholicism seems to have done just that in the last years of Philip II's reign and that of his son Philip III (1598–1621). The scope of royal justice and the base of governmental resources declined, as whole towns and villages, with the jurisdiction over them, were sold or granted away to nobles. Military administration became decentralized, as it became easier to contract for troops or ships from entrepreneurs—with consequent loss of quality control—than to administer the war effort directly. Successive royal bankruptcies were surmounted only by pledging more and more of the crown's future revenues to the payment of interest-bearing bonds.

Even the strong links between the crown and the Catholic faithful wavered as popular prophets began from the 1580s to denounce the weight

Peter Paul Rubens's painting of an imaginary discussion between himself, his brother, a friend, and Justus Lipsius testifies to Lipsius' influence both as an educator (he taught Philip Rubens at the University of Louvain) and as an interpreter of the Stoic ideas of Seneca, whose bust presides over their conversation.

of taxation, the failures of justice, and the inadequacy of some of the churchmen promoted by the king. One prophetess, who correctly predicted the defeat of the Armada in 1588 and went on to foresee Philip II's replacement by an apocalyptic king who would take her as his queen, numbered among her sympathizers three dukes, one councillor of state, a noble canon of Toledo, and the prior of the Madrid Franciscans. Cooler heads than hers also worried about the state of Spain. By the early seventeenth century a range of political writers or *arbitristas* were analysing Spain's apparent *declinación* from military dominance, economic health, and moral vigour and prescribing a range of often mutually contradictory remedies. Their ideas struck a chord amongst the men who came to power at the end of Philip III's reign; they helped to propel Spain simultaneously into convulsive internal reforms and the violent external struggles of renewed war with the Dutch and Catholic partisanship in the Thirty Years War. The results, at length, were dire.

The Impact of Religious Change

The most influential variable in the development of sixteenth-century states was the impact of religious change. The kings and emperors of medieval Christendom had always invoked divine blessing on their rule, and by the fourteenth and fifteenth centuries the parish clergy were used to disseminate news of military victories and lead prayers for further success. Through concordats with the papacy or pressure on their subjects, most later medieval rulers steadily engrossed greater control over the distribution of senior ecclesiastical posts in the lands under their control; they tied these into systems of reward for their clerical councillors or for the younger brothers of loyal noblemen. By the turn of the sixteenth century, princely patronage of reforming movements in the Church such as those of the Franciscan Observants was becoming a badge of pious magnificence for rulers such as Louis XII of France, Henry VII of England, Ferdinand and Isabella in Spain, and the Sforza dukes of Milan. Throughout the century, engagement in the crusade against the infidel retained its medieval attractions as a kingly duty, at least for the Iberian rulers. Charles V mounted major campaigns against Tunis and Algiers and dreamed of a descent on Constantinople; young King Sebastian of Portugal vanished in battle against the Moroccans in 1578, leaving his people to yearn in the cult of *Sebastianismo* for his messianic return in years to come. But the greatest key to the tighter intermeshing of politics and religion was the development of the Reformation and Counter-Reformation.

Elector John Frederick of Saxony's political leadership of German Protestantism brought him to grief in 1547, when he was captured at the battle of Mühlberg. Yet he refused to disown the Reformation. Here, comforted by a verse from the Psalms, he is shown impervious to the assaults of the beasts about his feet with their bishop's mitre, cardinal's hat, and papal tiara.

The official adoption of reformed religion contributed to the power of different rulers in different ways. One, Albrecht of Hohenzollern, made a hereditary secular principality for himself from scratch, by secularizing the Prussian branch of the Teutonic Order, of which he was the Grand Master. Many others, notably Henry VIII in England, Gustav Vasa in Sweden, Christian III in Denmark, and a dozen leading German princes, confiscated church property within their territories or absorbed into their states adjoining bishoprics or monastic estates. Most stepped up taxation of the clergy, took control of clerical promotions, and integrated the church courts' system of moral controls more closely into their own judicial structures. Most took a firmer grip on education from school level to the universities, and introduced state-run poor relief to replace the charity of dissolved monasteries and hospitals. In these ways, as in the wars to defend the new religion, many spent much of what they gained from confiscating the wealth of the Church in the first place. No other went as far as Henry VIII did in declaring himself supreme head of the English Church—a step the leaders of continental reform found distastefully blasphemous—but many trumpeted their role as godly princes, wielding the sword of justice and the book of God's word to govern their people in unquestionable righteousness.

Secular and ecclesiastical bureaucracies expanded in parallel and became intertwined, as the Reformation helped consolidate a more intensive form of state. They provided the means to regulate, down to parish level, changes which had the potential to reach every subject. New orders of service were introduced at the prince's command, as were new marriage regulations to foster the godly family and the stability of patriarchal control. They operated together with the more spontaneous effects of the blending of Protestantism, national identity and dynastic loyalty to produce the united commitment of the Swedes behind their Protestant warrior king Gustavus Adolphus (1611–32), or the bonfires and bells that enlivened the parishes of England on the anniversaries of Elizabeth's accession (17 November) and the delivery of James I from the popish gunpowder plot (5 November). Similarly, though the Protestant cities of Germany and Switzerland often adopted the Reformation earlier than the princes and under more intense pressure from their citizens, they derived many of the same benefits in the expansion or clarification of the control of secular magistrates over church property, clerical conduct, patterns of worship, poor relief, education, marriage, and morality.

The Protestants had no monopoly on such changes. By the 1540s, the Wittelsbach dukes of Bavaria were the most powerful remaining Catholic princes in Germany, the leading patrons of the German Jesuits as they had been the patrons of Luther's early opponent Johann Eck. Yet just as they were not shy of working in the complex politics of the 1540s and 1550s to limit Charles V's power in Germany to the benefit of all the princes, they were not shy of taking closer control of the Church in their territories and beyond if such action might strengthen their own and the Catholic cause. Tridentine concerns about pluralism notwithstanding, one Wittelsbach cadet was thus installed by 1618 as bishop of Liège, Hildesheim, Münster, and Paderborn, and Archbishop-Elector of Cologne. Other ecclesiastical princes were encouraged to contribute to what was effectively a Bavarian standing army under a series of Catholic leagues, culminating in the army of General Tilly, which was to dominate the early stages of the Thirty Years War. Within Bavaria, the dukes taxed the Church hard and governed it through a spiritual council manned mostly by lay lawyers; by the early seventeenth century they maintained surveillance of their subjects' spiritual, moral, and political behaviour through a network of secret informers paid by the volume and quality of information supplied. Ducal commissioners accompanied the Jesuits as they toured rural areas in the 1590s to reconvert Lutheran peasants and confiscate their heretical books. Already in the 1560s the resistance of Lutheran nobles in the estates had been broken in a combined assertion of Catholic dominance and princely control. Gradually a Jesuit-educated nobility of the court combined with the ubiquitous jurists to form a ruling élite more attuned to the dukes' purposes. Where Bavaria led, others followed, notably the surviving prince-bishoprics and the Habsburg provinces ruled by cadet princes: Styria, Lower Austria, and above all the Tyrol, blueprint for the baroque Catholic Danubian monarchy of the later Austrian Habsburgs.

The Impact of Religious Division

At length, as we shall see, the religious tensions stimulated by the extension of such policies to the wider Habsburg realms plunged most of Europe into war. But already in the second half of the sixteenth century there were states beyond the German Empire not consolidated but torn apart by the effects of the Reformation. France was the first and largest casualty. Long wars against the Habsburgs had left its monarchy financially weak and its nobility alarmingly dependent upon military service and royal reward. It was then struck by a double blow. In July 1559 King Henri II died from a wound incurred in the tournament held to celebrate the peace of Cateau-Cambrésis. In May of the same year the rapidly growing French Protestant Church held its first national synod. By 1563 there were perhaps 1,200 or

1,400 congregations spread across the nation, though with concentrations in Normandy and the south. Noblemen, whether because of their readier access to new ideas, their preparedness to follow great patrons who had declared for the new faith, or perhaps their general sense of alienation amidst economic and social change, were disproportionately common amongst the Huguenots, as the Protestants soon became known.

Henri's heirs were too young to rule effectively, and the fate of France's religion was seen to hang on the outcome of the struggle to control the government conducted in their name. Here noble faction at court and the reliance of government on the chains of clientage linking courtier nobles and provincial governors to local élites formed a combustible mixture with the religious issue. The Guises, powerful in the north-east and dominant in the short reign of François II (1559–62), were bent on the extermination of heresy. The Bourbons, more closely related to the royal house in blood and powerful in the south, identified with the Huguenots. The Montmorencys, influential at the courts of François I and Henri II, were split by generation, the elders Catholic but old rivals to the Guises, some of the younger, led by Admiral Coligny, vigorously Huguenot. Between them all the Queen Mother Catherine de' Medici, regent from 1562 for her second son Charles IX (1562–74), manœuvred with hopes of some sort of toleration.

Resolution of the issues at a national level proved impossible; local religious tensions initiated the first of a series of disjointed but bitter civil wars in 1562–3. These were made nastier than ever by the nationwide massacres of Protestants connived at by the crown in 1572. As war succeeded war, both Protestant and Catholic towns became in effect republics, which banded together to form confessional states-within-states, above all in the Protestant south. Some nobles became little more than robber-barons. Some provincial governors became virtually independent local rulers, who ignored central authority when it suited them and dabbled in alliances with the different religious factions, as Henri de Montmorency-Damville did in Languedoc. Henri III (1574–89), the last of Henri II's sons to rule, found himself at odds with both his Protestant and his Catholic subjects as the latter, led by the Guises, took over Paris and tried to coerce him into pursuing the policies of their Catholic League. At the nadir of the crown's fortunes Henri tried to cut his way out of trouble by having the duke of Guise and his brother the cardinal of Guise assassinated, only to die himself by the knife of a Parisian friar ten months later. His heir was the Bourbon Henri IV, who brought France under control again after nine more years of war against the Catholic League and its Spanish allies. He renounced his own Protestantism to secure the submission of Paris, offered specific rights and guarantees to Protestants by the Edict of Nantes (1598), and did his best to reunite France around his predecessors' policies of strong government and opposition to Habsburg hegemony.

Religious division brought turbulent politics elsewhere in western Europe. The Scottish Reformation was enacted against the royal will and eventually brought the deposition of Mary Queen of Scots and a troubled minority for her son James VI. The failure of the Reformation in Ireland made Irish resistance to Tudor government ever more a matter of religious as well as national antagonism. The Catholic Sigismund I lasted eight years on the throne of Lutheran Sweden, but was then overthrown in favour of his uncle Charles IX. More drastic change still resulted in the Netherlands. There, as in France, the wars of the 1550s left the government financially and politically weak, and Philip II's uncompromising but absentee rule did little to repair the situation. Philip was bent on the persecution of the growing Protestant movement and refused pleas for toleration from the urban élites and the high nobility. He must have regarded with particular distaste an attempt by a group of leading merchants to buy toleration from him in the interests both of conscience and of smooth business with the English and Germans. When the Protestants turned unsuccessfully to armed insurrection in 1566, he resolved to crush resistance with a Spanish army under the duke of Alba.

Alba was strong enough to repel invasions in 1568 and 1572 coordinated from his German estates by William of Orange, the former Habsburg client prince of mixed German, Burgundian, and Brabantine descent who emerged as leader of the opposition to Philip's policies. But the duke's ruthless executions, heavy taxation, and insensitive billeting of Spanish troops prepared the ground for further revolt. In 1572 much of Holland and Zeeland welcomed rebel forces headed by the Sea Beggars, Protestant pirates who had been operating out of English ports. Waterlogged and well fortified, these provinces resisted the Spanish reconquest until Philip went bankrupt in 1576, his army mutinied and sacked Antwerp, and the whole Netherlands combined against Spanish occupation.

Religious and social polarities, however, might work against rebel movements as much as against governments. The populist Protestant regimes which soon sprang up in cities such as Ghent, Bruges, and Arras horrified the Catholic nobility dominant in the southern provinces. Their reaction was understandable when, for example, the Ghenters' idea of solving a disagreement with the duke of Aerschot, governor of Flanders, was to arrest and imprison him. In 1579 the southern provinces combined in the Union of Arras and returned to the Spanish obedience. In the same year, the northern provinces combined in the Union of Utrecht, and in 1581 they formally deposed Philip as their prince. That left the geographical and economic core of the old Habsburg Netherlands, Flanders and Brabant, as a battlefield for decades of exhausting war, interrupted by a truce from 1609 to 1621 but terminated only in 1648.

Spanish success was so dramatic in the 1580s that reconquest of all the rebel provinces looked within their grasp, but thereafter the Dutch began to push the border back. After unsatisfactory attempts to find a foreign sovereign, they attained a rough-and-ready political equilibrium, constituting themselves as a decentralized federal republic with a prominent military role for the descendants of William of Orange, who had been assassinated in 1584. The reforms of Maurice of Nassau, William's son, made the Dutch army a match for the Spanish. The transfer of mercantile capital and expertise from devastated and blockaded Antwerp and the emigration of skilled workers from Flanders and Brabant—partly to find religious toleration, partly to escape the war zone—stimulated an economic boom which made it possible to fund a war against the world's greatest empire. The chance to attack that empire at its weakest points overseas—notably the Portuguese Spice Islands, conquered in 1605—reinforced the boom. And the mantle of diehard opposition to Spain attracted alliances with England (from 1585) and Henri IV of France (from 1588, even before his accession as king), both wary of Spanish dominance in European affairs. These allies diverted Spanish effort away from the Netherlands into three Armadas against England, two marches into France to relieve Paris and Rouen from siege by Henri IV, the installation of Spanish garrisons in Kinsale and several Breton strongholds, and the defence of the Caribbean against Drake and other raiders. Though France left the war in 1598 and England in 1604, the United Provinces fought on to secure a truce in 1609. By then the Netherlands were on their way to being one of the leading European powers of the seventeenth century.

The Weak Monarchies of the East and the Coming of the Thirty Years War

Some polities had barely begun to intensify state power before they were diverted from the task. Poland-Lithuania, ruled as the kingdom of Poland and the grand duchy of Lithuania by rulers of the Jagiellon dynasty until 1572, was bound into a single commonwealth by the Union of Lublin in 1569. Its enormous area, twice that of France, predisposed it to a regionalized rather than a centralized system of politics and government. Under the union the Lithuanian nobility shared all the extensive privileges secured by their Polish peers in the fifteenth and early sixteenth centuries, notably the right to elect the king and to sit in the diet or *Sejm* in which individual noblemen could veto decisions. These privileges were confirmed and extended in the bargaining which preceded a series of disputed elections to the crown between 1572 and 1587. Blessed with assured religious toleration (many adopted Calvinism or Unitarianism), life tenure of provincial governorships, a recognized right to rebel against a king who broke his coronation oath, loyal followings amongst the gentry, and almost unlimited power over the serfs who worked the great grain-growing estates to supply the hungry west, the Polish noblemen were the most secure in Europe. It was still possible to rule Poland-Lithuania after a fashion, through negotiation with the magnates, the exercise of the declining fund of royal patronage, and successful military leadership against the Muscovites. However, it proved impossible to extend the powers of central government. King Sigismund III attempted to reverse the constitutional balance in 1606–9, when he proposed to create permanent taxation and a standing army, and to allow the diet to proceed by majority decisions. He was at once confronted by a petition bearing more than 50,000 names and then by a rebellion. He defeated the rebellion, but withdrew his proposals. His successors in the next two centuries, faced with neighbours growing in military and political strength, would preside over the decline and dismemberment of a state too republican for its own good.

The Polish example was not lost on the nobilities of the Habsburg lands to the south and west, again often Protestants under Catholic princes. The territorial estates they dominated retained influence across the sixteenth century, by exploiting their rulers' need for taxation to fund the Turkish wars. By the early seventeenth century, however, noblemen faced the combined reassertion of princely authority and Catholic religion. In Hungary they rebelled in 1604 against the violent re-Catholicization which was being pursued by the Habsburgs in Transylvania as part of the war against the Turks and, in parallel, in royal Hungary itself. In the peace that ended the war, they secured religious toleration and the continuing independence of Transylvania from Habsburg or Ottoman control. In the diet that followed the peace, they secured the expulsion of the Jesuits and the appointment of a Lutheran magnate to the viceregal post of palatine. As divisions between the Emperor Rudolf and his brother and eventual successor Matthias fatally weakened Habsburg policy, noble opposition movements in Bohemia, Moravia, Silesia, and Austria spent the next few years extracting from their rulers guarantees of their religious and political freedoms.

In every part of the Habsburg realms, however, local Catholics continued to promote Counter-Reformation. In Matthias's heir presumptive, the Archduke Ferdinand of Styria, they found a dedicated figurehead, educated at the Bavarian university of Ingolstadt and counselled by Jesuit confessors. Moreover, for the first time since Charles V's abdication the advocates of Austrian counter-reform could hope for Spanish support. For a generation after the succession disputes and religious compromises of the mid-century, the two Habsburg dynasties viewed each other warily. They then began a long series of cousinly intermarriages in 1570, which were genetically disastrous but politically reassuring. By the 1610s successive Spanish ambassadors in Vienna urged their local friends to look to Madrid for help. In 1617 Ferdinand was elected as king of Bohemia and Hungary in reversion after Matthias. Yet within a year the Protestant nobles of Bohemia had staged a coup against the provocative Catholic councillors installed by Ferdinand at Prague: they threw two of them out of an upstairs palace window in the celebrated 'defenestration'. Soon Lusatia, Silesia, Upper Austria, Lower Austria, and Moravia joined in revolt against Ferdinand, and Bethlen Gabor, prince of Transylvania, allied himself with the confederates. Within six months of Matthias's death in 1619, the Bohemians deposed Ferdinand and elected in his stead the Elector Palatine.

Elector Frederick V was leader of the aggressively Protestant group in the uneasy religious politics of Germany. In recent decades the pacification of Germany's religious struggles arrived at in 1555 had come under increasing strain for a number of reasons. Protestants looked to protect their co-religionists from persecution in the newly aggressive Catholic principalities. Catholics looked to prevent the secularization of further church lands by bishops or abbots who turned Protestant. Both Catholics and many Lutherans feared and obstructed the spread of Calvinism in the 'second Reformation', while it was the Calvinists, led by Frederick, who were keenest to challenge the Counter-Reformation, whether in Germany or in the Habsburg lands, where the palatine court had many contacts. The leader of Germany's militant Catholics was Frederick's distant cousin, Duke Maximilian of Bavaria. He coveted both Frederick's electoral title—his right to vote in the election of the Holy Roman Emperor—and his territory of the Upper Palatinate, adjacent to Bavaria. For the transfer of these to his line by imperial authority, Maximilian was happy to step in to save the Habsburgs from their rebellious and heretical subjects. To save the family honour and the Catholic faith, the Spanish Habsburgs were prepared to do the same, thus aligning the Dutch more readily than ever with the German and Bohemian Protestant cause. Already in 1610 German religious politics

The election of Frederick, Elector Palatine, as king of Bohemia inspired militant Protestants across Europe but set off the Thirty Years War. In this Dutch print intended for the English market, the Hebrew name of God shines blessings on him and his wife Elizabeth, daughter of James I, while Luther, Calvin, and the Bohemian reformer Hus confer over the Bible, and Catholic clergy flee.

had threatened to ignite European war, as Protestant and Catholic claimants vied for the succession to Cleves and Jülich with Dutch and Spanish support. Henri IV of France was preparing to intervene on the Protestant side when he was assassinated by an outraged French Catholic, and the crisis was gradually defused. In 1618–21 no such check diverted the onrush of Armageddon. Power after power became sucked in by dynastic alliance, strategic interest, or religious duty; strengthened armies, fleets, taxation systems, bureaucracies, and religious identities were put to the test. Europe descended into a more general and destructive war than any yet seen.

II

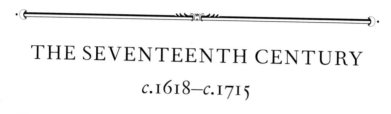

THE SEVENTEENTH CENTURY
c.1618–c.1715

4

Colonies, Enterprises, and Wealth: The Economies of Europe and the Wider World in the Seventeenth Century

R. A. HOUSTON

Introduction: Europe and the Wider World in 1600

Europe had gone through unprecedented change during the sixteenth century. The religious unity of Christendom, so long in conflict with Islam, had in the end been sundered from within by the 'Protestant' ideas of Martin Luther and his successors. The Renaissance monarchies which had emerged as the dominant political form at the end of the Middle Ages were beginning to give way to different types of state. The supranational monarchy presided over by Charles V had been divided between the Spanish and Austrian branches of the Habsburg dynasty, and the Low Countries hived off from the Holy Roman Empire to the crown of Spain. But the compact nation states which were to dominate political and military life by the eighteenth century were still emerging from obscurity—England, France, and Prussia. Warfare was the principal motor of these changes and had in turn profound implications for social and economic life. Europe was never truly peaceful at any time during the sixteenth or seventeenth century and at some periods all European powers were engaged in warfare both within the continent itself and across the known world.

If Europe's leaders were restless and bellicose, Europe's economies were far from static during the sixteenth century. Population had been more or less stable since the Black Death of the mid-fourteenth century but after *c.*1550 rising fertility and falling mortality combined to produce growth rates of 1 per cent a year—unremarkable to our eyes but unprecedented since the end of the thirteenth century. Agriculture had not risen to the challenge of feeding more mouths, for the poor had become a large and permanent class during the sixteenth century. Inflation fuelled by rising demand and the increased production and importation of bullion created serious social problems not only for the lower orders. Famines ravaged the continent in the 1590s.

The richest parts of Europe were the lands owned by the Habsburgs in Spain, northern Italy, southern Germany, and the Low Countries. The countries of northern Europe were politically insignificant, geographically marginal, and economically peripheral. Four-fifths of England's exports were wool or undyed woollen cloth. Her largest single import after textiles was French wine. The economic powerhouse of Europe was the Mediterranean, where European cultures met those of North Africa, the Middle East, and the Far East. Building on the first tentative voyages of discovery made by Columbus and Magellan, Europeans forged sea routes to the East Indies round the Cape of Good Hope. They established footholds in central and southern America and on the west coast of Africa. Oceanic trade began to supersede the ancient caravan routes from the heart of Africa northwards, and the silk and spice roads overland from the distant east to Constantinople. By 1600 the Iberian powers, Spain and Portugal (ruled by Spain 1580–1640), between them had the first empires on which, it could truly be said, the sun never set.

But by the time of Philip II's death in 1598 the first cracks in the dominance of the Habsburgs were appearing. Philip's commitments had become hopelessly overstretched. He had failed to suppress a revolt begun over thirty years earlier among his subjects in the Low Countries. Lurching from one financial crisis to another, he had chosen not to confront the economic problems which were becoming apparent both in Castile and in his north Italian lands. In the four years after his death Spain may have lost as many as a million inhabitants to a devastating plague. Commercially too the Habsburg Empire was beginning to weaken, its merchant fleet subject to merciless attrition at the hands of Dutch and English privateers. English exports of cloth, as opposed to raw wool, were rising; the lightweight textiles which were ultimately to invade the Mediterranean were already in production, if not yet quantitatively significant. The balance of economic power was about to undergo a dramatic and irrevocable change.

People

Severe as this outbreak of plague between 1598 and 1602 undoubtedly was for Spain, she was not alone in her demographic problems. Contemporary writings bring out the appalling human and social costs and for some communities we have figures showing dramatic surges in mortality. But, like many other aspects of early modern life, it is often difficult to be precise about this important event. The seventeenth century was to all intents and purposes a non-statistical age. Minimal bureaucracies, evasion, fraud, and patchy survival of documents all make time-consuming and imperfect the creation of even the most basic series of economic data. Jean Bodin opined that a state's only strength and riches came from its people; but early modern rulers had a rudimentary notion of the size and composition of their populations. France was the largest nation state with at least 16 million subjects by 1600 and 19–20 million by 1700. The only territories with appreciable population growth were Ireland, Portugal, and Scandinavia. England's population grew steadily from 3 million in the 1540s to 5.5 million in the 1650s but did not reach that level again until the 1730s. Under the impact of disease and warfare numbers fell in Spain and Germany. The city of Augsburg lost half its inhabitants during the 1630s and 1640s. Overall, the population of western Europe remained static at perhaps 70–80 million souls. The population of the world is largely a matter of guesswork: a figure of 200 million is as good as any.

Men and women lived in a very different material environment to our own, and in some respects the ideological assumptions and cultural patterns which influenced their lives are alien to us. In other ways, life for ordinary people was close to our modern experience. Europe's people generally lived in family groups whose size and structure we would readily recognize. Living alone was unusual except for widows and widowers. The family was the basic unit of consumption and of biological and social reproduction. But, in addition, the household was the locus of production and welfare to a much greater degree than in the modern developed world. In north-western Europe households were simple and families small—husband, wife, and unmarried children with the possible addition of unmarried young people of both sexes called servants. These were not just domestics but performed a range of jobs in agriculture and industry where the closest equivalent was a (male) apprentice. Service in another household was a normal part of growing up for most ordinary people as they passed from being adolescents to full adults.

Service was a distinctive feature of early modern societies, which declined with industrialization and modernization; but other important transition points in life occurred at roughly the same time as they do for us. Women married for the first time in their mid-twenties but perhaps a sixth never married during their childbearing span. Marriage coincided with the creation of a separate household in the west. This north-west European marriage pattern exerted a powerful check on fertility and population growth—important in societies which either did not know about, or did not practice, contraception as we understand it. Once married, women produced children every two or two-and-a-half years. Except for the élites who employed wet-nurses, it would be wrong to assume that women were constantly pregnant between the ages of 25 and 45 years; the average woman would spend no more than five years pregnant.

This pattern of late marriage is very much a north-west European one. In eastern and southern Europe family forms and social organization were more reminiscent of some modern third world countries. Here, households were often large and complex, comprising more than one married couple. Servants (and indeed hired labour generally) were much rarer. Most labour was family labour. Marriage was universal except for those who took religious vows and most women were married by the age of 20 years. Newly married couples simply joined a larger household and men were commonly in their forties before they became a head of household. These profound differences in social organization may be the result of timeless and enduring cultural preferences. The mixing of generations may have enriched family life and helped preserve peasant values. But extended families may also have been sustained in the east and south by rich and powerful lords who kept the peasantry in their thrall through economic, legal, and even military means. The fact that a lord was able to dictate what labour should be provided by a farm helped to dictate the size of the family unit which occupied the farm buildings.

Serfdom east of the river Elbe was an extreme example of patterns of landholding and power which obtained across Europe. In exchange for access to the products of the land, people there were subject to the lord's justice and had to provide labour for his lands. Peasants required the permission of the lord to move from one farm to another or even sometimes had to ask the lord and the village community's consent to marry. Some peasants were richer than others and the exact conditions of serfdom varied from one region to another. Economic inequality was ubiquitous across Europe, whatever its social variety. But the system of serfdom in general was characterized by restricted personal freedom and the exploitation of the peasantry by legal and political rather than economic means.

In the long term, serfdom and its successor, seigneurial domination, either decayed or was swept away by revolutions like 1789 or 1917. In the seventeenth century, economic change did not always bring with it more modern forms of social organization. Powerful landowners east of the river Elbe reacted to growing western demands for grain by exploiting more intensively their feudal privileges over serf labour. The rights of Russian lords over their peasants were consolidated and extended by comprehensive laws passed in 1649. Even in Britain, which Karl Marx saw as the cradle of capitalism, feudal power and mentalities died hard. In response to shortages of skilled labour in the coal and salt industries, a statute of 1606 (not repealed until 1799) bound Scottish colliers for life to the owner of the coal, giving them the legal status of serfs.

Serfdom was much rarer in the west, but the legal status of a farmer still played an important part in determining how much of the fruits of their labours he and his family would enjoy. The other crucial determinant of well-being was, of course, whether the landholding was sufficient for subsistence. Most farmers were tenants of one kind or another. For them, the amount of land held and the level of rents and taxes determined their standard of living. Holdings large enough to support a family were unusual in north-eastern France but more common in Scandinavia. Some peasants held land on a year-to-year basis at the whim of the lord; others might have leases which allowed them to enjoy the land at a more or less fixed rent for up to three generations. Landlords in Brittany and other parts of western France extracted a large percentage of the surplus created by their peasants through exploiting their extensive feudal rights. In Burgundy certain sharecropping contracts allowed farmers only a third of the produce they had worked so hard to create. Ecclesiastical, royal, and seigneurial taxation took at least 20 per cent of the gross income of a farmer in north-eastern France. While few Europeans were completely divorced from the land, many of them had only a toehold on it. Scotland and Ireland had their 'cottars' or 'cottiers'—a large but (to historians) almost invisible rural underclass who, with their families, provided the bulk of agricultural labour. In some parts of Europe the polarization of landholding and wealth were extreme. Three-quarters of the population of Andalucia and New Castile were landless labourers or *jornaleros*. England, parts of southern France and Scandinavia were the only parts of Europe with large numbers of peasant proprietors. Western European peasants were generally 'free' but that did not make them rich.

The world was an uncertain and dangerous place for rich and poor alike. Fire, warfare, bandits, fraudsters, even the elements, could wipe out in min-

The Three Lilies brewery on the river Spaarne at Haarlem was owned by Johan Claesz. van Loo. Clean water was brought in barrels from unpolluted rivers or filtered through the dunes. Brewers also sold fresh water to the inhabitants of major towns whose supplies were too contaminated to drink.

utes a hard-won fortune, for insurance was not commonly available except to cover shipping until the eighteenth century. Life itself might be cut short by deadly diseases like smallpox, typhus, typhoid, and of course plague, which continued to scourge European towns until the Marseilles outbreak of 1720–1; by accidents or violence; through ineffective or even counter-productive medical care like bleeding. Chronically high mortality from disease explains why population levels barely changed across much of Europe. Anxieties produced by a threatening and poorly understood environment might be assuaged by religious belief; but there was still the fear of God's judgements or the supernatural. Most early modern people had some kind of disfigurement from accidents or childhood afflictions like smallpox, polio, or rickets. A recent speculation is that at least one person in twelve was blind or crippled.

We shall see below that, with so many expensive new products coming into Europe, the seventeenth century was an exciting time to be rich. Some of these commodities eventually became 'essentials'—tea, coffee, sugar,

and tobacco. But for most people adequate food and clean water were the most important necessities of life. Few European cities had supplies for populations which were either expanding or developing greater demands for water. Mid-eighteenth-century Paris had 65 public fountains: one for every 10,000 inhabitants when one for 1,000 would have been needed to meet demand. Edinburgh had just eight public fountains in the late seventeenth century for roughly 30,000 people. Only towns like Namur, where the ratio was roughly 1 to 500 had anything like adequate provision of fresh water.

Polluted water, basic or non-existent sanitation, and the diseases carried by flies and people made towns very unhealthy environments. Not surprisingly, it was said to be possible to smell eighteenth-century Berlin 10 kilometres away. One child in three born in seventeenth-century London would die before its first birthday compared with one in seven in the countryside. High fertility made up for swingeing infant and child mortality, with perhaps a third of the population comprising those aged 15 or younger. Conversely, there were relatively few people aged 60 or above. Life expectancy at birth for the rich bourgeoisie of seventeenth-century Geneva was 36 years—hardly inspiring but nevertheless twice as long as a badly housed member of the labouring classes could expect. For comparison, the average life expectancy at birth in France was about 30 years and in England about 35 years.

Land

We might imagine that such an environment would breed a sense of fatalism. Early modern people tolerated uncertainties and injustices which modern westerners have now largely forgotten. But their mental world was in many ways similar to our own and seventeenth-century Europeans met life's challenges head-on. Land had to be worked, stomachs had to be filled, rents had to be found, taxes had to be paid. On its part, the growing needs of the state for information on its subjects prompted the investigations of early political scientists. The Englishman Sir William Petty 'anatomized' Ireland *c.*1649–51. Later in the century Louis XIV's minister Vauban conducted a detailed investigation of national wealth with an eye to reorganizing and increasing taxation. Gregory King, one of the first true 'political economists', published an intensive analysis of England's economy and society in 1688. Very approximately, King estimated that 40 per cent of gross national product came from agriculture; 20 per cent from the domestic market for goods and services; 10 per cent from exports; and 30 per cent from overseas imports and re-exports. All other European countries except perhaps the Netherlands would have had an even higher percentage of national wealth generated by agriculture. If, as Bodin said, all wealth came from people it was primarily the product of their labours on the land.

Most people lived on the land. Many documents of the period do not trouble to give a man's occupation because it was assumed he was a farmer. Access to rights in land was fundamental to wealth. Landowning conferred social cachet but it also formed the basis for political power. In some countries the right to vote for representative assemblies like the English Parliament depended on being a freeholder of some substance. Improvements in agricultural output were at the core of sustainable economic growth in traditional economies. Most industrial raw materials came from or were nurtured by the soil: flax, wool, leather, and wood, for example.

Vital as it was, European farming was poorly developed in comparison with later centuries. Except in pockets of the Low Countries, England, and northern Italy, agricultural output was dismally low. In much of eastern and southern Europe yields per acre and output per worker stagnated. The ratio of seed sown to grain crop harvested averaged one to three or four across much of the continent—dangerously close to subsistence after taking into account rents and taxes, animal fodder and seed for the following season. New crops were introduced from America and Asia, most notably maize, which was extensively cultivated in northern Italy, south-western France, and Spain by the end of the seventeenth century. Maize, rice, and, in the following century, potatoes reduced dependence on grain and offered more calories per acre.

Progress was being made. In some countries productivity in agriculture grew significantly during our period. This involved reorganizing land use by enclosure and consolidation of holdings, introducing new crops and different rotations, improving the soil, and linking pastoral and arable husbandry. Used together in one area or by regions specializing in certain products, these innovations allowed improvements in output which were dramatic by the standards of the day. The falling price of grain and the growing convergence of prices across England were attributable to increases in yields and the creation of integrated national grain markets. Together, these allowed some regions of Europe to break out of the long-established cycle of subsistence. In England and the Netherlands one peasant could feed his own and half of another family in 1600. By 1700 a comparable worker could feed his own and another whole family. English agriculture improved so much during the seventeenth century that it became a net exporter of grain.

Agricultural improvements might allow more mouths to be fed. More importantly, they might create a higher standard of living. Thus people could afford to buy items other than food and basic necessities such as clothing. They could aspire to buy the products of trade and industry within an economy which could feed those who provided them. This seems to have happened in seventeenth-century England. As population pressure eased after 1650 and as agricultural output per head rose, real wages (the purchasing power of money wages) also increased. But this was not the only pathway to economic change. Even in the sixteenth century the Dutch had imported as much as a third of their grain needs from the Baltic, allowing specialization within pastoral agriculture alongside a level of urbanization and industrial employment unthinkable if their economy had been closed. More than anything else, it was commerce which made the Dutch so economically successful. Their success testifies to the possibilities for diversification and growth even within 'traditional' and, to modern eyes, apparently 'backward' economic systems.

This lively engraving shows women selling fish. Most retailing was conducted in the open market-places of Europe with women prominent among the purveyors of food and drink. Shops only sold a limited range of goods to a restricted clientele until the eighteenth century. The depiction is none too sympathetic as we see a customer holding his nose, presumably because the fish has gone 'off', and two women egg-sellers fighting.

The level of demand for goods and services depends on disposable incomes and cost on the one hand and the marketing which makes them available on the other. In parts of Europe more than four-fifths of workers' expenditure went on food but in England it was no more than a half. What remained could be spent on manufactured goods, making specialization of production and economic diversification possible. Even if most peasants tried to be self-sufficient in food, all but the very poorest both needed and, above all, wanted to enjoy well-made goods made for them by others. In north-western Europe it is unlikely that most households made items such as clothes from scratch for their own use. The manufacturing process from raw material to finished garment was far too complicated and time-consuming. Even in the more isolated economies there was a considerable degree of specialization. Most women had jobs (in the conventional sense as well as looking after the household) which were usually separate from those of their husbands, and which would not have left time to do anything except perhaps mending clothes. Thus there were opportunities for growth and change even within apparently backward economies.

Yet the pace of economic development was slow compared with the nineteenth century. One reason is that land was significant not only as a source of food but also of energy. Taking into account the elementary technology available we should not be surprised that much of the energy for domestic and industrial uses came from the soil. Wood or charcoal was still the main fuel in Mediterranean and central Europe but peat was the principal energy source for households and industries in the seventeenth-century Netherlands. Coal was used increasingly in Britain. While stocks of coal were, to all intents and purposes, infinite, growing demand for wood and peat created serious environmental problems and shortages of supply. So much peat was dug out of the bogs of Schieland (around Rotterdam) and the Haarlemse Meer (site of Amsterdam's Schipol airport) during the seventeenth century that they turned into lakes. Windmills kept the water at bay but it was not until the nineteenth century that steam technology made it possible to drain and reclaim large tracts of land for agriculture.

More generally, the sorts of fuels used help us to understand the inherent limitations on economic growth in this period. Energy came from rivers, wind, animal or human muscle, or by burning wood, coal, or peat. In the case of wood the source of energy was renewable, but only slowly. The iron and glass industries of the late medieval English Weald had all but disappeared by 1650 because there was no longer enough wood to make charcoal. Productivity horizons were limited by the use of renewable energy. In the absence of significant new technologies, the 'organic' economy of early modern Europe was constrained by the productivity of the land. Iron-ore, clay, and sand could be used to make iron, pottery, and glass. These 'mineral-based' sectors formed only a small percentage of any European economy. English coal production at least trebled in the course of the seventeenth century to a level which was five times as great as the rest of the world put together but it was still less than 3 million tons annually. The average Lancashire coal mine of the later seventeenth century employed a mere three men with output of just 400 tons a year. Swedish exports of bar iron quintupled over the century but only to 30,000 tons a year. Europe's economies certainly diversified and grew during the seventeenth century, but the level of industrial output remained modest in manufactures which would later become the core of the industrial revolution.

Cities

In one way or another, all the inhabitants of early modern Europe depended on the land. People who lived in cities could not wholly escape this dependence. They generally did not produce their own food but had to buy it from rural producers; if they were manufacturers their raw materials were almost always sourced in the countryside. In exchange for the means of subsistence they offered an industrial product, a service, or a trade good which rural dwellers could not, or would not, make or locate for themselves. Townspeople paid farmers for food and thus enabled them to buy the goods and services available in cities. Rarely this simple in practice, the relationship between town and country was nevertheless a powerful force for economic change.

Most of Europe was not densely urbanized in our period. There were few cities of more than 100,000 inhabitants even in 1700: Amsterdam, Lisbon, London, Madrid, Milan, Palermo, Paris, Naples, Rome, and Venice. More typical of the urban experience was Germany which had hundreds of towns, but most of them with only 2,000–5,000 inhabitants. Tiny by our standards, a town of 10,000 or more inhabitants would be counted large by contemporaries. Perhaps 8 per cent of the population of north-western Europe lived in such conurbations in 1600 and around 13 per cent in 1700. Most of the growth can be accounted for by a doubling in the urban proportion of England's population. London grew from 200,000 to nearly 600,000 during the century and from less than 5 per cent of the national total to more than 10 per cent. As early as the end of the sixteenth century nearly a third of the Dutch lived in towns but here and elsewhere in continental Europe the percentage did not grow. Individual cities waxed and waned—noteworthy successes included Liverpool and Nantes on the back of the tobacco trade; a singular failure was Toledo after Philip II shifted his capital to Madrid late in the sixteenth century—but the continent as a whole was barely more urbanized in 1700 than it had been in 1600.

Despite their often small size and low proportion of national population, towns were the motors of economic change in the seventeenth century. Some exchanges involved barter or payments in kind but European economies of the period were highly monetarized. In a curious sense, Europe had a 'single currency' since any coin with a precious metal content could be used anywhere in Europe. For example, Swedish, Dutch, French, and English coins were in common use in seventeenth-century Scotland. To the bewildering array of coinage in circulation we can add trade tokens issued by retailers such as apothecaries. Not all money was metallic and the seventeenth century saw the origins of modern banknotes, originally called bills of exchange. These were promissory notes from one individual to

Rotterdam. Within an area 200 metres square we find a microcosm of a successful pre-industrial economy: tightly packed stone housing, ships thick along the quays, shipbuilding, windmills, brewery cranes, and the proximity of farming to the heart of the city.

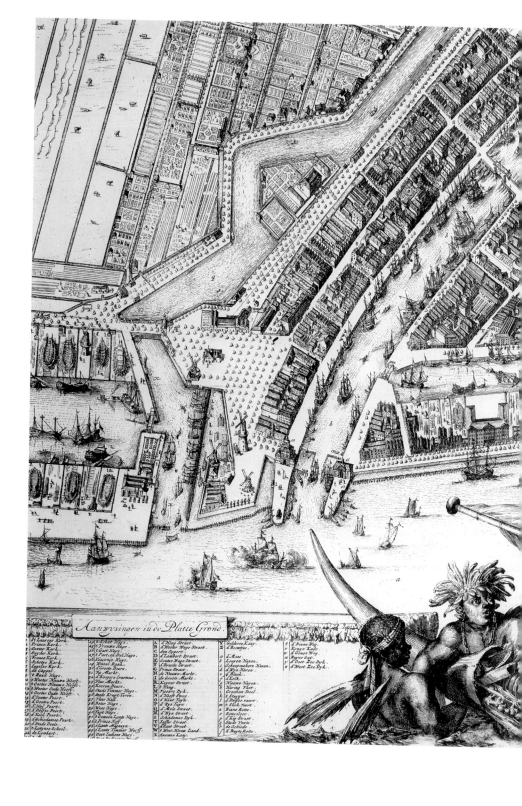

Aanwysingen in de Platte Grond

another which could be assigned to other parties. Bills of exchange were an increasingly sophisticated extension of the ubiquitous institution of credit. Webs of debt and credit linked communities and economies. Borrowing and lending lubricated the wheels of commerce, agriculture, and industry.

From the poorest (who used pawnbrokers and friends) to the rich landowners (who used lawyers, merchants, and even the crown) all levels of society borrowed money to fund current expenditure. Social groups prominent in lending included professionals such as the clergy and notaries, widows and other rentiers, goldsmiths, and Jews who had traditionally been untroubled by Christian reservations about charging interest. Some people obviously had more money than others and were sources of cash, but even they might also be borrowers. Landowners whose incomes came from the sale of crops or agricultural rents paid seasonally are an example. Mortgages became an established aspect of estate management throughout the British Isles during the second half of the seventeenth century. Debt was ubiquitous. With 160,000 ducats a year coming in, the Spanish duke of Medina Sidonia had an income more than 5,000 times greater than the day labourers on his estates. But men of his social class could still die hundreds of thousands of ducats in debt. The Spanish state borrowed money at high rates of interest and relatively low risk, even if defaults on payments were not unknown. This diverted investment from industry and commerce into arguably less productive areas such as funding bureaucracies and armies.

Even in the seventeenth century the exchange of goods was vital to economic growth but the ability to manipulate money was also of fundamental significance to the creation of wealth. Some credit was extended free as part of neighbourly or lordly charity. Most lenders charged for the use of their money. During the sixteenth century interest rates had been high—perhaps 10 per cent a year. During our period they fell substantially to settle at 5–6 per cent in England and 3–4 per cent in the Netherlands. The origins of modern banking can be traced to the seventeenth century. The Bank of Amsterdam (1609) issued notes and honoured bills of exchange against deposits of specie. Neither it nor the 1614 *Huijs van Leening* (Lending House) of Amsterdam actually provided much credit but they did help merchants efficiently to operate their own lines of borrowing and lending. The Bank of England (1694) was founded to provide money for William of Orange's war against the French and to tidy up the mess of unfunded public debt that had accumulated through three Anglo-Dutch wars. However, it too had beneficial effects on private finance. A pamphleteer writing in 1695 (the same year as the Bank of Scotland was founded) declared that the competition provided by this fledgling institution had 'almost crush'd several sorts of Blood-suckers, mere Vermin, Usurers and Gripers, Goldsmiths, Tally-Jobbers, Exchequer Brokers and Knavish Money-Scriveners, and Pawn-Brokers'.

While the Bank was the way of the future it is worth remembering that very few individuals did business with it. Even its role in government finance was far from exclusive. Indeed, the Exchequer extracted far more from the public by offering interest annuity lotteries in its struggle to fund the War of Spanish Succession 1710–13 than was attracted by the Bank from private investors. Fondness for lotteries testifies to early capitalists' proclivity for gambling even if Sir William Petty denounced them as a tax on 'unfortunate self-conceited fools'. One way of coping with an uncertain world was to try to profit from the uncertainty. Hazard took other forms. The business books of Scottish merchants of the seventeenth century sometimes contain records of wagers alongside their double-entry book keeping. By entering into tontines men even bet on how long they would live.

Both the sophistication and the imperfections of early modern financial markets are neatly illustrated by the rise and fall of a humble flower. First imported from Turkey in the 1560s, tulips were the orchids of the day. By the 1620s they had become the ultimate horticultural fashion accessory for the monied classes of the Netherlands. By then, strong demand and fat margins attracted many more growers into the market. By the early 1630s tulips were within the reach of almost every purse and the nation had become obsessed with them, not only as objects of beauty but also as investments. Between 1634 and 1636 a bulb of the basic 'Gouda' variety doubled to three guilders—an artisan's weekly wage. At the peak of the boom in the winter of 1636–7 a rare tulip bulb could cost as much as a fine house. In 1636 tulip 'futures'—the right to buy the next season's crop—were available on the Amsterdam exchange. But then prices plummeted in the last phase of the classic speculative cycle as blind greed turned to caution and then to naked fear. Similar 'bubbles' occurred in England in 1682 and in both England (the 'South Sea Bubble') and France in 1720–1. The French crisis was precipitated by the ill-founded schemes of a gifted, if flawed, Scottish financier called John Law of Lauriston. Standards of honesty were not high and information flows were far from perfect. For example, earlier in the century money had continued to come into the English Virginia Company long after it became apparent that no dividends would ever be paid.

Imperfect information flows were primarily due to serious communications difficulties. Around 1700 it took two weeks for news from Antwerp to reach Venice, five weeks from Dublin, and nearly six from Constantinople

(Istanbul). Military tensions meant that in the Levant the conventional adage 'the sea united but the land divided' did not apply. The problem everywhere was that information could only travel as quickly as a man on horseback or on a ship. Bandits continued to prey on travellers in remote areas and even in some interstitial regions where they could hide from the authorities of one country over the border of another. If rural roads were often slow, dangerous, and deserted, urban thoroughfares experienced serious overcrowding. One solution to Amsterdam's problem of traffic clogging its narrow streets was a one-way system in some areas from 1615 and the banning of wheeled private vehicles from the town centre after 1634. Sleighs were allowed because they were quieter and slower (therefore safer) than wheeled coaches.

News was hungrily sought by high and low alike. Commercially sensitive information was exchanged in newsletters which were the precursors of modern newspapers. But the quickest way of gathering information was in person and thus people tended to congregate in places where information was communicated. It is no accident that London's stock market and its insurance industry began in coffee-houses. With open sides, the first Amsterdam *beurs* (stock exchange) looked like any other covered market place—though only men milled around in it. Venice, Seville, and London were important centres but Amsterdam, Europe's leading port, was the premier information exchange of the seventeenth century. It is not surprising that men like Blaeu also made Amsterdam the leader in cartography.

Ramshackle, dishonest, and bizarre as these financial structures appear to us they undeniably helped to generate riches. Growing wealth and changing priorities also stimulated more general improvements in urban amenities. Paris is said to have had the first lantern system paid for by local taxes from 1667. Amsterdam replaced poorly observed regulations, common to many cities, requiring private households to put lights above their doors, with a public system of oil lamps in 1669 and the Hague followed suit in 1678. Amsterdam had 133 lamps by 1679 and 2,400 by 1689. In many senses, this was the dawning of an 'age of light'. Even during the day, lighting in the narrower streets and closes of the congested cities cannot have been good. The tightly packed houses made good use of space and conserved heat more effectively than detached ones but many people would have had to use artificial light or work on the doorstep unless they lived on an upper floor or in an advantageously located building. Not surprisingly then, the lives of early modern people were lived much more publicly than our own.

The main 'consumer durable' was the dwelling-house itself and at least a third of gross fixed investment was in domestic accommodation. Few rural vernacular buildings of the pre-seventeenth century survive. Those we can visit nowadays are the stone- or brick-built dwellings of the urban middle classes or the rural élites. Again, the plush decorations of a castle and an institutional building like a German *Rathaus* (town hall) or *Zunfthaus* (guildhall) were far from typical. Certain decorative objects such as pictures, looking glasses, and window curtains became more common as the century wore on but mainly in the homes of the richer bourgeoisie. The first decorated wallpaper, imported from China, was fabulously expensive. In all European towns it was much more common for ordinary people to rent rather than own their home. The contribution of housing to the economy lay in building it and in feeding and clothing its occupants rather than in decorating, refurbishing, or purchasing durables for it.

Yet, the sometimes lavish material lifestyle of baroque Europe was beginning to be formed around this time. Only one in ten Londoners' inventories after death mention clocks in 1675 compared with more than half by 1715. Almost no English home had china plates or cups during the reign of Charles II but one household in six had them by the accession of George II. The real cost of textiles like linen and calico fell by a half over the seventeenth century in England. Falling prices helped people to afford some of the new consumer goods. Imports of tea into Europe were small and irregular until the eighteenth century—when rum and molasses also became commodities of mass consumption. When first imported into Europe in the early seventeenth century, tea was a great luxury and was considered medicinal. The Dutch scholar Constantijn Huygens used it to treat his toothaches. But elsewhere in Europe wealth was so polarized that only a small proportion of the population could aspire to enjoy the new 'groceries' being imported from the Indies: for example, coffee, sugar, and tobacco. Even fruit and vegetables were only affordable by the richest fifth of Madrid's population.

Towns generated wealth by marketing the products of agriculture and commerce and through what we now call 'financial services'. But they also made things. Even in commercial cities like Venice, London, or Hamburg industry was the largest employer because of the need to build and equip ships, to store and process imports. The Venetian arsenal employed 1,500 skilled craftsmen and 1,000 labourers. The most important industries were those involved in feeding and clothing people. Half the adult male population of the towns of Cordoba (Spain) and Northampton (England) made leather goods around 1600. Available in different strengths and types, beer was an important food item for domestic consumption and on board ship.

The Scots' tally was 1.7 litres a day for every man, woman, and child. Haarlem and Amsterdam together produced a third of all the beer brewed in Holland around 1660. At its peak around 1648 Haarlem alone was producing 67 million litres a year. Wealth also brought political power and in 1618 fully 21 of the 24-man *vroedschap* (town council) of Haarlem were brewers. The political life of Newcastle was dominated by coal shippers, of Bordeaux by wine merchants.

In all sorts of ways, towns were special environments. They housed ecclesiastical and secular governments. Most crafts and trades were organized into guilds which performed an economic, social, and sometimes even military function. Guilds were quasi-governmental institutions important to monarchs for administrative and fiscal purposes. In Louis XIV's Paris even the lemonade sellers were guildated. The aristocracies of Italy and Spain had their power bases in towns and even the landed classes of Britain were beginning to see the attractions of seasonal residence in cities and spa towns. Concentrations of rich people created demand for professional legal and medical services rare in the countryside. Advanced schools were to be found in towns and most communities of any size would have had a printing press in 1600. Literacy was universally high. Urban living promoted social mobility and the ready interchange of ideas and experiences. Only in towns do we find a rudimentary mass political consciousness. Rich and poor were literally face to face with each other. Ports saw unrivalled exchanges of goods and mixing of people. The only exception to this image of urban dynamism was east of the Elbe. Towns in the east were less economically dynamic and socially precocious than in the west, being mere extensions of the military and administrative power of the state and of the crushing economic dominance of the lords.

Manufactures

Cities were special in many ways. Yet in others they formed part of a single economic and social continuum for, as Adam Smith was later to argue, town and country were mutually dependent. If anything, that dependence grew over time. For much industrial production was located in the countryside of seventeenth-century Europe. Taxation documents show that across north-western Europe between a sixth and a third of all men living in the countryside were primarily employed in non-agricultural jobs such as textile manufacture. These were both independent artisans producing for local markets and dependent employees whose work might reach international markets. In reality, industry was probably even more important. Take the example of textiles, which were easily the largest industrial employer. Weavers were usually men but at least four women and children and perhaps as many as ten would be employed to prepare and spin enough flax or wool to keep a single loom at work. In order of numbers employed commerce came a long way behind agriculture and industry. This may have been a 'pre-industrial' age but it would be a serious error to see it as 'non-industrial'.

The advantage of rural domestic production or 'cottage industry' was that it was cheap and flexible. Breaking free of guild restrictions on quality, price, and employment, entrepreneurs were able to find plenty of eager workers among the underemployed poor of rural Europe. In the major cloth-producing areas such as Picardy in north-east France or the English West Country entrepreneurs bought raw wool or flax to be prepared and spun into yarn. They then gave the yarn to specialist weavers and bought back cloth which was then taken for finishing and finally for marketing, often in national or international markets. Urban specialists added more value to the product by dyeing cloth and tailoring it but the majority of ordinary woollen and linen fabric was made in the countryside by 1700. Putting-out thus embodied important 'modern' elements. Capital was controlled not by individ-

These clothes from a bog burial belonged to a man aged about 20 years, some 5' 4" tall and lame in one leg. He was murdered by a blow to the back of the head by a right-handed assailant some time around 1700 and his body thrown into a peat bog at Arnish Moor south of Stornoway on the Isle of Lewis, Scotland. The peat which hid the crime also preserved his much-repaired woollen clothing. The clothes of the poorer classes were mended and patched until they literally fell to pieces, then were collected by rag-gatherers to be made into paper. However, this young man's clothes were professionally made and, remarkably for such a remote corner of Europe, followed the fashion of the day.

ual workers but by entrepreneurs; the production process had a clear division of labour; workers were paid wages for, while some might own their own looms, the only commodity they were selling was their labour.

Putting-out appears more modern and 'capitalistic' because the components of the production process are separate and specialized, and because the ownership of the means of production is not located with the workers who produce the cloth. However, small-scale production organized by master weavers rather than merchants continued to characterize the woollen cloth industry of seventeenth-century Leiden or Lille. Even within a single English county like Yorkshire putting-out and independent artisan cloth production coexisted. Sometimes they even competed as when English cloth merchants became adept at forging the seals on bales of Venetian luxury cloth then reselling these bogus fabrics to the Venetians themselves.

Articulated artisan production was not only appropriate to local or regional markets. In Edinburgh, Leiden, and Lille small commodity production was favoured over putting-out for social and political reasons. The Lakenhal (now a museum) was the heart of Leiden's woollen cloth industry. Clothmakers brought their work there to be inspected and a lead seal was fixed to the bales as a hallmark of quality. These seals have been found all over the world in places as far apart as Indonesia, South Africa, and South America where Leiden cloth was sold. And while it may be possible to characterize some aspects of rural domestic industry as 'modern' we also know that when the industrial revolution came it was located not in the peasant household but in towns and factories.

Industrial innovation in town and country alike was closely associated with mobile labour. Religious refugees like the French Huguenots helped diffuse the manufacture of silk, glass, and clocks across northern Europe. The Liège region was the world leader in iron smelting and working at the turn of the seventeenth century. It was from there that skilled craftsmen were recruited to organize the industry in Sweden. Communications may have been poor but the population was far from immobile. Half of those granted citizenship at Frankfurt am Main 1600–1704 were immigrants to the town. Seasonal migrants moved from the mountains of the Alps or Pyrenees to the plains of southern France or northern Italy. Poor and overpeopled countries like Scotland haemorrhaged inhabitants to Ireland and the countries of the North Sea and Baltic basins. On Europe's eastern fringes the steppes were being peopled. Those who left Europe temporarily or permanently for the New World were merely extending an established tradition of extensive internal geographical mobility.

States, Colonies, and Commerce

The incentives for European expansion were numerous. Authority over distant lands, the revenues they were said to provide, supervising the conversion of their inhabitants to Christianity: all added lustre to the reputation of a ruling house. Even the Dutch, Europe's leading capitalists, had a military agenda pursued across four continents and seven seas during their independence struggle against the Spaniards between the 1560s and 1640s. However, private individuals pushed much harder than public figures in north-western Europe. The government of the Dutch Republic (1648) was to all intents and purposes an extension of commercial interests. The pressure for the French and English crowns to back colonization came from courtiers, financiers, and merchant magnates. The crown's role in early English colonization was as a public promoter of private enterprise—for example, recognizing the existing Virginia as the first 'crown colony' in 1624. Direct control over certain colonies only came after the restoration of Charles II to the English throne in 1660. Early modern states were more likely to respond to economic change than to initiate it, attempting to profit from new sources of wealth rather than to create them.

States had what might loosely be termed economic policies, conventionally given the label 'mercantilism' to distinguish them from the notions of 'laissez-faire' which dominated economic life in the later eighteenth and nineteenth centuries. Mercantilism itself was not really a 'movement' in economic thought—let alone a coherent theory—so much as a 'tendency'. Said to embody the economic spirit of the age, mercantilism was an umbrella term for a set of more or less shared assumptions. Lobby groups for private interests found that certain themes appealed to rulers. These were: maximizing the wealth and power of a kingdom by self-sufficiency in food and manufactures; preventing the outflows of precious metals (the basis of all good coinage at the time); protecting native trade and increasing the nation's share of a fixed volume of commerce by taking it from others.

The early modern state was better as a protector and facilitator rather than as an initiator of commercial enterprise. Yet, the fact that states followed rather than led many aspects of economic development should not detract from its significance. Government demand was important for certain sectors such as armaments and ships; the state was anxious to protect existing commercial enterprises by force and by legislation. Aimed against the Dutch dominance of sea-carriage, the English Navigation Acts (from 1651) allowed colonial as well as metropolitan enterprise to prosper. Similar laws passed by the French halved the Dutch share of the Bordeaux wine trade 1651–84. In contrast, the state's attempts to shape economic life by creating new industrial enterprises were of limited importance. The textile manufactory of Villenouvette at Clermont de Lodève was founded by Louis XIV in 1679. It had mixed fortunes over the following century but never fulfilled its intended function of leading the modernization of cloth production in the French Midi. The Swedish imposed tolls on copper produced in Thuringia, Westphalia, Bohemia, Moravia, and Poland and marketed through the Baltic while occupying most of the ports there in the 1630s in order to raise the price of their own copper exports. Again, any enduring effect on industry was small.

Political control of economic life might facilitate economic development but when there were competing interests political priorities almost invariably outweighed economic ones. The regional economy of Spain's capital, Madrid, was rigged by the crown to ensure food supplies for the populace and luxuries for the bureaucrats and aristocrats who congregated there. Virtually all manufactures were imported from abroad, causing market development to be distorted and agricultural change to be retarded. By 1700 Madrid and Castile had become locked in a rigid economic relationship which also perpetuated a polarized social structure and a sharply unequal division of wealth and power in town and countryside alike. In contrast, Barcelona and its hinterland developed a healthy symbiotic relationship. Commercial interests often took second place to imperial needs. The Spanish crown tried to wage economic warfare against its rebellious subjects in Holland during the 'Eighty Years War' (which ended with the creation of the Dutch Republic in 1648) but its efforts backfired badly, setting the seal on Spain's economic as well as political decline. Indeed, poorly informed and politically motivated intervention could be disastrous. All early modern governments were chronically short of cash. Philip III's debasements of the coinage up to 1608, and again in 1617 and 1621, merely accentuated Spain's economic decline. The English crown's Cockayne project of 1614 proved a costly failure. Economic 'policy' was too often subordinated to short-term fiscal exigencies.

Whatever the state's role in it, overseas expansion was perhaps the essence and the greatest achievement of seventeenth-century capitalism. Europeans apparently used military power to exploit weaker economies. By doing so, they short-circuited some of the inherent constraints on economic growth within traditional economies. The legendary profits concentrated in the hands of capitalists helped to fund further economic development while beneficial side effects like improved financial systems hastened the process. Historians conventionally believed that international

The flyboat was the key to Dutch dominance of European trade. The most significant technological developments occurred in economic sectors with political and military importance, notably weapons, printing, ships, and navigation. Western ships became better armed, more elaborately rigged, and easier to handle with fewer crew.

trade, especially with the New World, was the prime force behind the primitive accumulation of capital which eventually led to the industrial and commercial revolutions of the nineteenth century.

Overseas trade could therefore convey benefits far beyond simple buying and selling of goods. Longer voyages required more sophisticated financial instruments and new ways of spreading risk such as joint stock companies. Transportation and transaction costs would be reduced by innovations in carrying. Ships had to be built, outfitted, and victualled, further stimulating production. New ship designs reduced transaction costs and made possible a large expansion in the carriage of grain and shipping supplies from the Baltic. These *fluijts* were cheap to build and man, meaning that operating costs were much reduced. Better financial services and improved organization of storage and distribution made a contribution here and to the Atlantic trade. However, demand for Indian cotton textiles and Chinese porcelain grew quickly in spite of rising shipping costs. The new designs were for bulk carriage as well as traditional low-volume, high-value commodities like spices. Successful merchants could diversify into industry for entrepreneurs of the age were usually merchants (sometimes landowners) rather than 'industrialists'. The spread of local, regional, and international trade in raw materials and manufactured goods brought about important changes. Production for exchange rather than use became the norm and with it a specialization of function or 'division of labour'. The really significant transport developments were in water-borne types, including an extended canal network in Holland. Passenger transportation by road was improved to a degree but it remained at least five times more

William Okeley and his shipmates were taken by Turkish pirates in the English Channel en route for the West Indies in 1639. Imprisoned for three years in Algiers they finally escaped to Majorca. While the horrific illustrations in the pamphlet were standard propaganda against Muslim pirates, designed to sell copy rather than add to the story, the captives were well-treated in this instance and were even able to attend Christian religious services. In reality, Christians made more barbarous pirates than Muslims.

Turks taking the English.

Selling slaves in Algiers

Execution with A batoone.

Turks burning of A Frier &c

Divers Cruelties

Makeing the boat & their Escape to Ma

expensive to send bulky goods overland than by water. The backs of horses and mules (and people) were more widely used than carts or sleds.

Individuals might leave Europe 'to improve their estates'—population had grown strongly during the second half of the sixteenth century and colonial labour shortages meant that skilled craftsmen could generally command a much higher standard of living than in the Old World. Motives were complex, sometimes rational, sometimes emotional. Indeed, contemporary writings about voyages of discovery convey a vivid sense of adventure. The men who undertook them have the appearance of adventurers rather than capitalists, gamblers rather than merchants who were motivated by desire for glory and greed for gain. The English East India Company (given a charter in 1600) was originally a privateering operation. Piracy itself was probably a major branch of economic activity but, like smuggling, it is difficult to quantify. Famous or notorious even now, these adventurers were far from typical of early modern businessmen and investors as a whole. For most of the latter were strongly averse to risk. Prosperous London merchants of the late seventeenth century had just 3 per cent of their total assets in shipping, 20 per cent in real estate, and the remainder in loans, stocks, leases, and government debt. This breakdown is based on inventories of possessions after death but throughout their careers early modern businessmen showed a strong preference for liquid assets and for low-risk investments like land. Agricultural land was perceived to offer a lower yield but much higher growth than urban buildings. Property was valued as a multiple of annual rental called 'years' purchase'. Evidence given by Sir Robert Murray to a House of Lords committee in London during 1669 included a statement that 'land near Edinburgh will give 20 or 22 years' purchase'. Within the city itself dwellings were sold for just twelve years' purchase meaning that they gave a high yield but limited growth prospects.

Indeed, overseas expansion was less spectacularly significant in reality than contemporary propagandists and some historians might lead us to expect. Fewer seventeenth-century merchants diversified into industry than was the case in the eighteenth and nineteenth centuries. The rich tended to invest in land which was not only a secure asset but also conferred social status on the owner. The Whitbreads are an example of a landed family founded on the proceeds of trade—beer in this case. Indeed, it is debatable whether the urban élites of seventeenth-century France were 'bourgeois' in any meaningful sense. Most aspired to belong to the nobility and, when able, tried to ape their social norms and economic behaviour—including a disdain for trade and a preference for conspicuous consumption.

France's richest men were courtiers, bureaucrats, and financiers—men like Louis XIV's famous minister Jean-Baptiste Colbert. Many of the richest men of the seventeenth century profited from the inability or unwillingness of central authorities to document and exploit human and natural resources. Those who received monopolies or licences from the crown did well. Those who collected royal taxes in exchange for a proportion of the assessment—'tax farmers'—were able to exploit the administrative network for their own gain. France under Louis XIV had one bureaucrat for every 1,200 inhabitants compared with one in seventy nowadays.

Trade with the wider world created many more opportunities for consumption than production. The advantage of colonies lay not in being markets for manufactures. Asian markets were closed to European goods and far eastern products had generally to be paid for in specie. The number of settlers in the Americas was too small to create much demand. The total population of all English settlements in North America was probably no more than 10,000 people c.1625 and Boston, the largest town in North America around 1700, could boast only 7,000 inhabitants. Spain found to its cost that colonists became increasingly self-sufficient, halving the tonnage of exports from Seville to the Americas 1600–50. Instead, colonial imports stimulated demand for European goods within Europe itself as people sought to sell their products in order to buy china, silks, spices, sugar (and later rum), tobacco, coffee (and later tea). Exports to the New World made up only a sixth of the value of England's' overseas trade in 1700 but colonial goods accounted for a third of imports. In the seventy years after 1637 tobacco imports into Britain rose from 1.5 million pounds annually to 38 million. Around 1600 profits could be astronomical—as they had been in the early years of the spice trade. But when the volume of trade in 'groceries' really took off after 1650 returns per unit slumped.

Whatever the glamorous image of New World commerce, its power to change European economies should not be exaggerated. Only a fortunate few became rich from overseas trade; many made an adequate living; countless more went bankrupt. Scotland's only attempt to establish a colony at Darien (modern Panama) was a disastrous failure which showed the hazards of such enterprises and the triumph of greed and optimism over realism. Connections between elements of the primitive 'world economy' remained tenuous and liable to interruption, profits from international trade fluctuating and uncertain. Throughout the seventeenth (and eighteenth) century Europeans bought and sold far more merchandise from each other than they did from other continents.

Except for Britain, most countries' overseas trade was overshadowed by their commerce with the rest of Europe at the end of the seventeenth century. Three-quarters of French imports came from Europe around 1700 and nine-tenths of her exports went to other European destinations. Even the Dutch, the world's greatest traders in the seventeenth century, saw the traditional Baltic routes as 'the mother trade'. Unglamorous both in locations and goods shipped, this trade nevertheless generated large amounts of wealth. Three-quarters of the Baltic grain which came through the Sound between modern Denmark and Sweden was carried in Dutch bottoms and around 1670 a similar proportion of the capitalisation of Amsterdam's *beurs* was accounted for by Baltic commerce. The tonnage employed in Spain's New World trade was only 1 per cent of that used by the Dutch in the Baltic. Overall, no more than 4 per cent of western Europe's GNP was accounted for by intercontinental exchange.

Colonies were a fascinating new area of economic life during the seventeenth century. If one characteristic of a 'colony' is that it provides primarily raw materials for a more developed 'metropolitan' economy, then Europeans hardly needed to look beyond the boundaries of their own continent. Ireland had provided wool and livestock for English markets since the Middle Ages but Spain too, once among the most 'developed' nations on the continent, was reduced to supplying wool to English West Country weavers by the 1680s. The number of looms working in Segovia fell by two-thirds in the century before then. Late seventeenth-century Spain's case was unusually parlous for not only was its manufacturing base contracting. Even against a backdrop of falling population it had not been self-sufficient in grain for over a century. Taxation was rising and confidence ravaged by repeated debasements of the coinage. But in many ways its fortunes were symptomatic of the general economic malaise of the Mediterranean. Milan turned out 3,000 bales of cloth a year in 1640 compared with just 100 in 1705. High costs, technological backwardness, and unwillingness to adjust to new demand patterns damned many basic industries in Spain and Italy.

After two centuries of aggressive expansion, even the awesome military machine of the Ottoman Turks was falling apart as the empire failed to respond to the economic, social, and demographic challenge of static frontiers. The spread of hydraulic silk mills across Europe from the end of the sixteenth century killed off much Ottoman silk weaving by dramatically reducing the costs of production. The Turks became exporters not of cloth but of raw silk. As a source of the once lucrative spice trade, the Levant or eastern Mediterranean was in terminal decline by the end of the sixteenth century. The collapse of Venice's dominance over the silk and other trades in that region during the mid-seventeenth century allowed the English and later the French to establish powerful commercial interests there.

Similar changes were occurring in the economic powerhouses of the New World. Until 1650 Brazil accounted for half the total New World sugar production—even if the contribution only amounted to perhaps 30,000 tons annually. The sugar and spice trade helped to make Lisbon the third largest city in Europe around 1600. By 1710 the focus of the sugar trade had shifted to Amsterdam and London (later still to Hamburg), following a change in the location of production as the British West Indies took over the leading role from Brazil. The stage was set for the rise of the North Atlantic economies which came to dominate the world in the eighteenth and nineteenth centuries.

Europe and the Wider World

Established for religious, commercial, and military reasons in the most diverse range of environments the globe had to offer, New World colonies varied enormously in character. For example, Massachusetts was a theocracy, Carolina quasi-feudal. Brazilian colonies attracted women from Portugal more readily than elsewhere. The families they helped to create gave the settlements a greater permanence than some of the purely military or trading outposts in the East. Outnumbered two or three to one by men, young women easily found husbands in the English Atlantic colonies while on Barbados 'a whore, if handsome, makes a wife for some rich planter'.

In the seventeenth century planters, married or single, sought to avoid labour shortages by using bonded servants or slaves. Transportation of convicts did not begin in earnest until after 1718 and most white migration to the Americas before then was voluntary. The northern colonies of New England attracted whole families but the characteristic movement to the southern settlements was by young single males. Between a quarter and a third of white settlers in the American colonies of the seventeenth century were indentured servants, four-fifths of them young men. Socially, the migrants were a cross-section of English society and not the 'rogues, whores and vagabonds' of legend. When whites began to choose not to go to the southern and West Indian colonies from the 1680s their place was taken by black Africans for whom the move was anything but voluntary. Two million slaves were shipped to the sugar plantations of Brazil and the West Indies in the course of the century. Between 1670 and 1730 the ratio of whites to blacks on the rich island of Jamaica fell from 1 : 1 to 1 : 10. In the New World as much as the Old we find a competitive individualism, an acquisitive materialism, and an exploitative attitude towards labour which were among the keynotes of early capitalism.

The most important intellectual export from Europe was Christianity (generally Catholicism), imposed or adopted to a greater or lesser extent everywhere the Iberians went. The other enduring legacy of the first two centuries of European expansion was language: Portuguese in Brazil and parts of West Africa, Dutch in Surinam and Java, Spanish in the Philippines and Mexico. Despite—or perhaps because of—the Europeans' arrogance, the peoples of the wider world showed little inclination to accept other aspects of their culture.

Looked at the other way, it is equally striking just how little difference to European outlooks contacts with new peoples made. We can only admire the courage and determination of men like Abel Tasman who discovered Australia in 1644 while looking for a passage from the East Indies to South America for the VOC (*Verenigde Oostindische Compagnie* or Dutch East India Company). Service in some stations was deeply unpopular. So bad were conditions on the northern coast of South America that sailors used to use the phrase 'go to Berbice' in the same way that they would tell someone to 'go to hell'. This makes the determination of those who explored, traded, and settled the New World all the more impressive. The voyage to the East Indies took about eight or nine months but most of those who went signed up for at least five years. An astonishing figure of one million young men left the Netherlands to work for the VOC between *c.*1600 and *c.*1800. An equally remarkable 600,000 died during their tour of duty.

But, whatever their fine qualities, Europeans seem mostly to have dealt with new cultures by ignoring, simplifying, or dehumanizing them. At best, the culturally advanced, commercially adept, and politically sophisticated Chinese and Japanese were granted a grudging respect. Disapproval and contempt were the more normal attitudes. Stereotypes of African culture emerged at this period which have endured until the present day. Richard Hakluyt set the tone in his influential *Principal Navigations* of 1589 by describing negroes as 'a people of beastly living, without a God, law, religion, or common wealth'. Feared and distrusted, black Africans were seen as the antithesis of Europeans in their colour, lack of civilization, sexual immorality, stupidity, brutality, and idleness. The next two centuries of increasing contacts saw the myths founded by Hakluyt and others expanded and reinforced rather than questioned. It is fair to say that the spectacular widening of the geographical horizons of Europeans in the century after 1550 was not paralleled by an opening of their minds.

Nor was tolerance any more apparent within Europe's frontiers. Muslim

and Christian fought at the gates of Vienna in 1683, continuing the battles of centuries. Catholics and Protestants insisted on the exclusive truth of their respective paths to salvation: France's Louis XIV revoked the rights of the minority Protestant Huguenots to worship in 1685 and finally rooted them out of their last stronghold, the mountainous Cévennes, by military force during the early 1700s. Jews were still subject to murderous pogroms in eastern and central Europe. Spain expelled its remaining Moorish or Morisco population between 1608 and 1614. Western European culture influenced small numbers of the Polish and Russian élites (who used French or German to distinguish themselves from the Slav-speaking masses) but otherwise its effect was only superficial. There were no printing presses in Russia until two centuries after Gutenberg. The idea of individual ownership of goods was subordinated to that of a family or community interest. Europeans traded and warred with the Ottomans but beyond a few borrowed objects there was no real interchange of ideas and behaviour. The 'iron curtain' in seventeenth-century Europe was a religious and cultural one: to a degree erected between the Orthodox east and the west but much more so between Christian and Muslim.

Conclusion: A New World Economy?

Attitudes towards those who were different on account of creed or colour was one of many continuities the seventeenth century displayed. There

Pernambuco plantation showing a house and sugar factory with hydraulic mill, grindstones and boilers. Sugar and tobacco were the most important growth products among colonial imports into Europe during the seventeenth century. On the left is the planter's imposing house.

were other links with the past which simply manifested themselves in different ways. British Caribbean pirates were only continuing a long-established tradition of Mediterranean robbery and ransoming by Muslims of Christians; just as the Mediterranean world had possessed its colonies in Africa and the Middle East throughout medieval times; and just as Arabs had for centuries traded in black slaves in the Indian Ocean. The English themselves took over Portugal's flourishing African slave trade in the 1600s. The north Italian city states may have faded as trading powers but Italians (especially Genoese) still numbered among the most eminent financiers in key commercial cities such as Lyons, Marseilles, and Barcelona.

The seventeenth century saw substantial continuities in many areas of economic and social life. But there were also fundamental departures from traditional ways. The economic hub of Europe had shifted irrevocably from the Mediterranean and Germany to the north-west seaboard. At the core of Europe's economy in 1550, Portugal found itself very much on the periphery by 1750. The once great inland trade centres like Leipzig or Nuremberg had become backwaters by 1700 as trade flowed to the thriving Atlantic ports of Bordeaux, Nantes, Bristol, Liverpool, and in the eighteenth century Glasgow and Hamburg. Even mighty Amsterdam was entering a period of stagnation. With the changing economic focus went political leadership and, to a degree, the centre of intellectual and cultural life. Versailles, not Venice, was to be the model for building, literature, and

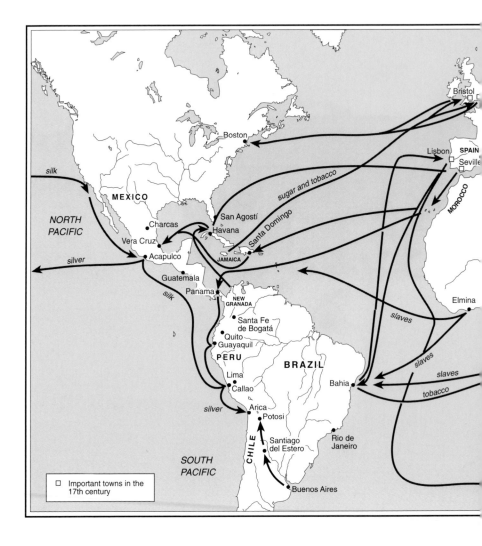

language from the end of the seventeenth century. Wool or undyed woollen cloth remained a significant component of English exports but during the 1700s and 1710s the re-export of colonial goods was growing rapidly.

Clearly, economic progress did not happen overnight. Equally, its pace was not uniform across Europe. To an allegedly 'general' crisis in the first half of the century we can add appalling famines which decimated the populations of France, Scotland, and Scandinavia during the 1690s: shortages which show the limits of agricultural development, transportation, and the administration of social welfare. Towns helped to modernize the economies of north-western Europe but they had little effect on Iberian or

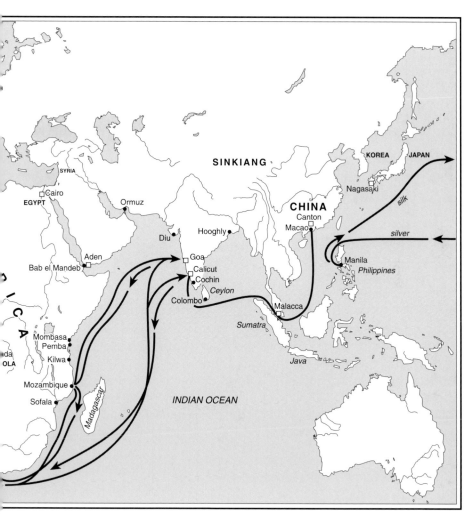

WORLD TRADE ROUTES IN THE SEVENTEENTH CENTURY

Russian agriculture, trade, and industry. Involvement in European or world commerce was a social solvent in England and the Netherlands but involved a hardening of traditional relationships east of the Elbe. At every turn, the extent of economic change was influenced by existing social forms, cultural priorities, and political structures. Its effects were also contingent. Trade was important in creating the wealth necessary to patronize the arts but other influences such as a court or foreign embassies were needed because while Amsterdam was an important centre for painting during the seventeenth century Rotterdam, the second port of the Dutch Republic, was not.

The paths to progress also differed. The Dutch succeeded by dominating the commerce and shipping of northern Europe and then expanding into the Far East. Yet they were eclipsed after the 1650s by English expansion of the Atlantic trade based primarily on colonies. At the other end of the spectrum the reasons for failure were depressingly similar: high production costs; inadequate transportation; extreme wealth polarization and heavy-handed political intervention which inhibited rather than facilitated economic change. Poor economic performance had deep-rooted social causes and long-lasting consequences. The dismal economic showing of the rural south and east of Europe was, for example, associated with profound illiteracy until far into the nineteenth century.

Incomplete as it was even in 1700, the development of a truly European economy had progressed during the century. From being a conglomeration of parcellized regional economies, continent-wide exchanges of grain and of certain raw materials and manufactures helped to create a more unified entity. A rudimentary 'world economy' was also in the making, founded on trade in 'groceries' and semi-durable goods—and human beings. The mercantilist assumption of a 'fixed cake' was becoming outdated by new products and new markets. Ideas of intervention and stasis were being replaced by laissez-faire and dynamic growth. There was still a long way to go before technological change broke down the barriers within traditional economies and made possible two centuries of exponential growth. But the stage was set for agricultural, industrial, and commercial revolutions which would utterly transform the world.

5

Embattled Faiths: Religion and Natural Philosophy in the Seventeenth Century

ROBIN BRIGGS

Intellectual life in the seventeenth century was not confined to the religious and scientific spheres, yet in different ways these were the most dynamic or dominant elements, and virtually all other forms of thought were closely related to them. Religion and science were not distinct entities in the seventeenth century, nor were they widely seen as being in direct conflict. Knowledge of the natural world was also knowledge about the divine purpose. Nearly all the major intellectual figures who contributed to the 'scientific revolution' did so in a distinctly religious spirit, while numerous clerics were strong supporters of the new science. In many respects religious and scientific thought were indeed developing along parallel tracks, supporting rather than hindering one another much of the time. Both were powerfully impelled by a sense that reform was at once necessary and possible; this was arguably as true of the Catholic Church as it was of the Protestant denominations. Although there were some resounding clashes over the respective significance of scriptural and experimental evidence, on closer examination these were always very complex affairs, with the opposing positions far more nuanced than is apparent at first glance. This is hardly surprising, for most of the contestants were very sophisticated thinkers, whose shared culture was based on an intensive educational system. Just because their categories and concepts may seem strange to modern eyes, we should not underestimate the virtuosity with which they deployed them.

The Legacy of Renaissance and Reformation

The sixteenth century had been an exceptionally creative period, whose legacy was a rich yet confusing one. The Reformation and the new discoveries overseas were merely the most spectacular manifestations of this fertility. A whole range of new ideas had entered the intellectual bloodstream of Europe. Genuine innovations such as those of Paracelsus, Copernicus, and Vesalius were probably less important, in the short run at least, than the reappearance of so many challenging writings from antiquity. The apparently timeless scholastic Aristotelianism of the Middle Ages might survive in the official curriculum, but only by absorbing a range of other doctrines which undermined it from within. Europe had rediscovered its own intellectual history, in a profoundly subversive way. What gave this process such exceptional force was a simultaneous revolution in the means of transmission. The advent of printing combined with a huge expansion of educational facilities to create a literate public and a market place for ideas on a quite new scale. The media and the messages merged into a tidal wave of concepts and information, which swept away those modest control systems which had previously seemed quite effective. The ruling élites, far from joining forces to defend the old orthodoxy, at first proved highly susceptible to the seductive charms of the new approaches. For the most part they saw these less as a threat than as potential sources of wealth and power. Although outright religious innovation, with its obvious threat to the established order, might rapidly polarize opinion, other major intellectual shifts aroused far less opposition.

The result was a ferment of ideas, many of them highly speculative or fanciful. The world was interpreted in multiple fashions, with significance being wrested from some very unlikely material. The tone might be literally apocalyptic, as it had been with large numbers of early Protestants, for whom the Reformation heralded the fall of the papal Antichrist and the Second Coming. Repeated disappointments were far from having destroyed this millenarian enthusiasm by the early decades of the seventeenth century. Meanwhile Neoplatonism, alchemy, astrology, hermeticism and their like flourished, at least as strongly in Catholic courts and intellectual circles as anywhere else. Religious conservatism did not carry any clear implication of narrow orthodoxy on other fronts. Such doctrines made much play with the images of secret or occult knowledge, accessible only to the initiated, and widely thought to have been lost since earliest times. There had allegedly been a *prisca theologia* or ancient learning; even partial recovery of these arcane mysteries would endow mankind with powers to control the natural world and predict the future. Such ideas can also be seen as evidence for the continuing domination of theory over facts; intellectuals used the latter to support preformed concepts rather than to test them, so that referential accuracy was still low on most people's scale of values. The world was widely construed in terms of balances and harmonies, so that the health of both individuals and societies could only be assured if these were maintained. At the same time monsters and prodigies were regarded as peculiarly important, with their very abnormality carrying significant messages. For most thinkers of the time change for the better usually implied a return to an allegedly superior past, through the removal of corrupting elements. A significant minority, however, were coming to see their own civilization in more positive terms; among them were some remarkably talented advocates of economic and technological advance, full of ideas about new machines, agricultural practices, and so forth.

These concerns emerged in different ways, from ambitious encyclopedic projects trying to organize knowledge meaningfully to sensational pamphlets aimed at a quick profit. Some historians have argued that an occult philosophy had permeated European thought, constituting the necessary basis for the development of a truly modern natural science. However dubious the immediate claims to manipulate nature, some of the techniques and aspirations were forerunners, they would claim, of those which later proved so fruitful. Others object that the whole occultist approach was so flawed that it was more an obstacle than a help. An excessive reliance on arguments by analogy, speculative theorizing, and inherited error made it an intellectual regression rather than an advance, from which delivery could not come too quickly. Even a brief glance at individuals suggests, unsurprisingly, that both positions are far too extreme. The great astronomer Johannes Kepler was also a practising (yet sceptical) astrologer; he was driven by an almost mystical fascination with celestial harmonies. On the other hand, he displayed a remarkably tough mathematical approach, relied on direct observation for his data, and ruthlessly identified the English natural philosopher Robert Fludd as a pretentious windbag. Many other leading figures display similar ambivalence; Francis Bacon, who has often been claimed as the standard-bearer of a new rationalist mode of scientific proof, also turns out on closer inspection to have been much influenced by the magical tradition. In the end modern distinctions between hard science and occultist nonsense are almost impossible to apply until late in the seventeenth century.

It remains likely that the ultimate effect of the multiple world systems on offer was positive, because their very incompatibilities invited further debate. In the end the new science would very largely define itself by opposition to older views, whether these were Aristotelian or occultist. This does not imply a generally negative relationship, however, because these critiques necessarily originated within the very systems they attacked. In this they resembled religious unorthodoxy and even outright atheism, threats which generally worried clerics far more than any perceived challenge from scientific thinking.

Religion: Rigour and Reform

These fears must have been increased by the hardening of religious differences across Europe in the aftermath of the first shock of the Reformation. By the beginning of the seventeenth century the Protestant challenge had fairly obviously passed its peak, despite the lingering hopes of some zealots that the Roman Antichrist might still be destroyed. As boundaries became clearer, so the competing faiths geared themselves up for a long and bitter struggle. Their leaders saw this as much in terms of internal discipline and reform as of direct confrontation. Since God was the final arbiter, his hand must surely be with those who pleased him the most, by the scrupulous observance of his commandments. Dissenting opinions and sinful behaviour were therefore doubly offensive, for not only did they threaten local harmony, they also risked provoking some disastrous manifestation of divine anger. Only the truly godly state could have confidence in its security against internal and external enemies.

Religious conflict readily acted, in other words, as a stimulus to repressive, authoritarian versions of Christianity, which aimed to reinforce hierarchy and tradition. Such movements were not merely negative, for they often mobilized great spiritual fervour, and this in turn made them difficult partners for secular rulers. One of the great paradoxes of the whole period was the frequency with which nominally conservative doctrines turned out to have dangerous, even revolutionary, aspects. This was one of the reasons why the apparently promising alliance between Church and state frequently turned sour. Significant numbers of both clerics and laity, in all the major religious denominations, were making a strenuous attempt to live out true Christianity as they understood it. In the process they rejected numerous traditional compromises, recognized only absolute moral standards, and tried to extend the sacred into all areas of life. These enthusiasts were always a minority, but more tolerant—or perhaps lukewarm—Christians often found it difficult to resist them openly. Scripture, the Church Fathers, and logic itself appeared to be on their side. Their ultimate aim was to turn passive Christians into active ones, who did not just participate in ritual activities stage-managed by others, but internalized the faith as a moral code and a way of living. Conversion and a change of life were key concepts here, built around the inspirational power of the word. Preaching and religious writing were to carry the message round Europe, where missionaries were just as necessary as they were in heathen lands beyond the seas. Popular ignorance, superstition, and sinfulness were great enemies to be overcome. To the credit of the reformers, many also saw the greed, ostentation, and worldliness of the rich as comparable problems.

This great project for religious reform naturally came in different forms, and was always mixed with other elements. Nevertheless, it was largely shared by Catholics and Protestants, for the post-Tridentine Catholic Church had mounted a formidable counter-attack on the Reformation, which aimed to compete on the same terrain. Without fully realizing it, the churches were setting out to revise or even destroy most of the subtle understandings and compromises on which European Christianity had functioned for many centuries. The much-repeated call for a return to the values of the primitive church implied a radical condemnation of much of what had happened since. In principle at least the standards for true membership of the Church were being raised abruptly, to levels which only a devout minority could really hope to attain. The obvious corollary, that the elect were few and the reprobate many, was widely drawn, even by Catholics. Another shared view was that the failings of the medieval Church had one fundamental cause, the corruption of the clergy; the people had been led astray less by their own innate failings, it was supposed, than by those of their spiritual leaders. This rather simplistic notion had great attractions, because it suggested that once the clergy had been reformed one might expect a transformation in religious life more generally. Across Europe a slow and expensive development of colleges, academies, and seminaries made it possible for the clergy to receive the necessary education, so that professionally trained pastors gradually replaced the older generation who had learned their trade mainly through the traditional mode of apprenticeship on the job. Remarkable successes were achieved in this first stage; disillusionment rapidly followed, however, as the scale and intractability of the broader enterprise became apparent at parish level. Over the course of the seventeenth century the devout were to suffer a whole series of crippling defeats, yet the aspirations and the style they had set would remain deeply influential.

Ultimately this type of reforming Christianity tended to fragment as much as it united. The closer the bonding between the enthusiasts, the sharper the divisions between them and their opponents; the practice of defining oneself against the 'other' was much in evidence here. Internal splits could be ferocious, or lead to such paradoxical results as were seen in the Dutch Republic, where a highly disciplined and exclusive Calvinist Church had to accept the civic toleration favoured by the magistrates. On the international scene confessional tensions remained high, for despite the similarities between the creeds they continued to regard one another as mortal enemies, while as churches became more national this hostility might be reinforced by xenophobia. Different countries vied for the position of the 'elect nation' specially favoured by God. Notions of this kind might intermesh with the general belief that human history was following a predetermined pattern, dictated by divine will. Millenarian and eschatological visions were one possible outcome, perhaps based on the idea that once the fixed number of the elect had been completed the Last Days would begin. None of these beliefs was stable or universal, which makes it impossible to measure their influence accurately, but they were certainly very pervasive. There were some obvious motives for rulers to associate themselves with religious reform, which offered a boost to their power and prestige, and a means to trump potential critics. On the other hand, it was scarcely possible to conduct either foreign or domestic policy on strictly devout lines, for in most cases these required compromises with a range of allies and interest groups. Even the kings of Spain, who found it easier than almost any of their rivals to match (Catholic) orthodoxy with perceived self-interest, could not resist occasional underhand help to the French Protestants.

Religious Motives in Politics and War

The mingling of secular and religious motives was so widespread that it creates great difficulties for modern interpreters of the period. There is a constant temptation to expose the realpolitik behind virtually every decision, then treat the religious elements as little more than a sham, a cynical attempt to cover up the brutal self-interest which was the real driving force. The French government did indeed go to great lengths at the time to present Spanish policies in this light, with the Catholic cause allegedly misused as the cloak for the true design of European domination. In his famous *History of the Council of Trent* the Servite friar Paolo Sarpi, defender of Venetian liberties, shaped an ostensibly dispassionate narrative into a biting analysis of the political cynicism behind the Council's decisions. Yet this type of reductionism risks being wildly misleading when applied uncritically. Religious belief and allegiance were immensely powerful forces in their own right, possessing a durability and strength in depth far exceeding that of merely pragmatic alliances. Among the rulers of the first half of the seventeenth century, moreover, we find an extraordinary number whose personal piety carried over into their policies. Philip IV, Louis XIII, Emperor Ferdinand II, Gustavus Adolphus, James VI and I, Charles I, Maximilian of Bavaria; these were the men at the heart of European affairs for two or three vital decades. The dominant statesmen of the period, Olivares, Richelieu, and Oxenstierna, are equally incomprehensible in purely secular terms. We have to understand how such men did twist religious ideas to suit themselves, while remaining aware that such manipulation could only take place within strict limits, and at a largely unconscious level. Where the Catholic rulers were concerned, one corollary was a great rise in the political influence of the royal confessor.

The great conflict which enveloped Europe after 1618, the Thirty Years War, was at once a war of religion and a struggle for power. In fact virtually all participants were drawn into the war unwillingly, and with the possible exception of the Elector Palatine Frederick V their initial concerns were defensive. A sequence of unlikely events allowed the Catholic forces to overcome a seemingly impregnable Protestant ascendancy in Germany, to the point where normally cautious Habsburg ministers in Madrid, Vienna, and Brussels could briefly dream of a spectacular triumph over the heretics. In 1628, with Wallenstein's troops on the Baltic coast, the divided and irresolute Protestant powers had reason to fear the worst; memories of this appalling crisis would linger for decades. No doubt the threat was not what it seemed, for if Wallenstein could not even take the city of Stralsund, Spanish hopes that he might implement their Baltic plan and strangle the Dutch economy were hardly realistic. The Emperor and his generalissimo were probably unenthusiastic about such schemes anyway, for each of them had his own agenda. As usual their opponents saw deep-laid plots and coherent strategies where there was really only opportunism and growing division. The nearer the unwieldy Catholic coalition came to winning the war, the more fissures appeared within its ranks, and the more blunders its members perpetrated. One of these deserves mention, for it was an extreme case of religious commitment overriding political prudence. Ferdinand II, under the influence of his Jesuit entourage, pushed through the 1629 Edict of Restitution, which would have restored great tracts of confiscated land to the Church. At a blow he destroyed all hope of a viable settlement within the empire, just as fortune turned against the Habsburgs and their allies on a grand scale.

Dragonnades (forcible billeting of troops and harassment) against Huguenots in the reign
of Louis XIV. Such images of military brutality employed to force conversions to Catholicism became a staple of Protestant anti-French propaganda. Although the artists drew on
conventional ways of portraying the horrors of war, and should not be taken as offering a
literal record, the persecution was real enough. It shocked many Catholics and displeased
the Pope.

Within a few years the position had been transformed. When the 'Lion
of the North', the Protestant champion Gustavus Adolphus of Sweden, fell
in battle at Lützen in December 1632 his victories had already shattered the
Imperial position beyond hope of repair. Meanwhile the Dutch had
resumed the offensive in the Netherlands, as Spanish resources dwindled
and the southern provinces threatened revolt. From this point the idea of a
forcible religious reunification of Europe was effectively dead. This did not
of course mean that future conflicts lacked a religious dimension. The
French wars with the Dutch after 1672, and then also with the British from
1689, aroused new and intense fears of this kind. The Revocation of the
Edict of Nantes in 1685, with the related diaspora of French Protestants in
exile, caused former French allies such as the Elector of Brandenburg-
Prussia to change sides. At an earlier stage the English Republicans had
conceived the project of formal union with the Dutch to form a new Protestant superpower, only to make war on their intended partners when this
bizarre offer was rejected. What must be admitted is that over the century
alliances between Protestant and Catholic states became relatively routine
events, which no longer aroused the same level of anxiety as they had earlier done. However unwillingly or unconsciously, most people were com-

ing to accept that confessional boundaries were there to stay. There are no real parallels in the second half of the century for the forcible Catholicization of Bohemia after the 1618 revolt; the attempted elimination of the Protestant minority in France by Louis XIV was a very different affair, causing some disquiet to foreign Catholic observers, including the Pope himself. The occasional German princes who changed their faith after 1648 would find it politic to abandon any claim that their subjects ought to follow them.

Although Catholic and Protestant groupings may have possessed some reality earlier in the century, one hugely complicating factor had been the attitude taken by France. Her hostility to Spain and the Habsburg powers more generally was so long-standing, so deeply incorporated in political rivalries across much of Europe, that the occasional truce or royal marriage did little to soften it; one of its aspects was a constant battle for influence in the papal Curia, so that religious authority itself became entangled in the conflict. French kings had traditionally allied themselves with German and Dutch Protestants, and even gone to the lengths of making treaties with the Ottomans, who were infidels, not just heretics. By the seventeenth century this last practice had become more or less obsolete, as Ottoman power waned; the Thirty Years War, on the other hand, saw France drawn into acting as the mastermind of the anti-Habsburg coalitions. This did create serious internal debate, with a powerful dévot faction opposing the policies of a first minister who was also a cardinal. As an even more curious detail, Richelieu's chief adviser on foreign policy was the Capuchin Father Joseph du Tremblay, a man of great austerity and piety who was obsessed with the need to restore Christian unity in order to mount a new crusade against the Muslims, and regarded Habsburg secular ambitions as the great obstacle to his designs. The ministry also mounted an extremely shrewd (if disingenuous) public defence, harping on Spanish iniquity and perfidy, while trying hard to limit any unwelcome religious consequences of its policies. This apparently anomalous case can actually be used as evidence for how seriously the religious dimension of both foreign and domestic affairs was taken in this period.

Dogma, Faith, and Society

The highly charged atmosphere of the early seventeenth century predictably generated numerous signs of tension within the creeds as well as between them. Bitter quarrels repeatedly broke out over the crucial question of the terms for salvation, as the ancient dispute between St Augustine and the Pelagians was renewed. On the Catholic side the papacy struggled to preserve a compromise by refusing to pronounce on some of the central issues, while enforcing silence on the disputants. This policy of sensible moderation lasted rather longer than might have been expected, but in the end the pressure was simply too great, and from the 1640s the Augustinian views of Cornelius Jansen and his followers were furiously debated.

Between November 1618 and June 1619, 31 Dutch and 28 foreign Calvinist theologians met in the town of Dordrecht. Their main business was to condemn the Remonstrant minority who followed the more liberal doctrines of Arminius (over 150 ministers subsequently lost their positions), but they also dealt with other business, such as commissioning an official Dutch translation of the Bible.

Among the Protestants the Calvinist orthodoxy on predestination and free will was challenged by the Dutch theologian Arminius, whose views found much support in England as well as in his native Holland. At the Synod of Dort in 1618–19 the Dutch Reformed Church reaffirmed its hardline Calvinism, with the assistance of numerous foreign divines, but this proved a pyrrhic victory. Such exclusivism made it impossible for the Church to extend its base in Dutch society, so it had to remain a minority state Church within a remarkably tolerant nation. In England the disputes over theology, ceremonies, and discipline were to prove exceptionally divisive. It remains unclear how far this should be attributed to the ineptitude of Charles I and Archbishop Laud, whose heavy-handed tactics did much to convert isolated opponents into a national resistance movement. Whatever its manifold other causes, the 'English Revolution' is unimaginable without the powerful religious dynamic that made civil war possible. The explosion of sectarian enthusiasm which followed—from Diggers, Baptists, Quakers, and their like—was an extraordinary demonstration of the vitality and diversity latent within Christianity at the popular level. Any idea that conformity and orthodoxy could be inculcated through the Bible and the catechism could hardly withstand this practical evidence to the contrary.

The effects of the Civil War were of course paradoxical. The zealots and the radicals might have terrified polite society, but they had also exposed their own disunity and proved unable to carry the nation with them. The Restoration monarchy tried to put the clock back through coercion, only to find that all available instruments broke against the sheer obduracy of the Dissenters; after 1688 it was plain that Anglican hegemony could only be sustained at the price of limited toleration. In their different ways the Dutch and the English had both been forced to abandon the heady visions of a 'godly nation' based on a single communion, to fall back on a civil society which guaranteed certain basic rights to all, even if religious discrimination still operated within it. Religious attitudes gradually began to change, even among the devout, so that by the end of the century many Dissenters seemed as distrustful of 'enthusiasm' as their orthodox neighbours. They were less interested in theological issues than in the past, placing the main emphasis on godly living and loyalty to the religious community. If God's providence was still seen as active all around them, it was in very individual or local forms, and had lost its wider Millenarian implications. Much Protestant spirituality had of course always been of this type. Regular fasts, linked with prayer sessions and preaching, had been a central feature, alongside the ideal of the godly household. The power of this faith should never be underestimated; quite apart from its political manifestations, it dominated many people's lives in a more internalized fashion. The spiritual diaries, correspondence, and pious literature of the time testify to the intensity of their experience. Introspection and self-examination could lead to violent crises, when the believer was overwhelmed by a sense of personal inadequacy and doubted his or her salvation. For most, however, belief seems to have triumphed in the end, allowing them to achieve great fortitude in the ultimate test, and make that 'good death' which was widely held to be a sign of election. When the Essex clergyman Ralph Josselin was thinking about the deaths of his son and a close friend in 1650, he wrote in his diary:

My heart trembled, and was perplexed in the dealings of the Lord so sadly with us, and desiring God not to proceed on against us with his darts and arrows; looking back into my ways, and observing why God hath thus dealt with me, the Lord followed me with that, 'sin no more, lest a worse thing happen unto thee'; and the intimation of God was that he would proceed no further against me or mine, and he would assist me with his grace if I clave to him with a full purpose of heart, which I resolve; oh my God help me, oh my God fail me not! For in thee do I put my trust.

This curious yet moving blend of perplexity, guilt, and consolation takes us somewhere near the heart of seventeenth-century religion, as it was experienced by the devout within all denominations.

Intense feelings of this kind are as likely to be found among members of the 'mainstream' Protestant confessions as among the sectaries, although clearly any national Church included many lukewarm or nominal Christians. In large parts of Germany and Scandinavia there was a high degree of unity within state boundaries, with the secular and religious authorities combining to enforce moral discipline. Here too the trend was towards a more inward-looking faith, whose radical tendencies had been largely subsumed into a drive for conformity. One should be cautious about interpreting this as evidence for declining commitment, however; it might equally well be seen as the development of more realistic and effective positions. Catholic Europe moved in similar directions, as the élites were increasingly attracted by self-consciously polite lifestyles, with an emphasis on orderliness and decorum. There were, nevertheless, important differences between the major confessions. The reformed churches, through their massive simplification of church structures, had made it much easier for their pastors to teach unified and potentially revolutionary doctrines. Despite its initial appeal to the laity, Protestantism rapidly evolved into a new and highly demanding form of clericalism, whose rigid doctrines and intense moralism were ill-suited to win general support. In the face of widespread passive resistance the clergy were simply too few and isolated to make much progress. Where they could muster serious lay support, either from the rulers or from systems of consistories and elders, the discipline might be enforced with a fair degree of success. In such circumstances, and in smaller sectarian groups, great fervour might be generated, but usually at the cost of isolating the godly from the mass of the population.

The Catholic Church, on the other hand, had preserved its complex internal structures, which the Council of Trent had merely sought to bring under better control by enhancing the authority of the Pope and the bishops. Although it took considerably longer for reform to gather momentum within this elaborate and cumbrous system, there were some significant advantages in terms of manpower and flexibility. The dynamic expansion of new orders such as Jesuits, Capuchins, and Oratorians, alongside revitalized older ones, gave the Counter-Reformation most of its initial drive. They also staffed many of the seminaries and colleges which sprang up to train the secular clergy, and to provide education for the élites more generally. Feminine orders made their own major contribution to teaching and to nursing the sick. A great wealth of overlapping agencies characterized the Catholic Reform, arguably giving it an institutional strength in depth which its Protestant counterpart could not match. There were of course corresponding drawbacks; jealousies and rivalries proliferated, while the divide between clergy and laity was often emphasized. If a new determination to impose true celibacy responded to many long-standing complaints, it simultaneously erected another barrier between clerics and the surrounding world. A hostile view of the family and of kinship loyalties as enemies of true spirituality was one of the rather unexpected consequences, although the influence of such austere doctrines is hard to measure accurately. Another striking feature was a persistent mistrust of the various lay associations which made a vital contribution to the texture of ordinary religious life. Whether the agencies were confraternities, charitable organizations, or groups of moral reformers, they had to battle against this deep-seated suspicion on the part of the hierarchy. Many kinds of fervour and involvement were therefore discouraged, at least in principle, primarily because they were thought to contain the seeds of possible deviance.

There are serious dangers in taking such analyses too far, because the formal positions taken by theologians and canon lawyers can be very misleading as a guide to reality at parish level. In practice many of the clergy continued to offer their parishioners the religious services they wanted, without paying too much attention to the formal rules. Those who tried to be more rigorous might find that the bishops preferred to compromise when local protest ensued. Whatever systems of control were established, they always remained vulnerable to local silence and complicity. There was also something very ambiguous about the great campaigns for moral reform. Were they genuinely seeking to release a new wave of spiritual energy, or were they primarily a drive for greater social control, which would keep the unruly lower orders in their place? While the former may often have been the intention, there was a constant danger of slipping towards the latter. This was all the easier because most contemporaries would have seen the two aspects as being natural partners, and thought there was every reason to pursue them simultaneously. In the end one may actually doubt how far the élites (a relative handful of zealots and missionaries apart) really wished to see the general population turned into pious active Christians in the new style. Ignorance, superstition, and ungodly living had their own place in the scheme of things. They provided justification for the rule of the few over the many, while reassuring the educated and sophisticated that only they passed the first test for divine election. The widespread insistence on a proper knowledge of Christian doctrine as the basis for true membership of the Church might be seen as a filter of this kind. It is noticeable that only for a few decades after the Revocation of the Edict of Nantes in 1685 did the French political and religious authorities make a serious attempt to move towards general elementary education—as a means to ensure orthodoxy among the new converts. As this issue lost its urgency, so did enthusiasm for schooling.

More generally, the attempt to assert the primacy of Christian ethics was dangerous as well as over-ambitious. The churches were drawn into endless compromises and difficulties, so that instead of sacred values coming to prevail over secular ones, as the reformers intended, a paradoxical reversal occurred. Through their own efforts to apply their doctrines rationally, they became to a considerable degree the unwitting agencies of secularization. The idea that the whole of life must be lived as a kind of willing servitude to God obliged them to take positions on everything, from childcare to business ethics, taxation, and international relations. In effect the tacit understanding that there was a boundary between the sacred and the secular spheres was being challenged, without any recognition of the problems that would ensue. Supposedly absolute rules were brought into much closer and more extensive contact with messy realities, conflicts of interest, and human passions. In the end it was inevitable that the rules themselves would have to bend, while their whole basis might ultimately be challenged. The furious arguments about the atheistical implications of particular theological positions show that some contemporaries did have intimations about these trends, but no one at this time could or did appreciate their deeper significance.

One of the most confusing and difficult areas in which to assess the impact of religious change is that concerned with familial and gender relations. It used to be thought that Protestantism, with its abolition of clerical celibacy and its stress on the godly household, had nurtured a more companionate vision of marriage. Recent work has questioned this view, pointing to the traditional sources of most writing about the household, the renewed emphasis on patriarchal authority, and the failure of disciplinary bodies to take effective action against abusive or philandering husbands. The theoretical equality of believers before God looks a rather feeble sop in comparison. On the Catholic side the multiple activities of feminine religious orders and the devotion to the Virgin Mary can plausibly be seen as offering opportunities and consolation to women. Here the downside is the very hostile view of the family evident in nearly all religious writing, and the *cordon sanitaire* which came to surround a clergy which tried so hard to repress its own sexuality. Despite all the qualifications, there was a sense in which religion did retain a special capacity to empower women, even if mystics and deviants who spoke out of turn were usually harshly treated. Christian teachings could be employed to defend women's rights on earth as well as in heaven, while perhaps only fervent belief was likely to give individual women the courage necessary to attack the whole structure of male domination. On a limited scale at first, the challenge which had been implicit in later medieval feminine piety might now become explicit.

On the whole the feminine piety of the age was far more conformist, turning as it so often did towards mysticism and self-abasement. As one reforming French nun, Charlotte Le Sergent, put it, 'I only know that all that is performed by his creatures is nothing but impurity, so that God is obliged to glorify himself.' She thought that the human spirit was always liable to slide into self-esteem—'if the soul wishes to act of its own volition, it opposes its base and lowly action to that of God. This inclination to act is a residue of past actions which one must destroy and make flow into God in order to give the abandoned soul over to him.' It is interesting, however, to note that this was advice given by a devout woman to a man, while abandoning oneself blindly to God might lead to the kind of behaviour which discredited later mystics like Mme Guyon. Such faith certainly enabled pious women to bear great hardships and exercise astonishing self-control. Mary Rich, countess of Warwick, had lost her children, then had to watch her much-loved husband dying slowly in terrible pain, which often

The painter Philippe de Champaigne, who painted this austere and powerful 1643 portrait of Marie-Angélique Arnauld, abbess of Port-Royal, was himself a Jansenist whose daughters were educated in the famous schools run by the nuns. The buildings in the background would be systematically destroyed on the orders of Louis XIV in 1710–11, causing widespread outrage.

made him very unkind to her. At times she thought the Devil was tempting her to blame God for his cruelty, but her diary records how she repeatedly transformed such feelings into remorse, praying 'that it [remorse] may turn all my sorrow into the right channel, that my tears may no more be poured out for my friend's ill usage of me but . . . for my crimson sins against thy constant and unmerited goodness to me.' She consoled herself with meditations on 'love to Christ's person', reminding herself that 'Heaven would make amends for all my troubles' and that her 'afflictions would work an exceeding greater weight of glory'. Evidence for the humble and unlettered is harder to find, but there is Bunyan's touching account of overhearing 'three or four poor women sitting at a door in the sun', who

talked how God had visited their souls with his love in the Lord Jesus, and with what words and promises they had been refreshed, comforted and supported against the temptations of the devil . . . And methought they spake as if joy did make them speak; they spake with such pleasantness of Scripture language, and with such appearance of grace in all they said, they were to me as if they had found a new world.

Only the most blinkered reformers could afford to ignore feminine concerns, when women so often showed themselves more pious than their menfolk. By the end of the seventeenth century some male observers at least were coming to doubt those general beliefs in women's inferiority and sexual fallibility around which the case for their subjection had been constructed; it seems probable that their religious performance had much to do with these first intimations of change. Where actual treatment of women is concerned, however, there continued to be important differences by region and social class, which appear to reflect long-standing traditions more than doctrinal allegiance.

The Decline of the Devil

Ideas about women's moral and intellectual weakness reappear in a very unpleasant fashion in one specific area, that of witchcraft persecution. This phenomenon has been grossly misunderstood by those who have seen it as a deliberate campaign led by Church and state against female healers, midwives, or followers of ancient pagan cults. In fact most suspects were accused by their neighbours, not by sadistic witch-hunters, while many of the accusers were themselves women, and around a quarter of those convicted were men. Belief in malevolent witchcraft was general among the peasants and artisans of the time, and should be regarded as an independent social reality, however erroneous the thinking behind it may have been. At its core lay the explanation of misfortune as the result of envy and ill-will, with the associated idea that thoughts can harm or kill. These traditional notions linked up with the growing emphasis on the power and ubiquity of the Devil, to encourage belief in an anti-religion dedicated to worshipping the Devil and subverting the community. It was therefore predictable that the main purpose of the imaginary witches' sabbats should have been to damage the crops; this was a simple inversion of the normal purposes of local rituals, designed to protect fertility. Persecution was only possible because governments, lawyers, and clerics took these imaginings seriously, so it was clearly related to the febrile religious climate of the age. On the other hand, there was always considerable doubt and uncertainty about how best to proceed. Reactions varied enormously, from the witch-hunts instigated by some Catholic prince-bishops in Germany around 1630, or encouraged by the Presbyterian Kirk in Scotland on several occasions, to the outright scepticism which rapidly developed in the Italian and Spanish Inquisitions. The same divisions are apparent at an individual level, with some clerics acting as witch-doctors or helping to organize persecution, while others defended suspects they saw as innocent victims.

The Scottish case shows how the ideal of a godly state might encourage witch-hunting, but wider European experience disproves any necessary connection. The most powerful states of the time—France, Spain, and England—were characterized by official caution and low rates of both persecution and executions. Endemic witch-hunting over several decades occurred almost exclusively in weak states, where local courts or even forms of lynch law could take charge of the process. By the middle decades of the century an abrupt decline in persecution was apparent almost everywhere in western Europe. Although there were still some local outbreaks, and groups of vocal would-be persecutors, polite opinion had moved decisively against practices which were seen as founded on popular superstition and ignorance. There was also great anxiety about miscarriages of justice, made more acute by the growing role played by children as accusers. Few people denied that there might be witches, yet many had come to think that attempts to punish them were futile or dangerous, and might do no more than play the Devil's game. Some shrewd observers noted that persecution merely encouraged popular beliefs, so that witches multiplied where they were most severely treated. In the end it was probably the linked fears of contamination by superstition and allowing justice to be perverted by popular action which did most to end this tragic episode.

The Devil too was slowly going out of fashion. Whatever theological subtleties they employed to avoid outright Manicheism, both Protestants and Catholics had originally espoused a dramatic view of the world as riven by a cosmic struggle between good and evil. On the one hand Catholic doctrines of the real presence were regarded as diabolical, images of saints became graven idols worshipped as gods, and the Pope was Antichrist himself. On the other both Luther and Calvin were denounced as agents of the Devil, while their followers were supposedly fit only for extermination. Ascetic leaders of both creeds agreed that the conventional religion of ordinary people, with its protective rituals, spells, and magical practices, amounted to trading with the Devil; all such activities supposedly involved an implicit pact with the great enemy. Again it was the middle decades of the seventeenth century which saw a subtle yet perceptible change in this rhetoric, with sin envisaged more as the result of specifically human and social weaknesses. Other people were now the primary source of danger, to such an extent that some moralists advocated an almost total withdrawal from the world and a renunciation of human society. Meanwhile groups of zealots launched repeated campaigns against prostitution, gambling, theatres, low-cut dresses, and other manifestations of sinfulness. Success in these endeavours was predictably limited and temporary at best, while charges of hypocrisy and self-interest became routine. Although stories about divine judgements on blasphemers, adulterers, and their like did not disappear, this was another genre to suffer from a process of banalization and marginalization.

Reason and the 'Crisis of Conscience'

Such changes, alongside the freethinking and worldliness of many eighteenth-century intellectuals, have tempted historians into identifying a 'crisis of conscience' around the end of the seventeenth century. Internal contradictions and the impact of growing scientific knowledge were allegedly bringing the whole basis of orthodox Christianity into question. The 'pre-Enlightenment' of Spinoza, Bayle, Locke, and Leibniz is thus seen to lead into the much greater and more radical movement of the eighteenth-century Enlightenment. In purely intellectual terms much of this story is convincing. We can trace a growing scepticism about hell and eternal torment, while atheistical arguments were patiently elaborated by clerics whose own immediate concern was to demolish them. Both the intellectual leaders among the clergy and the natural philosophers were often deeply concerned about the religious implications of new mechanistic theories of the universe, many of whose dangers they did to some extent anticipate. In

the very long run these fears were indeed justified; scientific and technological advance has transformed human life and ideas more radically than any
seventeenth-century prophet could have imagined. Knowledge really is
power, as Bacon said it was; it also turns out to be corrosive of all fixed systems and moral absolutes. Historians who have been born into such a world
have enormous difficulties in dealing with its antecedents. In almost everything we write about the past we naturally select out those 'modernizing'
and 'progressive' factors which we believe to have contributed to the making of our own very peculiar and exceptional situation. The great risks are
those of distortion—grossly exaggerating the significance of marginal tendencies in their own time—and of determinism—supposing that 'good'
ideas were bound to succeed simply through their own inherent merit.

The later seventeenth century is a case in point. There may have been a
lethal time bomb ticking away amidst the most advanced thought of the
epoch, but only a few observers saw matters in such dramatic terms. Anxieties of this kind were usually attached to specific issues, such as particular
views of the nature of God and his relationship to the cosmos, rather than
to a putative subversion of all religion. There was a concern that the primacy of ecclesiastical scholarship might be undermined, and another general worry that any threat to orthodox religion would damage the social
order, supposedly maintained by the belief that even secret sins would
inevitably be punished by an omniscient deity. Meanwhile scientific ideas,
briefly fashionable around the 1660s, later attracted a good deal of criticism, even ridicule, when they failed to deliver either practical benefits or
easily understood major discoveries. While Christian orthodoxy was—as
always—adjusting itself subtly to the spirit of the times, to most observers
the established churches were evidently reinforcing their dominance. If
dissent was tolerated in some areas, it was also marginalized and policed.
As European colonization and trade spread across the world, ideas about
'noble savages' were insignificant beside a huge missionary effort designed
to bring other cultures into the Christian fold. New knowledge about the
natural world was gradually assimilated into a celebration of God's bounty
and wisdom on behalf of his creation, the so-called 'argument from design'
which most educated people would ultimately come to see as a satisfying
union of science and theology (although this trend did not gather its full
force until the early eighteenth century). Moreover this is not to say that
religious thought had become complacent or sterile, for there were still
plenty of violent controversies within the major denominations, which
attracted far more attention than the threat posed by scientific discovery.
Among them we can discern the germs of further surges of enthusiasm

which would mark the next century, through a variety of pietistic and evangelical movements.

The continuing vitality of religion at this period is such that we cannot really argue for anything beyond a series of smaller 'crises of conscience', which were more inherent to the system than a direct threat to its wellbeing. It is only through the generous use of hindsight, and with some huge chronological leaps, that we can link these issues to the long-term fate of religion in the West. There is certainly a Weberian sense in which the 'rational religion' of the later seventeenth century marked a natural development of the internal logic of Christianity, moving towards the 'disenchantment of the world'. At the level of systematic theology, at least, what was being offered was a range of austere moralizing creeds, which encouraged political and social conformity on just about every front. The more highly charged magical and apocalyptic visions of the world had become unfashionable, as they were increasingly identified with popular credulity, and tainted with suspicions of fraud. This process was not uniform across Europe, of course, and an old-fashioned 'magical' intellectual like the Jesuit Anastasius Kircher could retain his prestige at the court of the Habsburg Emperor through the 1660s. Such exceptions formed part of a wider phenomenon, for as Latin slowly gave way to the vernacular tongues, communication across national boundaries could actually become harder.

The Reception and Resumption of the New Science

One of the most important developments of the later seventeenth century was the creation of a network of agencies whose main purpose was to foster interchange and collaboration. Societies and academies, scientific or literary journals, and that elusive wider community known as 'la republique des lettres' were all vital elements in this largely self-defined world of intellectuals. The two most significant creations were the Royal Society and the French Royal Academy of Sciences, which both took shape in the 1660s, but this is more apparent in retrospect than it was at the time. Most of the groups which came into existence were less formal, and often less permanent; they commonly pursued a diverse range of intellectual interests, among which natural history, antiquarianism, and the collection of curiosities were much more prominent than physics or astronomy. This does not really lessen their importance, which lay above all in building up a climate of opinion open to new ideas and intellectual debate. From the 1680s onwards a major contribution was made by the French Protestant exiles, whose international links gave them a special place; to some extent they were following in the paths established by earlier Central European migrants such as Hartlib and Comenius. Several were among those who sought to commercialize scientific knowledge, whether through public lectures and demonstrations or in publications aimed at a more popular market.

The rather artificial disputes of the 1690s over the respective merits of ancient and modern authors were necessarily inconclusive, yet they did allow advocates for the moderns to emphasize the major scientific achievements of the last century. This was no bad thing, for as already suggested, something of the gloss had rubbed off the new science by this time. After a series of spectacular discoveries, a phase of consolidation and uncertainty had set in. If in retrospect the publication of Newton's *Principia* in 1687 now appears as the apogee of the 'scientific revolution', the immediate impact of this masterpiece was relatively muted, not least because of the highly technical form in which Newton chose to present his findings. In England there was enough sense of his importance for others to proffer simplified versions of his work, but for many foreign scholars his central claims proved highly controversial, so that it would take more than forty years for Newtonianism to find any real support in France. To modern eyes the continuities between Newton and his immediate predecessors seem so obvious that resistance of this kind is puzzling; in order to understand it we must go back to the earlier work on which he drew. The great innovations of early modern science can, predictably, be traced back far into the past— not for nothing was Newton himself a great believer in the *Prisca Sapientia* or ancient wisdom, supposedly known to biblical prophets and ancient philosophers, which he saw himself as destined to help recover. One strand was that of the experimental method, something which went beyond the painstaking accumulation of observations about how nature really behaved, rather than was said to behave. For all its virtues, on its own this technique could only lead into the dead end of Baconian induction, since without some directing intelligence it was useless to multiply facts. The vital step was developing a more sophisticated vision of how experiments could be devised to test central propositions about the physical universe.

The practical difficulties here were enormous, when it was hard to measure anything accurately, and the vital element of time could only be calculated in very rough terms. Most of the great discoveries of the time related to two major problems already identified in classical antiquity, the motions of the heavens and those of falling bodies. Aristotelian science had failed ignominiously here; as Thomas Hobbes waspishly remarked about the scholastic theory of gravity, 'So that the cause why things sink downward, is an endeavour to be below: which is as much as to say, that bodies descend, or ascend, because they do.' The Ptolemaic version of planetary motion was avowedly designed to 'save the appearances', without any plausible reason being offered for the wandering paths taken by the planets. These matters had therefore been intensively discussed for many decades; the great advances made by Galileo and Kepler would have been impossible without such predecessors as Copernicus, Tycho Brahe, and the Paduan natural philosophers. This is not to diminish the genius of two daring thinkers, who brought a new level of mathematical rigour and scientific insight to bear on the old problems, to find solutions which were substantially correct. Kepler made the heliocentric system work properly, by establishing that the planets moved in ellipses with the sun at one focus, and adding a second law governing their speed, under which they swept out equal areas of their orbits in equal times. These two laws allowed him to calculate celestial motions with unprecedented elegance and precision. His third law, relating the periods of the planets to their mean distances from the sun, only came into its own within Newton's system.

The reception of Kepler's discoveries was patchy, not least because of the convoluted way he presented them. As early as 1611 the English scientific group led by Thomas Harriott had grasped the significance of the first two laws, however, and by the 1660s the Keplerian astronomy was widely accepted. In contrast Galileo's *Siderius Nuncius* of 1610, with its forceful advocacy of his telescopic observations, was a superb piece of self-promotion. The moons of Jupiter, the phases of Venus, sunspots, and the irregular surface of the moon were used to demonstrate the physical reality of the heliocentric system. This brilliant observational and rhetorical performance deservedly won its author instant celebrity, yet it was not Galileo's most important conceptual achievement. This emerged primarily from his studies on falling bodies and projectiles, leading into the development of the 'mechanical philosophy'. In essence Galileo established mathematical laws for moving bodies, which involved the vital idea that friction, whether from other bodies or the surrounding air, prevented these laws being observable in pure form. He and his disciples went on to elaborate a vision of the world as composed of particles in motion, opening up the possibility that one set of laws could explain both celestial and terrestrial phenomena. Unfortunately Galileo's highly combative style, and his fondness for drawing broader philosophical and even theological conclusions from his work, led to his famous confrontation with the Catholic Church. Several ingenious theories have been advanced to explain his condemnation, which does not in fact seem particularly mysterious. His first trial in 1615–16 was clearly provoked by his own determination to force the issues, and it is hard to see how the theologians could have acted otherwise than they did without abandoning all their established principles. The condemnation was deliberately mild, requiring little more than a show of obedience. The much harsher treatment of 1632–3 followed an act of deliberate defiance, the publication of the *Dialogue on the Two World Systems*, which Pope Urban VIII not unreasonably believed to include open mockery of his own opinions.

Did the trial matter to anyone but the immediate protagonists? We know that Descartes was so alarmed at the news that he delayed publication of some of his work, but his friend Mersenne—a pious Minim friar—would soon go to great lengths to arrange the publication of Galileo's last and greatest work, the *Discourses* (1638). From the start many French Catholics seem to have seen the whole affair as another example of papal perversity, while there is little sign that French scientific thinking was inhibited. The situation in Spain, Italy, and the Austrian Habsburg lands was rather different, for here the Church usually had a firmer grip on the intellectual world, and Roman decisions were regarded with less suspicion. There was no sign of any general move to persecute individuals or groups for holding irregular scientific or philosophical opinions, so long as these were not proclaimed too loudly; on the other hand, free debate was inhibited, while all formal teaching remained very conservative. This might well have been the situation had Galileo never been tried, so perhaps he was right to force the issue, and mainly at fault because he fought his corner so ineptly in political terms. In the end the Catholic Church was left with an embarrassing ruling which it would take a ridiculously long time to rescind; it suffered a good deal of damage to its own credibility, while quite possibly advancing the theories it tried to condemn. There was certainly a serious temptation for Protestants to react by embracing the new philosophy just because the Vatican had condemned it.

Matter and Void: Descartes's System and its Opponents

Whatever worries Descartes may have felt about theological orthodoxy, they did not finally prevent him from giving fresh impetus to the mechanical philosophy, which became increasingly identified with the new science. His audacious attempt to provide a complete model for a new world system, built entirely around the laws of motion and impact, was really no more than a brilliant fiction. On points of detail he was repeatedly wrong, even managing to distort and misapply Harvey's great discovery of the circulation of the blood. Yet there is a sense in which these errors were unimportant, compared with the excitement and stimulus he created. Cartesianism was never a rigid school of thought, for all the significant thinkers who espoused it did so in a distinctly critical spirit; much of its importance was as a model for how a mechanistic world might operate.

Like his friend Hobbes, Descartes carried highly subversive ideas derived from science into the broader philosophical arena. His mechanical philosophy required a radical separation between mind and body, for material objects could not retain inherent qualities of the type previously ascribed to them. The physical world was governed by mathematical rules, not by sympathies, harmonies, and all the other purposive features imagined by both scholastic and occultist thinkers. Ideas were not something inherent to the cosmos; they were products of the human intellect, which had to be modified or discarded if they clashed with observed reality. This subjectivism, which found its most famous expression in the claim 'I think therefore I am', has become such an inherent part of modern thought that it is now hard to recognize just how revolutionary it was when first revealed in the 1630s and 1640s. Descartes had every reason to fear trouble with the Church, when his materialist position had drastic implications for the theory of transubstantiation, and his ontological proof of God's existence scandalized traditional theologians. As it turned out his long residence in the Dutch Republic may have been an excessive precaution, because yet again the French authorities took a relatively liberal attitude, and as a private scholar he ran no serious personal risk. It remains true that the public teaching of Cartesianism was later banned in France, while some overt supporters were excluded from the Academy of Sciences when it was established in 1666. This did not stop the broader aspirations and methods of the new philosophy from exerting enormous influence, when they were developed by such figures as the great Dutch scientist Christian Huygens and the French philosopher Nicolas Malebranche. One should also recognize the less spectacular yet widespread interest in the ideas of Descartes's contemporary and rival Pierre Gassendi. If his modified atomism was less clearly expressed as a system, it was just as challenging and subversive in its implications.

When Descartes defined matter as extension he committed himself to the concept of a densely packed world, in which any void was a logical impossibility. His universe was composed of a great number of interlocking vortices, within which particles spun round, and since motion was conserved, once the system was propelled into action it would run perpetually. The anticipation of some of the key concepts of modern physics is striking, yet there were major objections to this formulation. Above all, the 'subtle matter' which allegedly filled the insterstices between larger particles was really a clever evasion, since it possessed contradictory properties as both matter and a kind of non-matter. The void rapidly became one of the most hotly disputed issues around, partly because two ingenious new experimental techniques were brought into play. The first was the barometric experiment, based on the work of the Italian Toricelli but most effectively publicized by the Frenchman Blaise Pascal. In 1648 Pascal organized a scheme whereby the height of a column of mercury in a tube was compared at the base and the top of the Puy de Dôme in the Auvergne, to demonstrate that the variations related to different air pressures, and that the space in the tube must be a void. Soon the principle of the air pump, originally designed by the German Otto von Guericke, was developed by Robert

Otto von Guericke organized this striking event, observed by the Emperor Ferdinand III, in 1654. The two metal hemispheres, which had been emptied of air, could only be pulled apart by the horses after the vacuum was released. The various public experiments demonstrating the existence of the void played an important part in advertising the potential of the new science.

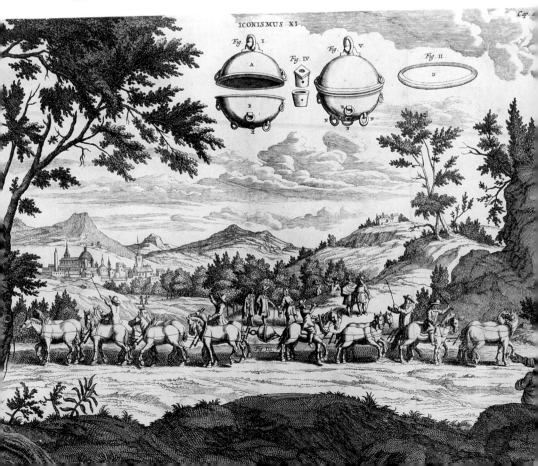

Boyle in England, then taken up by Huygens. This device evacuated the air from a glass receptacle, so that various experiments could take place inside it. Neither experiment was truly conclusive, and indeed neither produced a genuine vacuum, but they did cast grave doubt on this central Cartesian position. Newton's theory of universal attraction, which required bodies to affect one another across an intervening void, went much further, for it directly repudiated some of the central principles on which Descartes had built his system. Here was a universe mostly composed of empty space, in which invisible forces bound together exiguous atomic particles, by means that no one could understand. Attraction at a distance was so repugnant to most mechanical philosophers in Europe that they resisted Newtonianism for decades.

New Instruments and New Sciences

As already pointed out, it was extremely hard to devise convincing experiments; for a few years the air pump was regarded as a great curiosity, becoming one of the routine showpieces of the Royal Society and other scientific organizations. Rather paradoxically, interest waned once commercial models became available to any interested amateur. More generally it has been suggested that there was a particular desire to secure authentication for the new science, by staging public demonstrations witnessed by members of the ruling élites, whose involvement was more important than any purely intellectual argument. On this argument Boyle was a peculiarly valuable asset to the Royal Society because of his status as the son of an earl. There is clearly something in this view, which reminds us of the highly stratified nature of seventeenth-century society, within which the fashionable pursuits of aristocratic dilettanti might be very influential. In fact the emergence of a more elaborate culture of leisure and consumption among the élites was very important, not least because it provided a market for books, periodicals, scientific instruments, and the like. If the telescope and the microscope proved curiously hard to exploit for front-line scientific purposes, once their early impact had passed, their broader role as serious playthings is not to be despised. However ambivalent many among the élites may have remained—like Charles II when he mocked his 'madmen' in the Royal Society and their attempts to weigh the air—their interest does seem to have been caught and (perhaps precariously) held.

The telescope was an essential tool for a new generation of astronomers, who set out on the long and tedious task of mapping the heavens, just occasionally observing some more spectacular phenomenon. Halley's brilliant explanation of the comet of 1682 was one moment when advances in knowledge became unusually evident. What was most significant in the long run was the creation of a new body of data, far more precise and extensive than anything known to Kepler or his predecessors. This was no easy matter, as the long sad history of the relationship between Newton and the Astronomer Royal John Flamsteed should remind us; although the delays and errors in the supply of data about the moon were not wholly the latter's fault, they gave rise to some of the rudest letters imaginable. The royal observatories at Paris and Greenwich were rare and important recognition that science might deserve state patronage, however qualified or niggardly. Monarchs and ministers understood that some kinds of knowledge might really matter, when they improved their ability to control their own territories and acquire new ones. The prestige of sponsoring new discoveries was incidental compared with the potential advantages of better maps, charts, and navigational techniques as agencies of power and profit. The microscope had no comparable prospectus to offer; after Hooke's early exploitation of compound instruments to display the fascinating details of small creatures and objects serious work rather languished. The great exception was the solitary and humbly-born Dutch microscopist Anton van Leeuwenhoek, who worked with single lenses which were effectively just glass beads, at almost unbelievably high magnifications. It is hard to understand how he achieved so much with these primitive devices, which admittedly avoided the optical problems that dogged the compound versions. His observations of bacteria, spermatozoa, and other micro-organisms were astounding feats, but ones which ran ahead of anything the biological theories of his day could handle satisfactorily. The nature of

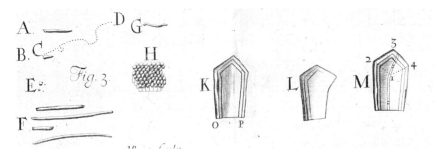

The humbly born Dutch microscopist Anton van Leeuwenhoek (1632–1723) was remarkably unsqueamish about his subject-matter. This 1684 plate shows bacteria scraped from between his own teeth. Like many of his other observations, this one was well in advance of the theoretical knowledge required in order to make sense of it.

generation, corruption, and related processes remained largely obscure, amid a welter of mostly inaccurate speculation.

Doctors were prominent among those involved in scientific inquiry, while at the same time medicine remained in many respects an amateur pursuit, at which anyone could try their hand. Successful therapy was a hit-and-miss affair, and medical intervention was often very dangerous, especially when the traditional remedies of bleeding and purging were employed. Seventeenth-century advances were marginal here, although a few doctors were beginning to see the advantages of minimalist approaches. Some diseases were properly identified for the first time, which might tie in with a growing concern for public health and sanitation measures; the very concept of diseases as independent entities was an important novelty in many respects, even if the causes were rarely understood. By the end of the century western Europe had achieved one striking success, with the virtual elimination of bubonic plague, the great terror of the previous three centuries; this seems to have resulted primarily from the introduction of very tight quarantine in the ports and along the land frontier with the Ottoman Empire. There were also major advances in both human and comparative anatomy, although these had few practical consequences at the time. Public dissections were among the most frequent activities of scientific societies for some time, until everyone tired of these rather repetitious activities. The description and classification of living creatures and plants was another important area of research, which demonstrated the value of close observation, and merged into inconclusive debates on such issues as the modes of reproduction. The earth sciences also started to emerge, with discussions of earthquakes, fossils, rock strata, and the like. Here there was the potential for very fraught debates about the nature and age of the earth; some highly speculative theories about the creation were already causing controversy in the 1680s. Meanwhile chemistry was struggling to emerge from the alchemical chrysalis, with only limited success in this period. Newton's own passionate interest in the subject has troubled historians, unsure whether to classify him as an alchemical adept or to emphasize the methodological rigour he brought to his work. Here if anywhere he does appear to fit Keynes's description of him as 'the last of the magi', hoping for a great breakthrough not even his talents could bring to the confused heritage with which he was compelled to work. Where he was surely right was in intuiting that the world-view he had helped create would only be complete when the microscopic structure of matter was understood in the same terms as the macroscopic structure of the planetary system. Furthermore, the final triumph of the industrial revolution would only be possible when

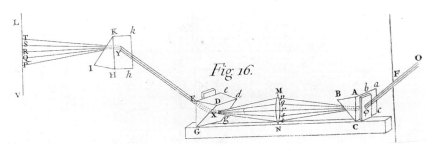

Newton's experiments with prisms, which established that 'white' light was actually composed of the colours of the spectrum, dated back to 1666, and formed the basis of a controversial publication of 1672. This diagram of the 'crucial experiment' in which light was separated and recombined through a series of prisms is taken from his *Opticks* of 1704.

chemistry became an effective science, still a distant prospect when Newton died. The other great area in which he was celebrated was his work on optics, with his demonstration of the compound nature of 'white' light through the use of prisms to reveal the spectrum. Most of the major thinkers of the century from Kepler onwards were concerned with the nature of light, refraction, the theory of lenses, and kindred questions.

The Quest for Practical Applications

Alongside the isolated major discoveries of the decades before the 1660s there had existed a much broader concern for science as a means of improvement. This ranged very widely, from attempts to find the philosophers' stone of the alchemists (supposedly capable of making unlimited gold and curing all ailments), through projects for more or less feasible machines, to down-to-earth techniques such as fen drainage. While the many vicissitudes of these ambitions cannot be traced here, they had great influence on the early scientific societies. Those who advocated and planned these bodies were naturally anxious to convince patrons of their utility. With sincere but generally misplaced enthusiasm they held out the prospect of great strides in technology, usually based on the notion that once proper scientific method was applied to artisanal processes the latter could readily be improved. This facile assumption disregarded several inconvenient facts. Craftsmen were very sensibly resistant to suggestions that they hand over their well-guarded secrets, on which their livelihoods depended. Even if such contacts were established, scientists were rarely capable of understanding the processes properly, still less of making useful changes to them. Labour-saving devices, which might have been possible on a limited scale, had little application in an economy where labour was cheap and governments worried about the social implications of unemployment. One has to balance admiration for the vision of future possibilities against the fact that many projects were wildly unrealistic. Even the more sensible ones might end up in abject failure, like Benjamin Worsley's saltpetre scheme, backed by Samuel Hartlib and his associates, then subsidized by the Commonwealth government. The Royal Society's ambitious range of improving committees, and its projected *History of Trades*, turned out to be starry-eyed fiascos. The gap between ambition and results was so vast that it risked bringing discredit on those involved, and was still being mocked by Swift in *Gulliver's Travels* decades later. Not every effort was in vain; a book like John Evelyn's *Sylva* quite probably encouraged better management of British woodlands. In France Pascal and his friend the duc de Roannez were involved in draining marshland, using wind-driven pumps adapted from Dutch designs, and in organizing a Paris bus service. They also seem to have experimented with a primitive steam engine; although this vital development took so long to mature, and was largely brought about by practical engineers, there was sporadic interest and involvement by members of the scientific community.

Like so many other promising ideas, the steam engine was held back by a range of different obstacles. The social and intellectual gap between upper-class virtuosi and those who worked with their hands was a major factor, but so was a rather surprising lack of imagination about the potential of a new source of power. The latter becomes more explicable if we recognize how hard it would be for the new technology to outperform water and wind power even a century later. By the later seventeenth century many very ingenious mechanical devices were being suggested, which often, like Robert Hooke's universal joint, had enormous potential. In practice they rarely worked satisfactorily—and sometimes not at all—because it was virtually impossible to make them to the required standard. Machines were normally constructed with wood, cord, and other organic materials, which wore out rapidly; the primitive and costly metal-working techniques of the day might have improved on this to some extent, but were still inadequate to the need. The theory of superior cog-wheels using the epicycloid, first suggested by the French mathematician Desargues in the 1650s, was well understood by the 1700s, yet was still virtually unused. There were some marginal exceptions to this technological impasse. Clocks and watches improved greatly, with major contributions from men like Huygens and Hooke, a trend which had important implications not just for social and economic practices, but for how people conceived their world. It was not

By 1695, when this handsome bracket clock was made, London had become the international capital for the manufacture of fine clocks and watches. Leading makers were in constant touch with scientific circles, while both the skills and the workforce were also employed producing scientific instruments.

merely a casual metaphor which construed the Newtonian Deity as the divine clock-maker. Scientific instruments themselves (often constructed by the same people who made timepieces) played a very important role in demonstrating that higher standards were possible, albeit at a cost. Surveying and mapping were now possible to a far higher standard than before, with the aid of much improved instruments and tables.

This was one area which held direct attractions for governments, to the point of inducing them to offer financial support. The process turned out to be both laborious and costly, however, so that results were often delayed by decades; maps and charts appeared with desperate slowness. The greatest prize of all was the discovery of a method for determining longitude at sea, the subject of excited speculation and innumerable projects from the beginning of the seventeenth century. In the 1660s Huygens was working on the right lines, attempting to make a marine chronometer to the high standard of accuracy required. While he blamed his failure on the (admittedly abysmal) mishandling of his instrument by the French navy, we can now see that he was still far short of solving the problems. It was more than a century later that John Harrison finally won the £20,000 prize on offer from the British parliament since 1714, with the most famous timekeeper ever made. On its own the chronometer would have been useless without the general improvement in other navigational instruments and the capacity to use them; in this sense the efforts of pioneers like the Gresham College professors of the decades before the Civil War were far from futile. Another area in which rulers had a direct interest was the coinage, where new techniques for pressing coins and milling their edges finally made it possible to defeat counterfeiters and clippers. It was Isaac Newton himself (appointed as Warden of the Mint from the end of 1695, then as Master in 1699) who took charge of the major English recoinage of 1696. His extraordinary success in his second career as an administrator was one more indication of the ways in which scientific abilities could be turned to practical ends. The careers of Wren and Hooke as architects were further instances of the same phenomenon.

The application of mathematical and statistical techniques on a much wider scale had enormous long-term implications, not least in the political and economic spheres. Probability and the theory of games had interested exceptional earlier thinkers like Cardano and Galileo, but it was only in the 1650s and 1660s that a new conception of probability suddenly became a major theme, with Pascal and Leibniz among its outstanding exponents. The word 'probable' itself was in the process of changing its meaning from 'supported by authorities' to 'likely in view of all the evidence'. Behind this shift one may reasonably detect both questions of scientific proof and a drive for bureaucratic rationalization. Among the authors who took up the issues were the pioneering English statisticians Sir William Petty and John Graunt. While Petty's mathematical and logical skills were not very impressive, the range of military, economic, medical, and other issues to which he sought answers was highly original. His 'Political Arithmetic' lies at the very roots of economics as a coherent discipline; he even proposed a national statistical office. Graunt's work on London bills of mortality has a similar status in relation to demography. In practice it was a long time before governments came to understand the potential of such techniques, for both information and disinformation. What they were interested in was calculations of life expectancy, because in both the Dutch Republic and Britain the state began to raise money by the sale of annuities. In 1671 the Dutch statesman John de Witt seems to have got his sums right, so that the terms offered were slightly favourable to the state overall, yet offered a good deal to any purchaser who lived longer than the average. In contrast the British government displayed a truly awesome incompetence, despite having access to excellent tables compiled by such men as Edmund Halley and Abraham de Moivre.

Conclusion

A summary listing of the intellectual changes of the seventeenth century is bound to give a misleading impression, which exaggerates their speed and initial impact. This is why this chapter has tried so hard to emphasize the durability of conventional religious beliefs and the multiple limitations of early modern natural philosophy. We must always remember the crucial distinction between what contemporaries perceived and the historian's retrospective view. This is peculiarly important here, because what is at stake is the massive and complex set of shifts which can be seen as the birth of modernity, to which we must ascribe such huge significance. The *ancien régime* of kings, nobles, and priests was sailing in serene unawareness towards its doom, as industrial society gradually emerged to replace its agrarian predecessor. This long-term process was only possible through a vast intellectual revolution, which saw referential accuracy triumph over concept affirmation as the criterion of truth. Authority gradually lost its association with antiquity; claims about the world must more and more expect to be tested against new evidence and close observation. Passionate opinions about the primitive Church or the ancient wisdom, which had played such a large part in stimulating and justifying the intellectual radicalism of the seventeenth century, would be among the eventual victims. This is particularly ironic when we note how important they had been to men like Pascal and Newton. Theories of probability, statistical testing, and experimental method were perhaps the most important of the insidious yet profound shifts which were at work here. If their true subversiveness remained hidden, the reasons lie in the situation described in this chapter. Religion still provided the framework within which everything was set, so that there appeared to be little difficulty in absorbing new intellectual trends within Christian doctrine. Meanwhile even the wildest enthusiasts had no real notion of how far technology might transform the conditions of human life.

It is hardly surprising that the future remained a closed book to the seventeenth-century mind, when what lay ahead was so revolutionary as to be unimaginable. With the advantage of hindsight we can now see that the development of cognitive specialization, in combination with the concept of a single, rule-based nature, open to endless exploration and manipulation, had staggering implications. Human beings have progressively acquired unprecedented power to manage their environment and satisfy their material wants. In the process they have inevitably transformed their relations to one another as well, to find themselves adrift in a heartless universe increasingly devoid of moral purpose. It seems likely that from the later seventeenth century, at the latest, this evolution was inevitable; Pandora's box had been opened, and the ideas which had been released were simply unstoppable. Perhaps the most curious twist to the story is that no one really tried to block the changes effectively, because for so long they seemed of such marginal importance, and could be assimilated into much conventional thinking. It was however in this realm of ideas that the most revolutionary changes of the century occurred, to unleash powerful forces which increasingly dominate our lives today.

6

Warfare, Crisis, and Absolutism

JEREMY BLACK

Seventeenth-century Europe was dominated by war, and it was through war that the major political changes occurred. Bourbon France emerged under Louis XIV (1643–1715) to become the leading power in Europe. Sweden rose during the Thirty Years War (1618–48) to become the dominant power in northern Europe and then during the Great Northern War (1700–21) lost much of its empire to the Russia of Peter the Great (1689–1725). War was also the means by which the Turks were repulsed by Austria in 1683, and Austria subsequently conquered Hungary (1684–99). All these developments focused on warfare, and were accompanied by a dramatic increase in military strength. Military expenditure and army and navy size increased greatly: Louis XIV had the largest army in western Europe since the days of the Roman Empire. This greater military strength was related to the development of what were subsequently termed 'absolutist' monarchies, although the power of monarchs rested as much on the cooperation of the nobility as on the size of the army.

The Expansion of Europe

Military strength was crucial to another fundamental aspect of early modern European history, namely relations with the outside world. In 1618–1715 more of the world's land surface was brought under the control of European powers and these powers strengthened their position on the major sea-trading routes.

In Asia the expansion of Russian power across Siberia to the Pacific brought a vast, but little populated area under European control. Okhotsk on the Pacific was founded in 1648. In this advance the Europeans enjoyed a definite technological edge. Their opponents had no gunpowder weaponry and many existed at a very primitive level of military technology. The native peoples were also subjugated by the Russian construction of forts which maximized the defensive potential of firearms and anchored their routes to the Pacific. Furthermore, resistance was weakened by the small size of the native population, by the lack of unity among the tribes, and by the absence of a resource-base and governmental structure able to sustain permanent forces to resist the Russian advance. The Russians were helped by the mutual hostility of many of the tribes and were able to obtain military support from several. Those who resisted were treated barbarously. Due both to this and to the introduction of new diseases, numbers fell dramatically. Nevertheless, resistance continued, especially among the Chukchi and Koryaks of Kamchatka, and the Russians made scant progress there until the eighteenth century. Expansion left Russia in control of a vast extent of territory, but these possessions did not make her an active Asian or Pacific power. The hostile nature of the Siberian environment exacerbated the impact of distance, while there was no warm-water route along the coast of Siberia and into the Pacific. The concentration of population, resources, and government on the European side of Russia, especially after Peter the Great moved the capital from Moscow to his new city of St Petersburg, ensured that Siberia was peripheral to the Russian state.

Elsewhere in Asia, the European impact was minimal; in any case, what the European powers sought in South Asia was trade, not territory. As yet, European contact with the Pacific and Australasia was limited, although in the western Pacific Spain, operating from the Philippines, acquired the Marianas in 1668 and the Caroline Islands in 1696. The direct European impact on Africa was largely limited to coastal regions, but interest in these increased in this period: the Dutch founded Cape Town in 1652 and the British, Dutch, and French founded bases in West Africa. The Portuguese were the most aggressive. They sought to expand their colonies of Angola and Mozambique. In both areas, however, the limitations of their musketeers were revealed. Their slow rate of fire and the open-order fighting methods of their opponents reduced their effectiveness, and the Portuguese failed to maintain their position on the upper Zambezi. In 1698 the Portuguese base of Fort Jesus at Mombasa fell to an Omani siege.

In South America, Spain and Portugal were steadily extending their power, and there was a considerable expansion of British, French, and Spanish territorial control and settlement in North America. The French

View of the Binnehof in The Hague, by Berckheyde. The Hague was the centre of federal government, but the real centre of Dutch strength was the economic and financial power-house, Amsterdam. Until their European resource base and commercial position were badly hit by wars with England and France in 1652–78, the Dutch were the most globally expansive European power of the century, the power that best combined military force and commercial skill; but, thereafter, their overseas enterprise was reduced and, in relative terms, the Dutch declined in the face of rising English trade and naval power.

founded Quebec in 1608, the Dutch New Amsterdam (later New York) in 1625, and the Spaniards established a garrison in Pensacola in 1696. As in the sixteenth century, it would be mistaken to think simply in terms of a struggle of European versus non-European. Both within and outside Europe, the European powers competed vigorously. Their common concern to dominate trade routes ensured that this competition was often more intense than that between European and non-European powers. Thus the Dutch drove the Portuguese from the Moluccas (1605), Malacca (1641), and coastal Ceylon (1638–58), but failed to do so, to lasting effect, from Angola and Brazil (1624–54), while the English drove the Dutch from New Amsterdam and renamed it New York (1664). Similarly, in Africa, the Near East, India, and the Orient struggles between local powers were more important than those with European states.

Warfare as an Agent of Change

Military effectiveness was affected by internal political crises in mid-century in a large number of states, including Britain, France, Russia, Spain, China, and Turkey. Thereafter, there was a general process of domestic consolidation and a growth of governmental power. This led, despite the widespread demographic stagnation and economic problems of the period, to a marked increase in the resources at the disposal of the state. This manifested itself in the greater military activity in the late seventeenth century of a number of powers, most obviously France, England, Austria, Prussia, Russia, Savoy-Piedmont, Turkey, and China. Some of this activity was directed against peoples with looser governmental structures, as with the Russians in Siberia, the Chinese in Mongolia and Tibet, and the establishment of the French in Louisiana: but most was deployed against other states with comparable governmental structures. Thus warfare both defined and reflected the respective strength of states.

This created an unstable context for domestic developments. To contemporaries, international relations were crucial. They were a central focus of political activity and attention. Aside from those directly affected by death and devastation, taxation, food shortages, and recruitment brought the effects of war home to most. The monarchs, ministers, diplomats and generals of the period faced a hazardous and difficult international and domestic situation. Information was difficult to obtain and often unreliable. Rulers were short of money, generals of men. Activities, whether military operations or the journeys of couriers, depended on weather and climate, the condition of the roads, the crops, and the countryside. Chance factors of birth and death played a major role in creating and influencing a diplomatic agenda in which dynastic circumstances were often paramount. The nature of monarchical authority and power ensured that the personal views of rulers, such as Louis XIV or Charles XII of Sweden, were extremely important. The unpredictability of developments cannot be disguised by terms such as 'balance of power' and 'natural interests' which imply that a hypothetical international system operated according to some rules.

The 'Thirty Years War' in Europe, 1618–1648

Such unpredictability was well demonstrated in the cause and course of the major struggle that convulsed Europe in the first half of the century, the Thirty Years War (1618–48). This, the longest conflict of the period, was in fact the combination of a number of different but related struggles. The

most important was the attempt by the Catholic Austrian Habsburg dynasty to resist the challenge to their authority in their hereditary lands, particularly Austria and Bohemia (now part of the Czech Republic) and to gain greater control within the Holy Roman Empire (roughly modern Germany and Austria). The war initially began as a rising of 1618 against Habsburg authority in Bohemia. The Protestants turned to the Calvinist Frederick V, Elector Palatine, and elected him as king in 1619. This was a direct challenge to the position of the Habsburg, Ferdinand II, who was elected as Holy Roman Emperor two days later.

In 1620 Bohemia was invaded by superior forces and the Bohemians were crushed at the battle of the White Mountain outside Prague (8 November). Habsburg authority was then reimposed and Bohemia was catholicized. At the same time Spanish troops from the Army of Flanders overran the Rhineland territories of Frederick, whose rule in Bohemia had been so brief that he was known as the 'Winter King'. They did so in order to protect the communication routes between the Spanish bases in north Italy, particularly Milan, and the Spanish Netherlands (modern Belgium), known as the 'Spanish Road'. These were crucial routes because in 1621 the Twelve Year Truce between Spain and the Dutch came to an end and war resumed. The Dutch then encouraged opposition to the Habsburgs in Ger-

The Thirty Years War, here shown in Callot's engraving, was a conflict of great brutality. The cruelties shown to civilians owed something to religious animosities, but much to the inadequacies of the structures for the financing, supply, and control of European armies. However, by global standards, European military administration was well developed. Martial élite culture was transformed as knights became officers. This helped to ensure the continuation of ancestral political and social privilege, but their technically different battlefield roles required a more predictable and disciplined response. As a result, the relative effectiveness of European forces improved.

many. Ferdinand II, however, entrusted his troops to a Bohemian military entrepreneur, Wallenstein, who defeated the Dutch-subsidized Ernest, count of Mansfeld at Dessau (25 April 1626). Christian IV of Denmark was then encouraged to intervene on the Protestant side, not least by his ambition to secure Catholic prince-bishoprics in north-west Germany. At Lutter (27 August 1626) Christian was defeated by Count Tilly, the general of the Catholic League, which was led by Duke Maximilian I of Bavaria. The Danes were then driven from northern Germany and in 1629 forced out of the war.

Ferdinand II then dominated the empire, but he failed to use this period to win support and consolidate his position. He was to be challenged by Gustavus Adolphus of Sweden (1611–32). This warrior monarch had spent his early years fighting Denmark (1611–13), Russia (1611–17), and Poland (1617–18, 1621–9), but in the late 1620s he became increasingly concerned about growing Habsburg power on the German shore of the Baltic. He was encouraged to act by France. France and Spain had maintained passable relations in the 1610s, and the French had done nothing to help the Bohemian rebellion; but after 1624, when the anti-Habsburg Cardinal Richelieu became the leading minister of Louis XIII (1610–43), relations deteriorated. Within France, Protestantism was destroyed as a politico-

military force with the successful siege of La Rochelle (1627–8) and the Grace of Alès (1629). Abroad, however, Richelieu was eager to ally with Protestant powers in order to cripple the Habsburgs. France and Spain fought the War of the Mantuan Succession (1628–31) over control of northern Italy. Richelieu wanted to undermine Habsburg dominance of the empire and therefore encouraged Gustavus to invade in July 1630.

Landing at Peenemünde, the Swedes overran Pomerania and Mecklenburg and won French subsidies. In April 1631 Gustavus moved south into Brandenburg. The brutal sacking of Protestant Magdeburg, after a surprise storming by Tilly, helped to lead Brandenburg into Gustavus' camp and when Tilly advanced into Saxony that Electorate followed. On 17 September 1631 the two armies met at Breitenfeld. This was the largest battle, in terms of manpower, of the war: Gustavus had 42,000 men, Tilly 35,000. Gustavus' victory was due to his numerical superiority, to the resilience of the Swedish forces in the face of the collapse of their inexperienced Saxon allies, and to the extent to which the Swedish defensive position allowed them to use their firepower, particularly their greatly superior artillery, against the attacking forces of Tilly's army. The battle of Breitenfeld led many Protestant princes to rally to Gustavus; he meanwhile advanced into central Germany, taking Würzburg and Frankfurt, while the Saxons took Prague.

In 1632 Gustavus planned to overrun Bavaria and then conquer Austria. Tilly was killed at the river Lech when he failed to stop the invasion of Bavaria and Munich fell on 17 May. Ferdinand II, however, reappointed Wallenstein, who had been dismissed because of his unpopularity with the German princes, and the general's threat to Saxony led Gustavus to return northwards. The Swedes were unable to drive Wallenstein from a heavily fortified position at the Alte Veste; instead, they lost heavily from desertion due to supply problems in the devastated countryside. Wallenstein then convinced himself that the campaign was over and began to disperse his troops. Gustavus attacked him at Lützen (17 November 1632), a fog-shrouded and largely inconclusive battle in which both sides lost about a third of their strength and Gustavus, 'the Lion of the North', was killed.

Cardinal Richelieu, by Philippe de Champaigne. Despite presenting himself as an impartial guardian of national destiny, Richelieu was a deeply partisan politician who used a system of profitable cronyism to control the government and bring himself great wealth. Never in total control, Richelieu had to confront Louis XIII's willingness to turn to other advisers. War with Spain helped to undermine French finances and led to the serious crisis of the *Fronde*.

The initiative then increasingly passed to the Habsburgs. Wallenstein, now following his own policies, was murdered on the orders of the Emperor (25 February 1634), and at Nördlingen (6 September 1634) a joint Austro-Spanish army heavily defeated the Swedes. This led to the Swedish loss of southern Germany and to the Peace of Prague (1635) by which Saxony abandoned the Swedes. Most of the German Protestant princes were now reconciled to the Emperor, and the war was increasingly one in which foreign powers contended with each other on the soil of Germany.

Worried about Habsburg success, France entered the war in 1635, and thus began a gruelling struggle in which it was not possible to win a decisive victory. Louis XIII and Richelieu hoped to achieve victory over Spain in one campaign. Like Philip IV of Spain and his first minister, the count-duke of Olivares, they did not seek a lengthy or attritional war. However, it proved impossible to create the large armies required to achieve the bold strategic plans that were devised. Armies were badly affected by supply problems and desertion. In 1636 the Spaniards invaded France, advancing

Jan Asselyn, *Gustavus Adolphus at the Battle of Lützen*. Lützen was a bitterly fought, fog-shrouded, and largely inconclusive battle in the Thirty Years War. The Swedes under their warrior king attacked the Imperial forces under Wallenstein on 16 November 1632. Gustavus died in the mêlée, shot three times. Both sides lost about one-third of their strength and Wallenstein retreated to Bohemia, leaving the Swedes in control of Saxony.

as far as Amiens and Corbie. This invasion showed the vulnerability of France to attack from the Spanish Netherlands, and caused great anxiety there, but it failed to overthrow Richelieu. After Corbie, the French launched attacks into the Spanish Netherlands, conquering Artois with the fall of Arras in 1640. Breisach was captured in 1638: its fall cut Spanish routes between northern Italy and the Army of Flanders, and opened the way into Germany. Perpignan fell in 1642. The French were helped by rebellions in the Spanish Empire, particularly in Catalonia (1640) and Portugal (1640), as the financial burdens of the war interacted with strong regional antipathy to rule from Madrid and to its attempts to share the cost of the conflict.

The period is commonly presented in terms of French triumphs, especially over the Army of Flanders, most famously the 22-year-old Louis de Condé's victory at Rocroi (19 May 1643); but these victories were offset by defeats and logistical problems. Furthermore, the consequences of Rocroi have commonly been exaggerated: the Spaniards speedily regrouped. After the mid-1640s it was not so much that the French suffered defeats, but rather that they failed to make much progress: certainly they made insufficient headway to defeat Spain before France's heavily indebted finances collapsed. Despite major efforts in the mid-1640s, the Spaniards resisted French attacks and the French were unable to exploit anti-Spanish rebellions in Palermo and Naples in 1647.

The conflict in Germany was meanwhile drawing to a close. The second half of the Thirty Years War has never seemed as dramatic and important as the first, but this is misleading. In 1636 the Swedes were nearly driven back to the Baltic, but in 1639 they advanced as far as Prague. In 1643–5 Sweden overwhelmed Denmark in a conflict that showed how decisive warfare could sometimes be in this period. Joint Franco-Swedish operations succeeded in 1645–8 in defeating the Austrians and Bavarians in southern Germany; as the war ended, the Swedes were besieging Prague, the original site of the conflict.

The treaties that ended the Thirty Years War were signed at Münster and Osnabrück, and are collectively known as the Peace of Westphalia. The Austrian Habsburgs were left in secure control of their hereditary lands: they were not to lose Bohemia until their empire collapsed at the end of the First World War. The Swedes gained much of Pomerania as well as the ecclesiastical principalities of Bremen and Verden; these gains brought control over the estuaries of the Elbe, Oder, and Weser, and consolidated Sweden's position as the leading Baltic power. Brandenburg-Prussia also gained much territory, and emerged ahead of Saxony as the leading north

XILIO SOCIOS, QVI FORTIBVS ARMIS
ENDIT LÆSACVE IVRA DEI

Rulers were expected to be bellicose and successful. Although no Gustavus Adolphus, Louis XIII, here depicted by Philippe de Champaigne crowned by Victory, led his army to Béarn in south-west France in 1620 in order to coerce the local Huguenots into accepting royal authority and Catholicism. In 1622 he marched through west and south France capturing Huguenot positions and in 1627–8 commanded when La Rochelle, the last Huguenot stronghold, was besieged and starved into surrender.

German Protestant state. France gained control over much of Alsace. Calvinism was recognized as an acceptable religion in the Holy Roman Empire and the German princes were in effect left free to pursue their own foreign policy. France and Sweden were made guarantors of the peace, and thus given opportunities to intervene in German politics. The war had caused terrible devastation in Germany, but the religious and political compromise it brought helped to lessen conflict within Germany for nearly 100 years.

Conflict between France and Spain

The Franco-Spanish struggle was not ended by the Peace of Westphalia. The French lost much ground when Spain took advantage of the *Fronde*, the French civil wars of 1648–53. These arose from the unpopularity of the ministry of Richelieu's successor Cardinal Mazarin, an unpopularity that owed much to the taxation and other burdens produced by the war. Spain's attempt to intervene directly in the *Fronde*, by invading Gascony in order to help Mazarin's opponents in Bordeaux, was a failure; but during the *Fronde* the Spaniards regained the major naval base of Dunkirk, which they had lost in 1646, and also Catalonia.

The end of the *Fronde* did not bring victory for France. The Spaniards captured Rocroi in 1654. Defeats at Pavia (1655) and Valenciennes (1656) led France to offer reasonable terms, only for Philip IV to reject them in 1656. Valenciennes was a spectacular victory, in which the French baggage train and supplies were captured, but it does not enjoy the fame of Rocroi because it does not fit in with the conventional view of the inevitable decline of Spain and rise of France. The war ended after the intervention of fresh English forces on the side of France tipped the balance in Flanders. Oliver Cromwell's Ironsides helped Marshal Turenne to defeat the Army of Flanders at the battle of the Dunes (23 June 1658), as the Spanish force tried to relieve the siege of Dunkirk. The Spanish army was outnumbered, its artillery had not arrived, the terrain prevented it from taking advantage of its superiority in cavalry, and its flank was bombarded by English warships. The battle was followed by the capture of Dunkirk, and Turenne was able to threaten an advance on Brussels. This led to the Peace of the Pyrenees (1659), signed at the Isle of Pheasants at the western end of the mountain chain. France made valuable gains, principally Artois and Roussillon, but the peace was more of a compromise treaty than is usually appreciated: the French had failed to drive the Spaniards from the Low Countries or Italy as had been planned. The Spanish Empire remained the largest in western Europe. One loss was Dunkirk, given to England as a reward in the peace only for the recently restored Charles II to sell it to Louis XIV in 1662.

The British Civil Wars

Charles II was restored in 1660 after a protracted political crisis in mid-century Britain. This was the most serious of the crises in various countries in this period often collectively known as the 'mid-seventeenth-century crisis'. The outbreak of the English Civil War was the result of a political crisis in 1640–2 that stemmed from risings in Scotland (1638) and Ireland (1641). In Scotland the absentee Charles I's support for bishops and his autocratic handling of Scottish interests and patronage led to a Presbyterian and national response which Charles failed to suppress. He turned to England to raise the necessary resources, but the Long Parliament rejected his authority, though many members of both Houses subsequently fought for him. Fighting broke out in 1642. The Royalists made considerable gains in 1643, but failed to take London, the centre of the rebellion. In 1644 the Scots intervened on the side of Parliament, and the Royalists were defeated at Marston Moor, losing the north of England. In 1645 the Parliamentarian army, its cavalry commanded by Oliver Cromwell, defeated Charles at Naseby. The Royalists were beaten, but the Parliamentarians fell out with the Scots, leading to a Second Civil War in 1648. Cromwell beat the Scots at Preston, and Charles was then formally tried and executed (30 January 1649). England was declared a republic and the House of Lords abolished. Largely thanks to Cromwell, English forces then conquered Ireland (1649–52) and Scotland (1650–2), and for the first time the British Isles were united.

Under Cromwell as Lord Protector (1653–8) Britain was relatively stable; but he faced difficulties with the Parliaments that were called, and unpopularity in the localities over the decision in 1655 to entrust authority to 'major generals', instructed to preserve security and create a godly and efficient kingdom. Cromwell's willingness to sacrifice constitutional and institutional continuity, and the Protectorate's transfer of local power to those who were not members of the social élite, were not generally welcomed. Neither were the religious reforms of republican England, such as the introduction of civil marriage, attacks on the churching of women after childbirth, the readmission of the Jews, and the toleration of a range of sects and practices that were anathema to many. Political, social, and religious conservatism remained strong. When Cromwell died in 1658 he was not an Alexander cut short in his prime; the unpopularity and divisions of the regime were readily apparent. Cromwell had neither led the latter-day children of Israel to the promised land as he had sought to do, nor had he created a stable government that would maintain and further his achievements. His successor as Protector, his son Richard, was unable to command authority; the republic collapsed in division and disorder, paving the way for the restoration of the Stuart dynasty.

British history is often treated separately from that of the continent of Europe, but that is particularly inappropriate for the seventeenth century, as there was little contemporary sense of distance. Furthermore, events in Britain revealed the potential fragility of the established political order and the radicalism that could exist, especially in religious circles. Elsewhere in Europe, while a radical politico-religious agenda was in part offered by the rebels against Habsburg authority in Bohemia and Austria in the early stages of the Thirty Years War, none the less an important aspect of the disorders of the 1640s and 1650s was that religion played little role in most of them. The Protestant Huguenots had been crushed in France in 1626–9, particularly by Richelieu's successful siege of their stronghold of La Rochelle in 1627–8, and they played no role in the *Fronde*. Unlike conditions in the earlier Dutch Revolt, religion was similarly absent from the crisis in the Spanish Empire. Instead, these crises reflected a combination of unease over the political complexion of regimes (especially the Mazarin ministry in France), the burdens arising from war, and regional particularism.

In some respects the results of the mid-seventeenth-century crises revealed the strengths of prevailing political systems. Despite severe economic conditions, population decline (which reduced society's ability to cope with the savage financial burdens of governmental tax demands), seemingly intractable conflicts, and unpopular governments, there was no sustained fundamental challenge outside Britain to the political, social, and religious bases of society. A radical movement in Bordeaux, the *Ormée*, had very few members. The particularist uprisings in Catalonia and Portugal were essentially reactive calls that responded to governmental actions or problems, rather than attempts to produce a new political order. The same was true of the early stages of the British rebellion.

'Absolutism'

In reaction to the crisis, greater emphasis came to be placed on social and political cohesion. 'Absolutism', the term most frequently used to describe the governing system of the late seventeenth and early eighteenth centuries, is in many senses misleading. Until recently, absolutist states were seen as powerful entities, characterized by a government monopoly of power and the growth of central institutions, such as the court, the standing army, and the administration. According to this older view, purpose was provided by the will of the ruler, and absolutist states shared similar objectives: centralization and the coercion of domestic and foreign opponents. A detailed examination of governing practices suggests that such a stress is misleading. The power of the ruler was limited by three significant factors: first, resistance to the demands of the government; second, the often tenuous control of the ruler over the emerging 'bureaucracy'; and third, the constraints of prevailing attitudes towards the proper scope of monarchical authority.

The first is readily apparent. The habit of obedience towards authority was matched by a stubborn, and largely successful, determination to preserve local privileges. This helped to ensure that the focus of authority was often a local institution or a sense of locality, rather than a distant ruler. This was exacerbated by the failure of dynasticism to provide the ideological context for unity that nationalism was to offer in the nineteenth century.

The size of central government bureaucracies was limited and their sphere of operations was not conducive to administrative efficiency. Communications were poor, states were permanently short of money, and, in a largely pre-statistical age, it was difficult to obtain information necessary to make informed choices or to evaluate the success of policies. Most central governments had only a limited awareness of the size or resources of their population. Therefore the most effective way to govern was in cooperation with those who wielded social power and with the institutions of local authority. The appearance of power contributed crucially to the reality of power: but, behind the façade of absolutism, the imposing palaces built in imitation of Louis XIV's Versailles, and the larger armies, governments were dependent on local institutions and sought the co-operation of the influential. This was particularly the case in the larger states. Thus the stress usually placed on Louis XIV's use of intendants (officials sent to the provinces by the central government) can hide the fact that intendants had to cooperate with local institutions such as the provincial *Parlements*, and that much power remained with the *gouverneurs* of provinces who were generally major aristocrats. Similarly, the impact of Brandenburg-Prussian government was limited on the estates of the aristocracy. Indeed, in practice, 'absolutism' tended to mean trying to persuade the aristocracy to govern in the interests of the ruler—a far from novel objective. It was only in small states, such as Denmark, Savoy-Piedmont, and Portugal, where it was easier for a strong ruler to supervise government personally, that the connotations of the term 'absolutism' became appropriate. Even there, the difficulties of coping with factionalism among the officialdom and of inculcating notions of state service and efficient administration were considerable.

Furthermore, over most of Europe clear hostility to the idea of despotism, and conventions of acceptable royal behaviour, limited the possibilities for monarchical action by setting restrictive limits of consent, in both theory and practice. Monarchy was expected to operate within a context of legality and tradition, and this made new initiatives politically hazardous and administratively difficult.

Louis XIV

The monarch who most clearly personified absolutism was Louis XIV (1643–1715). Born in 1638, he came to the throne as a child and did not assume effective rule until the death of Mazarin (1661), the Italian-born cardinal whom Richelieu had left as first minister. Europe was awed by Louis's strength and frightened by his actual and supposed ambitions. He extended France's boundaries, though at considerable cost. On the domestic scene, Louis XIV renewed harmonious relations with the social élite. These had been lost during the period of the cardinal-ministers, because they had based their position on the support of that section of the élite that was willing to back them. This broad-based cooperation with the nobility, rather than any supposed absolutist agenda of centralization and bureaucratization, brought stability to France. Louis quarrelled with the papacy and the Jansenists and revoked Protestant privileges (1685), creating a diaspora of critics, who also spread French culture. A charismatic figure, Louis was a major patron of the arts, especially of triumphalist works. He expressed and strengthened his power and pursued his *gloire* in war. Louis's triumphs, such as the crossing of the Rhine in 1672 and the successful sieges of Maastricht (1673), Mons (1691), and Namur (1692), were celebrated with services and paintings of commemoration. Sieges provided suitable stage-managed opportunities for Louis to demonstrate his power and military prowess and until he became too old to do so he enjoyed such campaigning.

Recent scholarly work has emphasized the limited nature of improvement in the French army during the administrations of Cardinals Richelieu and Mazarin and its continued weakness. These necessarily throw the achievements of Louis XIV into greater prominence. Certainly the major increase in the size of the French army from the 1670s was not the consequence of tactical developments. Instead, it is appropriate to emphasize the stronger domestic position of the French monarchy under Louis, and how far this lent weight to his assertive foreign policy. The army increased in size because the king believed that was necessary to give weight to this policy and could obtain the soldiers, thanks to the domestic stability he brought France. It did not do so because any tactical or technological innovations encouraged any such change.

Louis XIV's Foreign Policy

Under Louis, France became the most dynamic military power in western Europe and shattered Spain's European empire. The foundations of French military power were clear. A population of about 20 million, far greater than those of England and Spain combined, gave France the strongest military potential in western Europe. Much of the French agrarian economy was generally buoyant. Though the French were not at the forefront of new agricultural techniques, as the Dutch were, much of France was fertile and well watered.

Louis's first war was a relatively modest affair, the War of Devolution (1667–8). Motivated by an opportunistic claim on part of the succession of his late father-in-law, Philip IV of Spain, Louis was helped by the diplomatic isolation of Philip's handicapped son Carlos II. The French rapidly captured a number of fortresses in the Spanish Netherlands, including the strategic one of Lille (1667). The Spaniards were in no position to offer effective resistance, but, concerned about France's success, England, the Dutch, and Sweden formed a Triple Alliance (1668), and Louis found it appropriate to bring the war to a close with the Treaty of Aix-la-Chapelle with Spain (1668) by which he kept Lille.

The Dutch War (1672–9) was a more protracted conflict. It arose from Louis's anger at the Dutch role in the Triple Alliance and his contempt for them as merchants and republicans. Louis was influenced by the prospect of easy alliances and quick victories held out by Turenne, one of his leading generals, but there was little sense of how the war would develop diplomatically or militarily. Rather than planning to take Amsterdam, Louis hoped that Spain would come to the aid of the Dutch and that he could, therefore, resume the conquest of the Spanish Netherlands.

Having gained the alliance of Charles II of England by the Secret Treaty of Dover (1670) and of most of the German princes, Louis attacked the

The conquest of the Franche-Comté. Having invaded this strategic Spanish-ruled area on his eastern border during the War of Devolution (1667–8), Louis XIV finally conquered it in 1674 and was ceded it by the Treaty of Nijmegen of 1678. This success, never reversed, indicated the ability of *ancien régime* warfare to effect major territorial changes. It also greatly contributed to the misleading sense that Louis was in control of events.

Dutch in 1672. His army crossed the Rhine and rapidly advanced into the Dutch republic from the east, but was stopped by flood water when the Dutch opened the dykes. The war then broadened out as the Emperor Leopold I and the 'Great Elector' Frederick William of Brandenburg-Prussia joined the Dutch, who were energized by William III of Orange. The crisis produced by the war had given William an opportunity to wrest control of the crucial province of Holland from the anti-Orange republican faction led by the De Witt brothers, who were murdered. Louis XIV was abandoned by Charles II in 1674, and his Swedish ally was defeated by the Great Elector at Fehrbellin (1675). At the Treaty of Nijmegen (1678) France gained Franche-Comté, Freiburg, and more of the Spanish Netherlands.

Louis's gains can be seen as part of a territorial strategy designed to break Habsburg encirclement. There was certainly little sign of any attempt to reach the supposed 'natural' frontiers of the Rhine, Alps, and Pyrenees. Louis does not appear to have thought in these terms, and was rather concerned to acquire positions that could extend his power beyond these lines, such as Freiburg and Casale. Unable to rely on her allies, as was demonstrated by Sweden and the United Provinces in 1648 and by England in 1674, France appeared in a vulnerable position, provided a large number of her enemies could unite. Defensive considerations were as important as opportunism in Louis's policy. Nijmegen gave France a more defensible frontier with the Spanish Netherlands, and this was strengthened further by a programme of fortress construction organized by Sébastien Le Prestre de Vauban, who became Commissioner General of Fortifications in 1678, and by the *réunions*, a series of territorial gains obtained through force and dubious legal means in the years after Nijmegen.

In 1688 French forces advanced into the empire in order to enforce Louis XIV's views in disputes in the Rhineland. This gave William III an opportunity to invade England successfully and to replace his unpopular Catholic uncle and father-in-law, James II (1685–8) in the so-called Glorious Revolution. By the summer of 1689 Louis was at war with Austria, Bavaria, Britain, the Dutch and Spain, and in 1690 the leading Italian ruler, Victor Amadeus II of Savoy-Piedmont, joined the alliance. Louis's isolation was a significant diplomatic defeat and influenced the course of the conflict: France's operations in Europe were largely confined to her borderlands, although colonial conflict raged from Hudson's Bay to India. In a hard-fought struggle the French were unable to dominate the war in the Low Countries and their attempt to support James II in Ireland was crushed by William III at the battle of the Boyne (1690). By the Treaty of Rijswick (1697) Louis lost his earlier gains of Philippsburg, Breisach, Freiburg, and Kehl.

In a startling turnabout, Louis and his bitter enemy, William III, then sought to defuse tensions over the forthcoming succession of the childless Carlos II of Spain (1665–1700). However, the infant Bavarian prince selected to inherit most of the dominions by the First Partition Treaty (1698) soon died; and the compromise suggested by the Second Treaty collapsed when Carlos died in 1700 and left his entire inheritance to Philip duke of Anjou, Louis's second grandson. This was challenged by the other claimant, Leopold I's second son, Charles. The War of the Spanish Succession broke out in 1701. William's hostility to Louis and a series of provocative acts on the part of the latter, including the recognition of James II's son as king of England, led Britain and the Dutch to join the conflict on the side of Leopold in 1702.

British intervention was to play a crucial role in the conflict. In 1701 William appointed John Churchill, later 1st duke of Marlborough, as Captain-General of the English forces in the Netherlands, a post he held until 1711. Marlborough skilfully held the anti-French coalition together, and his bold generalship played a major role in turning the tide against the French. In 1703–4 a combination of France, Bavaria, and rebels against Austrian rule in Hungary appeared about to extinguish Habsburg power. The crisis was averted by Marlborough's bold march at the head of an Anglo-German army from Koblenz to the Danube. This, the most decisive British military move on the continent until the twentieth century, led to his subsequent victory, in cooperation with Prince Eugene of Austria, at Blenheim (1704). Marlborough displayed there a mastery of the terrain, of the retention and management of reserves, and of the decisive stroke. Blenheim was followed by the clearing of Germany. After another victory for Marlborough at Ramillies (1706) the Spanish Netherlands were conquered, while the French attempt to reverse this was thwarted at Oudenaarde (1708).

The anti-French Grand Alliance, however, had less success in conquering Spain and invading France. The course of the war reflected the respective strategic strengths of the combatants. France had a relatively secure home base protected by a large army and excellent fortifications and was largely immune to British amphibious attack. From there, her forces could take the offensive: the French ability to campaign simultaneously on a number of fronts was a testimony to her military, fiscal, and administrative strength. Yet France's opponents were also effective. The British sustained the coalition, in large part with financial support made possible by growing British foreign trade. Marlborough totally broke the image of French military superiority. Yet the Dutch, Austrians, Savoyards, Portuguese, and the lesser German princes were also crucial: they provided the armies to resist France and, by staying together for over a decade, eventually forced France to accept terms that marked the end of French diplomatic predominance. War weariness in Britain led to the creation of a Tory ministry that negotiated the Peace of Utrecht with France (1713). By this the Spanish inheritance was divided, reflecting the fortunes of war. Philip V (1700–46) retained Spain and Spanish America, while Charles, the Austrian claimant to the Spanish throne, now the Emperor Charles VI (1711–40), gained the duchy of Milan, Sardinia, Naples, and the Spanish Netherlands. Victor Amadeus II of Savoy-Piedmont gained Sicily, while Britain kept two Mediterranean bases, Gibraltar and Minorca, which she had captured in 1704 and 1708 respectively. The British also gained the profitable right to send an annual ship to trade with Spanish America, an important breach of the Spanish commercial monopoly, as well as Nova Scotia, Newfoundland, and Hudson's Bay in North America. The Protestant succession in Britain was also recognized: the French thus renounced the cause of the exiled Catholic male line of the Stuarts.

These terms marked a new political order. Austria was now the dominant power in Italy, and far stronger in Germany, than in the 1600s and

1610s. Britain was a leading power. Louis XIV had been unable to sustain the leading position of his early decades. Growing discrepancies between the official rhetoric of triumph and the reality of French defeats helped to tarnish the royal image. There was also a shift in style from the 1680s, as Louis and his advisers adopted a new strategy. Although the use of the device of the sun in glorification of the 'Sun King' was never abandoned, it lost its earlier importance. Attempts to draw connections with Alexander and Augustus also declined. There was a new emphasis on the statistics of conquered territory and population. A less 'glorious' note was struck.

Yet it would be inappropriate to close any account of Louis XIV's reign on a note of failure. His wars had brought heavy costs and eventual failure, but it is also important to note the king's successes. His reign did not see the precarious evasion of crisis that had characterized his grandfather Henri IV. Under Louis XIV royal government was considerably strengthened and an important measure of domestic stability created. Partly as a result, the minority of his successor, his great-grandson Louis XV, was less disturbed than his own or that of Louis XIII had been. In international terms, the revival of Austrian strength which was so important in the period 1620–1732 did not lead to a reversal of France's gains on the crucial eastern frontier. Dynastically the Bourbons won the great prize: the throne of Spain. Compared to the gains of Austria in Hungary and of Russia in the eastern Baltic, these advantages may appear of scant consequence, but Louis XIV was not operating on Europe's open frontier. His successes helped to re-establish the domestic and international prestige of the French dynasty and government. Louis's successors were to squander an impressive political legacy.

Vienna Saved

Since 1606 the Austrians and Turks had fought only one, brief, war in 1663–4. The Turks had been more engaged in conflict with Safavid Persia (Iran), had suffered from domestic instability, and had devoted 1645–69 to a lengthy, but eventually successful, conquest of Venetian-ruled Crete. Their energies and strength were revived by the grand viziers of the Köprülü dynasty. After brief wars with Poland and Russia, the Turks exploited a rebellion in those parts of Hungary ruled by the Habsburgs in order to attack Austria. In response, the outnumbered Leopold I sought general support, while Pope Innocent XI pressed Catholics to unite in a crusade. King John Sobieski of Poland and a number of German rulers

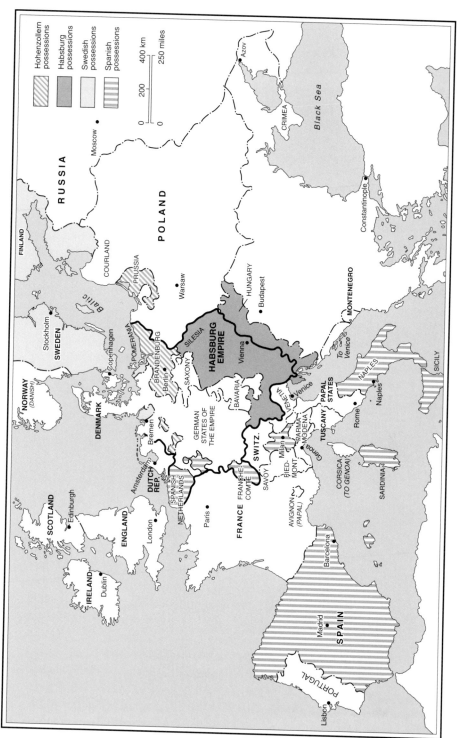

EUROPEAN STATES c. 1660

Hohenzollern possessions
Habsburg possessions
Swedish possessions
Spanish possessions

400 km
200
0
250 miles
0

Moscow

RUSSIA

FINLAND

POLAND

Black Sea

CRIMEA

Azov

Constantinople

COURLAND

PRUSSIA

Baltic

Stockholm

SWEDEN

Copenhagen

NORWAY (DANISH)

DENMARK

POMERANIA

BRANDENBURG

Berlin

SAXONY

SILESIA

Warsaw

HUNGARY

Budapest

HABSBURG EMPIRE

Vienna

BAVARIA

Bremen

Amsterdam

DUTCH REP.

GERMAN STATES OF THE EMPIRE

SPANISH NETHERLANDS

MONTENEGRO

To Venice

VENETIA

Venice

PAPAL STATES

NAPLES

SICILY

Naples

Rome

TUSCANY

GENOA

PARMA MODENA

Milan

PIED-MONT

SWITZ.

SAVOY

FRANCHE-COMTÉ

FRANCE

Paris

AVIGNON (PAPAL)

CORSICA (TO GENOA)

SARDINIA

SCOTLAND

Edinburgh

ENGLAND

London

IRELAND

Dublin

Barcelona

SPAIN

Madrid

PORTUGAL

Lisbon

came to the relief of besieged Vienna in 1683. The relief army crushed the besiegers and Christian Europe celebrated the relief of its most prominent bulwark.

Between 1683 and 1718 the Turks were defeated and pushed back by a Christian power as never before. Suleiman the Magnificent's failure at Vienna in 1529 had been a check but not a defeat. The failure of 1683 was, however, followed by the reconquest of most of Turkish Hungary. In 1684 a Holy League of Leopold I, Innocent XI, Sobieski, and Venice was formed and in 1686 Buda was successfully assaulted. The Turks were defeated at Berg Harsan (1687), Zalánkemén (1691), and, crucially, Zenta (1691) and by the Peace of Carlowitz (1699) Austria kept Transylvania and most of Hungary. The Venetians captured southern Greece, the Poles Podolia. In 1715 the Turks drove the Venetians from their Greek conquests, but, when war resumed with Austria, they were crushed by Prince Eugene at Peterwardein (1716) and Belgrade (1717). The Peace of Passarowitz (1718) left Austria with the rest of Hungary, Belgrade, western Wallachia, and northern Serbia. Thanks essentially to Austrian military success, the 'World Question' between West and East had resolved into the Balkan question.

The Rise of Russia

Under both Ivan IV, 'the Terrible' (1547–84), and Alexis (1645–76), Russia had displayed a powerful capacity to press on her western neighbours. In both cases, however, Russian advances towards the eastern Baltic had been repelled, although by the Truce of Andrusovo (1667), Alexis had been able to keep his gains of Smolensk, Kiev, and the eastern Ukraine. Under Alexis's son, Peter I 'the Great' (tsar from 1682 although he did not acquire complete power until 1689–1725), Russia came to play a more dynamic and successful role in international relations. This was largely as a result of Peter's massive development of his army during the Great Northern War with Sweden (1700–21). A major reorganization carried out in 1699–1700 created numerous regiments designed to fight like the troops of the other European powers. In 1705 a system of general levies was introduced: every twenty taxable households were ordered to send one recruit. By 1707 the army was about 200,000 strong. Peter recruited foreign officers and munitions experts, developed an armaments industry based on the metallurgical resources of the Urals, founded artillery and engineering schools and generally energized Russian military life.

The Great Northern War led to the collapse of the Baltic empire created for Sweden largely by Gustavus Adolphus. The accession of the young Charles XII of Sweden (1697–1718) encouraged hopes of Swedish weakness in her neighbours, and led to the formation of a hostile league composed of Peter the Great, Augustus II of Saxony-Poland, and Frederick IV of Denmark. Charles, however, responded rapidly in 1700, knocking Denmark out of the war and defeating Peter at Narva: 8,000 Swedes defeated 23,000 Russians, benefiting from their own greater professionalism and from the favourable direction of a snowstorm. Charles then invaded Poland, eventually dethroning Augustus in 1704. In 1708 he invaded Russia, but by then Peter had built up his army. Supply problems, the severity of the winter of 1708–9, and the hope that he would win support in the south led Charles to turn towards the Ukraine. However, the swiftness and brutality of Peter's military response in the Ukraine and the savageness of the winter of 1708–9 undermined the value of Charles's move south. Hopeful of regaining the initiative, Charles attacked the entrenched Russians at Poltava (1709), but was repelled with heavy casualties by the larger Russian army. Charles took refuge in Turkey where he stayed until 1714. In the meantime the Swedish position around the eastern Baltic collapsed. Augustus regained the Polish throne and in 1709 Peter occupied Courland. Viborg, Reval, and Riga were seized by the Russians in 1710, Finland in 1713–14. When peace finally came at Nystad in 1721, it left Peter with Livonia, Estonia, Ingria, and Kexholm. Russia had emerged as the dominant power in the Baltic and power had shifted away fundamentally from divided Poland.

Peter was less successful against the Turks. He had captured Azov from them in 1696, but when he invaded the Balkans in 1711 he met with a humiliating failure. The expected support from Balkan Christians did not materialize and Peter was outmanoeuvred by far larger Turkish forces at the River Pruth and forced to sign a humiliating peace. The Turks were not to be decisively defeated by the Russians until the war of 1768–74.

Peter also had a dynamic effect within Russia. He sought to modernize his country. Major administrative and economic reforms were pushed through, though many were only partly implemented. Peter helped to give Russian government and élite society a western orientation, widening the gulf between them and the bulk of the population. The new capital he founded at St Petersburg symbolized the new westward-looking attitude. Moscow, the epitome of old Russia, was abandoned as a capital. Peter impressed many, including Voltaire, who wrote a life of him; but he was unpopular with the bulk of the population, among whom he was widely regarded as a diabolical changeling.

Conclusions

Peter's reign was important for a number of reasons. With his determined emphasis on novelty and a breach with the past, it marked a potentially radical departure in the use of state power. In practice novelty and radicalism were tempered by the weakness of the administration, in particular the difficulty of creating new bureaucratic mechanisms, and by the continued dominance of the government by the nobility. The myth of Peter was in some ways more important than the reality. Nevertheless, Peter's aspirations looked forward to those of the 'Enlightened Despots' later in the century. As with them and with his predecessors, however, Peter's major concern was supporting his military capability. War continued to dominate the political agenda and governmental systems of European rulers. It was the sphere in which 'state' activity most affected the people of Europe.

Yet Peter, with his (apparent) stress on novelty and change, was unusual. The dominant theme in the early eighteenth century was continuity, not change. Continuity manifested itself not only in the persistence of markedly inegalitarian social, economic, and political relationships, the continued centrality of religion and the Christian moral code, and the persistence of a predominantly low-efficiency agrarian economy; but also in a society and a political culture that continually referred back to the past. There was little sense of future progress. Instead, the eighteenth century opened, in both the international and the domestic spheres, with a traditional agenda of political concerns, objectives, ideals, and methods.

III

THE EIGHTEENTH CENTURY
*c.*1715–*c.*1789

7

A Widening Market in Consumer Goods

JAMES C. RILEY

Population

At the beginning of the eighteenth century Europeans numbered some 95 million. By the century's end their numbers had jumped to 146 million, and their share of global population had risen slightly. Sustained population growth began in the eighteenth century, not just in Europe but more forcefully there than elsewhere in the world. The rate at which new people were added to the population also increased. In the century's first half population growth in western Europe, for which quantities are better known, averaged about 0.3 per cent a year, a rate familiar from the past, albeit never previously sustained in the long run. In the second half of the century, the growth rate rose to 0.5 per cent, on its way toward the rapid pace of increase of nearly 1 per cent that Europe would achieve in the nineteenth century.

This growth brought some rearrangements in settlement density, with economic and political implications. Western Europe, led by France and England, gained people at the fastest pace: France's population rose from 21.5 million in 1700 to 28 million on the eve of the French Revolution, and England's between 1700 and 1800 from 5 to 8.6 million. The population grew elsewhere in western Europe, too, but less in the east. The result was a redistribution of people and resources toward the west, a redistribution that helps explain both the growing military importance of west European powers and the primary position of western states in economic growth.

Population growth followed from small conquests over mortality and in England, but probably not elsewhere, from a temporary increase in fertility. Bubonic plague, a disease made frightening by its lethality as well as its disfiguring symptoms, had retreated in the 1670s. Its place in the mortality scheme was taken by other diseases that remained commonplace: smallpox, dysentery, typhus, typhoid fever, influenza, among others. War remained endemic, but civilian casualties diminished, perhaps because the typhus introduced so often in earlier times by unwashed troops took fewer lives as the eighteenth century progressed. Inoculation with active smallpox matter caused a mild case of the disease, in which some one in a hundred died rather than the one in seven who died from natural smallpox. Yet only in England were large numbers of people inoculated for smallpox before the last decades of the eighteenth century. The rising number of people seems to have outstripped agricultural output, but the distribution of somewhat smaller per capita supplies of food improved enough to compensate, so that subsistence crises—the coincidence of harvest shortfalls and mortality peaks—occurred less often. Final height—which in the eighteenth century was achieved around age 24—has been put forward as a decisive arbiter of welfare, on grounds that a gain in height signals better nutrition during growth years, and a loss poorer nutrition. But from the evidence about height trends it is unclear whether the last part of the eighteenth century was a period of improvement or deterioration. Across the continent people became more concerned about environmental sources of disease. Long before the advent of germ theory, and drawing on ideas from classical Greece rather than new epidemiologic theories, they attributed epidemic disease to environmental filth, and set out to discover ways to avoid disease. At the century's end the rate of decline in mortality would be sharp enough to constitute a revolution. The modern rise in life expectancy, in which the average number of years infants could be expected to live rose from about 30–5 to more than 75 years, began in a small way in the population of north-western Europe, from France to the Nordic lands, towards the end of the eighteenth century.

Europeans entered the era of the old regime in a state of epidemiologic equality. The rich lived better than the poor, they ate more, especially more protein. They were taller and their housing was more spacious. But they did not live longer, and may indeed have lived slightly shorter lives, as the English peerage seem to have done in comparison to the population at large. Social status, which counted for so much in the influence that people could bring to bear on local and national policies, did not yet count also as a means of greater longevity. This additional means of inequality emerged in the eighteenth century: the English peerage gained an advantage over the population at large by the second quarter of the century. This advantage is manifest, even blatant, from the studies that historians and sociologists, some contemporary and some academic, have conducted of the conditions of life in the first half of the nineteenth century.

Formerly regional differences, especially residence in town or village, had counted the most in distinguishing people according to their potential to survive. Towns and cities were so densely peopled that they could sustain infectious diseases which, like smallpox, required a constant supply of non-immune hosts, whereas villages could not. Thus important infectious diseases, which caused the death of about half of each cohort between birth and age 20, remained endemic in cities, but merely epidemic in the countryside. As a result, villagers lived longer lives than did townspeople. But by the century's end socio-economic status mattered as much. Whereas the urban–rural differential would fade across the nineteenth century, the socio-economic differential would sharpen itself and persist through the twentieth century.

Marriage, reproduction, sickness, and death all seem likely to be linked to economic conditions. French historians studying the seventeenth century detected a link between temporarily higher food prices and higher mortality, and that combination remained strong in eastern Europe in the eighteenth century. But it rarely occurred in western or central Europe. Harvests failed across much of Europe in the early 1740s, but only Ireland and Norway suffered a simultaneous mortality crisis; in 1817, when there was another harvest failure, no people suffered from it in the way that had been so common in the seventeenth century. The eighteenth century was still an era of periodic poor harvests without any longer being an era of simultaneous mortality crises.

Work and Income: One Conundrum

From one point of view the most important watershed in the eighteenth century consisted of the invention of mechanical equipment to make cloth and the reorganization of labour around the new equipment. Industrial modernization made western Europe richer. From another point of view the most important divide was the reorganization of work, not toward creating a factory system, but instead in expectations about the work that individuals within a family would perform, and how that work would be associated with output. In the traditional economy all the members of the family worked. From young ages, around 6, children collected animal manure, tended livestock, and watched siblings. Later, at 12–14, youths took on more formal tasks. They learned a trade by apprenticing to masters in the trade, farming by working as an agricultural labourer, or domestic work by apprenticing as a domestic servant to a householder. In any case they often left home by age 14. Adults shared the work tasks that had to be performed outside the home, women working alongside men at many of the tasks of farming, transport, artisanship, and other trades. Other tasks were assigned either to men or women; in England women dairied, cultivated the garden, and sold its produce in the market, supervised domestic servants, and often kept the farm's accounts. Russian peasant women tended poultry and livestock and slaughtered poultry; wove, spun, and bleached fabrics; collected and spun hemp; harvested rye; and weeded flax. Other members of the household, in northern Europe domestic servants and labourers, and in southern Europe those plus members of an extended family, also contributed to the household's work.

This work scheme changed in most respects between the late eighteenth century and the late nineteenth. By the latter time children were schooled up to the age of 12 or 14, or higher. The young no longer trained as apprentices, learning all the steps in the hand manufacture of an item, but learned on the job how to perform a single step in machine production. Women first entered the labour force as wage earners, and then withdrew from it: by the late nineteenth century wives were meant to stay at home and to run the home. Men were meant to work outside, earning the wages that sustained the entire family, but it is not unusual to encounter testimony of men performing such household chores as tending the children or carding wool. At more or less the same time that mechanized capital equipment began to take over some of the tasks of production, work and expectations about work within the family began to be reorganized.

The withdrawal of so many people from the labour force must have had important consequences. But those effects do not show up in the income data. Income is measured in the traditional circumstances by assigning the household's output to the householder, rather than dividing it among individual members. In the first half of the nineteenth century women and children emerged as wage earners in Britain, Belgium, and some other places. They make an appearance in the income accounts, before disappearing in the second half of the century when they were caught up in education, domesticity, and uncompensated work.

This new model of the household economy influenced economists when they set out in the twentieth century to measure output and income in the national economy. Income accounting noticed wages but overlooked uncompensated work. Economic historians then applied this accounting model to the nineteenth and the eighteenth century, trying to reconstruct income. They took over the implicit assumptions of the model about which work should be assessed, and sought to discover how much income might have been earned by males in the eighteenth century, had those men worked for wages. In fact most men did not work for wages, or not for wages alone, in the eighteenth century. They were paid also in kind, wholly or in part, in services, and by being granted access to land or equipment. And this model disregarded the work of family members. Income accounting influenced the appraisal of the eighteenth century in another way, too. Assigning value only to product and income, this accounting system overlooked the quality of life, and such gauges of that as literacy, life expectancy, and housing.

If we take the income accounting approach, the most distinctive feature of the eighteenth century is its poverty. In the Dutch Republic, the Southern Low Countries, England, and parts of France, Italy, Spain, and Germany people were notably richer than were their counterparts in the Nordic lands and eastern Europe. Travellers from each realm remarked these differences in what was the most popular literary form of the age: the journal of a journey. But all of them were poorer by far than they would become in the nineteenth century. According to one estimate, in 1820 Britain was the richest land in Europe with a per capita GDP of $1,450 (in 1985 US relative prices, corresponding to £1,115 at a 1985 rate of $1.30 = £1), and Finland at $639 (£491) was the poorest among those lands for which an estimate may be ventured. By 1989, making the comparison in constant terms, which adjusts for inflation, Finland had advanced to $14,015 and the UK to $13,519. The differences in 1820, and earlier, too, bulk small against the gains over time.

But three important elements are disregarded. First, these estimates, and others like them, leave out the things people grew and made for themselves at a time when those were important elements in household income, and they leave out barter exchanges. Workers paid in a combination of kind and wages, which was a commonplace means of payment, count only for the wages they earned. Second, these estimates disregard the work of women and children, and the non-wage-earning work of men. Such work is also omitted from twentieth-century income accounts, but the point is that work of that type contributed much more to household well-being in the eighteenth century than it does in the twentieth. Both omissions end up understating income in the eighteenth century, and exaggerating its growth since then.

The third overlooked element is actually a congeries of things comprising all the characteristics of life that influence its quality but remain uncaptured by income. If, between countries or among individuals, income

varied in much the same way as these various gauges of the quality of life, then the omission would not matter. But it did not. Sweden, for example, was relatively poor. But, compared to other lands, it was rich in the literacy of its people, their life expectancy, the rural nature of its population, and its prospects. Sweden would remain poor throughout the nineteenth century in GDP, but it would hold its lead as the land where people lived the longest.

The conundrum has two aspects: how much better off will old-regime people be seen to have been when the traditional and the modern economies are compared on the same terms? How much will the appraisal of differences among countries be changed by taking into account other measures of the quality of life? This is a research agenda, one that also has much to do with differences in the way less developed and more developed economies are compared to one another in the twentieth century.

Agriculture

Across the continent, at the beginning of the eighteenth century and the end, more people worked to produce food, fodder, and textile crops than at any other tasks. At the century's beginning most of them worked with little dependence on markets for food, fibres, or labour; they produced most of the goods they consumed. Nevertheless specialized agricultural areas, which had appeared much earlier, developed more rapidly in the eighteenth century than they had done previously. The great European breadbasket, stretching eastward from the southern Baltic across Prussia, Poland, and Ukraine supplied much of urban northern Europe with grain, channelled through the Amsterdam market in the seventeenth century but more often in the eighteenth century moving directly from the Baltic to ports across north-western Europe. Mediterranean Europe drew on the Levantine coast for grain. The coastal lowlands of France's Atlantic south-west furnished salt in commercial quantities. Across the eighteenth century Europeans consumed exotic foodstuffs and spices with increasing frequency, depending for the supply of cane sugar, chocolate, coffee, tea, and other items on the East and the West Indies, and on North America for the tobacco they

Painted in 1739, this depiction of a servant returning from the market shows some of the items that householders, even those with servants, no longer made for themselves. Here she carries a fowl or a hare, and two loaves of bread. By the eighteenth century the concept of 'the market' referred to the wholesale exchange that business people frequented, and to the open air or sheltered market patronized by householders.

smoked in pipes or took as snuff. More and more town residents drank French wine and brandy in place of, or in addition to, their local beers. The most important changes in agriculture occurred in the development of markets and the expanding use of new crops and more productive crop rotations.

For people who lived in cities, specialization was axiomatic. Cities supplied their hinterlands with religious, political, and commercial services and, increasingly, they were also centres for the manufacture of household goods of better quality than what rural folk made for themselves. They could exist because the countryside produced surplus food, textile crops, fuel, and wood for building. Cities and towns provided the sites for the markets where these goods and services were exchanged, and often, but not always, controlled the terms of exchange. In the eighteenth century it is appropriate to think about the terms of trade—the changing relative value of goods and services moving in trade—between nations and also between town and countryside.

If specialization provided the means for cities to exist, for people in the countryside any step away from self-sufficiency and toward dependence was fraught with risk. Compared to townspeople, villagers had little power to influence the terms of trade and the value of goods and services. In years of crop failure, it is true, they sold the smaller quantities of their crops for higher prices. But a system of subordination existed in the pricing of rural versus urban goods and services. Land and agricultural labour on average earned smaller returns than did urban capital and urban labour, so that for the same investment of money or time, townspeople got more. Villagers also paid more in taxes, tithes, and seigneurial dues than they received in benefits. Thus the terms of trade were biased against the countryside in a structural way.

Specialization and dependence on outside suppliers was fraught with risk for rural people also because they bore the costs of any failure associated with shifting towards specialization. By tradition rural people worked the land in household units, growing a variety of crops and livestock calculated to meet their own needs and produce that surplus required to obtain the outside goods and services they wanted and to pay the taxes, dues, and rents they owed. If they specialized more, focusing their energies on raising livestock, growing grain, or on whatever single activity earned them the highest returns, they gained the promise of larger revenue at the risk of having to buy from the outside more of the things they had formerly supplied for themselves. On paper, as any introductory student of economics will be eager to explain, specialization should be advantageous for everyone. It uses resources more efficiently. But in the old regime taking such a step meant that rural dwellers would be dependent on the vagaries of weather elsewhere and on markets, trading routes, and entrepreneurial talent which they did not control and which were not very reliable. Peasants owning or leasing land in the Paris basin could depend on the urban market as an outlet for the foods and fibres they grew and as a way to supply their needs. They could afford to specialize. But in rural Valpolicella, in Italy, peasants scattered their fields rather than consolidating them, they mixed their crops rather than specializing, and they practised intricate schemes of land tenure. They were, as a consequence, poorer than their counterparts in the Paris basin. But they were also safe.

For agriculturalists something else, too, made specialization hazardous, and this thing is the central fact of economic life in the old regime. The land was not highly productive. Its yields were modest. Moreover, working the land required an inefficient use of time; if there was barely enough labour available to plant and harvest, there was through most of the year too much inactive labour.

In modern agronomy crop yields are measured in output volume per unit of land. For the old regime it is easier to estimate the ratio of seeds harvested to seeds planted. For wheat and rye, the most important crops in value and quantity, average yield ratios ranged from a low between 3 and 4 in eastern Europe to a high between 9 and 14 in Britain and the Low Countries. At their best, those amount to about one-third of modern yields. In

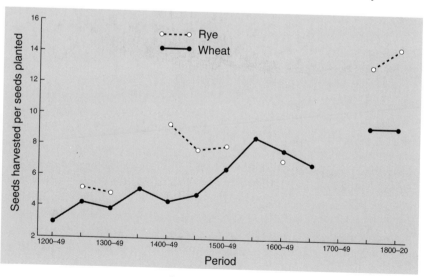

Wheat and rye yields

western Europe, Germany, and the Nordic lands, but not in Poland, Russia, and along the Baltic coast, those yields were somewhat higher than what had obtained in the seventeenth century, and markedly higher than they had been in the medieval era. In these terms, agricultural progress came gradually, keeping pace with population growth until the later eighteenth century.

Improvements in output during the eighteenth century derived first from more intensive use of the land, and secondarily from reclamation of new arable lands. As the demand for foodstuffs grew, lands not previously cultivated because of their low quality were put into cultivation, usually with improvements in the way they were cropped. Prussian Silesia added 15 per cent to its arable during the eighteenth century, but France only 2.5 to 4 per cent. Fields already in use were cropped more often, even continuously, by the introduction of techniques for controlling soil fertility. Farmers had typically counted on a rotation between cropping and fallow, and grazing livestock on fallow, to maintain the fertility of their fields. In the era of the Renaissance, Flemish farmers began planting fodder crops that allowed them to maintain larger livestock herds, thereby producing more manure, and they began to rotate nitrogen-dependent grains with nitrogen-fixing turnips and clovers. The nitrogen-fixing plants converted atmospheric nitrogen into soil nitrates, though this is knowledge gained later. Those techniques, which spread slowly before 1650, afterwards moved into England and Scotland as well as some regions of France, Spain, Italy, Germany, Sweden, and elsewhere, acquiring characteristics that suited them to the locale. In Prussia, for example, the Hohenzollerns persistently introduced new crops, promoted livestock breeding, and tried in other ways to increase agricultural output.

Astonishingly complex rotations emerged under such names as the Norfolk system and stall feeding, all sharing the feature that they supported larger livestock herds which produced more manure and in that way enlarged the output of crops that people ate. These new schemes of land use flourished where proximity to urban markets made feasible the heavy investments that they required, and where also the people who worked the land could depend on cornering the benefit of their investment. Output rose also as people acquired a taste for potatoes, a New World plant available in the sixteenth century but not widely cultivated and eaten until the second half of the eighteenth century. The potato required more hands for cultivation and harvesting than traditional grain crops, but it repaid that investment with far higher yields in weight and calorie content.

Nevertheless, it is misleading to think of the old regime as an era of agricultural revolution. Most people continued to work the land using traditional methods, to derive traditional yields, and to farm for subsistence. Two field rotations, alternating grain with fallow, and three field rotations, alternating grain, pulses (peas and beans), and fallow, remained common. In France at the end of the century still at least three-quarters and perhaps nine-tenths of the land under tillage was worked by sharecroppers. They held short leases that militated against the investments in the land that heavy manuring required. Across Europe most agriculturalists also owed the prince, the church, the seigneur, and the landowner so much in rents and dues that they may be characterized as bound rather than free labourers. The *mezzadri* (peasants) of Altopascio, in Italy, borrowed seeds to plant and grain to eat, becoming so dependent on their landlords that the lords had to periodically forgo the debts. Only in eastern Europe were they formally bound by serfdom, which tied a family to the land. But their putative freedom in western Europe was closely restricted by the taxes they owed the prince, the monopolies and dues in cash and in kind that they owed seigneurs, the tithe that the parish priest collected to supply local church activities, plus rents. A family of four could have fed itself on little more than one hectare—two or three acres—of good land, growing wheat. But in practice the family required much more acreage because of these obligations.

Bread—made of wheat, rye, or often a mixture of the two grains, or of other grains—made up the principal item in human diets. Adult males in France ate 1–1.5 kilograms—2–3 pounds—of bread a day, and women and children smaller amounts in proportion to their weight. People who did not eat bread usually ate large amounts of pancakes, gruel, and other foods made from grain. Everyone consumed grain indirectly, in the form of beer, drinking 115 litres or more a year per capita, and, in small quantities, the meat of livestock raised partly on fodder grains. Vegetables appear in dietaries of the era, but they made up only a small part of calorie intake. Medical authorities often characterized fruits as dangerous. Apples and pears were widely consumed as cider, but it is not apparent whether people took their doctors' advice, staying away from raw fruit, or whether fruits were too perishable to appear either in the price currents listing items sold at market or in lists of the foods eaten by people living in institutions, which supply most of the dietaries. The most widely distributed manual of advice about diet in the age, written by Luigi Cornaro who lived to 98 or so and claimed the right to give advice about how to live a long and healthy life, urged people to avoid vegetables and fruit, to eat bread, soup, and eggs, and always to eat much less than the appetite demanded.

Town population
- ⊙ 200,000
- ○ 100,000
- ○ 30,000
- • less than 30,000
- ■ Financial centres
- Metallurgical industries
- Textile industries

St Petersburg
Stockholm
Vilna
Königsberg
Danzig
Glasgow
Edinburgh
Dublin
Birmingham
Bristol
Haarlem
London
Amsterdam
Antwerp
Lille
Brussels
Hamburg
Berlin
Warsaw
Leipzig
Breslau
Frankfurt
Paris
Strasbourg
Nantes
Vienna
Budapest
Lyons
Bordeaux
Bayonne
Bilbao
Toulouse
Turin
Milan
Venice
Bologna
Florence
Marseilles
Leghorn
Lisbon
Madrid
Barcelona
Rome
Sofia
Seville
Cordoba
Valencia
Naples
Salonica
Malaga
Granada
Palermo
Messina

MANUFACTURING AND FINANCIAL CENTRES IN EIGHTEENTH-CENTURY EUROPE

Manufacturing and Industry

Manufacturing and trade made up the most dynamic visible sectors of economic activity in the eighteenth century. Nearly everywhere their contribution to output rose more sharply than did that of agriculture. The number and share of people working in these sectors increased. From the perspective of the industrial revolution, the important manufacturing activity of the old regime focused on textiles and metalwork, which were the specific products around which manufacturing was first revolutionized, and on the mining of coal, which powered steam engines. From the perspective of the things that people bought and consumed, however, the description of what was important widens to include household furnishings, beer and ale, building implements and artefacts, transportation routes and equipment, decorative items, apparel, shoes and hats, glassware, pottery, and many more goods and services. The emerging factory draws attention to large enterprises employing hundreds rather than tens of people. But the reality of manufacturing in the eighteenth century remained the workshop, where a handful of people made and finished goods by hand, with the aid of implements driven by water, wind, and sometimes animal power, assisted by a number of individually modest technical innovations. In Barcelona large firms manufactured printed calicoes, called indianas, for sale in Catalonia and the rest of Spain and, from the 1770s, also in the Americas. Spanish consumers, like their counterparts in northern Europe, preferred cotton to woollen garments. These large enterprises existed before the invention of mechanical spinning, which assisted their growth by further reducing the cost of the fabric they produced. But in eastern Europe and much of the west, too, yarn and cloth were still made chiefly in rural households by a workforce consisting of family members, children and adults. Some of the work in these household workshops, producing yarn and cloth, prefigured mechanization and the factory system. In Bohemia in 1731 Count Johann von Waldstein's manufactory employed 223 weavers and spinners scattered about the village of Horni Litvinov, and 250 to 300 more spinners working in their homes. Specialization of task (nearly a half century before Adam Smith urged the greater efficiency of specialization) allowed the employment even of unskilled workers, with their lower wages. But much household production remained traditional: family members made yarn and cloth in order to clothe themselves.

At the end of the eighteenth century capital intensive factories, new technologies, and factory-disciplined labour could be found in west central England—the Midlands—and in the eastern parts of the Southern Low

Countries. Traditional manufacturing thrived in many more regions, including a large part of the Dutch Republic, the Southern Low Countries, England, France, Bavaria, and Prussian Silesia, as well as Upper Saxony, the region around Berlin, Lowland Scotland, the Austrian portions of the empire, in Barcelona, and in Russia around St Petersburg and Moscow.

The recognition that ordinary working people acquired more possessions adds a new range of questions to the things historians need to explore. When the old regime could be seen, at least in the early industrializers of England and the Southern Low Countries, chiefly as a prelude to industrialization, the pressing questions were these: how were the new technologies devised? How was financing amassed? And how was an industrial labour force created? Much has been learned about these issues. Yet even before they have been satisfactorily answered, new questions have appeared, questions that relate not so much to the origin of supply factors, as those questions about the sources of industrialization do, as to the origin of a surging demand for consumer goods. Why did people, élites and commoners alike, but especially commoners, who were so numerous, decide that they needed or wanted so many additional items of clothing, furniture, and ornamentation? The questions deal also with issues of wealth, its scale and distribution: how did ordinary working people, who are usually depicted as poor and therefore unable to afford amenities, manage to become consumers? And they deal with familiar economic issues: what forces promoted the growth of workshops and manufacturing? So far historians have expended much more time and energy on seeking answers for the questions about supply than for those about demand.

Answers to those questions about supply reveal more about the foundations of modern economic life than they do about why industrial modernization should have become so sharply focused in England and the Southern Low Countries. During the eighteenth century the pace at which solutions were devised to practical problems in manufacturing quickened, and inventors enjoyed some success at cornering profits made from their work. But if invention had been a key factor, then Scotland was a place far likelier to have industrialized than the Southern Low Countries. During the eighteenth century the rich saved money in increasingly liquid form, investing in government securities on capital markets in Amsterdam, Paris, London, and elsewhere. Grasping for a windfall, they sunk fortunes into the South Sea and the Mississippi bubbles, grand Ponzi schemes in which incoming resources were employed not to build the commercial ventures that had been promised but instead to pay dividends high enough to attract new investments. In sum, people who had money to invest put it into safe and secure investments and also into get-richer-quick schemes. Sometimes they invested also in mundane manufacturing enterprises. But the new industrialists mostly financed their projects from their own resources or with loans from friends and family members, rather than from credit obtained on capital markets. If capital, or even the cost of credit, had been the key factor in industrial modernization, then the Dutch Republic was a far likelier place for revolution than England. There the cost of credit remained the lowest in Europe. Industrial modernization emerged first in England for banal reasons. England possessed more advantages than any other region so that its uniqueness lay in the combination of its resources rather than in their singularity. England possessed coal, waterways for transport and water for supplying power, a dense and migratory population, well-developed cottage industry, trade routes providing access to foreign markets, in short, more advantages than any rivals, except the Low Countries.

Among supply factors, historians have in recent years paid particularly close attention to the creation of an industrial labour force. Men, women, and children whose descendants would work ten- or twelve-hour days in nineteenth-century factories worked in the seventeenth century to an overwhelming extent in cultivating crops and raising livestock. Their work year was irregular, mixing bouts of stupendous activity, such as at harvesting, with long periods of near inactivity. Their skills were widely possessed, and in any case focused on the key decisions and techniques of planting, tending, and harvesting crops. The answer that has emerged is that, in many more or less isolated regions scattered across Europe, beginning in the sixteenth and seventeenth centuries these agriculturalists added some new off-season activities. They began to card, spin, weave, or knit in their homes. Merchants supplied them with raw textile material, and agreed to pay a certain price for the steps that household members took in the multistage process of transforming raw wool, flax, and cotton into cloth. By tying this off-season work performed by farmers to later industrial modernization, the historians who studied it saw the need to characterize it anew. They changed their description of the activity called in earlier periods 'putting-out' (the term used in Chapters 1 and 4 above), or domestic industry, to a word expressing this link: proto-industrialization. Yet if proto-industrialization had been the key factor in industrial modernization, then the industrial revolution might have begun first where this activity first appeared, which is unlikely to have been England, and would have thrived by the end of the eighteenth century in many regions scattered across Europe rather than a few.

Rural women knew how to make cloth, though the cloth they made was not as finely spun or as richly dyed as that made by urban craftsmen. Presumably they taught these skills to their husbands and children when the householder rented or bought a loom or a frame and began using off-season time to perform one of the tasks involved in making cloth. This kind of work seems to have focused attention more effectively on the cost of labour, a factor examined dispassionately by the merchant-entrepreneur putting material out, and on production bottlenecks. Proto-industrialization also transformed the nature of work. The men and women who performed tasks at home discovered the relationship between skill and time, on one hand, and compensation on the other. Under this system, far more than under the agricultural tasks that had dominated work in the past, it is plausible to examine the value that workers attached to their time, and the value that employers attached to it. Whereas formerly leisure had been an inescapable feature of long stretches of the year, in domestic industry household members could choose whether to work and earn money. From limited evidence, they seem often to have adopted a leisurely pace early in a week, only to make that up with strenuous work towards the week's end. For the most part they made such choices in circumstances dictated by merchants who controlled compensation, and who set the price of labour at the lowest level and managed to prevent many workers from making their way up the scale into entrepreneurial positions. In the past agricultural labour had been valued at a lower rate than labour in nearly any other field of work. That hierarchy remained in place as proto-industrialization developed, and it was extended to domestic work. On one hand, therefore, proto-industrialization added in a substantial way to the efficiency of labour. Men, women, and children who had not worked most of the year because there was nothing gainful for them to do found a gainful activity. Labour resources were thereby used more efficiently. Moreover, output expanded sharply, and passed out of the control of urban craftsmen, who had monopolized it and profited from their monopoly. The new goods were not as fine, but they were also much cheaper. On the other hand, agricultural households were drawn into domestic industry on unfavourable terms, which enriched the merchant-entrepreneur far more than they did the working family.

A putting-out system developed also in urban manufacturing, where it sometimes rivalled and sometimes overlapped the traditional system of handicraft production. Nails and pins, for example, were increasingly made

What is on view in this character painting by Giuseppe Nogari? Is it more the dignity of this old and timeworn woman? Or the simple elegance of her shawl?

by urban workers employed not as apprentices, journeymen, or masters but instead as piece-rate labourers. In the traditional system master craftsmen controlled the quantity and the quality of output by setting limits to the number of masters the guilds they controlled would accommodate. In the proto-industrial system entrepreneurs controlled quantity and quality in a fashion much more responsive to market conditions than capable, as in the guild system, of setting market conditions. In the guild system young men—most guilds excluded women—entered apprenticeships and, if they completed them successfully, became journeymen. As apprentices they took less important jobs around the shop, and gradually learned how to perform the tasks of their master's trade. As journeymen they made the products of the shop, often under the master's supervision. If they were journeymen to a master artist, they painted parts of the portraits, still lifes, and other paintings being produced in the master's shop. But the master designed the painting, planned and scheduled its execution, and claimed artistic as well as financial credit for it. Such, at least, is the theory of mastership. In practice the situation was messier. Guildsmen rarely stood so completely apart from piece-rate labourers in the eighteenth century. Partially trained apprentices and journeymen set themselves up outside the towns, serving country people and sometimes slipping their goods and services into guild-controlled towns.

In both of these parallel and overlapping worlds of work, unemployment and underemployment possessed a character different from that in agriculture. Peasant farmers who held land, or who contracted to share their crops, had employment, even though they worked full days only part of the year. The things they grew in the weeks and months of strenuous activity were meant to suffice to support that family. But people working for piece rates, in the countryside or the city, had employment on terms much more akin to those of an agricultural day labourer. The day labourer could count on work and income during the busy seasons of the agrarian year, and correspondingly could count on being out of work for much of the rest of the year. One estimate, based on observations from Arthur Young about the 1770s in England, suggests that if a large farm with a progressive crop rotation required seventy people in March and August, only twenty-five were needed in other seasons of work.

Piece-rate workers faced the same prospect of part-time employment, with one difference: they could not so easily forecast when they would be active and when inactive. They depended on the entrepreneurs who engaged them to supply work, and in turn the entrepreneurs depended on the demand for their goods. Little is known yet about the storage of finished goods. To appearances entrepreneurs tried to anticipate demand in the short run rather than to make output balance demand at the end of a longer period. Few people worked throughout the year. It does not appear to be true that, in piece work or in handicrafts, workers ever took nearly as much time off as implied by the number of religious holidays on the calendar. But it does appear to be true that seasonal or intermittent unemployment characterized the world of work in the eighteenth century, albeit less so for people who moved successfully between the two worlds of agricultural and piece-rate work.

For agriculturalists this pattern mattered less than it did for townsmen. Peasants in all but the most market-oriented regions literally earned their livelihoods, cultivating and harvesting most of the things they consumed. Thus they stored produce gathered in the several harvest seasons of the year. Townsmen, however, had to buy food throughout the year, whether or not they were actively employed. Largely for that reason there emerged in towns, but not in the countryside, a network of private and municipal pawn banks, where people borrowed against the artefacts of everyday life in hard times and redeemed their loans in good times. In that way the pawning system became a motivator of consumption. People stored wealth in household artefacts. The more goods a household possessed, goods easier to protect from theft or feckless spending than cash itself, the more the family could pawn in bad times. The rural counterpart was a prosperous peasant, a landlord, or perhaps a notary, who lent money against livestock, implements, or the crop itself. These characterizations contrast starkly with the classical picture of rural and urban life, noteworthy for its simplicity. In the old regime, as we are just learning, even ordinary people possessing only commonplace work skills often lived complex lives requiring seasonal migration and astute financial planning.

In some ways the new structure of manufacturing seems more capitalist than the traditional styles. Compared to guild masters, merchant-entrepreneurs defined their interests more narrowly around the cost of factors of production, especially labour, and set their sights more aggressively on profits. What is more, the new system embodied conflict between workers and owners. The very eagerness of entrepreneurs to raise profits by lowering factor costs prompted the people who worked for them to define their own economic interests more aggressively, and to recognize the degree to which they were at odds with, rather than allies of, their employers. Proto-industrialization not only laid foundations for industrial modernization. It also set the terms of the attitudes that workers and employers would adopt towards one another.

Trade and Transport

In the most dynamic national economy of the old regime, Britain, the largest volume of growth came neither in manufacturing nor in agriculture but in services. Around 1800 services accounted for some 44 per cent of output, compared to about 35 per cent in 1700, and made up the largest sector. More people worked in agriculture, but more value was produced in services, which already bulked large in the economies of the Low Countries, France, Italy, and urban regions elsewhere.

The growth of the service sector remains the largely untold part of the history of commercial development. Much more has been learned about long-distance and international trade than about inland transport, retailing, and other service activities. Well before the opening of the eighteenth century the actual movement of goods to Europe and across Europe had become regular enough to drive markets towards integration with one another. The prices of basic goods on different markets moved together, not merely in the short run, which might indicate merely similar weather patterns, but also in the long run. That characteristic signals increasing specialization, and means that shipping facilities—ports, the merchant marine and the skill of merchant seamen, ship technology, and the flow of commercial news—were all regular enough to allow further development toward specialization. The invisible hand of the market, which Adam Smith described so effectively, had been at work for a long time. During the eighteenth century coal, sugar, and tobacco from the New World, and coffee, tea, and cotton from Asia joined the inventory of goods regularly in transit (wheat, rye, precious metals, wool, wine, spices, iron, silk, hemp, flax) while the quantity of such goods continued to grow. In the seventeenth century certain markets, especially Amsterdam, had held the status of entrepôts, meaning that goods were transshipped and stored there temporarily. Eighteenth-century merchants found ways to bypass entrepôts, which undermined Amsterdam's position but made for greater overall efficiency.

Trade promoted empire, and empire in turn fostered transoceanic trade. European merchants had discovered earlier that they could manipulate and exploit people living in Asia, Africa, and the Americas; exploitation flourished in the eighteenth century, especially in the form of slavery. Slave labour in the Americas, even more effectively than enserfed labour in Prussia, cheapened production costs, making possible the popularization of New World foodstuffs, which were too expensive for widespread consumption if grown by smallholders. Some historical sociologists argue that

Peasant market gardeners set off to market, carrying the produce they hope to sell. This painting offers a picture of rustic country people attuned to market forces, thus belonging at once to the traditional and the modern.

this exploitation was the keystone of a world system, in which Europe enriched itself by forcing the remainder of the globe into a position of dependence on it. That argument does much to describe the long-range effects of colonization and exploitation in Asia, Africa, and the Americas. But it is very difficult to show that the wealth extracted from the colonial regions was grand enough in scale to make Europe rich. It was icing—sugared chocolate, mocha, or coffee—on a cake made in Europe.

Trade remained prey to war. Merchants eagerly followed news of diplomatic tension, and the price of such important war-making commodities as saltpetre and Swedish iron, because they knew how effectively a conflict between major powers could shut off trade. Suppliers, merchants, and consumers alike adjusted to the undependability of trade links, rushing large quantities into the European trade network immediately at the conclusion of a war. They seem to have been able to anticipate upcoming conflicts, for there is evidence of surging shipments on the eve of war, too.

In the eighteenth century on a far grander scale than in either of the two preceding centuries Europeans imported gold and silver from the New World. Most of these imports they made into coins, enlarging the money stock at a quickening pace and permitting the monetarization of economic life in regions which had relied on barter. From 1701 to 1800 Europe added an annual average of 324 tons of silver and silver equivalent to its stock of precious metals, not counting re-exports, mostly to Asia. Already in 1700 transactions were regularly referenced to money, even when they often occurred via barter. During the eighteenth century, however, even people living at some distance from urban markets found it easier to acquire money. Merchants also created money in larger quantities, drawing bills of exchange to cover commercial transactions and more confidently circulating those bills in the two or three months between their creation and final settlement of the transaction they financed. Coins and commercial instruments alike fed an increase in the money stock, which promoted higher prices but also fostered economic growth.

Theorists and rulers understood some aspects of these developments. By pursuing objectives called mercantilist, they meant to expand the stock of precious metals within a country, as well as to advance the manufacturing interests of that country by fostering the output at home of goods being imported. But seventeenth-century mercantilists conceptualized the economic world as a pie of fixed size, and saw the rivalry among states as a struggle over redividing that pie, rather than enlarging it. The notion that an enlargement was possible emerged strongly in the eighteenth century. Frederick the Great of Prussia, influenced by cameralists who sought to understand the structure of things, used an algebraic formula to explain how a ruler might augment the resources at his command by fostering growth in population and economic activity. Mercantilism also came under attack by Adam Smith, who argued for markets regulated only to prevent unfair competition, and by François Quesnay, who favoured unregulated markets even for grain, long in France a commodity so sensitive that its export had been prohibited. Mercantilism represented a traditional outlook, which stressed the capacity of government to set and pursue objectives, while Smith's ideas comprise classical liberalism, a novel theory that assigned only two tasks to government: taking care of people needing assistance, and preventing unfair competition.

The State Sector

The chief business of government in the old regime consisted, first, of high finance and, second, of war and war finance. The state dominated capital markets, which had been created in the seventeenth century in order to raise credit for governments. That had been a fabulously successful enterprise. By the eve of the French Revolution, every major and secondary power, excepting only Prussia, had amassed a debt large enough to make servicing it the leading item in state spending. Second only to the task of paying interest and sometimes also repaying some capital on existing loans was the business of borrowing anew to meet the costs of fresh wars. In the old regime, as earlier, states levied taxes sufficient only to meet their needs in peacetime, which condemned them to borrowing money to fight wars. The solution to that problem seems obvious: fight fewer wars. But these states existed in a competitive system. Wars involving major powers and intended to add to or merely to protect existing territory were fought in nearly half the years up to 1815.

Even so eighteenth-century rulers foresaw other aims of taxing and spending. The enlightened despots among them, especially Joseph II of Austria, foresaw a state that would fund education, health training and services, assistance to the poor and disabled, and other tasks central to modern social democracies. Like Adam Smith, who in an era of conflict and hardship envisioned a laissez-faire world of harmony and prosperity, Joseph II dreamed the enlightenment dream of a world bettered by new avenues of state spending, and managed to disregard the fiscal peril that Austria faced. Such dreams as these, which directed taxing and spending towards social programmes rather than towards state building, could only become plausible through some combination of economic growth and debt annulment. Most states wrote off their insupportable debts during the wars of the French Revolution and Napoleon, entering the long post-war peace in far better financial shape than they had been in during the old regime.

Despite the burden of debts and debt service, it was not merely the idea of a larger role for the state that emerged in the eighteenth century, but also some explicit action in that direction. To deal with the growing threat of famine, which they anticipated on the basis of population growth outstripping output, Spanish monarchs revived the institution of public granaries; by 1773 some 5,225 had been built. They held enough wheat and flour to feed the entire population of Spain for two months, a generous barrier against famine. Several governments introduced settlement programmes meant to invigorate agriculture. Frederick the Great drew 300,000 or more German immigrants to Prussia; Austria shifted 150,000 or more people to Transylvania and other parts of the eastern empire; and Catherine the Great enticed large numbers of Germans to settle on the Volga.

Even so, the leading theme of taxing and spending in the old regime

must be a theme of constraint. It was an era in which novel and imaginative ideas about fiscal policy circulated freely, unbound by the weight of reflection on their prior use and the lessons of that experience. But it was also an era in which the state could rarely free up resources for new projects.

Consumption

In the eighteenth century many ordinary people, especially people living in towns and cities, began to acquire consumer goods and to form the attitudes of materialism. Moreover the society at large built a more refined infrastructure, more roads and canals, a larger housing stock, more frequent and more dependable postal services, more spacious and open towns and cities. The creation of consumer goods, the stronger emergence of a desire to possess material objects, and improvement of the infrastructure describe a take-off toward material society. To a substantial degree, the greater wealth that European economies would produce from the eighteenth century forward has consisted of material objects, which people, even élites, had theretofore consumed in comparatively small quantities. In the traditional outlook economy in possessions was preferred, especially among the bourgeoisie. In the new outlook people found that they needed an array of material amenities, oft-times in duplicate. The process of growth in consumption was evolutionary, but its effect was revolutionary.

There are some economic answers for the question why acquisitiveness thrived so in the eighteenth century. Possessions, ordinary people discovered, were a good way to store wealth in an age in which people did not have the option of putting their money in a savings bank. Estate inventories, themselves an important historical source testifying to the developing habit of consumption, reveal how little money people kept, and how much of their wealth they stored in artefacts. Possessions could also be pawned to assist a family over periods of sickness or joblessness. But the desire to possess arose not only from economic motives. Nor did it arise merely from a desire of the bourgeois to mimic the aristocracy, or working people to mimic the bourgeoisie. Certainly that is part of the story. Domestic servants were intermediaries who spread the word about what the rich owned. But some of the new habits and attitudes arose first among working

Various commercial objects are on display in this middle-class family portrait from 1669. At the centre a medical service—bloodletting—is being performed by the surgeon, Jacob Fransz. Hercules on his brother Thomas. Hercules' family surrounds him, in the proper hierarchy. They show us much of the material environment of bourgeois life in a Dutch town at that time.

people. Across western Europe working people first organized non-profit mutual societies to compensate themselves for wages forgone during bouts of sickness, and their heirs for the cost of a respectable burial.

Before the mid-seventeenth century the homes, wardrobes, and milieu of the élite included many amenities and artefacts of which ordinary people owned few counterparts. After the 1650s, as inventories of their possessions made after death reveal, ordinary people began to acquire these counterparts, plus many new items. They slept on mattresses rather than loose straw, and more and more often on beds rather than on the floor, and by the century's end the parents slept apart from the children, not yet in separate rooms but in separate beds. To the sparse religious ornaments that adorned their walls people added paintings, often of food or flowers, and mirrors. They bought additional clothing, woollen and cotton, so that ordinary people came to own not merely the garments on their backs but additional outfits, while bourgeois consumers changed wardrobes as fashions shifted. By the late eighteenth century ordinary consumers sometimes bought ready-made garments rather than apparel cut and sewn by tailors or by members of the household. Women owned more clothing than men. And, to store these things, people bought wardrobes and dressers. With increasing frequency ordinary city dwellers adorned their houses with wallpaper. They followed the progress of the day with clocks and pocket watches; they bought chamberpots and razors, enamelled buttons and snuff boxes. It was the dawn of the age of the shopkeeper, in which small home-shops proliferated.

Ordinary people began to drink tea and coffee, and some of them who did not live in viticultural regions drank wine and, more often still, brandy, but they continued to drink large quantities of local beer, ale, or wine. They ate a somewhat more varied diet, in which potatoes figured increasingly often as a staple, supplementing grain, and they ate cane sugar, chocolate, and other items grown in distant places. They ate off pottery rather than wooden plateware or bread itself, and they drank more often out of glasses than from wooden cups. They washed somewhat more of their bodies, their faces and arms rather than just their hands, and bought soap to cut dirt. They lit their uncomfortably small, low-ceiling homes with candles and lamps. They bought toys for their children, and books, newspapers, and broadsheets for themselves. At least in Paris they ate more prepared foods, bought at take-out counters. They wore more cotton clothing, stockings, and hats, the styles of which changed more rapidly, and they carried umbrellas. More and more often they hired instructors and tutors so that their children might learn to be literate and numerate. They replaced

Overland transport remained far more expensive than water transport throughout the early modern era. Neither the more extensive networks of roads built in the later eighteenth century nor the canals constructed in the Dutch Republic, Britain, and France overcame the problem of cost. Moving bulky goods across country remained often too expensive until the railway age.

informal medical practitioners with formal practitioners, shifting from wise women, bonesetters, and leech suppliers to apothecaries, from whose shops they purchased medicaments, and to surgeon-general practitioners.

In the eighteenth century the consumption of space also changed. People wanted larger houses with higher ceilings and more rooms. They also wanted towns and cities with open spaces. And they wanted an environment less offensive in its smells. Public money was to be spent on the public's health, to ventilate and lavate the town, just as the householder ventilated his or her residence and washed it out. Smell signalled the danger of epidemic disease, in the prevailing medical theory. Actions to combat the smells of human, animal, and vegetable waste constituted patriotism, in the definition of the latter decades of the eighteenth century. Patriots proposed the relocation of intramural cemeteries to sites outside the town.

On the side of infrastructure, old-regime Europeans constructed roads more rapidly than any generations before them had, and spent more to maintain their roads. The journey from Paris to Marseilles, which required seven days at 48 kilometres a day in 1765, was cut by 1780 to a mere three days at 112 kilometres a day. Carrying forward an older idea about national or even international networks of inland water transport, they built canals, channelled rivers, and drained swamps. And they built ships on an unprecedented scale, both to compensate for the brief working life of wooden vessels and to meet the rapidly growing demand for shipping stock. Lining hulls with copper or another metal extended ship life, especially for vessels operating in warm waters. The most easily noticed part of shipbuilding and transport improvement lies in the large merchant vessels built for the increasingly active transatlantic trade. But these Europeans also constructed fleets of ships for the coastal trade, plus large numbers of barges for river and canal traffic.

Too little is yet known about the timing of the consumer revolution and its origins. By the 1730s rapid growth in the number and proportion of people employed in supplying services—as opposed to products—was already complete in London. Thereafter the proportion would continue to grow, but slowly. Peak demand may have occurred even earlier in the cities of the Dutch Republic, perhaps in the 1670s, when the growth of Dutch trade slowed. In Paris and nearby Versailles, too, a peak seems likely to have occurred during the reign of Louis XIV, but there a broadly based revolution occurred only toward the end of the eighteenth century. Elsewhere a sharply higher demand for consumer goods appeared in the late eighteenth century. In each city and country the consumer revolution predated industrial modernization, which has mistakenly been assigned much of the credit for growth more closely associated with output using traditional means and equipment. The origins of consumer demand seem to lie in the secularization of attitudes and behaviour, which denigrated asceticism and exalted materialism. According to one specific hypothesis, the development of the modern novel with its idea of romantic love and the rise of a distinctively modern hedonism, preoccupied with pleasure and sensory experience, show the force of a romantic ethic. People learned to want to experience what theretofore they could only imagine; imagination became a guide to reality as it could be.

The growth of employment in providing services was one part of the consumer revolution. Another part lay in an expansion of the manufacture of familiar but heretofore not commonplace goods, using traditional means of production. London remained the British centre of manufacturing throughout the eighteenth century, notwithstanding the rapid growth of Midlands industrial cities. London manufacturing, like its counterpart in other capitals, employed skilled workers to finish goods with high value, such as watches and clocks, rather than to mass produce goods of low value per unit.

Wages and Prices: Another Conundrum

Two trends, seemingly irreconcilable with one another, coexisted in the eighteenth century. First, the price of basic goods, especially food but also firewood and some other necessities, increased at a faster pace than did wages for most of the century and in most places. The more rapid rise of prices than wages means that real wages declined. Hence, apparently, the ability of people earning wages to buy goods shrivelled.

Second, inventories of goods owned at death, including the inventories of large numbers of working people, show that from one generation to the next ordinary people—domestic servants and artisans—owned much more numerous and varied consumer goods. This transformation occurred in Vienna, Paris, Amsterdam, Delft, and elsewhere in western and central Europe. Somehow the very people who seem to have suffered at the hands of secular trends in prices and wages seem also to have found a way to step toward modern mass consumption and consumerism expressed in a rising working-class demand for and possession of household artefacts, apparel, and other goods. Each body of evidence—about prices and wages, on one hand, and about household possessions, on the other—has been tested and retested. If, as appears to be the case, that evidence is incontrovertible, how is this possible?

Part of the explanation lies in the terms of trade between consumer goods and other items. Where production of consumer goods flourished— in Florence in the sixteenth century, in much of England and the Dutch Republic from the seventeenth century forward, in Paris, Vienna, and other cites in the eighteenth century—the price of those goods declined relative to the price of other goods and services. On the price evidence alone, the consumer revolution implies marked growth in productivity. Hence buying consumer services and new and more especially secondhand consumer goods was easier from one year to the next. But the relative price trend is not by itself sufficient.

Two other explanations suggest how this apparently contradictory evidence can be reconciled. One poses the hypothesis of an 'industrious revolution'. People earned less as time passed, and paid more for food and for some other goods, too, but more than made up the difference by working longer hours and more days during the year, and by the addition of women and children to the wage labour force. That is, the transition to a long work week of 50, 60, or 70 hours and the working year approaching full-time employment, plus the wage-earning work of women and children, which has so often been identified with the early nineteenth century and the initial stages of industrial modernization, actually began earlier, in the workshops and homes of the old regime. It was not motivated by the discipline of the factory and the submissive position of labour during industrialization. Nevertheless, were people compelled to sacrifice their leisure, in the way that declining wages in British textiles in the late seventeenth century forced women and children into the wage labour force? Or was the shift mostly spontaneous and voluntary, driven by a quest for more possessions and a life of greater adornment? Those questions may even be premature. Because the evidence remains to be gathered and weighed, it is merely speculation to say that more people worked more of the time so that they could possess more in the way of consumer goods and services.

A second hypothesis about how real wages could shrink but purchasing power increase derives from the rise of market and money exchanges and a growing share of labour agreements paid in cash rather than kind. At the beginning of the century comparatively few workers were paid wages in cash, which provide the sources from which historians have extracted information about wage rates, and highly skilled workers earned much more than less skilled counterparts. As the century progressed, more of the labour market moved from the kind to the cash economy, working no longer for board, housing, plus a small payment but instead for cash wages. The mixture of jobs paid in cash shifted from mostly urban skilled trades which earned high wages, to a broad market in which poorly compensated jobs formerly paid in kind began to be paid in cash and thus to appear in the sources historians consult for information about the wage level. In France, for example, more and more trades show up in the sources as paying wages. A wage trend can be estimated by averaging across all occupations, upon the observation that wages changed in each occupation at more or less the same pace. Or a trend can be estimated by taking into account the continuing addition of occupations to the ranks of wage-paying jobs. The quandary revolves around deciding how to take the new wage-earning jobs into account. Do they mean that wages rose slowly because more and more low-paying jobs have been added to the mixture, and thus that workers were progressively less able to afford food, housing, fuel, and other items? Or do they mean that new consumers joined the market because their low-paying jobs were converted from kind to cash compensation?

Population growth and the rising number and size of cities promoted both the monetarization of payments to labourers, and the integration of labour markets. An important force behind this shift to cash for labour consisted of migration to cities. Young men and women from rural areas, where they earned low wages paid mostly in kind, moved to cities, where higher cash wages prevailed. But the people who stayed in the countryside also earned wages in cash rather than kind more often as the century progressed. In 1700 cities and towns comprised a world of cash work, and the countryside a world of largely work for kind. By 1800 in western and central Europe cash work prevailed in both areas. At the later date labour markets were also more integrated, which implies that workers migrated in search of jobs.

Both explanations—the industrious revolution and the cash labour hypothesis—remain speculative. Each claims to solve the conundrum by finding an error in the way historians have measured the standard of living. In the hypothesis of the industrious revolution, the measurement error lies in how much time each household allocated to work. According to it, buying consumption goods was possible because people converted leisure time to work time. In the cash labour hypothesis, the measurement error exists in the composition of the jobs under scrutiny; purchasing power is said to have increased because the shift from a labour market composed of a few high-paying jobs to one made up of many trades earning varied wages creates the misleading appearance of shrinkage in wages. According to it, consumption rose because more people entered the market-place for consumer goods. That implies no fundamental change in attitudes, but instead a shift from autoproduction and autoconsumption to production and consumption through the market and thereby a shift from a world in which material possessions consisted of the few things a household could make for itself to the larger range of goods than could be obtained through the market. If the cash labour hypothesis is correct, then the most important things requiring explanation are the forces promoting the monetarization of payments to labour.

Conclusion

Probably both hypotheses have some power to solve the wage–consumption conundrum and explain the early development of consumerism. Whether or not that is so, however, the key issue to which this puzzle calls attention is another version of the origins of modern economic growth. The advent of a consumer revolution, one in place across much of urban western and central Europe, implies that a leading factor in the initiation of modern economic growth lay not with solving problems of supply by making textiles and later a widening range of goods more cheaply via industrial modernization. It implies that modern economic growth originated before steam engines and factories, and not in a capital-intensive output of familiar products at cheaper prices. Modern economic growth emerged instead in the demand of urban consumers for larger quantities and a sharply diversified variety of goods and services, a demand that was satisfied largely by artisans and craftsmen working at home or in small shops. And it emerged more in growth of the number of people producing and consuming goods and services—one estimate suggests that the French bourgeoisie grew from 700,000 to 800,000 people in 1700, to 2.3 million in 1789, far faster than the French population—than it did in innovations in scale, use of technology, or investment. Industrial modernization is often said to have promoted 'capitalism', meaning not merely investment in productive assets but also a rapacious quest for profits. The consumer revolution calls attention, in contrast, to an enlargement of traditional means of production and therefore to the growth of working-class capitalism.

To discover the rise of urban consumerism is to enliven the economic history of the old regime. How far did this increasing demand for material goods extend into towns and villages? Did the new demand drive economic activity so strongly that it makes industrial modernization more a story about how manufacturers reduced overheads than an account about how modern economic growth was initiated? More fundamental still, how is the initiation of this widening market in consumer goods to be explained? Did it arise from new desire to amass possessions and therefore a new, less ascetic attitude toward the conditions of life? Or did it arise because ways were discovered to satisfy long-standing wants, which people had not been able to do? The theory of a consumer revolution poses fresh questions about the origins of economic growth, with important implications for the ongoing effort to understand how to spark sustained economic growth or, once growth is underway, how to sustain it. Moreover, this theory obliges economic historians to acknowledge that the market, where options are weighed, is a product of deeper cultural forces.

8

The Enlightenment

NORMAN HAMPSON

The Scale of Change

Many of the people who lived in western Europe in the first quarter of the eighteenth century probably felt that things were changing for the better in all kinds of ways. Life was becoming a little more secure, more predictable, and also more interesting. The period of general warfare that had followed a generation of civil and religious mayhem came to an end in 1715, to be followed by a generation of relative peace. There seems to have been an improvement in the physical climate, which meant better harvests and less hunger. After the final outbreak in Marseilles in 1720, there were no more visitations of plague, except in Italy. More people were born and more of them stayed alive. The broadening of European horizons that had begun with the discovery of America was now extended to embrace the entire globe. This operated at all kinds of levels. The educated began to understand that different cultures, especially that of China, had a validity of their own. The less intellectual started to drink tea and coffee and the coffee house became a new centre of sociability. Such changes in social habits could have appalling consequences, as the insatiable demand for sugar fuelled the growth of the slave trade, but it was not Europeans who paid the price and few of them devoted much thought to what was being done to Africans.

With these changes came a shift in the mental climate. If we are to appreciate the novelty of an outlook that now seems so familiar, we have to realize how things had appeared only a short time before. Cromwell's contemporaries had seen man as a tragic actor, seeking personal salvation from a jealous and punitive God, in a world where nature was a succession of portents, challenges, and ordeals. Many were called but few were chosen, and escaping from the damnation that was the fate of the majority meant satisfying God on his own terms—if one could be sure what they were. In the claustrophobic world of *The Pilgrim's Progress*, it had been fear that sent Christian on his way. Salvation could not be earned by leading an upright life: the town of Morality was the home of Mr Worldly Wiseman, and Save-all was one of Christian's tempters. The book ends, not when Christian and Hopeful enter the Celestial City, but when they are followed there by Ignorance, who has led a good life and triumphed over all temptations, but is cast down into hell for theological errors whose obscurity is likely to baffle the modern reader. Writing at the end of the century, Archbishop Fénelon held somewhat similar views, however he may have disagreed about the content of the saving theology. When his hero, Télémaque, visited hell in his search for his father, Ulysses, he discovered that the lowest depths were inhabited by people whose impeccably moral lives had been no compensation for their irreligion. Fénelon described them as 'philosophers'.

This dark and enclosed world was now challenged by a new vision that opened everything out in space and time. Scientists showed the universe to be far wider than anyone had previously suspected. Fontenelle, in his *Dialogue sur la pluralité des mondes*, speculated that the planets of the solar system and unknown planets orbiting other stars might be inhabited by beings who shared man's intelligence, whatever the differences in their physical characteristics. Fénelon, despite his traditional views on theological orthodoxy, asserted that, viewed from the summit of Mount Olympus (i.e. *sub specie aeternitatis*), the earth was no more than a particle of mud, whose inhabitants fought each other for a blade of grass. Hitherto it had been generally agreed that the universe had been created around 4000 BCE, and Sir Thomas Browne, at least, had not expected it to last much longer: ''Tis too late to be ambitious.' This was perhaps a personal idiosyncrasy, but people whose thoughts revolved around the Old Testament were inclined to look backwards towards a history of examples, rather than forwards to a future of infinite possibilities. To challenge the date of Creation too bluntly was to invite accusations of unorthodoxy; but Montesquieu, in the first great work of the Enlightenment, his *Lettres persanes* published in 1721, had one of his Persians affirm that 6,000 years ago was 'only yesterday' and speculate that Adam was perhaps the survivor of a succession of unrecorded Floods. What mattered was not any precise idea about the age of the universe, but the fact that people were quietly lifting the lid from a box that had not allowed time for geological change and biological evolution.

The scientific progress of the seventeenth century had probably been largely self-generating, and it was often inaccessible to ordinary people; but its result was to transform educated men's perception of the world in general. Future generations were to ascribe this new vision to Newton, but the rationalism of Descartes, however ultimately discredited where physics was concerned, pointed in a similar direction. Fontenelle remained a Cartesian to the end of his long life, but he was as convinced as any Newtonian that he inhabited a world that was regulated by universal laws. It was still a divine creation, but the lessons it held for man were general rather than particular and inspirational rather than minatory. Human intelligence, by observation and deduction, could understand the nature of the plan that divine wisdom and benevolence had instituted for human happiness. It remained as true as it had always been that God would reward those who conformed to his commandments and punish those who did not, but to observe the laws of God now meant to discover those of nature—including those of human nature—and they made no distinction between Christians and unbelievers.

Throughout Enlightened Europe Sir Isaac Newton was seen as the symbol of a new conception of the universe, as a rational system whose laws were accessible to humanity through science, rather than through religious revelation.

Locke's empirical study of the human mind and his use of newly available anthropological evidence to show that values were not universal, led him to deny the existence of innate ideas, implanted by God. All ideas, he thought, were the product of sensation and reflection, which implied that men brought up in different environments were bound, and in a sense right, to come to different conclusions. What they called 'good' and 'bad' was merely their way of referring to pleasure and pain. *If* one tacked on the prospect of eternal bliss or damnation, this could coexist with a belief in Christianity, but it did not encourage theological fastidiousness—and there was no logical necessity for that 'if'.

In this changed climate people's perceptions of God altered too. The jealous and exclusive Jehovah made way for a beneficent Creator who had designed the universe with a view to human felicity in this life, not as a kind of commando training to identify the handful who might qualify for it in the next. One of Montesquieu's Persians drew the appropriate conclusions: 'The first objective of a religious man must surely be to content the Divinity who established the religion that he professes. The most certain way of attaining this end must surely be to observe the rules of sociability and the rights of humanity.' To someone like Bunyan, the tone of easy confidence would have been as shocking as the upside-down theology. Instead of man being required to satisfy God on his own exacting and exclusive terms, God was almost being told that what was congenial to man must coincide with his own intentions. God was becoming equated with Providence, and Providence was assumed to operate in ways that human reason could both understand and accept.

All this suggests a kind of linear progression that would be oversimplified at best and can be seriously misleading. In practice, things were not so simple. The great Newton himself was attracted by alchemy and his later admirers preferred to ignore some of his more mystical speculations. Fénelon, as we have seen, could appear both modern and traditional. He condemned absolute monarchy and aggressive war, but he also insisted that the duty of the state was to enforce without questioning the inspired teaching of revealed religion. Télémaque's tutor, Mentor (who was, in fact, Minerva, or divine wisdom) drew up a code of institutions for Salento that had much in common with age-old Christian ideas about the nature of the good society—and also anticipated the opinions that the French revolutionary radical, Saint-Just, was to formulate in 1794 in what became known as his *Institutions républicaines*. The men of the Enlightenment were rarely content to rest quietly in the pigeon-holes to which we are inclined to assign them. Most of them grafted new perceptions on to more traditional stocks.

To complicate matters further, the movement had scarcely got under way before it provoked reactions that could combine elements of conservatism with anticipations of future attitudes. Anyone who aspires to confine the Enlightenment within a few ingenious formulas will find himself playing Procrustes.

If we think of the Enlightenment as a period of European history, rather than an intellectual debate, the situation becomes even more involved. Its perennial concern was to apply reason or philosophy to public life, in politics, economics, and sociology. In each of these fields it developed in rather different ways. It also meant different things to people in different situations. To reforming rulers and their ministers, it signified practical efficiency; to educated people it implied a more secular attitude to life; it meant a more purified religion to some; to others it was almost an intellectual game. Ordinary people, unaware of the learned polemics that went on over their heads, were conscious of it as it was reflected in the changed behaviour of their social superiors. They might still believe in the existence of witches, but they were not allowed to burn them any more. Similar ideas could take on different appearances in dissimilar national contexts. Catholic and Protestant churches did not respond to the challenge in uniform ways, but the latter tended to find it easier to assimilate. Governments could be welcoming, indifferent, or hostile. In Russia, the reception of the Enlightenment was part of a process of Europeanization; in Spain it was resisted as a European encroachment on national tradition. It was as pervasive as it was Protean. There can be no question, in a short essay, of doing justice to its complexity and its ramifications. Any analysis of its more salient components is liable to give a misleading impression of cohesion and uniformity, and one has to remind oneself all the time that it is a world to explore rather than a puzzle to solve.

Man in his Universe

The central preoccupation of the Enlightenment concerned man's place in the universe and the attributes of the good life. What emerged was not so much a choice between conflicting points of view, each internally consistent but incompatible with the others, as a new way of looking at the problems involved. This was common to most of the protagonists, with the result that men who differed radically in their conclusions shared a common perception of the issues, which set them apart from their predecessors. The collective sense of what was at stake was more significant than the attempts of individuals to produce coherent syntheses of their own.

As we have seen, the progress of science had offered eighteenth-century observers a new awareness of the scale and complexity of the universe and of the laws that appeared to regulate its evolutions. Perhaps the most poetic evocation of the new vision came from the materialist, d'Holbach: 'Suns become encrusted and die, planets perish and scatter in the wastes of space; other suns are kindled, new planets take shape, to perform their evolutions or strike out new paths, and man, a minute fraction of a globe that is itself no more than an imperceptible point in the immense whole, believes that it is for him that the universe was created.' From this new perspective, God became necessarily more remote than the Jehovah who had spoken to Moses, operating by general laws rather than particular admonitions, the playwright rather than the producer. At the same time he was, in a way, more accessible since the understanding of nature was the key to an appreciation of the working of the divine intelligence.

Locke's epistemology, which established its hold over much of Europe, insisted that all knowledge was derived ultimately from sense impressions. One consequence of this was to discredit metaphysics. In other words, at the same time that man's knowledge of how the universe worked was expanding, he was eternally debarred from understanding why. All knowledge was a matter of reasoning about phenomena.

In the short run, both of these changes in attitude pointed in the direction of deism. A created universe in which all parts were adapted to their function and operated in accordance with universal laws, seemed to imply an intelligent creator. At the same time, to identify this cosmic being with any particular revelation to a small fraction of the earth's population and to validate the claims of local religions by the testimony of miracles that constituted violations of the laws that God himself had established, came to appear increasingly implausible.

From the omniscience of the Creator to his benevolence was not so much a quantum leap as a change of perspective. Christianity, of course, had always insisted on God's love for his creation, but he had loved mankind on his own terms, as Adam and Eve discovered to their cost. As Leibniz argued, an omnipotent and benevolent deity would necessarily create the best of all possible worlds. No one argued about that. The question was: best from whose point of view? The new concept of benevolence, which the deists shared with many Christians, assumed that even if God did not exactly see things from man's perspective, he had arranged everything for man's terrestrial convenience. When Pope urged his readers to

> Grasp the whole worlds of Reason, Life and Sense
> In one close system of Benevolence

he had already described happiness as 'our being's end and aim'. God, in other words, had so disposed things that those who complied with his laws, which were those of nature, intelligible through science, were ensured of felicity in this life. How far this constituted a revolution in people's attitudes can be illustrated by looking at the place of the humble teredo worm in the universal scheme. When its dietary habits damaged the Dutch dykes, Calvinist preachers in traditional style declared it to be a scourge of God, like the Egyptian plagues, intended to turn the Dutch from their evil ways. A French abbé, Pluche, had no use for such old-fashioned jeremiads. If it were not for the providential appetite of the teredo for the piles that supported Amsterdam, what (he asked his readers) would become of the Scandinavian timber trade? Voltaire enjoyed himself making fun of some of Pluche's wilder flights of fancy—and then went on to say that mountain ranges had been created to serve as aqueducts to drain the lands. If, as both Voltaire and Morelly believed, benevolence was also a natural attribute of man, this did not leave much room for original sin, which had been the common starting point for both Protestant and Catholic theologians.

This was nevertheless a road that deists and the more latitudinarian Christians could embark on together. God had created a universe in which all parts cooperated to their mutual advantage, although man alone was conscious of what he was doing. He played his assigned role by acting reasonably and benevolently, rather than by subscribing to particular theological beliefs. Hume, the sceptic, asserted that the proper office of religion was to regulate the hearts of men; and Pluche, despite his Catholicism, agreed that the good life did not involve the renunciation of those gifts that God had made to man for his enjoyment. Properly understood, self-love meant self-fulfilment; and God had so ordered things that the individual's pursuit of self-fulfilment automatically contributed to the common good. The 'providential' argument of the 'invisible hand' was invented by the moralists before it was appropriated by the economists.

Soon, however, the paths began to diverge. It was one thing to cast a tolerant eye on the various schools of Christian faith, but why stop at Christianity? Parson Adams, in Fielding's *Joseph Andrews*, in the course of a denunciation of Methodism, maintained that 'a good and virtuous Turk, or heathen, are more acceptable in the sight of their Creator than a vicious and wicked Christian, though his faith was as perfectly orthodox as St Paul's himself'. By a succession of barely perceptible steps, the men of the Enlightenment moved from the conviction that works were more important than faith to an ethical code in which humanity had taken the place of God. Helvétius asserted that 'every moral code whose principles are of public

If religion reflected humanity's response to the order of nature, it became impossible to see Christianity as the embodiment of exclusive truths.

utility must be in conformity with religious morality, which is nothing more than the perfection of human morality'. Montesquieu insisted that religious and civil laws should have as their main objective turning men into better citizens. Rousseau went a step further, to argue that the only permissible religions were those that encouraged the development of the rights of man, as individual and citizen. Lord Chesterfield described religion as 'a collateral security, at least, to virtue', which implied that virtue was the more important of the two. In Lessing's play, *Nathan the Wise*, the parable of the three rings signified that the virtuous or anti-social behaviour of believers could serve as the touchstone for assessing the validity of their differing faiths. In Mozart's opera *The Magic Flute*, Sarastro and his followers may be priests, but the criterion of virtuous conduct throughout the opera is not what might be pleasing to God, but what is worthy of man. All this was getting a long way from what the seventeenth century had understood by Christianity, but it reflected a gradual shift of emphasis rather than a brutal confrontation; and some Christians, like Pluche, allowed themselves to go with the tide. 'As soon as returning spring allows people to go outdoors, the earth hastens to deck itself out in greenery. That is the robe with which it adorns itself so that it may appear before its lord with the propriety and respect that it owes him.' Providence thought of everything.

That, however, was not the end of the road. If 'enlightened' self-interest ensured that people would identify their own long-term advantage with the good of the community, how did one account for evil? Where the great majority of the population was concerned, the answer was obviously their ignorance. As we shall see, the men of the Enlightenment were virtually unanimous in the belief that their message was not intended for those whom Burke was to describe as the 'swinish multitude'. Some of them even thought that traditional religion and the fear of damnation might still serve a useful purpose in keeping the masses in order. But intelligent and educated men were equally capable of behaving anti-socially. To suggest that this was their own fault was to revive the concept of sin, which might have awkward connotations. One solution was to blame society. As d'Holbach explained, since society was corrupt, men were 'inevitably conditioned to act badly'. Condorcet shared his point of view, although not his pessimism, saying that vicious habits were all the product of bad laws and institutions or of national prejudice. That left unanswered the question of why, in a corrupt society, some were relatively saintly and others were what had formerly been known as sinners. Perhaps this was due to an accident of their physiological and psychological make-up. D'Holbach thought that 'our life is a line that nature compels us to draw . . . without being able to depart from it for an instant'. If nature operated by invariable laws and man was merely the most developed natural species, his actions, like those of the other animals, would be no more than the inevitable consequences of causes for which he could not be held responsible. Even Montesquieu forgot himself so far as to write that our predisposition towards virtue or vice depended on our 'mechanism'. Diderot thought that one was either happily or unhappily born. None of them seemed to believe that they had had the bad luck to draw losing tickets. Even so, it must have been hard for them to concede that they deserved no credit whatever for their most altruistic actions. The road of enlightenment seemed to lead to the determinist abyss.

Towards the middle of the century the debate took on a new dimension as a result of the discoveries—and the mistaken hypotheses—of the biologists. Educated people were already used to thinking of a universe that stretched backwards in time far beyond the emergence of historical societies. It was becoming clear that, within this vast and indefinite period, the climate of the planet had seen many changes, including those in the appearance of its inhabitants. Diderot believed that the existing form of any animal was merely 'a particular and transient production' and he was inclined to think that all species were descended from a common ancestor. Biologists claimed to have observed the emergence of life from inanimate matter. La Mettrie explained that only the viable forms of such life would be able to survive and to perpetuate themselves. As the environment changed, the criteria of viability would alter too, and different forms of life would emerge and perish. As Hume put it, 'many worlds might have been botched and bungled ere this system was struck out'. This was to knock away the main prop for deism, the argument from design. Hitherto the most telling justification for the existence of an intelligent creator—one that Voltaire clung to all his life—was the difficulty of explaining by any other hypothesis the incredibly complex way in which all forms of life were shaped to meet the demands of their environment. Henceforth all that was needed was sufficient time. Survival was a matter of being 'fortunately born' and what did not fit did not endure. There remained, of course, the question of why anything should be there at all and whether it had been created or existed independently of time, but if Newton had relegated God from the role of umpire to that of watchmaker, more recent scientists seemed to have reduced him to a hypothesis that Laplace said he did not need.

There was a quite different way of approaching the problems of the human predicament, which appealed to some of the people whose views we have been considering. Locke's epistemology had, after all, been founded on sensation, which was a matter of feeling rather than of thought. It was a commonplace of the Enlightenment that what prompted men to action was their passions. From this it was an easy transition to argue that sentiment was not merely a necessary impetus to provoke people into doing something, but a better guide than reason to what they ought to do. Burke, echoing Sterne, wrote that 'men often act right from their feelings, who afterwards reason but ill from them on principle'. Morelly put it rather more strongly: 'On a thousand occasions your prejudices, your mistakes, your mad opinions are at odds with the wise perceptions of nature; your heart seizes on these quick and certain indications and seems to laugh at the vain and deluded pedantry of the mind.' Helvétius took this argument further. Sensible people were the prisoners of conventional ideas. Since these were usually erroneous, accurate reasoning usually meant being systematically wrong. Only the genius, who was a man of passion, could escape from the prevailing mediocrity and perform great deeds that were somehow admirable, whether they were good or evil. He had few followers in this anticipation of Romanticism. It was more usual to argue, like the heroine of Rousseau's *Nouvelle Héloïse*, that the mere recognition of the theoretical identity of self-love and social duty was insufficient to motivate people to act to their immediate disadvantage. What was needed was an emotional self-starter, in other words, conscience, the subject of many a passionate invocation by Rousseau.

Conscience, considered merely as the feeling that one 'ought...', was no problem to the materialists. It was merely a conditioned reflex, the product of education and the environment. For it to become a source of authority superior to reason itself, it had to be endowed with divine qualities, to become, if not a substitute for religion, at least the means by which the individual communicated with God. In Rousseau's case, this involved getting away from men and isolating himself in 'nature' in the ecological sense. This was another anticipation of Romanticism. As in the case of reason, conscience seemed at first to offer a new solution to old problems, but its implications were just as complex and even more dangerous. If it was regarded as the voice of God, its dictates were absolute and its message uniform and unambiguous. Each individual receiver must be tuned to the same broadcast. Everyone was therefore the beneficiary of the same imperative message of unimpeachable authority and universal application. Whatever others might believe in their ignorance or pretend in their hypocrisy, they had no right to disagree. The political implications of this were somewhat ominous. It was, in a way, a return to the religious attitudes of the seventeenth century, except that the source of authority was now individual inspiration rather than the corporate doctrine of the Church.

It cannot be emphasized too strongly that, if the Enlightenment was a product of the eighteenth century, the eighteenth century was not the product of the Enlightenment. For the great majority of the population, it filtered down, if at all, only through the changed attitudes and behaviour of their social superiors. In more elevated circles it could be ignored or vigorously contested. To regard the new ways of thought as the norm is to fall into the kind of anachronism that comes about when historians concentrate on one aspect of a period because it happens to be relevant to their own concerns and preoccupations. Most of the books published in France—90 in 1770 alone—were about religion, and the majority of them were orthodox and traditional. When the established churches responded to the Enlightenment, their attitude could take the form of either a movement in the direction of latitudinarian tolerance, or a more zealous spirituality. The latter could imply, as in the case of the French Jansenists and the British Methodists, an increased emphasis on man's inability to escape from sin without the succour of divine grace. It did not necessarily involve a more 'modern' outlook on the world in general: Wesley regretted that 'the infidels have hooted witchcraft out of this world'. There were renegades within the ranks of the Enlightenment itself. Swedenborg had enjoyed an international reputation as a scientist before he turned to religious mysticism. Mesmer may have regarded himself as a physicist, but to many of his supporters he seemed to be a kind of spiritualist. Masonic lodges, which could be centres of enlightened sociability and benevolence, became more and more involved with the mumbo-jumbo of their ancient rites and legendary origins. This is not the place to explore these counter-currents, but to ignore or underestimate them would be to get a false impression of the soil in which the Enlightenment had to grow.

Economy and Society

The new attitudes towards economic and social policy evolved in a somewhat similar way to the speculations about religion. This is not very surprising since they were held by the same men, who did not live in compartments, even if we have to dissect their views for the purpose of analysis. They were born into a society that expected fluctuation rather than development, where success or failure was in the hands of the Almighty, who sent fair weather or 'acts of God' to reward or punish. The economy itself might have evolved but economic attitudes still had something in common with those of the Old Testament. The purpose of the poor was to provide the rich with occasions for the manifestations of charity; God had assigned everyone to his appropriate station; and, whatever might happen to individuals, there was no ground for thinking that the system itself was likely to change more in the future than it had done in the past. Rulers ought to behave like the fathers of their people. In economic terms, this implied continual interference with the free play of the market, notably to protect consumers from exploitation by producers, especially in times of scarcity. During the seventeenth century the state had extended the range of its activities and economic policy had come to be seen as a branch of a foreign policy that aspired to establish a favourable balance of trade in a world where commerce was regarded as a kind of warfare.

The Enlightenment had little time for any of these attitudes. Economic activities, like everything else, must be regulated by scientific laws, which could be discovered by rational investigation. As in the case of the law of gravity, understanding these laws would not allow people to do whatever they liked, but it would teach them how to attain the limits of the possible. As a science, economics was morally self-validating; there was no possibility of conflict between the pursuit of individual self-interest and the good of the community. Thanks to the Invisible Hand, the two were synonymous. As Adam Smith put it, 'every individual exerts himself to find out the most advantageous employment of whatever his capital can command. The study of his own advantage necessarily leads him to prefer what is most advantageous to society.'

Economic liberalism was therefore a kind of anti-policy which aimed at destroying the 'artificial' barriers to trade that had been erected in what Lord Chesterfield described in another context as 'centuries of monkish ignorance', so that the laws of nature could operate unimpeded. If this were done, capital would gravitate naturally towards the activities where it would generate the highest profit and the backward would imitate the more successful in order to compete. In the same way that a dawning awareness of the possibilities of evolution changed people's attitudes towards nature and nature's God, economics took on a new dimension as it incorporated development in time. What enabled the labourer to generate a surplus over and above the cost of maintaining him in a healthy and efficient state was the enhancement of his productivity that arose from the division of labour. The extent to which this could be carried depended on the size of the market. The destruction of local tolls, customs barriers, and so on, was therefore in everyone's interest. Provided that all behaved in the same enlightened way, the creation of a free trade area meant that each region, indeed each enterprise, would specialize in whatever it could produce most efficiently. The fall in prices due to increased productivity would be more than compensated by the growth in the volume of trade. There was no reason why this beneficent process should stop at national frontiers. International free trade would profit the wine-growers of Aquitaine as much as the Lancashire cotton master and so on, if not *ad infinitum*, at least to an indefinite expansion of specialization and affluence. For perhaps the first time in human history, men began to situate the Golden Age in the future and to think in terms of accelerating change.

That was the view from the top. Economic liberals were inclined to argue that labour was a commodity and that if the system were to operate with maximum efficiency, governments should allow the price of all commodities to be determined by supply and demand. This implied that the rewards of prosperity would be reserved for the owners of capital, while those of labour would never get beyond subsistence level. The old moralists might be wrong when they proclaimed that the enrichment of some meant the impoverishment of others, but it looked as though the ever-increasing wealth of the entrepreneur was going to widen the gap that separated him from 'hands' condemned to vegetate just above the starvation line. In eighteenth-century economics, wages, to the extent that they were paid in cash and not in kind, tended to be relatively stable. What mattered most to town and country labourers was the considerable fluctuation in the price and availability of bread. The economic liberals were confident that they had the solution to this problem, in the long run. If prices were allowed to find their natural level in times of scarcity, instead of being artificially held down, as was traditional practice, capital would be attracted into cereal production and output would eventually increase. But as Keynes was to remind a later generation, in the long run we are all dead. The liberals' insistence that in the *short* run the traditional controls that tried, however ineffectually, to regulate prices and supply, must be abolished in the name of theories that the poor did not understand, was advanced with the self-confidence of men who had no personal fear of hunger or starvation. As Burke cheerfully explained, à propos the harvest failure of 1795, 'we, the people, ought to be made sensible, that it is not in the breaking of the laws of commerce, which are the laws of nature, and consequently the laws of God, that we are to place our hope of softening the Divine displeasure'. When viewed from a humbler perspective, the Enlightenment's commitment to benevolence might not be overwhelmingly obvious to those who suffered from its consequences. Some of the *philosophes* were inclined to regard the poor not so much as the victims of ignorance and superstition who must be rehabilitated by education, but as a kind of permanent underclass whose condemnation to a life of unthinking toil was the necessary price of the comfort of the minority. Rousseau thought that to educate them above their station would merely make them discontented. Voltaire was rather more blunt. 'We need men who have nothing but their arms and a willingness to use them.' 'Society itself could not exist without an infinite number of useful people who own nothing at all.'

Economic liberalism involved no necessary commitment to constitutional government. On the contrary, the powerful vested interests that would resist the abolition of trade guilds and internal tolls could only be overcome by a kind of legal despotism that would not be accountable to sectional pressure groups that claimed to represent public opinion. Constitutional machinery was a means rather than an end and what really mattered was the enforcement of the 'scientific' policies that alone would ensure prosperity, whether or not people understood what was good for them. That was another point of view with a long future ahead of it.

As in the case of religion and ethics, the new ways of thinking encountered resistance from traditionalists and provoked counter-movements. Old habits died hard. When the French revolutionaries, on 4 August 1789, declared that they had abolished 'feudalism', and committed themselves to what Marx was to call the 'cash nexus', the first reaction of the marquis de Ferrières was to write to his wife, 'all the bonds that attached me to the inhabitants of my lands are broken; henceforth we owe each other nothing'. A couple of months later he told her to increase her charitable donations: 'as long as Marsay is mine, I will not allow anyone to go short of food or clothing'. When Blake denounced the 'dark satanic mills', he may have been thinking of the mechanistic theories of Newton and Locke rather than the cotton industry, but his condemnation extended to all those whose vision was circumscribed to what could be weighed, measured, and priced. Necker, who saw himself as a *philosophe* as well as a finance minister, would not accept that property was a natural right and wages a commodity. He denounced 'that chilly abstract compassion for posterity that is supposed to harden our hearts against the cries of ten thousand wretched people who surround us now'. Robespierre too insisted that, whatever the general validity of economic laws, they could not derogate from the basic obligation of government to see that the people were fed.

Others were inclined to question more radically the assumed benefits of a developed economy. When Bougainville published an idealized account of what he had found when he visited Tahiti, Diderot was one of those who succumbed to the charms of that island paradise. Even Helvétius, who had once been a tax farmer, extolled the virtues of the simple life; he argued that the owners of capital were using it to buy out the small producers and reduce wages, and asserted that the natives in primitive societies lived better than French agricultural labourers. The most eloquent and extreme advocate of this point of view was Rousseau, who denounced economic progress as wholly evil. 'In every aspect of human work one should rigorously proscribe every machine and every invention that can reduce human labour, economize manpower and produce the same effect with less effort.' He thought that shipwrecks were 'truly beneficial'. In his advice to the Corsicans he extended his anathema against commerce to include the grain trade, although he reluctantly conceded that it might be necessary to indulge in occasional barter. This was going back, not to pre-industrial society, but to the Palaeolithic. Here again we see the Enlightenment generating a revolt against itself that pointed in the direction of Romanticism.

If we turn from economics to the consideration of society as a whole, we can observe a similar process at work: the demolition of the past led men further than they had originally intended to go, and each answer raised new problems. The initial hypothesis was the same: society must be regulated by natural laws that were not merely social conventions; the function of 'philosophy' was to discover these laws and to adjust social practices to bring them into conformity. One could begin pleasurably enough by attacking such obvious targets as clerical celibacy (it was assumed by most people that the proof of good government was an increase in population), pride of ancestry when divorced from merit, and the survival of antique habits and assumptions that no longer served any useful purpose. It was impossible to get far down this road before one encountered the problem of what was 'natural'.

Montesquieu claimed—probably not just to pacify the French censors—that his object was to make men more contented with the regimes under which they lived, by understanding their *raison d'être*. Apparently irrational practices, such as the aristocratic code of honour or the venality of judicial offices, had come about for identifiable reasons and, when properly understood and regulated, served useful purposes. What was 'natural', in the sense of being the logical consequence of social causes, was not, however, self-justified. It was liable to conflict with what Montesquieu believed to be absolute moral values: liberty and justice. On the whole, he seemed to think that these were self-evident qualities. Men of objectivity and goodwill could agree on what was desirable and, by cautious amendment and the example of their own conduct, inch society in the right direction. He was a modernist, in the sense that he welcomed the development of commerce, as something that bound societies together and encouraged peaceful cooperation. Proclaiming himself to be 'a human being of necessity and a Frenchman by accident', he regarded the European corner of the world at least as a single community. To the extent that people's behaviour was moulded by their environment, greater prosperity—provided that it was not too unequally shared—would make men better, as well as better off. If anti-social behaviour was, in part at least, the product of ignorance, superstition, and need, increasing affluence would reduce the last of these and education might do something to alleviate the first two.

Others were less concerned to improve the status quo than to repudiate it. To men who chafed at what they saw as the artificiality of aristocratic society, the cultivation of the primitive—from a safe distance—had an irresistible appeal, whether one identified it with the allegedly harmonious people of Tahiti or the more martial virtues of the American Indians. Voltaire himself succumbed to the spell in *L'Ingénu*. For most of the *philosophes* this was not much more than escapist fantasy; for Rousseau it was the heart of the matter. Man's natural state was one of independence, which implied self-sufficiency in every sense of the word. Economic interdependence destroyed his autonomy and enslaved him to the false values of possession, ostentation, and effeminacy. He conceded that the nations of Europe were indeed becoming parts of a single society, but he saw this as proof of their corruption. His own emotional commitment was to small embattled societies, each ready to spring to arms in defence of its autonomy, not Tahiti but Sparta.

The new evolutionary perspective encouraged more disquieting ideas about what was natural. Pope's cheerful affirmation, 'whatever is, is right', had been conceived in terms of a static harmony. Even on that basis, d'Holbach was inclined to challenge it, arguing that nature was morally neutral and that the totality of things could not have any purpose since there was nothing outside itself to which it could be referred. The apparent order that people claimed to perceive in nature was merely an anthropocentric delusion. Helvétius put in a word for relativism: to the insect in the grass, the sheep was a ravening monster and the lion an avenger of the innocent. If one threw in a dawning awareness of evolution, 'nature' became nothing more than an endless process of change and extinction, and it was difficult to invest it with any normative qualities—and difficult to answer the marquis de Sade when he claimed that his curious sexual practices were no more than the indulgence of his natural inclinations. Hume's pessimistic comment that 'doubt, uncertainty, suspense of judgement appear the only result of our most accurate scrutiny' seemed to have a more general application than he had intended.

Politics

The men of the Enlightenment approached the problem of politics with the same tendency to react against the past and against each other. Their predecessors had been inclined to see societies as organic wholes rather than as aggregations of individuals. Bossuet, the tutor to the son of Louis XIV, in a striking anticipation of Rousseau, thought that they were formed 'when everyone, renouncing his own will, transferred and united it with that of the prince and the magistrate'. Once this had happened, property and all other rights were derived from public authority or the state. Unconditional obedience was due to all rulers, even tyrants and those who persecuted the true religion, since they were vehicles of the divine will. Such doctrines were not the product of human calculation, as Hobbes imagined, but the revealed wisdom of God. Bossuet described the Jewish polity of the Old Testament as 'the government of a people whose legislator was God himself. Whatever the best governed states, Sparta, Athens, Rome, and Egypt itself, to go back to the beginning, achieved with all their wisdom, is nothing when compared to the wisdom embodied in the law of God.' Secular power was absolute but rulers were under a moral obligation to conform to tradition. The legitimate monarch, unlike the tyrant, consulted those whose birth or office entitled them to speak on behalf of the community. This process was essentially the same, whether institutionalized as in England or informal. During the seventeenth century the more effective concentration of power in the hands of the royal government, notably in France, had circumscribed the process of consultation without overthrowing underlying attitudes; as the first gentleman of the realm, the king respected the social status of his mightier subjects. To treat all subjects as equal was characteristic of the despotic practices of the East. European monarchies, especially Catholic ones, were to some extent diarchies, in which Church and state reinforced each other's authority, even if they disagreed about the frontier between temporal and spiritual from time to time. Some departments of what would now be considered government, notably education, public assistance, health, and the censorship of blasphemous or seditious libels, were accepted as being mainly the province of the Church.

The Enlightenment consigned much of this to the dustbin of history. It began by affirming the autonomy of politics. Whatever its protagonists' attitudes towards religion, they agreed in restricting the Church's influence to the preaching of morality. Religious belief was an essentially private matter, respected by the state, and perhaps useful in promoting appropriate habits amongst the unenlightened, but the Church as a corporate body had no right to intrude in the political affairs of a secular commonwealth.

Politics, of course, was a science. The laws that must regulate civil society, if properly understood by people who were beginning to regard themselves as citizens of a commonwealth rather than as subjects in a realm, would enable them to operate the system with maximum efficiency. In politics as in everything else, a beneficent Providence would ensure that conforming to the laws of nature delivered tangible benefits. If things were going badly, in terms of crime, civil disorder, or an unsuccessful foreign policy, that must be due to someone's mistakes. Politics might be a science, but it was a slippery one: to the man in the street—or more accurately in the study—the fault might seem to lie with the government, but ministers could always reply that their correct policies were frustrated by a coalition of prejudice and vested interest. Traditionally, state policy had always been a confidential business that it was not for ordinary people to applaud or criticize. In the new atmosphere both governments and their critics appealed to what they were beginning to call 'public opinion', in order to disarm the opposition. By the end of the *ancien régime* in France, ministers and their opponents (who were often their colleagues) were hiring pamphleteers to acclaim or denounce each other's policies and to influence business confidence, as reflected on the Stock Exchange.

The results of politics might be tangible, but they were not limited to the provision of material goods. They influenced the conditions on which the entire life of the nation, religious, economic, and intellectual, was conducted. Writers challenging intolerant orthodoxies were naturally vociferous in their demand for freedom of the press, even if they did occasionally appeal to the government for protection from their 'unscrupulous' opponents. Most of them believed that enlightenment involved a commitment to political liberty in a much more general sense. This opened a Pandora's box that no one has ever been able to shut again. Two main lines of thinking emerged, not necessarily or always in conflict, but implying a sharp difference of emphasis.

What may perhaps be described as the administrative approach commended itself to rulers impatient to maximize their power and resources, but it also attracted Voltaire. Despite his disclaimer, it seemed to be implied by Pope when he wrote:

> For Forms of Government let fools contest,
> Whate'er is best administered is best.

What mattered was the implementation of the correct policies. The best prospect of this, in a particular situation, might be to concentrate power in the hands of a ruler enlightened enough to use it only for the right purposes. Some of the French *philosophes* saw Frederick II of Prussia as just such a man. This was not merely because governments had to have strength to overcome demonstrably selfish interests. Representative institutions would transfer power to bodies like the French *parlements* which were the incarnation of traditional practices and values. The trade guilds and municipal corporations were not much of an advertisement for the dissemination of power, and Europe's few republics were in various kinds of decline. There remained the United Kingdom, whose practices were extolled with an enthusiasm that was partly due to ignorance and wishful thinking. When a man like Dr Johnson could say that, if he had been a great landowner, he would have evicted any tenant who refused to vote for his candidate, one comes up against the practical limitations of representative government in an age of widespread illiteracy and open ballots. The supporters of administrative autocracy may have been naïve in their expectations of a philosopher king, but it was difficult to disagree with their argument that any plausible form of representative government would tend to perpetuate the social and economic status quo.

To those in the second camp, this was not the main point. Montesquieu was the hero of those who put liberty first, and his *De L'esprit des lois* was their Bible. For Montesquieu, society, as a natural organism, took precedence over the state; politics was not the *raison d'être* of the citizen, but merely one aspect of an individual's interests and activities. 'Men are governed by many things: climate, religion, the laws and precepts of government, the examples of the past, habits, manners. From the sum of these emerges a general spirit.' The general spirit of a people determined its perspective on political issues, for freedom consisted in one's perception of one's liberty rather than in the observance of a set of rules. People were also governed by different kinds of laws: natural, divine, ecclesiastical, international, political, national, laws of conquest, civil and domestic laws. Individuals therefore found themselves at the points of intersection of their different circles of obligation. They were bound to differ, not merely in their interests but in their values, all of which enjoyed the same legitimacy. The general spirit of a people therefore consisted of a kind of amalgam of its different ways of being. A wise legislator might hope to modify it by the cautious manipulation of rewards and by the example of his own conduct, but to constrain the general spirit, however laudable one's motives and well intentioned one's objectives, was to act despotically and thereby destroy whatever one had aspired to create. In theory, one could envisage civil liberty under an enlightened autocrat; but in the long run freedom could only be guaranteed by the fragmentation of sovereignty. Montesquieu thought, or at least argued, that this was exemplified in England, with executive power in the hands of a king and legislative power divided between the representatives of the quality and the quantity.

That worked better in practice than in theory. Just as deism had come to look like a halt on the road to atheism, the search for a secular polity seemed to point towards democracy. If political power did not originate in divine delegation, where else could it come from except from the people themselves? *Philosophes*—unless they were Burke—could not take very seriously the argument that some people were more equal than others on account of their ancestry or the traditional privileges of the corporate bodies to which they belonged. Since, as they themselves often assured the authorities, they were abstract theorists rather than the compilers of political programmes, they did not have to concern themselves with the practicability of democratic politics in the eighteenth century. If they were to refute the democrats, it would have to be on grounds of principle.

The Enlightenment, with its substitution of rational for religious values, opened up a new division between an educated minority and the ignorant and superstitious masses. When a hot air balloon came down near Paris it was attacked by peasants who mistook it for a monster.

One line of attack was to challenge the wisdom of entrusting political power to those least qualified to know what to do with it. Helvétius in France and Hutcheson in Scotland might agree that the touchstone of good government was the greatest good of the greatest number, but government *for* the people did not have to be government *by* the people. When they contemplated the capacity of the masses to manage their own affairs, the *philosophes* were virtually unanimous. Diderot, whilst he conceded that all power derived ultimately from the people, thought that freedom of the press should be confined to the educated. His friend d'Holbach agreed that philosophy was not for the majority of the population. Rousseau, in the prize essay that established his reputation, warned against the dangers of popularizing what ought to be the preserve of the learned. Elsewhere he said that the masses would never understand and in *Émile* wrote of the difficulty of finding within the 'dregs of the people' a suitable wife for a gentleman. All of them would have agreed with Burke, 'what would become of the world if the practice of all moral Duties and the Foundations of Society, rested upon having their reasons made clear and demonstrative to every Individual?'.

One or two writers sought guidance from economics. The Abbé Sieyès, in his best-selling pamphlet of 1789, *Qu'est-ce que le Tiers État?*, produced the ingenious argument that governing a state was very much like managing a business, in the sense that success depended on the division of labour. He therefore proposed an electoral system in which 'active' citizens specialized in voting and 'passive' citizens in being governed. This was clever, but it appealed more to the educated deputies than to the passive citizens. There was a more general tendency to think of the polity as a kind of joint-stock company whose main purpose was to distribute dividends to the shareholders. There was something to be said for this point of view at a time when low productivity condemned the mass of the population to poverty, but it tended to equate citizenship with the ownership of property. This was Burke's attitude and the protection of property was a recurring *motif* throughout his diatribe against the French Revolution. If not a new attitude, this implied a new emphasis. As we have seen, Bossuet had included property rights within the compass of political sovereignty. Throughout the eighteenth century individual voices were to be heard disputing their claim to special sanctity. The Abbé Meslier, writing about 1720, advocated a form of primitive communism. A generation latter another abbé, Morellet, argued that the existence of private property was the main cause of man's alienation from nature, which he believed to be the only source of crime. It was a subject on which Rousseau could never make up

When some Enlightened thinkers tended to substitute an idealized conception of society for God as the source of moral obligation, they turned to the classical world for inspiration. The Brutus who had his sons executed for supporting Tarquin took the place of Christian martyrs.

his mind. On the whole, however, the economic liberals carried the day and they proclaimed the rights of property with more enthusiasm than discretion. This encouraged a revolt that, like the mirage of Tahiti, seemed to propose an alternative to a conception of society that did not offer much beyond the development of the economy.

The new vision incorporated the inheritance of Locke into an older view of society as an organic entity dedicated to the pursuit of moral objectives. If ideas were the product of experience it ought to be possible, at least in theory, to construct a society in such a way that all its members would be conditioned to behave socially, perhaps even, as Helvétius put it, to be *nécessités . . . aux actions héroiques*. If self-love and social duty were the same, as Pope had affirmed, in an ideally constructed state there would be no distinction between personal liberty and total self-subordination to the interests of the community. This was, in effect, to substitute the nation for

God as the source of moral obligation. People who felt this way tended to point to the classical republics as an example of the kind of society to which they aspired, but they were not merely indulging in a cult of antiquity or reviving Machiavellian civic humanism. To this inheritance they added sensational psychology, the belief that emotion took precedence over reason, and a commitment to equality that transcended the limited citizenship of the ancient world.

Rousseau was the most conspicuous advocate of this point of view. As early as his article on political economy in Diderot's *Encyclopédie* in 1755, he insisted that society was a moral entity with its own will, which was the criterion of what was just and unjust. This applied to humanity as a whole, but in practice people could only be expected to identify themselves with a particular state and local patriotism. On these grounds Rousseau preferred Cato and Rome to the universalism of Socrates and Athens. This embryonic nationalism received a more strident emphasis in *Émile*: 'Every partial society, when it is narrow and well-unified, cuts itself off from the great society. Every patriot is inflexible towards foreigners; in his eyes they are merely men [i.e. not citizens], in other words, of no importance.' To achieve this total social cohesion, the state should regulate the distribution of property and mould its citizens by public education, to insulate them from the corrupting influence of their parents. Rousseau amplified these views in his *Du contrat social* and they were to have a profound influence on the more visionary of the French revolutionaries.

This did not make Rousseau, at least in intention, a revolutionary. Like Fénelon, he thought that it was within the power of an almost superhuman legislator like Moses, Lycurgus, or Mohammed to transform the entire character of a people—but only in its youth. Old societies were so committed to their corrupt ways that to try to reform them was both dangerous and impracticable. Democracy was only suitable for a society of angels. 'The sublime conceptions of a God of wisdom and the gentle laws of fraternity that he imposes on us, the social virtues of the pure soul, which are the only cult that he expects of us, such things will always be beyond the grasp of the multitude.' When invited to offer practical advice about a constitution for Poland, his dislike of change, respect for social hierarchy, and aversion from economic development led him to make suggestions that were reactionary rather than merely conservative. Towards the end of the century Benjamin Constant described this school of thought as embodying an ancient, as distinct from a modern conception of liberty. In one sense this was true, but Rousseau had poured new wine into old bottles, with explosive results that were to be felt for a very long time.

Diversity across Countries and Regions

The Enlightenment, therefore, was not so much a specific set of opinions or beliefs as an attitude of mind. Its practitioners could be atheists or deists of the heart or head; they were not all economic liberals; some of them put their trust in enlightened absolutism and others opted for representative government. These divergent and sometimes contradictory conclusions were the product of a shared assumption that the human predicament could be explained without recourse to the mysteries of revealed religion, that nature and man's place within it could be understood in terms of general laws that were applicable to everything that existed. In this sense, the movement was international. Its seminal texts were promptly translated and assimilated throughout Europe. Catherine II in Russia founded a society for the translation of foreign books that published over a hundred texts. The wife of Klopstock, the German poet, wrote to Richardson, the English novelist, that she intended to breastfeed her own children, as recommended by Rousseau. The Enlightenment shared a common language in the literal as well as the metaphorical sense. Chesterfield told his son that a knowledge of French would allow him to make himself understood anywhere in Europe outside the Iberian peninsula. Dr Johnson was behaving like an English eccentric when he tried to get by with Latin. The Tsar Alexander I rarely spoke Russian.

Nevertheless, the situation in which the *philosophes* found themselves varied very considerably from one country to another. The dissemination of their ideas was conditioned by the extent to which there existed, in any particular country, a wide educated readership. The attitude of rulers and governments varied from hostility and suspicion to an eagerness to appropriate the ideas of the Enlightenment and to employ its devotees as agents of the state. This diversity of national climates meant that different aspects of enlightened thought predominated in different countries. What was of prime concern in one was scarcely relevant in another. If one thinks of the Enlightenment as a social phenomenon rather than as a mental attitude, its diversity is more obvious rather than its unity.

Shared conceptions about the nature of religion could look very different when refracted through the prism of national churches. In Roman Catholic countries each Church was a powerful segment of an international organization. The various national churches nevertheless offered very different kinds of targets to enlightened anti-clericalism. Throughout most of the eighteenth century the Spanish Inquisition dominated the intellectual life of the country and had no great difficulty in suppressing hetero-

Despite its wide local variations, the Enlightenment was an international phenomenon. The classical Tsarist Palace at Tsarskoe Selo was designed by an Italian, Bartolomeo Rastrelli, and enlarged by a Scot, Charles Cameron.

doxy. In Florence, on the other hand, although Galileo's works were still on the Index, the existence of the Inquisition did not stop a statue being erected in his honour. In Protestant states the Church was poorer and more dependent on the secular power; marriage and lay patronage integrated the clergy into civil society and they were usually less effective in persuading governments to defend them from their critics. The Orthodox Church in Russia had tended to restrict its role in the community to preaching morality. It had never concerned itself with the education of the laity. Closely subordinated to the state by Peter, at the beginning of the century, its impact on secular life was so slight that anticlericalism in Russia would have been a gratuitous irrelevance.

Some of the Catholic and Protestant clergy, like Morelly and Sterne, were active contributors to the Enlightenment. Others subscribed to the *Encyclopédie* or joined local academies and learned societies. The Richerist movement, which campaigned for the more democratic government of the

Catholic Church, could perhaps be considered as a current running parallel to the Enlightenment. Other movements took off in an anti-secularist direction: the German Pietists, English Methodists, and French Jansenists shared some common features while retaining their own distinctive character.

Politically speaking, the situation was equally complex, partly as the result of differing social conditions. In a rough and ready way, Europe was divided between the 'advanced' nations—the United Kingdom, the Netherlands, France, and Italy—on one hand and the east and the Iberian peninsula on the other, with Germany divided between the two. What characterized the former was the existence of an extensive educated society that generated its own newspapers, printing presses, and circles of sociability and education. The clientele of the Enlightenment was independent of government and public opinion existed as an autonomous force. Even within this camp, local conditions varied a good deal. In England the Enlightenment was a way of life rather than a movement of intellectual dissent. It was not greatly concerned either to challenge the government or to capture it as a vehicle for the transformation of society. To the Scots, whose intellectual contribution was a great deal more distinguished than that of their southern neighbours, it offered, among other things, an education in civilized sociability and a means of creating a new sense of national identity after the union with England in 1707. Perhaps as a result, the Scottish Enlightenment was orientated in a practical direction: there was all the difference in the world between the ineffectual French agrarian societies and the Scottish Board of Trustees for Trade, Manufacturing and Fisheries. In France itself the government on the whole regarded the Enlightenment with suspicion and disfavour. Diderot was only one of those whose writings earned him a stay in a state prison. Unable to influence policy and only intermittently intimidated by the ineffectual attempts of a weak and derided government to censor them, the *philosophes* were provoked into opposition and encouraged in utopianism by the knowledge that nothing that they wrote was likely to be put to the practical test. Under Louis XVI there was a dramatic change, and with Turgot in charge of finance and the Academy of Science invited to report on Mesmer's credentials, it looked as though the Enlightenment might become part of the Establishment.

In the east and in Spain, it is difficult to think of it as anything else. In Russia, if it was not quite the offspring of the German-born Catherine II, it was almost entirely indebted to her for its development. In her huge and backward country, the majority even of the nobles and provincial merchants were either illiterate or not in the habit of reading for enjoyment and instruction. There were no private printing presses until she encouraged them. She herself created and contributed to a literary magazine, inspired by the *Tatler* and the *Spectator*, intended to civilize its readers by poking fun at their traditional prejudices. She corresponded with Voltaire and d'Alembert and welcomed Diderot as her guest for a six months' stay. Whatever was done to bring Russian society into contact with the rest of Europe was largely due to her initiative. Austria was less backward but more subject to the repressive control of the Catholic Church. The Empress Maria Theresa saw the need for modernization but was inhibited by the fact that she shared most of the beliefs of her clergy. Her son Joseph II, co-regent from 1765 to 1780 and sole ruler for the next ten years, although a sincere and even fervent believer, anticipated some of the religious policies of the French revolutionaries in an attempt to restore the Church to what he believed to have been its primitive purity, and some of their secular policies in his efforts to turn his dominions into a new Sparta. In Prussia and Spain also, the Enlightenment, at least if one thinks of it in social terms, was the child of rulers, but in different ways. Frederick II of Prussia enjoyed arguing with *philosophes*, especially with Voltaire, but insisted that action was his own province; much of what he did was a development of previous Hohenzollern policies. Spanish traditions were a very different matter, and the small group of men who clustered round Charles III saw themselves as breaking down Spain's isolation and regenerating the country by the importation of foreign ideas. No *philosophe* went to Spain, and when Marat was looking for a job there he thought it prudent to pretend that he was scandalized by the irreligion of his contemporaries. When Charles III died things reverted to normal, with the result that some adherents of the Enlightenment welcomed French conquest in 1808 as the only way of attaining their objectives.

Whatever generalizations one is tempted to offer are riddled with improbable local anomalies. When Catherine created an Academy of Languages, the person she brought over from the Academy of Science to be its head was a woman. There were two female professors at Bologna, in the Papal States of all places. Such goings-on would have been not merely impossible but inconceivable in England or France. Rousseau's *Du contrat social* was banned, not merely in France, but in the republics of the Netherlands and Switzerland, although a German translation was allowed to circulate in Russia. La Mettrie's aggressive *L'Homme machine* got him expelled from the relatively tolerant Netherlands and invited to Prussia by Frederick II. Catherine's ideas about what constituted a liberal education were rather broader than Diderot's and, in theory at least, corporal punishment was banned in Russian schools when its necessity was taken for granted in England.

The French Revolution and the Enlightenment

Something that did exercise a unifying influence over the Enlightenment and, in a sense, brought it to an end, was the French Revolution. This was initially welcomed almost everywhere as a triumphal affirmation of the power of the new ideas to regenerate every aspect of a nation's life. Even from the start, however, the revolutionary message rested on a dangerous ambiguity: the Declaration of the Rights of Man, of August 1789, asserted both the need to divide sovereignty and the omnipotence of the general

The first years of the French Revolution were widely seen as the political fulfilment of the ideals of the Enlightenment: rationality, liberty, and the creation of a fraternal society. The three Orders of France are here combining to hammer out a new constitution.

tôt tôt tôt
battez chaud
tôt tôt tôt
bon Courage
il faut avoir cœur a l'ouvrage.

will. As revolutionary governments found themselves floundering among intractable social, economic, and political problems and intimidated by popular violence, Montesquieu succumbed to Rousseau, or at least, that was how the duc de la Rochefoucauld put it. Survivors of the great days of the *philosophes*, like Marmontel and the Abbé Raynal, condemned even the relatively liberal reforms of the Constituent Assembly. The only one who continued to support the republic, Condorcet, was proscribed and driven to his death in 1794. Paine, who had fled to France in order to escape arrest for sedition in England, been given French citizenship, and elected to the Convention, had already written off the revolution before the reign of terror began. He wrote to Danton on 6 May 1793: 'I now despair of seeing the great object of European liberty accomplished; and my despair arises not from the combined foreign powers, not from the intrigues of aristocracy and priestcraft, but from the tumultuous misconduct with which the internal affairs of the present revolution are conducted.' He was arrested early in 1794. Under the influence of Robespierre and Saint-Just the revolutionary government committed itself more and more to the implementation of what were believed to be Rousseau's ideas, notably with regard to education and the introduction of a civil religion; but Robespierre saw Rousseau as the enemy and victim of the *philosophes*, whom he denounced as 'proud in print and fawning in ante-chambers'. Both in theory and practice, the Terror was the negation of the Enlightenment. There was much less liberty than under the *ancien régime*; the press was censored; men were arrested wholesale and held in prison without trial; the academies were abolished. Lavoisier was executed because he was a tax farmer, not on account of his chemistry, but his death looked like a symbol of a regime which proclaimed that it had no need of *savants*. After the fall of Robespierre and Saint-Just in 1794 there was a not very successful attempt to return to the ways of the Enlightenment; Napoleon may be viewed as the last of the 'enlightened despots', but by this time the current of ideas was setting in new directions.

Outside France, the revolution soon came to be seen as a threat to the social order, especially when the French armies began their march across Europe. Reforming autocrats gave way to reactionaries. This was partly a matter of dynastic accident: Charles III, Frederick II, Joseph II, and Catherine II all died between 1786 and 1796. In the case of Austria, it was the intensification of a trend that had begun before 1789. Joseph's intemperate haste and impatience with anyone else's ideas had provoked revolt in Hungary and the Austrian Netherlands, where his cult of an Austrian fatherland held little attraction for conservative nobles and patricians. The Austrian Enlightenment was in retreat before anyone laid a hand on the

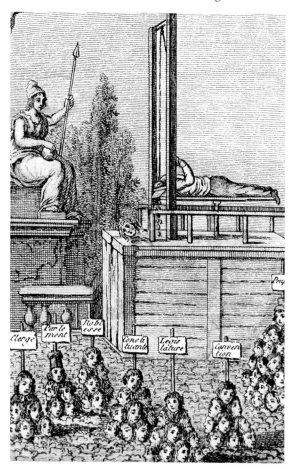

The Reign of Terror can be seen, from one point of view, as the consequence of an attempt to impose a vision of a utopian society on a recalcitrant population. Robespierre, after exterminating the rest of the French people, guillotines himself.

Bastille. As a result of the French Revolution, the reaction became general. Despite Robespierre's excommunication of the *philosophes*, they tended to get the blame. Catherine kept her head rather better than most rulers and there was not much of a witch-hunt in Russia. Radishchev, condemned to (quite comfortable) exile in Siberia for an attack on autocracy, was allowed to return before the end of his sentence and taken back into state service. Catherine was nevertheless inclined to regard the Polish constitution of 1791, which threatened her annexationist ambitions, as a product of 'Jacobinism'. She closed down the private presses, turned against the *philosophes* whom she had formerly admired, revived censorship, and banned the works of Voltaire. Everyone else was at war with revolutionary France and support for what had been French ideas was easily assimilated with sedition. In England, as in Austria, reform movements had become more radical in the years before 1789. After the outbreak of war in 1793 the government tended to panic and in its concern about possible subversion it abandoned some of the practices that had previously commended it to enlightened Europe. With the suspension of Habeas Corpus and the Seditious Meetings Act it began to attack political dissent in what had previously been regarded as continental ways.

When Europe was resettled after the Napoleonic wars, the old ideas survived, but they were temporarily submerged by a revival of dogmatic religion and a new reverence for the past that Romanticism created for itself. Rulers no longer aspired to be latter-day Lycurguses. Fear of revolution united monarchs and their nobles in defence of the status quo. When science, rationalism, sociology, and economics eventually reasserted their claims, everything had changed and the Enlightenment had passed into history.

Conclusion

The patient reader who has followed the story so far is probably wondering whether, in Michelin terminology, the experience *vaut le voyage*, and thinking that the Enlightenment was everything in general and nothing in particular. Its protagonists contradicted each other and were often inconsistent with themselves. The roads they took seemed to lead to T-junctions or dead ends. As a national experience, the Enlightenment took such different forms that it is perhaps best studied as a phase in each country's development, rather than a movement in its own right. Perhaps, in the Olympian language of the *Oxford English Dictionary*, the whole concept should be dismissed as an 'implied charge of shallow and pretentious intellectualism, unreasonable contempt for tradition and authority'.

What one makes of it depends upon one's personal make-up and the times in which one lives. Viewed from the end of a twentieth century that has supped full on horrors, its self-confidence and optimism look very much like a false dawn. Evil is not so easily dismissed as the remediable consequence of ignorance and superstition; knowledge is no guarantee of harmony or progress. It has enabled man, for the first time in human history, to acquire the ability to destroy his own species. All that may be conceded. The hopes of the *philosophes* are still unfulfilled and science has been made the instrument of barbarism. Nevertheless, in purely practical terms, the Enlightenment had lasting victories to its credit. People stopped burning witches, and the persecution of heretics, widespread at the beginning of the century, had almost ended by its close. Serfdom was on its way out, and the movement for the abolition of the slave trade had been launched. Judicial torture had been abolished in France, Austria, and Prussia, and the death penalty was coming under attack. One cannot divorce the Enlightenment and its attitudes from the take-off of industrialization which, with all its tragedies and destruction, was eventually to provide ordinary people with the means to live tolerable lives.

In the realm of ideas too, the Enlightenment was the gateway to the modern world. It asked new questions, for which we are still seeking the answers. If its own solutions appear jejune, we have nothing better to put in their place. It marked the transition from a world in which one took what one was given, in terms of religion, politics, and a way of life, to a world where man was seen as the architect of his own destiny. With the Declaration of Independence and the Declaration of the Rights of Man, the concept of universal rights replaced divine right, social hierarchy, and aristocratic honour. In some respects, our own century has seen a return to the perspective of the Enlightenment after the aberrations of social Darwinism. It is a commonplace for us, as it was for the people of the eighteenth century, that nature is not an adversary to conquer but a system to which we must adjust ourselves if we are not to perish. The Enlightenment is much more than a historical period. It helps us to understand the distant conclusions towards which certain assumptions lead, and to decide whether or not that is where we want to go. Whether we like it or not, it has helped to make us what we are. 'When me they fly, I am the wings.' It is not an anthology of unsatisfactory answers to oversimplified questions but the story of man's first attempt to come to grips with the contemporary world and all its unsolved problems.

9

Europe Turns East: Political Developments in the Eighteenth century

H. M. SCOTT

Political developments in eighteenth-century Europe have often been viewed through a French lens. There was, it must be admitted, considerable contemporary justification for such a perspective. At the beginning of the period, France was clearly the dominant European state. Her political leadership, based on abundant demographic and economic resources and Europe's largest and most powerful army, proved enduring, though by the mid-eighteenth century her relative military and international decline was becoming evident. Around 1700, however, France's army, monarchy, and system of government were all widely admired, as were her fabled court at Versailles and her élite culture, both of which set the standards for the other continental countries. Throughout the eighteenth century, French was the principal language of educated and aristocratic society on the continent, and was often used by rulers, statesmen, and diplomats in preference to their native tongues. The leading intellectual movement of the age, the Enlightenment, had important foundations in France. Above all, the revolution which began in Paris at the end of the 1780s seemed to confirm France's central place in the political world of eighteenth-century Europe.

The French Revolution's crucial importance for modern history has often distorted our view of eighteenth-century developments, which have been seen as a preparation for the dramatic events after 1789. France was and always remained a major state, yet its place in Europe's eighteenth-century history was less central than it has seemed. The key political developments of this period were located at the peripheries of Europe. In the

West, the British state rose to commercial, colonial, and eventually political pre-eminence. Simultaneously, new powers arose in eastern and central Europe: first Russia and Austria and then, from mid-century, Prussia. These shifts in the international order were in the long term decisive: the Pentarchy, the system of five Great Powers (Great Britain, France, Russia, Austria and Prussia) who collectively dominated Europe for two generations after 1815, was created by eighteenth-century developments, and its leadership was becoming apparent by the 1760s and 1770s. Yet in important ways the period before 1789 differed from this later age. 'Germany' and 'Italy' were not nation states, as they were to become during the third quarter of the nineteenth century, but geographical expressions. During the eighteenth century each was a territorially divided region which, at different times, served as a focal point for the rivalry and wars of the major powers. These divisions highlighted the lack of significant nationalist sentiment in eighteenth-century Europe, in contrast to the situation after 1800.

The international changes were accompanied and, in some degree, made possible by innovations in the internal government of leading states. The expansion of the authority exercised by rulers over their subjects was particularly evident in central and eastern Europe, where after 1700 such control increased significantly. To the west, state power was largely based upon relatively efficient fiscal systems supported by thriving agrarian and/or mercantile economies: here taxation and conscript soldiers were levied by governments and used to support their international adventures. These were also sustained by borrowing, which was less easy in the continent's eastern half, with poorer and more backward peasant economies with exiguous commercial sectors. There, taxation (though still levied) was less important, as rulers extracted more in the form of grain surpluses and, above all, compulsory military service from their subjects. Peasant conscripts filled up the rank and file, while noblemen were encouraged and, sometimes, forced into the officer corps. The two greatest political success stories of the age, the Prussian monarchy and the Russian Empire, were in this respect based upon rather different internal regimes from those to be found in western Europe. Everywhere, however, the principal and occasionally the only purpose of domestic government remained that of securing resources necessary for the waging of adventurous foreign policies and the wars these generated. As in earlier centuries, the needs of international competition and the expansion of administrative activity at home were organically linked. Throughout the eighteenth century, rulers and their ministers looked to their own subjects to sustain the rivalries which they pursued abroad.

The Wars of c.1680–1721 and Europe's Balance of Power

The changes in the international order were the product of a generation of near continuous warfare which stretched back to the 1680s and forward into the 1710s: the fighting in Europe did not formally cease until 1721. There were three conflicts which were distinct, though not entirely separate. The first was located in south-eastern Europe and was primarily a struggle between Austria (as the central European lands of the Habsburg monarchy, ruled from Vienna, were coming to be known) and the Ottoman Empire. It was the final act in the centuries-old Holy War between Christendom and Islam: the Crusade was proclaimed by the Pope for the last time shortly before 1700. This was one of the few major examples of enduring religious conflict. By comparison with earlier centuries, religion was a less divisive issue between states and within particular countries in eighteenth-century Europe, though there were exceptions and everywhere faith remained the basis of everyday life.

During the sixteenth and seventeenth centuries, Ottoman power had waxed and then, from the 1570s, stabilized. The Sultan's government, located in Constantinople (present-day Istanbul), dominated south-east Europe and, specifically, controlled much of the kingdom of Hungary, formally ruled by the house of Habsburg but in practice an Ottoman satellite. By the mid-seventeenth century, Constantinople's grip was slackening, as its overlordship came to be challenged, and from the 1680s a full-scale war of liberation was under way. The failure of a Turkish siege of Vienna in 1683 opened a period of intense campaigning. This was primarily between Austria and the Ottoman Empire, though Venice, Poland-Lithuania, and Russia also played minor parts in the fighting. In a series of campaigns between 1683 and 1699, and again between 1716 and 1718, Habsburg armies gradually gained the upper hand and conquered and reconquered much territory from the Turks. The peace settlement of Carlowitz (1699) gave Vienna control of all Hungary and Transylvania (except for the Banat of Temesvár) while that of Passarowitz (1718) added the Banat of Temesvár and northern Serbia. Though these latter gains were largely lost at the end of the 1730s, after a further and notably unsuccessful war against the Ottoman Empire, fought in partnership with Russia (1735–9), the changes in the territorial and military balance in south-eastern Europe were decisive and proved to be enduring.

Carlowitz closed two centuries when the power of the Ottoman Empire and the military threat it posed to its European neighbours had been a major factor in the continent's history and when Europe stood on the defensive. It was the first time the Ottoman Empire had signed a peace settlement—as distinct from a truce—with a non-Muslim state, and the first important occasion upon which it had handed back some of its earlier conquests. It opened two centuries during which the major European states had to tackle the problems posed not by Ottoman power but by Ottoman weakness, and when the Sultan's neighbours were attracted by the possibility of further and spectacular territorial gains from the once-feared Ottoman Empire. The notion of the Sultan's Empire as 'the sick man of Europe' first emerged in the late autumn of 1683, in a popular song which was heard in the Austrian territories during the immediate aftermath of its defeat at Vienna. The retreat of Ottoman power proved to be a prolonged process, and one that was periodically interrupted by significant periods of recovery, when Turkish armies once more put up a credible military performance. The Ottoman Empire had been forced onto the defensive, while its internal structure was increasingly backward by comparison with the more efficient states which surrounded it. Yet it remained a significant factor in eighteenth-century European history, though for rather different reasons than before.

The consequences for Austria were even more decisive. Throughout much of the early modern period, Vienna had been the front line of defence against the Ottoman threat, but it was now protected by the kingdom of Hungary, which resumed its late medieval role as a Christian buffer state defending central Europe against any revival of Ottoman military power. This new sense of security was apparent in the spectacular development of Vienna itself during the eighteenth century. Previously an exposed city inadequately safeguarded by fortified walls and largely confined within these limits, it expanded spectacularly between the 1680s and 1750s. Its population more than doubled, rising from around 80,000 to some 175,000, as the Habsburg court and government increased in size and leading members of the nobility took up residence in the capital for part and sometimes all of the year. The palaces built by the Habsburg monarchy's aristocracy in the city itself and then in the surrounding suburbs, together with the churches erected by the triumphant Catholic Church, and the residences and administrative buildings put up by the ruling dynasty, transformed Vienna. From a vulnerable fortress, it was rebuilt in little more than a generation as a baroque metropolis, the leading city in central Europe with a population of some 200,000 by the close of the eighteenth century.

Vienna's rise was part of a spectacular increase in Habsburg self-confidence and, less certainly, power in the decades around 1700. The extinction of the Spanish branch of the house of Habsburg in that year, with the death

One of the aristocratic palaces that came to dominate the skyline of Vienna, the Trautson Garden Palace was built for the family by the great architect and builder J. B. Fischer von Erlach, during the second decade of the eighteenth century. Simultaneously the family secured the exalted title and dignity of Prince of the Empire (1711). The Trautson family came originally from the Tyrol but was an important landowner in Lower Austria, and rose to prominence at the court of the Emperor Joseph I (1705–11). Its palace was the first to be built outside Vienna's city walls, and was located directly opposite the Hofburg (the main residence of the Habsburg family). Johann Leopold Donat, Prince Trautson, was *Obersthofmeister* at Joseph I's court.

of the wretched Carlos II, contributed to this. But it was primarily fuelled by Austrian military successes against the Turks and, to a lesser extent, in the wars against France. This new-found status rested on insecure foundations. The Habsburg monarchy's infrastructure was ramshackle even by the standards of the age, while its army was poorly organized and badly equipped: the victories over the Turks were due to the military failings of the Ottoman Empire and to a commander of genius, Prince Eugene of Savoy, rather than to the power of Austria's own forces, which were still raised privately by old-style noble military entrepreneurs and not by the government in Vienna. These colonel-proprietors exercised enormous power over their troops and ensured that, until the 1740s, the Habsburg army resembled a federation of regiments rather than a modern-style unified force.

Austria was also involved in the second series of wars: those against Louis XIV and the threat which France was supposed to pose to the other European states, or at least her neighbours in western and central Europe. The French monarchy's innate strength and the significant territorial gains secured during Louis XIV's reign made France clearly the continent's leading state when the century opened. Yet while it was dominant, especially in western Europe, it was far from hegemonic. This was due to the success of William III, Dutch Stadtholder and (after 1688–9) king of England, Scotland, and Ireland, in creating coalitions to oppose France. Fearing the French threat to his homeland, he had sought security for the Dutch Republic by emphasizing the potential threat of France's power to all her neighbours. This had led to the creation of Grand Alliances in 1689 and 1701, and these coalitions—headed by Great Britain, the Dutch Republic and Austria—had opposed Louis XIV and his allies in the wars of 1689–97 and 1702–13/14. The second of these conflicts, the War of the Spanish Succession, was initially fought to determine who would succeed to the worldwide empire ruled from Madrid, though behind this lay a broader question of predominance in western and southern Europe. The Peace of Utrecht, which terminated this conflict in 1713–14, awarded the vaunted Spanish inheritance to Louis XIV's great-grandson, Philip V of Spain (1700–46), with consolation prizes, principally in the Italian peninsula but also in the Southern Netherlands, for the Austrian Habsburgs, who had also advanced a claim to the throne in Madrid. Dutch concerns about security in the south were addressed not only by the establishment of Austrian rule over the former Spanish Netherlands but by the Republic's right to garrison a series of fortresses there, the famous Barrier.

The fighting in western Europe between 1689 and 1714 signalled the rise of one new state and the decline of another. The British state (in 1707 Scotland completed an incorporating union with England, which also ruled over Wales and Ireland) emerged as a major power during these wars. Though Britain's armies fought on the continent in the struggle against Louis XIV, after the Peace of Utrecht her horizons were to become increasingly colonial and her power dependent on her fighting navy, which increased dramatically in size and importance during the eighteenth century, and her strong commercial economy. It would be almost a century, in the struggle against Napoleonic hegemony, before British soldiers again made a substantial military contribution on European battlefields. Her rise to be one of Europe's leading powers after 1713 was striking and, in the longer perspective, the most decisive political consequence of the fighting. Britain's emergence highlighted her distinctive constitutional structure, created by the Glorious Revolution of 1688–9. In a Europe increasingly dominated by rulers who claimed to be absolute monarchs—and some of whom actually were—the British king shared power with his parliament. These distinctive consitutional arrangements were one source of Britain's eighteenth-century power and prosperity, and came to be much admired in progressive circles on the continent.

Britain's partner, the Dutch Republic, overextended itself and damaged its economy and fiscal system in these wars: it was never again to be the commercial or political power it had been during its seventeenth-century Golden Age. Dutch foreign policy now acquired a cautious and even neutralist tone, which it shed only occasionally during the rest of this period. Though retaining much of its prosperity, at least until the final quarter of the eighteenth century, the Republic was not the vital force which it had been during its earlier heyday. The Dutch economy now depended upon agriculture and investment rather than trade and manufacturing, and this was one source of its slow decline during these decades. Its eclipse was part of the general decline of republics at this time, in a Europe increasingly dominated by powerful monarchies. During earlier centuries, the republics of Venice and of the Northern Netherlands had been in the forefront of commercial enterprise, and had also been politically significant, but this was no longer true. Venice became a peripheral and declining city, famous only for its casino and, by mid-century, well on the way to its subsequent role as one of Europe's most famous tourist destinations.

The eclipse of a second leading seventeenth-century power, Sweden, was even more complete. This reflected the decisive outcome of the last of the three conflicts at this time, the Great Northern War (1700–21). The accession of a young and inexperienced king, Charles XII, to the Swedish throne in 1697 was the signal for a concerted attack three years later upon the Swedish state by Poland-Lithuania and Denmark, assisted by Russia. The place of Russia within the anti-Swedish coalition soon changed dramatically. The moving spirit behind this quickly came to be her energetic and ambitious ruler, Peter the Great (1689–1725). He was seconded by Poland-Lithuania's king, Augustus the Strong (1697–1733). The first ruler of the composite polity of Saxony-Poland is remembered principally on account of his sexual prowess, which was legendary in his own lifetime: it was said of him that he had fathered as many bastards as there were days in the year. His political achievements proved to be less memorable due to military reverses suffered at Swedish hands.

In the initial campaigns of the Great Northern War, Charles XII fought skilfully and inflicted several serious defeats upon the enemies who surrounded him. These early successes, however, fatally encouraged him to pursue a reckless military strategy and this was to be the principal cause of Sweden's eclipse. His attempt to invade Russia came to grief at the hands of Peter I's reconstructed and impressive army in 1709 at Poltava, which proved to be one of the most decisive battles of the entire eighteenth century. Thereafter the Swedish king was always fighting to avert a complete disaster, as Russia conquered much of the eastern Baltic empire that Sweden had secured through successful military imperialism during the previous century. Though Charles XII died in mysterious circumstances and amidst ill-founded rumours that he had been assassinated, while besieging the Norwegian fortress of Frederiksten in 1718, the war dragged on for a further three years. It was concluded by the Peace of Nystad, signed in 1721 and effectively dictated by the victorious Peter the Great, who now proclaimed himself Russian Emperor. Russia secured the lion's share of Sweden's former empire, annexing a string of territories in the Eastern Baltic (Livonia, Estonia, Ingria, Kexholm, and part of Karelia).

Sweden was now clearly a second-rank power, retaining only Wismar and a small stretch of western Pomerania as mementoes of her earlier imperial glories. The long years of fighting, and the enormous burdens these had imposed on the Swedish people, discredited the system of absolutist government created by Charles XI after 1680. Charles XII's death, without an heir of his own body, created uncertainty over the succession, and this was exploited to carry through a constitutional revolution in Stockholm which replaced royal absolutism with the rule of an aristocratic parliament. Adolf Frederik, Sweden's first king during the 'Age of Liberty' (as the period 1719–72 is known), was a constitutional king, not an absolutist monarch, and he was effectively controlled by the *riksdag* (parliament) and the state administration, both of which were dominated by the nobility. This political system was destroyed half a century later by Gustav III's *coup* in August 1772. It restored some of the powers of the monarchy, though there was no re-establishment of absolutism. Though Gustav III (1771–92) dreamed of reviving Sweden's former glory and military power, and consciously modelled himself on the great seventeenth-century warrior-king Gustavus Adolphus, the Age of Empire was clearly at an end. Sweden fought a series of small-scale wars during the eighteenth century, but these were all unsuccessful and were climaxed by the fiasco of her involvement in the anti-Prussian coalition during the Seven Years War, when her state finances collapsed and noble commanders in Germany were reduced to trying to support their military operations from their own pockets and private credit. Her military shortcomings in that conflict were highlighted by Frederick the Great when, in 1762, Sweden's plenipotentiary arrived at the Prussian camp to sue for peace. With one eye on the desultory campaigning in western Pomerania during the preceding years, Prussia's king sardonically enquired of the Swedish representative why peace was necessary when the two countries were not at war. The adjustment to small-power status was not altogether easy, but it was accomplished, while domestically Sweden was well governed, socially harmonious, and relatively prosperous throughout the eighteenth century.

Russia's mastery of the Baltic, and her leading position in northern and eastern Europe, were now established beyond question, and this supremacy would be consolidated during the eighteenth century. She was no longer landlocked, as she had been for almost a hundred years: she had recovered the lands ceded to Sweden in 1617 and made further gains to the south of the Gulf of Finland. Crucially, she again possessed a Baltic port through which the expanding trade with western Europe could be conducted throughout the year. One important source of the dominance Russia now enjoyed was the control over Poland-Lithuania, which had been established in the course of the Great Northern War. When that conflict began in 1700, the ruler of Saxony-Poland had been the senior partner in the coalition. The vicissitudes of Polish politics and the control over Poland's territory established by Charles XII during the early years of the struggle saw Augustus the Strong's deposition and his replacement by Stanislas Leszczynski, who was in turn swept from the throne. Augustus was restored to his Polish throne by Russian victories and Russian armies, and thereafter ruled as a puppet of St Petersburg. Control over its western neighbour was an important source of Russia's new-found power. It enabled Russian troops to move westwards through Polish territory, which simultaneously acted as a buffer protecting Russia's own lands from attack. This invisible empire was accompanied and made possible by Russian intervention in Polish domestic politics, which increased throughout the eighteenth century and which succeeded in maintaining Poland-Lithuania in a subordinate position.

The Burdens of War and their Impact upon Government

The generation of wars which came to an end between 1714 and 1721 had brought about considerable and enduring changes in Europe's international order. It had notably enhanced the power and importance of Great Britain, Russia, and Austria, while condemning Sweden to political eclipse and the Dutch Republic to a period of political and, eventually, economic decline. The scale and continuity of this fighting, moreover, had been unparalleled since the Thirty Years War, and may even have eclipsed the impact of that conflict. European armies reached their numerical peak in the decades around 1700: it has been calculated that at least one million men were under arms in 1710, while France—the leading military power—had had an army 300,000 strong in the 1690s. To support military forces of this size, European governments were forced to make unprecedented demands upon their subjects. In the relatively mature commercial economies of western Europe—Great Britain, the Dutch Republic, even France—these wars triggered recourse to borrowing on a new scale and this created problems of indebtedness and repayment when peace was restored, but such initiatives could only provide a small proportion of the sums needed. Everywhere the demands of the tax collector and the recruiting-sergeant became incessant.

The resulting burdens could be very great indeed, while losses on the battlefield also increased at this time, particularly in the wars against France. The adoption, first in the British army and then in the forces of some other states, of a new infantry musket (the famous 'Brown Bess') with an improved barrel which enhanced muzzle velocity and thus increased killing power, was part of the explanation. So too was the determination of the leading British commander in the War of the Spanish Succession, the duke of Marlborough, to fight decisive battles rather than wage a conventional campaign of manœuvres and sieges. But it was the scale and intensity of the fighting which did most to increase the burdens upon ruler and subject alike.

By the early decades of the eighteenth century, governments across Europe had assumed or were rapidly assuming direct responsibility for administering and equipping their armies. Soldiers now tended to be recruited directly by the state, which was then responsible for clothing, equipping, feeding, paying and housing the rank and file. Everywhere new institutions were coming into existence, and older administrative structures were being overhauled, to discharge these tasks, while barracks were being built and garrison towns created to house these men during peacetime, as armies continued in existence when wars ended. In maritime countries, governments created new ports and maintained impressive dockyards to support their fighting navies. State enterprises such as these did much to fuel an impressive economic expansion during the eighteenth century.

308

The resulting burdens upon state administrations which were invariably rather small and at times old-fashioned, not to say ramshackle, were considerable and becoming overwhelming. The generation of fighting around 1700 exposed many of the shortcomings of existing structures and provided one principal motive for the widespread administrative reforms throughout Europe during the early decades of the new century. These initiatives had two principal sources. Broadly speaking, in southern and western Europe the monarchy of Louis XIV inspired emulation; while in the north, the distinctive military and administrative system created by Sweden's Charles XI was the prototype.

France's importance was especially evident in Spain, where administrative models and practices came south in the baggage of the new Bourbon dynasty. The economic and political decline of seventeenth-century Spain had been striking, yet the considerable potential of the Spanish monarchy remained evident. The worldwide empire ruled from Madrid and especially the vast lands in Central and South America still appeared potentially a source of great wealth and power, if the governing institutions could be overhauled. One reason why many in the entourage of the dying Carlos II had favoured a Bourbon candidate for the throne was a conviction that French administrative techniques could awaken the Spanish colossus from its slumbers. A new administrative élite grew up in early eighteenth-century Spain, composed of young Spaniards such as José Patiño and Melchor de Macanaz, who willingly served the new, reforming regime. The streamlining of the central administration and the exclusion of the aristocracy from any real influence in government echoed developments in Louis XIV's France. Indeed, France's ageing king had urged his ambassador, who was the real mainspring in Spanish government, to permit the grandees to 'preserve all the external prerogatives of their rank, and at the same time to exclude them from all matters which might increase their credit or give them a part in government'. Instead Spain's administration came to be staffed by members of a service nobility. The division of the secretaryship of state into five separate offices was based partly upon the example of France, and gave administrative coherence and direction at the centre.

An even closer parallel with the situation north of the Pyrenees was the introduction of intendants. The royal provincial intendant, appointed by the crown and responsible directly to it, had been the key figure in the new system of monarchical government which had evolved in seventeenth-century France. Though his authority and thus his importance have been exaggerated, he was a significant figure, and he had come to symbolize the relative efficiency of Louis XIV's domestic regime. The introduction of intendants into Spain was a prolonged process, which extended over the first half-century of Bourbon rule. Efforts were made to establish these agents during the War of Succession and again in 1718, but these initiatives encountered stiff opposition from the existing agencies of provincial government: in the 1720s, the system was effectively suspended, with intendants remaining only in a handful of provinces where troops were stationed.

In 1749, however, under a new king, Ferdinand VI (1746–59), the system of intendancies was fully restored by another noted reformer, the marquis of Ensañada. Though his efforts were based on the 1718 initiative, there were important differences. A generation before, intendants had been made responsible for the four principal areas of domestic government, exactly as in France: these were taxation, the army, justice, and general administration. This was one reason why they aroused so much opposition. Ensañada now limited their duties to the military and fiscal spheres; it would be 1802 before the intendants recovered responsibility for law and general administrative matters. Nevertheless, the intendants provided new and more reliable links between the centre and the localities, and were one source of Spain's noted and accelerating eighteenth-century recovery, particularly in the economic sector. The Spanish empire survived intact until the early decades of the nineteenth century, while under the leadership of the new Bourbon regime in Madrid the country once more became a power in the western Mediterranean and the Italian Peninsula during the generation after the Peace of Utrecht.

Bourbon Spain exemplifies the way in which administrative reform blended a French prototype with the distinctive local situation. The fact that the new dynasty was French in origin increased the influence of Louis XIV's monarchy as model and inspiration, but there was no attempt simply to plant foreign institutions into Spain's unreceptive soil: a process of adaptation was clearly visible. A rather different blend of the same ingredients took shape in another of France's neighbours, the rising north Italian power of Savoy-Piedmont. This territorially compact state straddled and was divided by the Alps. Its strategic location between French and Austrian power offered diplomatic opportunities, and these were shrewdly exploited by the ambitious court in Turin. In the decades around 1700, it significantly enhanced its political standing by adroit diplomacy, becoming a kingdom through the acquisition in 1713 of Sicily, which was subsequently exchanged for another Mediterranean island, Sardinia.

The foundations for this enlarged European role were strengthened by a notable series of reforms carried out during the long and crucial reign of Victor Amadeus II (1675–1730). Once again there were strong echoes of developments in neighbouring France, with a streamlined central administration, especially in the 1717 reforms of finance and government, intendants (from the 1690s) and an economic regime reminiscent of the mercantilist policies pursued by Louis XIV's great economic and finance minister, Jean-Baptiste Colbert. Yet the continuities with the earlier Savoyard administrative evolution were much stronger than the influence of France. The intendants, for example, evolved out of the existing system of the *referendarii*, who had been established in the Duchy's Piedmontese provinces since the early seventeenth century. There was one even more crucial distinction: Savoyard intendancies remained venal offices, that is to say they could be bought and sold as a species of property, whereas in France the post was not venal and indeed had been created in response to the perceived deficiencies of the administration produced by the practice of selling posts in government. In Savoy-Piedmont, in other words, the French example was significantly less important than in Spain, and native evolution correspondingly more significant.

France's influence was strongest among its neighbouring states. Throughout Europe, however, Louis XIV's monarchy was widely admired and sometimes copied. Occasionally, this emulation could border on the ludicrous. Frederick III/I, the Elector of Brandenburg-Prussia (1688–1713) and (after 1701) king in Prussia, procured the exact dimensions of Louis XIV's wig so that a copy could be made for him. He also built a secret staircase in the royal palace at Berlin, to connect his own chamber with that of his *maîtresse-en-titre*, once again believing he was imitating French example. There were, however, more important reflections of France to be seen on the sandy plains of Brandenburg. When Frederick's chief minister, Danckelmann, died, the king briefly and unsuccessfully attempted to rule in person: exactly as Louis XIV had done after Mazarin's death in 1661, though with infinitely more enduring success. The Hohenzollern ruler's cultural policies and particularly the enlarged court which flourished in Berlin, also owed much to the example of Versailles. In Brandenburg-Prussia—as throughout Europe—the Sun King's political and cultural achievements, and the strengthened domestic base upon which these rested, were widely admired. The fame of Louis XIV's monarchy was spread by the noble travellers who visited France in increasing numbers, and also by prints and by medals advertising his triumphs: a Frenchman travelling in early eighteenth-century Russia was startled to be shown a medal of 'your king'.

On Europe's north-eastern fringes, however, a very different model was more directly influential. During the 1680s and 1690s, the Swedish King Charles XI had carried out a notable overhaul of his country's military and administrative systems, in an attempt to reconcile the imperative of defending his widespread Baltic Empire with the relative poverty and backwardness of his own territories. These initiatives built upon earlier arrangements for military recruitment and for government. Sweden's administration was streamlined, her finances were put in order and a budget was drawn up for the first time, while, most importantly, her army was placed upon a sounder footing. Soldiers and their officers were allotted specific farms, and these crown lands were expected to support army families: it was therefore known as the *indelningsverket* or 'allotment system'. In this way the considerable expenditure of supporting an army of the size needed to defend Sweden's empire was significantly reduced. In peacetime, the army lived as farmers, while when war threatened they joined their regiments. This mobilization was impressively swift by the standards of the age: as it had been in 1700, when Sweden was attacked at the beginning of the Great Northern War.

Sweden's modern administrative system, together with Charles XI's military reforms, came to be emulated because they appeared to offer a way of supporting and supplying a first-class army on the scanty economic and agrarian resources available to governments in Europe's more backward regions. Less of the state's demands came in the form of taxation, and more in the shape of conscript soldiers and grain levies. During the early decades of the eighteenth century, elements of this system were copied in Russia and Prussia. This development first took place in Russia during the Great Northern War. Her remarkable ruler Peter the Great carried out a wide-ranging overhaul of his country's armed forces and government. It built upon reforms carried out by his seventeenth-century predecessors and especially his own father, Alexis. These innovations, however, were more a response to the struggle with Charles XII and in particular to a shattering Russian defeat at Swedish hands in 1700 at the battle of Narva, which highlighted the shortcomings of Russia's army and government.

During the early years of the Great Northern War, Peter modernized the Russian armed forces at breakneck speed, in the process creating a Baltic navy for the first time. The army was totally reformed within less than a decade. The artillery lost at Narva was replaced, by the simple expedient of confiscating church and monastery bells and casting new guns from them, while the cavalry was increased in size and effectiveness, and new garrison and line regiments were created. Above all, a coherent and unified recruitment system was consolidated, in place of the haphazard mixture of peasant conscripts and volunteers who had previously filled the ranks. In early 1705, it was laid down that every twenty peasant households were to produce a fit soldier, aged between 15 and 20 years. Subsequently cavalrymen were levied in the same way at the rate of one per eighty households. This was the basis of the system which applied henceforth. These levies were at first frequent and burdensome. In 1706 there were no fewer than five: two for the infantry, three for the cavalry. The demands slackened after the victory at Poltava, but the system itself endured. It was to be the basis of Russian military and naval recruitment until the second half of the nineteenth century, and was a relatively efficient way of creating and reinforcing a powerful army from a large population. Yet the burdens it imposed were enormous: service was for life—later reduced to twenty-five years—and was in practice a death sentence for the peasant conscript unlucky enough to be chosen.

The burdens on the serfs who made up the overwhelming majority of Russia's population were increased by exactions of forced labour—to work in the shipyards or on building projects such as the Volga-Don canal and the building of the new capital, St Petersburg—and then by the poll tax

The building of the Twelve Colleges in St Petersburg, from an eighteenth-century engraving. The new administrative agencies established by Peter the Great required accommodation in St Petersburg, which was now the centre of Russian government. In 1722 an architectural competition—the first ever in Russia—was held. Architects were asked to submit designs, which were judged by the Emperor himself. The winner was Dominico Trezzini, who constructed the Twelve Colleges building between 1724 and 1732.

(literally 'soul tax') introduced in 1718 and directly collected by Russia's enlarged and modernized army. State activity and expenditure were over-whelmingly concentrated upon the armed forces: three-quarters of the budget during the final year of Peter's life was committed to military and naval expenditure. The imperative of organizing society for war also dic-tated the wide-ranging reform of Russia's ramshackle government during the second half of the reign. Here the debt to Swedish precedent, already apparent in the territorial system of military recruitment, was even more evident. Peter himself interrogated high-ranking Swedish prisoners of war about the details of government in their native land, and also collected information on the operations and structure of administration in Denmark and some of the German states. The outcome was an administrative system which blended foreign models with the needs of the Russian situation. Central to this was the creation of a series of Colleges, set up during and after 1718, which handled particular areas of business: there was, for exam-ple, a separate College to deal with foreign affairs and one to deal with war.

Central government was modernized and expanded during Peter's reign. It is important, however, not to exaggerate what was achieved. Shortages of money and trained personnel were endemic, while the accom-panying transformation of local administration with the division of Russia into *gubernii* (literally: 'governments') was far from successful: the units were too large, and reliable administrators could not be found, not least because many of the posts were unpaid. The Russian nobility were forced to accept the obligation of state service, and it provided an adequate supply of military officers. Noblemen, however, were less inclined to accept posts in the civil administration: this was one area where the Petrine changes were incomplete.

By the time of his death in 1725, Russia had changed enormously since his accession. It was now the leading Baltic state, symbolized by the build-ing of a new capital, St Petersburg, through which an increasing volume of trade with western Europe was conducted; it possessed a powerful army and (for the first time) a significant Baltic navy, together with a more modern system of government, particularly at the centre. This achievement was distinctly personal: with only a handful of trusted collaborators, Peter had himself transformed the military and administrative institutions of his state through the exercise of his own remarkable energy and will-power. This transformation, however, did not prove enduring. The acute dynastic instability of the next generation (1725–62) and the poor quality of many of Russia's rulers during these decades, undermined the Emperor's achieve-ments. It would be the 1760s before Russia would resume her advance.

Peter the Great's essentially personal style of monarchy had its counterparts all across Europe. A minority of states were either constitutional
monarchies—as were Sweden between 1719 and 1772 and Britain throughout the period—or republics. By far the majority were absolute monarchies, whose rulers claimed full sovereignty over their subjects and
personally directed the work of government. In 1716 Peter himself defined
his authority in the following terms: 'His Majesty is a Sovereign monarch,
who is responsible to no one for his actions, but has the power to rule his
state and his lands as a Christian lord according to his will and good understanding.' Half a century later the French King Louis XV went even further, declaring that 'It is in my person alone that resides the sovereign
authority of which the proper character is the spirit of counsel, of justice
and of reason. It is to me alone that belongs the legislative power without
dependence and without division. The entire public order emanates from
me.' These and similar affirmations of royal sovereignty were accompanied by monarchical involvement in the day-to-day business of government. Most eighteenth-century rulers worked extremely hard at the craft of
kingship, spending long hours consulting with their ministers, reading state
papers, and attending council meetings. Some rulers were lazy, while others
were inconsistent in their application to the business of ruling: France's
Louis XV was a case in point. Most monarchs, however, worked assiduously, and this was especially true of notably successful rulers such as Victor Amadeus II, Peter the Great, or Frederick William I.

The overhaul of the Russian administrative and military system was
admired and came to be influential in Prussia, her near-neighbour which
lay to the west of Poland-Lithuania and was divided by that country. Brandenburg-Prussia was a collection of widely separated territories which
were scattered across half of northern Europe, from the Rhineland in the
west to the river Niemen far to the east, and unified primarily by the person
of the ruler. The heartlands of Hohenzollern power were the territories of
Brandenburg (including the capital, Berlin) and eastern Pomerania, to
which a large tract of western Pomerania together with the important
Baltic port of Stettin, was added in 1721, at the end of the Great Northern
War: Prussia had joined the anti-Swedish coalition in the final stages of the
struggle. The other principal Hohenzollern territory was the duchy—from
1701, the kingdom—of East Prussia. These scattered and highly vulnerable territories offered an unpromising basis for state power: the soil was
notoriously poor and the agrarian economy backward by comparison with
the western half of Europe, while commerce was at a low level and cities
few in number and small in size. Above all, she lacked the crucial resource

of population: in the 1780s, after the substantial territorial gains made by Frederick the Great, the Prussian monarchy ruled over no more than 6 million subjects. Prussia's dramatic eighteenth-century emergence on these unpromising foundations was one of the miracles of the age.

Its foundations were laid in the reign of Frederick William I (1713–40). Prussia's autocratic king was an admirer of Peter's achievement in Russia: both men were hard-working and hard-drinking rulers, and sealed their friendship through several personal meetings. Frederick William I was motivated by the same love of his country that had underlain the Petrine transformation, and his reign established the domestic foundations of Prussia's later emergence as a leading European power. Its basis was the creation of a single unitary central administration for all his scattered lands. Hitherto, government had been organized on a territorial basis. Each group of possessions contained its own separate administrative institutions which were dominated by the local nobility and often entirely reserved for them, in theory at least. When Frederick William I ascended the throne in 1713, only two institutions of government existed which covered all the Hohenzollern territories. Both were military in nature, reflecting the army's position as the major institution covering all the Hohenzollern lands: the General War Commissariat and the General Finance Directory. These were amalgamated and were to serve as the basis of the General Directory, established in 1723. It covered all the Hohenzollern possessions, blended territorial with functional government, and was thus a major step towards a modern administrative system. Each of the four departments into which the General Directory was divided (five from 1740 onwards) handled a distinct group of provinces as well as certain kinds of government business for all the territories of the Prussian monarchy. The Third Department, for example, was responsible for the Electorate of Brandenburg and two enclaves of Hohenzollern territory in Germany (Magdeburg and Halberstadt), marching orders and the care of the army. Each was headed by a minister, assisted by four to five councillors, and had a separate day when its particular business was discussed. For the Third Department, this was a Thursday. The General Directory was at the apex of Prussia's administrative system and, by the standards of the day, it was modern and worked well. It was supported by a tier of local government which was also relatively extensive and efficient.

The Prussian government's purpose was to squeeze the necessary men and money to support a first-class army from the scanty resources available to the Hohenzollern king. In Frederick William I's reign, the military establishment doubled in size, rising from some 40,000 in 1713 to 83,000 in 1740.

During the reign of his more famous son and successor, Frederick the Great (1740–86), it would more than double again. One particular source of military strength was the cantonal system of recruitment, which took shape over a period of time and was finalized in the early 1730s. Like Charles XI's *indelningsverket* and the Russian recruitment system, which it so resembled, it enabled a poor country to maintain a powerful, modern army and provided abundant conscripts to fill the ranks. The Hohenzollern territories were divided into recruiting districts, based on the number of 'hearths'; each regiment was assigned a specific district and this was in turn subdivided into as many 'cantons' as there were companies to supply. All able-bodied men between 18 and 40 were registered for service, though there were numerous and significant exemptions: noblemen, merchants, industrial workers, even theology students. The burdens of conscription fell almost entirely upon the peasantry in the countryside. Each conscript received an initial period of training and subsequently returned periodically to the ranks for refresher courses which might occupy two months in any year. In peacetime, these men worked on their own farms and on the lord's estate, wearing their uniforms to church on Sunday, but in wartime they were ready to serve whenever required. Not all those cantonists who were enrolled actually served in Prussia's armies: it has been calculated that between 1727 and 1813 (when the system was abolished) less than half of those registered actually pulled on the blue Prussian uniform. Yet it remains true that the proportion of the population conscripted into military service quadrupled during the eighteenth century, rising from 4 per cent to some 16 per cent. By the standards of other contemporary armies, that of Prussia was relatively well supplied with recruits and the cantonal system was greatly admired: in the early 1770s an attempt was to be made to introduce it in its entirety within large areas of the Habsburg monarchy. Manpower was a serious problem for all eighteenth-century armies, and territorially based recruitment of this kind seemed the best solution available. This military service, however, was a further burden on the peasantry, many of whom also owed substantial labour services on the lord's estate.

Regiments needed officers and government agencies needed administrators. Both expanded significantly during the eighteenth century, thereby increasing the need for such trained personnel, who could only be supplied by the nobility: Prussia, like other states in central and eastern Europe lacked the kind of sizeable and ambitious middle class which was to be found in the mercantile countries on Europe's western seaboard and could furnish trained personnel for the expanded administrations of the age. The third element in Frederick William I's recasting of the Prussian state was the consolidation of the alliance between the Hohenzollern monarchy and its nobility, which was to make an important contribution to Prussia's eighteenth-century emergence. Prussian nobles were known, now and for the next two centuries of German history, as Junkers; the word probably derives from the Middle High German for young nobleman ('junk-herre'), though it would be the nineteenth century before it was universally employed. The Junkers were as a group less stratified and also generally less wealthy than many continental nobilities. This was due both to the poverty of the Hohenzollern territories and to the survival of partible inheritance among many noble families which militated against the full emergence of the kind of aristocratic élite found in most other countries by the eighteenth century. The Junkers therefore eagerly embraced the military and, to a lesser extent, administrative careers offered by the Prussian state, seeing these as a source of opportunities and much-needed income. These careers were available on an increasing scale, with the notable expansion of the officer corps as Prussia's army multiplied in size, and they were monopolized by the landed élite: in the final year of Frederick William I's reign, all sixty-three generals in the Prussian army, fifty-six (out of fifty-seven) colonels, forty-four (out of forty-six) lieutenant-colonels, and 100 (out of 108) majors were members of the nobility. By the early nineteenth century, around three-quarters of the Junkers in the Hohenzollern heartlands of Brandenburg and Pomerania were active or retired officers. These noblemen were also an important element in local government where they monopolized the key post of *Landrat*.

Frederick the Great and the Rise of Prussia

The remarkable integration between nobles, peasants and state machine achieved by Frederick William I established a strong military power on unpromising foundations. Until his death in 1740, however, this formidable force was confined to the parade ground, where the tall grenadiers which the king particularly delighted in collecting drilled side by side with their less lofty fellows. The Prussian army's potential only became apparent to the rest of Europe after his son's accession in the early summer of 1740. Six months later, Frederick II led his Prussian infantry across the border into the Habsburg province of Silesia, thereby launching the War of the Austrian Succession (1740–8). Prussia's success in conquering and retaining the rich province of Silesia signalled her dramatic political rise; until the very end of Frederick William I's reign, she had been a German and Baltic

state, rather than a truly European power, which she now became with remarkable speed. Vienna, of course, was unreconciled to the loss of income and prestige represented by Prussia's annexation of Silesia. Through skilful and imaginative diplomacy in the mid-1750s, the Habsburg foreign minister Wenzel Anton von Kaunitz assembled a powerful-looking coalition of Austria, France, Russia, and Sweden, supported by contingents of soldiers from the Holy Roman Empire, which between 1756 and 1763 fought to recover the lost province in the extended and destructive conflict known as the continental Seven Years War. Prussia's remarkable success in resisting this coalition, less formidable in practice than it appeared on paper, and emerging without any territorial losses, established her position as a fully-fledged great power.

Prussia's survival owed much to her own efforts: the resilience of her administration, the bravery of her people and her army, above all the leadership of her remarkable king, by 1763 generally known to contemporaries—and to history—as Frederick the Great. Her leading international position was always less securely founded than those of her rivals: scanty resources and dispersed territories could not completely be hidden by the towering personality of the ruler and the strength of the Prussian army, and for half a century to come, she would remain the weakest of the great powers. Even by the time of his death in 1786, Prussia's army was only the fourth—or possibly the third—largest in Europe, while despite the considerable territorial gains since 1740 she ranked tenth in terms of territorial extent and thirteenth in terms of population.

Prussia's monarch was by now recognized to be one of the wonders of the age, an eighteenth-century *stupor mundi*. Noble travellers making the increasingly fashionable grand tour frequently took in Berlin in the hope of catching a glimpse of the great Frederick. Yet they were usually unsuccessful, as the reclusive king increasingly lived and worked not in his capital but in the nearby garrison town of Potsdam, which had been his father's favourite residence. Secrecy and isolation were both public necessities and private goals for Frederick. Aloof, overbearing, sarcastic, and strongly

The Neues Palais, Potsdam, built for Frederick the Great between 1763 and 1769. Its principal architects were J. G. Büring, H. L. Manger, J. -L. Legeay, and K. von Gontard. The king never himself resided in the New Palace, which was used during his lifetime to house important visitors who were granted the privilege of direct access to the monarch at Potsdam. Its construction and even more its scale, at a time when funds were very scarce, were an attempt to underline Prussia's new-found status and pretensions after the Seven Years War and to camouflage the shaky domestic foundations upon which her enhanced international position rested.

misogynist, he rationed his own time quite ruthlessly. A disciple of the French Enlightenment, he wrote significant works of history and political theory, in addition to reams of bad French poetry. He was also a noted musician, playing the flute and, when his wind gave out, the klavier, and even composing some minor works. Prussia's reputation as the Sparta of the age did not prevent Frederick spending lavishly upon opera (his special delight) and architecture: he clearly understood the importance of what has come to be called 'representational monarchy', that is to say the use of large-scale artistic enterprises to highlight a ruler's power and wealth and that of his state. Above all he was acknowledged by the midpoint of his reign as the greatest ruler of his age. He towered above his fellow-monarchs as Louis XIV had earlier done, and like his French predecessor set the style for monarchy for a generation and more to come.

By mid-century, Prussia had replaced France as the monarchical paradigm for the rest of continental Europe. Her administration was admired and sometimes copied: when, at the end of the 1740s Vienna embarked upon a major administrative reorganization of the Austrian and Bohemian territories, its centrepiece, the *Directorium in Publicis et Cameralibus*, was closely modelled upon the General Directory and, for a moment, it seemed as if it might actually be named after it as well. The drill and equipment of the Prussian army were the inspiration for military reforms elsewhere, while during the Seven Years War (when Prussia and Britain fought on the same side), Prussian troops performed their distinctive drill and went through some manœuvres to the applause of an admiring crowd in London's Hyde Park. Above all, however, Prussia's monarch himself was venerated. Frederick's kingship was extremely personal in nature: he was his state's commander-in-chief, foreign minister, and head of its administration as well as ruler. He governed personally and, increasingly, directly from his own cabinet: exactly as his father, Frederick William I, had done. His powers of leadership and political intelligence were the principal reason why Prussia established and sustained a great power status on such limited resources. This new-found international position by 1763 was symbolized by the immediate construction of a resplendent 'New Palace', located at the far end of the park in Potsdam from Sans Souci and dwarfing that elegant and small-scale structure. Construction began in the same year that peace was concluded, and was completed by 1769, during a period of intense financial retrenchment by the Prussian government.

The principal victim of Prussia's rise was Austria, who lost her pre-eminence in Germany, where the house of Habsburg occupied the dignity of Holy Roman Emperor, and more generally her leading position in central

Europe. The Austrian Habsburgs fought three remarkably unsuccessful wars in 1733–48: against France, then the Ottoman Empire, and, finally and most decisively, Prussia and a coalition of other enemies. These conflicts exposed the shaky domestic foundations of Austria's great power position. The administrative and military reforms which every other major state underwent at some point in the later seventeenth and early eighteenth centuries were not introduced in the Habsburg monarchy at that time. Austria's increasing backwardness and vulnerability were slowly apparent to observers in Vienna, and the failures of the 1740s stimulated a significant series of administrative, fiscal, and military reforms undertaken after the return of peace in 1748, with the aim of preparing the ground for a war of revenge against Prussia. The Seven Years War, however, clearly demonstrated that much more needed to be done. The Habsburg home front was unable to support the war against Prussia, and a further significant series of reforms began in 1761, before peace was restored. The centrepiece was the foundation of the Council of State (*Staatsrat*), the first body to consider policy initiatives for all the scattered territories over which the Austrian Habsburgs ruled.

Modern States or Composite Monarchies?

The eighteenth century saw a significant increase in administrative activity, made possible by institutional reforms at the beginning of the period and again after 1750. This expansion was part of a more extended process by which government evolved from its traditional judicial function into a more modern administrative mode. It was under way throughout the early modern period and would extend into the nineteenth century. The principal catalyst was the new scale and increased frequency of warfare, which had been especially evident during the seventeenth century. A particularly decisive stage in this evolution was reached after 1700. Administrative activity accelerated, as both the institutions and activities of government expanded rapidly. By the eighteenth century, this expansion was assuming a particular form. This is a topic where generalization is especially difficult: individual governments were at distinct stages of development, and there was a world of difference between the relatively modern state apparatus created by Frederick William I's reforms in Prussia and the situation in neighbouring Saxony, a medium-sized German territory whose ruler was also king of Poland, where at least until the 1760s government was still an extension of the Elector's household administration.

The general trend, however, is clear. The eighteenth century saw the transition in many European countries to functional ministries, headed by an executive director. These new departments were responsible for a particular branch of government and not, as previously, a distinct geographical area. The earliest of the more elaborate and specialized departments of state to be created were those which conducted diplomacy, reflecting the pre-eminent importance of foreign policy for rulers at the time. France was in the forefront of this development, again providing the model for other countries to follow. The second half of Louis XIV's reign had seen the creation of a much larger and more sophisticated French foreign office, and broadly similar specialized departments were created in Spain (1714), Russia (1719), and Prussia (1728), though not until the 1780s in Britain, when the modern Foreign Office was established. This was followed before long by the creation of more specialized agencies for domestic affairs. The change was to be far from complete: even on the eve of the French Revolution, the older territorial arrangements had not been completely superseded. But the trend towards modern-style ministerial departments was securely established and probably irreversible. This, in turn, brought about a considerable gain in executive energy. The new ministries, by concentrating upon their own specialist area, were able to govern more efficiently and extensively than the older, territorially based agencies.

The eighteenth-century expansion of administrative activity was reflected in interesting changes in the terminology employed to describe it. New terms became established: in France, during the early part of Louis XV's long reign (1715–74), the word 'administration' came to be employed, while in English the term seems first to have been used in a modern sense in 1731. Around the same time, on the other side of the Channel, the term *gouvernement* ('government') came to be employed in its modern, absolute sense of the body of persons charged with carrying out administrative tasks, rather than its traditional meaning, that of the tasks and duties of ruling and directing the affairs of state. It has even been suggested that the word *bureaucrat*, signifying those who worked in a government office or *bureau*, can be found in France from the third quarter of the eighteenth century onwards. It would be the next century, however, before bureaucracy as a term and a concept came to be established.

These changes in nomenclature testified to the expansion of state authority that was under way. There were many more officials, especially in central government, and the pace of administrative activity simultaneously increased. This acceleration was especially marked during the second half of the eighteenth century, as rulers came to pursue more interventionist domestic policies, inspired to some extent by the ideas of the Enlightenment (see above, Chapter 8). The burdens upon officials were further increased by a growing preoccupation, during the generation before the French Revolution, with the collection of statistical information, as the gathering of such data became part of administrative culture and an essential preliminary to the adoption of new policies. This provided one illustration of a general search for more precise information by governments at this time, as they sought to push back the curtain of ignorance which all too often hindered their actions. It was most apparent in their sponsorship of large-scale mapping of their own territories, often for military purposes. In the North German territory of Hanover, ruled by Britain's kings *in absentia*, officials spent two decades drawing up a comprehensive topographical survey of the entire electorate. The eighteenth century saw considerable progress in this field, with the beginnings of the British Ordnance Survey through the work of General William Roy, and its remarkable Austrian counterpart, the famous *Josephinische Landesaufnahme*, which between 1764 and 1787 mapped the Habsburg monarchy's central lands in unique detail. This survey was primarily military in nature. Surveyors from regiments stationed locally carried out the necessary mapping. Yet they also marked every house, all rivers, roads, and woods, and even the number of livestock which they observed. It was in this respect a kind of eighteenth-century Domesday Book. Everywhere rulers anxious to centralize and extend their own authority sought more precise statistical and geographical information of this kind. As Joseph II remarked, 'If one is to rule countries well, one must first know them exactly.'

It is clear that these decades saw significant progress towards the kind of bureaucratic administration found in most European states by the midpoint of the nineteenth century. This is a different thing, however, from describing any eighteenth-century government as a bureaucracy. The great German sociologist, Max Weber, whose writings were seminal for the development of ideas about bureaucratic government, declared that this must exhibit certain pronounced features. There should be a distinct and self-conscious group of officials, with defined functions, a clear hierarchy of status among these administrators, together with an ability to work in a regular and routine way. These men must be recruited through open competition, should have at least some relevant and prior training or education, and should be paid regular salaries, as well as having an expectation of some kind of pension upon retirement.

In each of these areas, there was significant progress, particularly during the second half of the eighteenth century. With a clear decline in the number of clerics occupying posts in government, a growing number of administrators all across Europe were first acquiring relevant professional training in a university or college and were making careers in state service; many—though far from all—of these men, particularly in the western half of the continent, were of more middle-class origins than preceding generations of government servants. Especially in the central administration, there were improved salaries (though often paid late and not always in full) together with the emergence of administrative rules and practices. In significant respects eighteenth-century governments were acquiring some distinct bureaucratic attributes. Yet this evolution was far from complete, and it was defective in several important ways.

The most serious obstacle to the expansion of government was the structure of all eighteenth-century states, as some rulers and ministers tacitly or explicitly acknowledged. This was most evident in the case of the Habsburg monarchy. The lands of the house of Habsburg sprawled across central Europe, where its principal possessions were the Austrian and Bohemian lands and the kingdom of Hungary, which enjoyed a semi-independent status. Vienna also ruled over the distant Southern Netherlands and large parts of northern Italy, principally the duchy of Milan, while the grand duchy of Tuscany was governed by Maria Theresa's husband, Francis Stephen, from 1737 until 1765, and thereafter as a Habsburg *secundogeniture*, that is to say it was ruled by a minor branch of the family. Until the middle decades of the eighteenth century, each block of territories had been governed separately. There were, for example, distinct Austrian and Bohemian administrations. These were combined in 1749–61, and efforts were made subsequently to increase central control over the Netherlands and Milan. Yet Hungary remained relatively untouched by these centralizing reforms until the 1780s, when Joseph II's efforts to increase Vienna's control over the kingdom met significant resistance and ultimately ended in failure.

The ethnic, linguistic, and religious diversity to be found within the Habsburg monarchy was exceptional in scale, though far from unique. It resembled most other eighteenth-century states in its composite nature, consisting of a series of kingdoms, provinces, and territories of all kinds which remained only partially unified. This corresponded to the pattern in every country of any size. The eighteenth-century British state, for example, was imperfectly integrated. Scotland retained a government of its own in Edinburgh, while the administration of Ireland was largely handled through Dublin, where there was also a separate parliament. Denmark provides a particular clear illustration of this trend, remaining a composite monarchy throughout the eighteenth century. The kingdom's central government was divided on a geographical basis into two separate agencies. The Danish Chancellery governed Denmark itself, together with the crown's overseas possessions: Norway, Greenland, Iceland, and the Faroe Islands. The German Chancellery administered Holstein (which was also part of the Holy Roman Empire), Slesvig, and the ancestral territories of Oldenburg and Delmenhorst, while its head was also responsible for the country's foreign policy. Though certain specialist bodies, such as those for commercial affairs and finance, and the Danish Council of State (*Staatsrad*), dealt with the entire kingdom, most government continued to be conducted on the traditional regional basis.

This was symptomatic of a wider trend. Everywhere, efforts at centralization were making headway, yet these were only slowly breaking down the barriers of provincial separatism and the distinct law codes and, in some places, the territorial Estates which still protected local communities from the intrusions and demands of central government, at a period when the context of social, economic, and political life remained overwhelmingly local. Eighteenth-century states were far from internally united or uniform structures. On the contrary, the process of national unification, and with it the authority of central government, were everywhere incomplete and could sometimes be very limited indeed. A host of powerful individuals and corporate bodies—archbishops, bishops, towns, guilds, universities, even whole provinces—retained and defended their own way of life and especially their important privileges, which were usually legal and fiscal in nature. They were aided in this struggle by the small size of the state apparatus during the eighteenth century and by the difficulties posed by slow and unreliable communications, which magnified the fundamental problem of distance. Efforts to promote greater internal cohesion could make only slow progress in the face of the enormous strength of traditional structures and established patterns of life.

Many states still contained independent territorial enclaves where the ruler's writ did not run. Eighteenth-century France, though widely admired for her modern administrative structures, contained a number of such enclaves which were slowly integrated into the Bourbon kingdom. The last to be incorporated were the papal territories of Avignon and the Comtat Venaissin, which were occupied by the French revolutionaries in 1791. This symbolized the Janus-like nature of all eighteenth-century states. Taxation and conscription were heavier burdens than ever before on society at large, but central authority was in practice still limited in range and effectiveness.

In the second place, personal contacts were still the key to government:

later eighteenth-century administrations remained primarily reservoirs of people and ideas, rather than collections of formalized administrative structures. Personal initiatives and private connections oiled the wheels of the state machine, which was not yet driven by the bureaucratic routines of a later age. A good illustration of this is provided by Kaunitz, who was always searching for talented assistants and subordinates, whose careers he carefully advanced even if he did not always agree with their views and policies. The Council of State came to be staffed by a whole series of his protégés, who were also strategically located throughout the administration and the Habsburg monarchy's diplomatic service. He himself depended greatly upon Freiherr Friedrich Binder von Kriegelstein, his loyal and ever-reliable deputy, and upon specialists in various fields, such as the step-brothers Ludwig and Karl von Zinzendorf in that of public finance and commerce. A large number of these men had long been members of Kaunitz's entourage, while another important adhesive was provided by marriage to members of the state chancellor's extended family. He expected his friends and protégés to draw up and implement policy initiatives. This exemplified the continuing importance of personal connections and clientage within eighteenth-century state administrations.

To a significant extent monarchical authority remained essentially personal in nature. This was true in two distinct respects. In the eighteenth century, as throughout the early modern period, a ruler's strengths, abilities, failings, and weaknesses were transferred to the government over which he presided and determined the nature of his—or, less commonly, her—political regime. The personal element in monarchy was still immense: one reason for Prussia's dramatic eighteenth-century emergence was the two remarkable kings who reigned from 1713 until 1786. The relationship between ruler and ruled, moreover, remained extremely personal in nature. The reforms of Frederick William I gave Prussia one of the most modern and widely admired administrations in Europe. His son's accession, however, underlined that Hohenzollern kingship remained strongly personal and contractual in nature. Shortly after his accession, Frederick the Great extracted individual oaths of loyalty from his principal ministers and military commanders, and then toured his various territories, receiving the homage and the complaints of the provincial Estates. Everywhere, rulers personally bestowed prized commissions in the army upon noblemen, and thus enhanced their value at the same time that they reinforced the ties between the crown and the social élite. Such bonds remained crucial even in an age when the institutional framework was expanding.

The expansion of government was considerable during the eighteenth

The traditional nature of eighteenth-century polities: the Estates of the former Habsburg province of Silesia doing homage to their new ruler, Frederick the Great, in the town hall of Breslau in 1741, after the Prussian occupation in the winter of 1740–1.

century, yet it fell some way short of the levels needed to discharge all its tasks, which also increased significantly at this time. In part, this reflected the widespread difficulties encountered in finding suitable potential administrators in the numbers now required. In many countries, especially in the eastern half of the continent, there was a relatively small pool of qualified professionals who were able and willing to serve as officials, while recruitment was still remarkably haphazard and appropriate education difficult to find. Everywhere the number of officials in central and local government increased significantly, but administrative personnel continued to be relatively thinly scattered, especially at the provincial level. This was particularly so in later eighteenth-century Russia, a vast and thinly populated country, especially its non-European provinces, which as a consequence of its remarkable seventeenth-century expansion sprawled across much of the Asian continent and bordered China. The huge *guberniya* of Kazan, for example, contained some two-and-a-half million people, but in the early

1770s it was ruled over by a mere eighty officials. In these circumstances, it is scarcely surprising that the authority of central government was remote and frequently ineffective.

Catherine II's reign (1762–96) saw a significant restructuring of Russian government, with a doubling in the number of personnel shortly after her accession and some important changes in the practice of administration: civilian officials took over the collection of the poll tax (hitherto levied by the army), while centralized control of state finance, with a budget drawn up for the first time in 1781, replaced a chaotic situation in which as many as fifty separate agencies had the right to collect and spend taxation. Yet in the early 1760s, the vast Russian Empire was ruled over, according to one reliable estimate, by around 16,500 administrators in central and local government. (This was a dramatic increase in the figure only two generations before: later seventeenth-century Russia had been ruled by some 2,000 central administrators, together with an indeterminate number of local officials and scribes.) One of Russia's principal rivals, Prussia, was considerably smaller in terms of geographical size, but had almost as many government personnel. The figure for Frederick the Great's reign was around 14,000 officials, though the Hohenzollerns ruled perhaps only 1 per cent of the territory that Catherine II nominally sought to govern.

The way in which the expansion of government could have difficulty in coping with the increased pace of administrative activity is especially apparent from the figures available for the Habsburg monarchy. In 1740, at the accession of Maria Theresa, there were around 6,000 officials for the monarchy's entire central lands, that is to say the Austrian duchies, the Bohemian lands, and the kingdom of Hungary. By 1763—after the major mid-century administrative reorganization—this figure had increased by some two-thirds, to around 10,000. By the time of Maria Theresa's death in 1780, the total had swollen to 11,000, and there seems to have been a further increase during Joseph II's personal rule (1780–90). (These are rounded estimates and include the ever-increasing number in the Vienna City Bank, which was responsible for tax-collection, together with the personnel of the Habsburg court, between 1,000 and 1,500 over the period as a whole.) Though this expansion was significant, it was insufficient to keep pace with a simultaneous explosion of administrative activity. In the Habsburg monarchy the quarter-century between 1765 and 1790 saw the most wide-ranging programme of reforms attempted anywhere in later eighteenth-century Europe, with a series of radical religious, administrative, legal, social, and economic measures.

A convenient, though inexact, guide to the continually mounting burdens upon Habsburg officials is provided by figures for the average annual number of government edicts for the Austro-Bohemian territories. This grew from a mere thirty-six in the 1740s to ninety-six by the 1770s, and to an astonishing 690 during the 1780s: the decade of Joseph II's hectic personal rule, during which the total number of edicts was twice that for Maria Theresa's *entire* reign. A similar pattern emerges when the workload of the Lieutenancy Council in Hungary (which implemented policy decisions taken in Vienna) is considered. During the 1740s, it was handling an average of some 2,500 letters annually. There was a fourfold increase during Maria Theresa's reign: by the 1770s the Lieutenancy Council was dealing with more than 10,000 letters annually. During the same period, however, the number of administrative personnel only increased by a factor of around two-and-a-half, from fifty officials to 122. There was a further sharp increase in the early 1780s, when the average number of letters being received annually rose to over 16,000. These figures reveal that there was a considerable expansion of administrative activity during Maria Theresa's reign, followed by an exponential increase during the decade when Joseph II was in sole charge. The workload increased significantly faster than the number of administrators available to handle it. They in turn complained, sometimes vociferously, and were less and less able—especially by the 1780s—to keep up with the volume of business.

The second way in which the eighteenth-century expansion of government was incomplete related to local administration, which has been surprisingly neglected by historians. The hybrid nature of the eighteenth-century state apparatus was most apparent at the provincial and district level. Though it was acquiring some of the features of the modern bureaucratic state, it retained to a surprising extent characteristics of older conciliar and territorial administrations. Local government remained traditional—and enormously diverse—in form: the new institutions established by central government were often dwarfed by the existing bodies of Estates, provinces, and towns. Even in France, which at least until mid-century was widely viewed as the most modern administrative machine in Europe, the central authorities struggled to impose their wishes upon a confusing tier of local government made up both of established bodies at the provincial, town, and village level, together with an army of venal office-holders who were more concerned with status and income than good government. Eighteenth-century England was even more decentralized. There, the aristocracy and the landed gentry monopolized local government, dominating all areas of its activities and providing an amateur and independent tier of officials. Everywhere, at least in the larger states, the wishes of the monarch and his advisers were only imperfectly translated into policy initiatives at the local level. Central government lacked both the personnel and the institutional leverage to impose its views as it wished. One statesman who had a clearer sense of this than most was the Austrian chancellor, Kaunitz, who proclaimed in 1773—almost a decade after the major administrative reforms of Maria Theresa's reign had been completed—that the Habsburg monarchy's administrative structure was analogous to 'an inverted pyramid' and that it would have to be thoroughly overhauled before reforming measures could be fully implemented.

State authorities were not wholly lacking in alternatives to a reliable framework of local government. The large armies now maintained by most rulers of any standing could be used: as was done in Russia, where the troops collected the poll tax from its inception in 1718 until the 1760s, or in the Habsburg monarchy, where military forces were employed on Joseph II's celebrated land survey in the 1780s. The churches, Catholic, Protestant and Orthodox, with their parish structures which often extended further at the provincial level than the agencies of the state, could also be employed to publicize and, less certainly, to enforce the ruler's wishes. There might not be a priest or a pastor in every parish, but there was more likely to be one than an agent of the central government. The potential of this religious infrastructure was widely apparent. After 1780, for example, Joseph II set out to make the Catholic Church an agent of Habsburg government, decreeing that official edicts had to be read out after service on a Sunday. In an age where literacy was still uncommon and which largely lacked a mass media of the modern kind, the pulpit was an important way of communicating with the common people, who might only come together for church services.

These were important adjuncts to state authority. Everywhere, however, central government was dependent upon the territorial nobilities to govern at the provincial level. This was true both formally and informally. In most states, noblemen filled the majority—sometimes the overwhelming majority—of posts in local government. In Russia, for example, the rural nobility monopolized the provincial administration; while in Prussia the key post of *Landrat* was normally filled by a local Junker. Significantly, in both countries local administrators were often part-time and sometimes unpaid agents of central government. In each country, moreover, there was a real shortage of trained personnel who could only be drawn from the ranks of noblemen. This was not, however, the principal contribution of the nobility to eighteenth-century government. Public authority had traditionally been exercised by noblemen working in partnership with the crown, and

The apotheosis of aristocratic display: the Esterházy Palace at Fertöd, built between 1761 and 1781 at the astonishing cost of twelve million florins and quickly christened Esterháza. The original inspiration was Louis XIV's Versailles. It contained no fewer than 120 rooms and came to be the location of the Esterházy court during the time of Prince Nikolaus the Magnificent.

this was long the case. Everywhere they acted as an additional, informal tier of administration and continued to play a major role in the administration of justice. This reflected the way in which their traditional social leadership was intact, even in the later eighteenth century, and could be channelled to support the actions and enforce the decisions of the far-away central government. The corollary, of course, was that it was very difficult for policies which lacked noble support, or at least acquiescence, to be implemented successfully.

There was a clear hierarchy of wealth (principally in the form of land) and power within the nobility. At its apex was a relatively small number of aristocrats ruling vast estates: magnate families such as the Radziwill in the eastern regions of Poland-Lithuania, or the Esterházy princes in Hungary, who were the largest private landowners in all Europe with an estate complex that at its peak was over 4,000 square kilometres in size. Another Polish family, the Zamoyski, owned an equally vast domain in central Poland with (by the 1770s) 220 villages, ten towns, and a population approaching 100,000. Such *latifundia* were in practice independent kingdoms, where local aristocrats ruled as private sovereigns, with their own administrations and princely courts, dispensing justice and even collecting taxation. The Esterházy family had its own princely bodyguard, 150 strong. Members of its household received free medical treatment and even a pension (in cash and kind) when they grew too old or infirm to perform their duties. The Esterházy princes were notable cultural patrons as well as dominant figures in Hungary's eighteenth-century history. Prince Nikolaus the Magnificent, for example, head of the house from 1762 until 1790, was a celebrated Maecenas. He was the employer of the musician Joseph Haydn, who as *Kapellmeister* for almost three decades was obliged to appear every morning before his master in the distinctive blue livery worn by all the servants of the noble house of Esterházy, and enquire what musical entertainment might be required on that day.

The vast estates possessed by the Zamoyski or Radziwill, far less the Esterházy, were unusual, and more modest landed properties were the norm. Everywhere, however, the authority of the nobleman, whether great aristocrat or small landowner, was more immediate and direct than that of the state, which was often distant and could be quite remote. Throughout eighteenth-century Europe the nobility, through their dominance of the agencies of local government, wielded considerable authority. This was increased—where territorial military recruitment was established, as for example in Prussia and Russia—by the fact that the nobleman was also likely to be an officer in a regiment made up of peasant conscripts from that locality. Public authority and private leadership in society overlapped, and this generally worked to the benefit of the state, though it also placed restrictions upon the kind of policies that could be pursued. Eighteenth-century government always rested, in the final analysis, more upon cooperation than compulsion at the local level. The inroads made by centralizing reforms against the established framework of provincial life were usually limited and could be surprisingly slight. Some authority was yielded up to the newly enlarged and increasingly powerful central government. Far more obvious, however, was the enduring social and political dominance of the aristocracies and lesser nobilities all across Europe, the considerable powers still wielded by the territorial Estates (where these existed) and the separate legal and administrative systems which most provinces maintained and tenaciously defended. The size and the authority of central government had everywhere increased, but it was most effective when exercised in partnership with, rather than in opposition to, the established local élites and existing agencies of provincial government.

Enlightened Government

The limited size and range of government were the principal reasons for the uneven success of the reforming initiatives carried out across much of the continent between the 1750s and the 1780s. The generation before the French Revolution saw widespread efforts to reform many areas of state activity and social and economic life, inspired in part by the political philosophy of the Enlightenment. This has led historians to talk in term of a generation of 'enlightened absolutism'. Administrations and fiscal systems were modernized; various aspects of punishment were made more humane, for example by restrictions upon the use of torture and the death penalty, while comprehensive legal codes were drawn up. One of the most remarkable of these was the Prussian *Allgemeines Landrecht*: this was issued in 1794, but was the product of an extended period of codification primarily undertaken during the reign of Frederick the Great, who himself provided much-needed impetus behind this enormous task. Commercial and economic development was encouraged, by measures which ranged from protectionist tariffs and state encouragement of manufacturing enterprises to a liberalization of the domestic grain trade and improvements in communications. Among the most notable of these measures were the efforts of the Habsburg government to improve river transportation in Hungary and to expand road building throughout the Austrian and Bohemian lands, with the aim of stimulating internal trade.

Efforts were also made to improve agriculture, primarily through the establishment of Agrarian Societies which sprang up all across Europe and were to act as a conduit for new ideas about farming. Even more remarkably, efforts were made at this time to abolish the institution of serfdom where it existed, which was primarily to the east of the river Elbe. These initiatives were often abandoned when the difficulties involved and particularly the degree of noble opposition became clear. Both Catherine II in Russia and Frederick the Great in Prussia were opposed to serfdom, on the

grounds that it was economically inefficient and an affront to their cherished belief in natural rights. But each was forced to abandon wide-ranging schemes to abolish serfdom, when confronted with the opposition of their nobilities and made aware of the potential damage which emancipation could do to the fiscal-military bases of their own states. Both rulers, however, did something to ameliorate the condition of serfs who lived under their own jurisdiction: the 'state peasants' in Russia and the 'domain peasants' in Prussia. During his personal rule after 1780, Joseph II made a determined onslaught upon the institution of serfdom, but he too encountered strong opposition from the nobility and, though some amelioration took place, he was ultimately obliged to accept defeat. Only where the landed élite themselves championed the cause of serf reform, as in Denmark, could real progress be made. There, a relatively mild form of serfdom which had assumed its final form as recently as the 1730s, as a by-product of a new system of territorial militia recruitment, the so-called *stavnsbånd* (literally: 'bond of adscription'), was successfully abolished during the final decades of the eighteenth century by a campaign in which prominent Danish noblemen played the leading part.

One principal target of the reformers in Catholic states was the wealth—though this was sometimes more apparent than real—and the privileged legal position of the Church. A determined and in places successful attempt was made to channel some of the riches of the Roman Catholic Church into improved and increased pastoral activity, rather than to the support of monasteries and nunneries, which were reduced in number. Many of the characteristics of Counter-Reformation Catholicism and the baroque piety now associated with it, such as the swollen number of feast days and pilgrimages, were vigorously attacked by state authorities and even by reformers within the Church's own hierarchy. Efforts were also made to reduce its considerable legal privileges, through attacks on the right of sanctuary and on gifts in mortmain. Even more remarkably, significant measures of toleration of religious minorities (Protestants in Catholic countries and vice versa; Jews everywhere) were pushed through by the enlarged state administrations of the age, and achieved some success. The other principal area of reforming initiatives was education. In Catholic

One target of Catholic reformers: a mass with elaborate orchestral and vocal accompaniment, from an engraving by J. E. Mansfeld (1739–96). The 'Reform Catholics', who wished for a simpler, purer faith, believed that such elaborate and ostentatious music distracted from the main purpose of Christian worship. They advocated instead the adoption of silent devotions and the communal singing of hymns. In 1783 Joseph II's reform of church music regulated the use of the concerted mass and restricted expenditure upon it.

Europe these measures were a necessary response to the suppression in 1773 of the Jesuit Order, which had played a central role in teaching at all levels. University curricula were modernized and new and more utilitarian subjects introduced, while the provision of primary and secondary education was vastly increased at this time and, in some states, extended to girls for the first time. The high cost of such measures was everywhere an important limitation upon what could be achieved, and the level of educational provision in towns was always likely to be far greater than in the surrounding countryside.

In the context of the later eighteenth century these were radical and sometimes startling measures, though they subsequently became a commonplace and also enjoyed only limited success at the time. In particular the efforts to make primary and secondary education more widely available, to weaken the entrenched position of the Catholic Church and to ameliorate the situation of the serfs in central and eastern Europe were remarkable initiatives in the context of the times when they were attempted. This was even more true where religious toleration is concerned, an issue which was pre-eminent for the Enlightenment. It is nowadays taken so much for granted that it is difficult to conceive of a period when this was not so. In the eighteenth century, however, hatred and vilification of Jews was widespread, and coexistence between Protestants and Catholics far from common and perhaps even unusual. This makes the efforts of Catherine II and her leading minister, Nikita Panin, in the mid-1760s to stop the persecution of non-Catholics in Poland-Lithuania appear remarkable and praiseworthy, however distasteful the methods of Russian military intervention were in practice. The courage and the radicalism of Joseph II's edicts granting a measure of toleration to Protestants and Jews in 1781-2 are only fully apparent in the context first of Maria Theresa's renowned Catholic bigotry and notorious anti-Semitism, and also of the deep and vociferous public hostility which greeted the reforming measures. In a similar way, we now take law codes so much for granted that there is a danger of underestimating the herculean labours, often extending over several decades, that went into compiling them in the first place.

The remarkable extent and considerable success of these initiatives has been established beyond question. It is also clear that enlightened absolutism cannot itself provide a complete explanation for these reforms. In most European states there were important continuities as well as significant new directions in domestic policy at this time. The need to defend and uphold a state's international position, and thus to recruit soldiers and collect taxes, could set limits, particularly in the major powers, to the kind of reforms introduced. Enlightened absolutism was an additional layer of statecraft, and the principal origin of the radical and innovative measures introduced at this time. The movement of ideas known as the Enlightenment provided the broad intellectual context within which reforms were formulated, rather than the direct source of a particular measure: government policy was here creative rather than merely reactive. Certain areas of reform owed much to particular intellectual currents. The widespread religious reforms in Mediterranean Europe and the Habsburg monarchy were directly inspired by 'Reform Catholicism' and particularly by the ideas of Lodovico Antonio Muratori (1672–1750).

In the German-speaking lands and throughout northern Europe, cameralist doctrines were widely influential. These were a distinct body of economic ideas which emphasized the primacy of a state's wealth and the prosperity of its subjects. An increase in these would in turn facilitate a strengthening of military power, which in all the larger states was the main objective of government. In many ways cameralism resembled the kind of mercantilism associated with Louis XIV's minister, Colbert, though it endowed the state administration with a more interventionist role. Its advocates believed that the best foundation for a wealthy and strong state was a happy and prosperous population, and this led rulers to regulate the social and economic lives of their subjects in some detail. Another important source of agrarian and economic reforms was the ideas of the French physiocrats. Such initiatives, however, could also be inspired by non-ideological factors. Agrarian reform also owed much to the inspiration of Britain's eighteenth-century 'Agricultural Revolution', while her wealth and prosperity also inspired emulation. Finally, eighteenth-century populationist doctrines were influential, as governments came to believe that demographic strength was an important source of economic and political power.

The momentum behind this generation of reform was provided principally by Europe's monarchs great and small, assisted by their ministers and the enlarged administrations of the age, who drew up reforming schemes and then tried to implement them. The individual reforms were partly inspired by a fundamental transformation in the political philosophy which underlay government during the second half of the eighteenth century. Proprietary, divine-right kingship gave way to a new sense of the duties and responsibilities of monarchy. This was epitomized by Frederick the Great's celebrated aphorism that 'the king was the first servant of his people': a phrase that has often seemed the watchword of enlightened absolutism. The ruler's traditional sense of responsibility for his subjects,

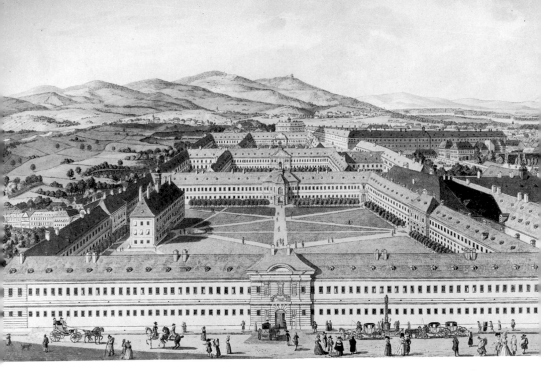

The new scale of public-health provision in the towns: the *Allgemeines Krankenhaus* [General Hospital], Vienna, built at the instigation of Joseph II and opened in 1784. By the end of his reign it had over 2,000 beds and incorporated an orphanage, a lunatic asylum, isolation wards, and a maternity unit for unmarried mothers.

rooted in Christian paternalism, now came to be accompanied and even superseded by the new doctrine of the social contract as the source of monarchical authority. The most radical statement of this was provided by the Grand Duke Leopold, who ruled Tuscany from 1765 until 1790, when he succeeded his elder brother Joseph II as ruler of the Habsburg monarchy and Holy Roman Emperor. Leopold was one of the most intelligent monarchs of the age, and rightly enjoys the reputation of being a model enlightened ruler in Tuscany. Writing in his political testament, he declared that 'a ruler, even a hereditary ruler, is only a delegate, a servant of the people whose cares and troubles he must make his own'. One of his leading advisers as grand duke, Francesco Maria Gianni, defined the duties which were consequently incumbent upon a ruler. 'Government is best,' he wrote, 'where the sovereign is best, who knows how to lead with legislation and administration toward the happiness of his subjects.'

The essence of enlightened absolutism is contained in these two quotations. It was as much a matter of aims and style, of attitudes and intentions, as of policies and actual reforms. Rulers came to approach the craft of kingship in a novel and radical way. They confronted the problems they faced in a new spirit and ruled, or believed they were ruling, in the interests of all the people; some even spoke of an attempt to promote the 'general good' or the 'general best'. The monarchs of the later eighteenth century aimed to provide better government and to improve the material conditions and advance the prosperity of their subjects and thus of themselves. This was a novel element in domestic policy during the generation after 1750. It coexisted alongside a state's traditional fiscal, military, legal, and administrative concerns.

Russian Expansion and French Crisis

The desire of the poorer states in central and eastern Europe to secure more wealth and subjects, and in this way enhance their own power, was also apparent in their foreign policies. It was one factor in a generation of dramatic territorial changes in eastern and south-eastern Europe which stretched from the 1760s to the 1790s and redrew the map of the region. The three eastern monarchies each made significant gains at the expense of the area's two declining powers. The Ottoman Empire lost vast tracts of land seized from its neighbours in earlier centuries, while Poland-Lithuania was partitioned out of existence. The greatest beneficiary was Catherine II's Empire, which expanded spectacularly at this time. Between 1725 and 1800, Russia's size increased by around 1,800,000 square kilometres, from 15,000,000 to 16,800,000. The spectacular territorial growth took place principally under Catherine II, and was the main element behind an equally dramatic demographic expansion during the Empress's reign, when Russia's population rose by over a half, from 23 million to 36 million: the largest in Europe. Two successful wars against the Ottoman Empire (1768–74; 1787–92), the second fought in partnership with Joseph II's Austria, together with the peacetime annexation of the Crimea (1783), established Russia as a major presence in south-eastern Europe and gave her a dominant position on the northern littoral of the Black Sea. This was symbolized by the founding of the new city of Odessa, the Greek version of Catherine's own name, which was established two years before her death. Though the Empress's achievements were spectacular, however, they were less dramatic than she had once hoped. Constantinople, where she had dreamed of re-establishing an Orthodox kingdom, remained in Ottoman hands, while Turkish control of the Straits was a considerable obstacle to Russian penetration into the Mediterranean. Yet Catherine's reign had established the basis of Russia's dominant nineteenth-century role in the region.

Russia's annexations from the three partitions of Poland-Lithuania (1772; 1793; 1795) were of equal significance. The first and last of these were undertaken in partnership with the other two eastern powers; the second with Prussia alone. The Empress's role in the destruction of the Polish state is, at first sight, surprising, in view of her western neighbour's satellite status throughout much of the eighteenth century and the real advantages that St Petersburg had derived from this. The principal architect of the first partition was not Catherine II but her ally during the 1760s and 1770s, Frederick the Great. The Prussian king had long dreamed of acquiring Polish Prussia, a broad swathe of territory which separated the Hohenzollern heartlands from the distant kingdom of East Prussia. He was able to do so in 1772 by skilfully exploiting the seemingly menacing situation which confronted Russia. Catherine II's control of Poland-Lithuania was threatened in the later 1760s by a Polish civil war and the emergence of serious armed resistance, Russia's impressive victories over the Turks did not seem to be bringing peace any closer, while a military faction in St Petersburg had for some time been urging the annexation of Polish territory on strategic grounds. The outcome to some complex diplomacy was the first partition, finalized in August 1772.

The seizure of Polish lands by Russia, Prussia, and Austria was unusual even within the ruthlessly competitive states system of eighteenth-century Europe, and attracted censure at the time. Some enlightened critics saw in it the principal defects of the rapacity and aggression characteristic of international relations. The transfer of territory was perfectly usual, though normally it took place at the end of a war, when the defeated power handed over lands to the victor or confirmed cessions that had already taken place: as Austria had done in the 1740s when Silesia was annexed by Prussia. The tripartite gains made from Poland-Lithuania in the early 1770s were unique in that the Polish state was at peace and had no serious political dispute with any of the eastern powers. Their avidity for more territory and demographic and economic resources, together with the diplomatic opportunism of Frederick the Great in particular, combined to bring about the first partition.

Poland's last king, Stanislas Augustus Poniatowski (1764–95), was powerless to resist this and subsequent encroachments upon his territory. A Polish nobleman and former lover of the Russian Empress, he owed his elevation to the elective Polish throne to Catherine II's belief that he would be an admirable vehicle for the continuation of Russian influence at Warsaw. In the event he proved to be more independent of Russia's control than had been anticipated and, in the aftermath of the first partition, provided much of the impetus behind significant, if limited, educational and administrative reforms within his kingdom. But Poland-Lithuania was a land of strong magnates and a weak king. It also lacked defensible frontiers and, crucially, the military means to resist voracious neighbours with their large, powerful armies and relatively modern state structures. Her army was limited in size to 24,000 men, tiny by comparison with the forces at the disposal of each of the eastern powers. This limitation had been imposed in 1717 by Russia, determined that Poland-Lithuania would never secure the means to escape from her satellite status. Russia's tutelage persisted for almost two decades after 1772, though by the later 1780s it was arousing increasing resentment and, ultimately, open resistance. In the first half of the 1790s, however, two further partitions removed the Polish state from the map of Europe. Once again the territorial ambitions of a Prussian king, this time the new ruler Frederick William II (1786–97), provided the political momentum. The Poles, under the inspired leadership of Tadeusz Kosciuszko, fought heroically but were defeated by Russia's overwhelming military power. To underline the disappearance of the Polish state, the partitioning powers then solemnly undertook never to use the name of the vanished kingdom in the future. The destruction of Poland-Lithuania had been swift and spectacular. Within a generation, Europe's third largest state, in size, had ceased to exist.

Russia gained most from this redrawing of the map of eastern and south-eastern Europe. Her vast territorial gains were the foundation of her nineteenth-century predominance in the eastern half of the continent. The three Polish partitions moved her frontier some 400 kilometres to the west, and made her for the first time a direct neighbour of Prussia and of Austria. This new-found status and especially her gains from the Ottoman Empire rested principally upon her large and formidable army. Russia's potential power had earlier been signalled by Peter the Great's victories over Charles XII at the beginning of the century. But the momentum Peter gave to Russian expansion had not been sustained after his death. For a generation after 1725 Russia had failed to exploit the position created by his victories, in part because of the weakness and instability of her government.

The origins of her later eighteenth-century predominance are to be found in her participation in the continental Seven Years War, when her troops for the first time played a decisive part in a major continental war. Though handicapped by poor generalship and by logistical problems that were magnified by the distances which her troops had to travel to reach central European battlefields, her armies had fought bravely and at time heroically. In particular they had won some significant victories over the formidable Prussian forces, above all in the two great battles of Kay (Paltzig) and Kunersdorf in 1759. Russia's military potential was increased by a notable series of reforms during Catherine's reign. The supply and transport services were improved, while the army was given a regular budget and a rudimentary high command structure, both of which had hitherto been lacking. Above all Russia's army reached an unprecedented size and was 300,000 strong by Catherine's death, when it was Europe's largest military force with the sole exception of the forces of revolutionary France, which had been swollen to wholly new levels by mass conscription after 1793. The Russian army was also better led than in the past, when it had been hobbled by poor and conservative commanders, and it adopted more modern, flexible tactics. Under A. V. Suvorov's inspired leadership it acquired an aura of near-invincibility, though during the generation after the Seven Years War the laurels of victory were won against Polish insurgents and the backward Ottoman forces and not modern European armies. Catherine II set out to exploit the enhanced European role created by these military victories. The Seven Years War had made Russia the arbiter between the two other eastern powers. By allying first with Prussia and then, after 1781, with Austria, the Empress established Russia's diplomatic leadership over the continent. By the final decade of her reign, her adopted homeland was clearly the dominant land power in Europe.

Russia's rise was facilitated by France's international decline. Until midcentury, Louis XV's monarchy was clearly the leading continental state. France's eighteenth-century position as a great power was always flawed, however, by her need to support two distinct and, increasingly, separate struggles: her traditional continental military role and the mounting demands of maritime and colonial rivalry with Britain. The strategic overextension which resulted was highlighted by the Seven Years War, when France was decisively defeated in both theatres. Britain's victory overseas established her as the dominant commercial and colonial power by 1763, when France was excluded from the North American mainland and saw her position in India all but destroyed. Within Europe, the shattering defeat of the French army at Rossbach (November 1757) by Frederick the Great destroyed her military reputation for a generation and thereby undermined her position as the leading continental state. After the Seven Years War a reversal of strategic priorities was apparent. France now concentrated upon her worldwide rivalry with Britain, and aimed only to neutralize the continent in the next Franco-British war, to the detriment of her own standing in Europe. This had been aided by Britain's effective disappearance as a European power between the 1760s and 1780s, as domestic and colonial problems consumed the attention of her statesmen. The ascendancy of the three eastern powers, so evident to contemporaries during the decade before the French Revolution, rested partly upon the problems and changed priorities of the two leading western states, Britain and France. French intervention in an American colonial rebellion (1775–83) against Britain weakened the commanding position she had secured in 1763. Two decades later the British government was forced to recognize the independence of the former American colonists and made some limited concessions to France and her Bourbon ally, Spain. France's success, however, was purchased at the high cost of further damage to her position in Europe and, more important, to her fragile state finances.

The French monarchy's financial problems went back to Louis XIV's reign, when the unprecedented scale and length of his wars had exhausted the capacity even of his populous and prosperous country to support spending on the scale demanded. The central problem came to be the level of borrowing needed to support the expenditure necessitated by the burdens of international competition. The early decades of Louis XV's long reign saw some temporary improvement during the generation of peace and prosperity which followed the settlement at Utrecht. The renewed cycle of warfare after the 1740s in which France played a leading part, however, significantly worsened the monarchy's financial position, while rising prices exacerbated the situation. Intervention in the American War made an already serious situation critical. It was paid for almost entirely by further borrowing, and by 1786 no less than half of the French state's annual income was committed to debt repayments.

One reason why the financial problems of the French monarchy were so overwhelming was the obstacles in the way of any modernization of the fiscal system. The need for this was widely recognized in ministerial circles, but few of the initiatives attempted at various points during the eighteenth century achieved much enduring success. Instead, successive ministries took refuge in a variety of fiscal experiments and periodic tax increases, which fell some way short of what was needed yet aroused considerable resentment and, eventually, opposition. There was a growing sense among those who paid the taxes that the government's finances were running out of control, and by the 1780s this was accompanied by a belief that the sole body which would enjoy the necessary authority to undertake major reforms was the Estates-General. Elsewhere in Europe the generation after 1750 was a notable age of reform, but in France it was the failure of innovatory policies that was more apparent.

The institutional rigidities of the French state and the lack of consistent royal support had together undermined a series of much-needed reforms. This was especially evident after 1786, when Calonne became the latest minister to be charged with the responsibility of solving the financial crisis. His plans were wide-ranging and imaginative, but his efforts were no more successful. Matters were brought to a head when the financiers went on strike and denied the government essential loans. The eventual outcome came to be the recall of the Estates-General, which had been in abeyance since 1614–15 but was summoned to meet in early May 1789. The elections took place against the background of an economic crisis and were characterized by political mobilization among all sectors of society, which was a portent of the struggles that lay ahead. Short-term political and economic difficulties, along with the emergence of fault lines within the French political nation and the structural problem of state finances, led to the collapse of the French monarchy, which by mid-1788 had lost control over events. The opening of the Estates-General on 4 May 1789 was the first act in the political drama of the French Revolution, which within a very few years would apparently transform eighteenth-century Europe beyond recognition.

Epilogue: The Old Order Transformed
1789–1815

T. C. W. BLANNING

The Outbreak of the French Revolution

The last quarter of the eighteenth century witnessed political instability in many parts of Europe. In Geneva, the Dutch Republic, Belgium (or the 'Austrian Netherlands' as it should properly be called at this time), Hungary, several German cities, Saxony, Sweden, Poland, and France, there were upheavals which in some cases led to violent changes of regime. Even in such an apparently stable state as Great Britain, the loss of the American colonies precipitated a crisis so severe that in 1783 a desperate George III contemplated abdication. As the century drew to a close, the old regimes of monarchs, prelates, and aristocrats appeared to face an irresistible challenge from below. This ubiquity of upheaval has prompted many historians of the period to dub it 'the Age of the Democratic Revolution'. Yet closer examination reveals that the similarities were only skin-deep and rarely went beyond coincidence. The revolts were often conservative rather than democratic (as in the case of Belgium and most of the German disturbances), abortive (as in the case of Hungary or Great Britain), *coups d'état* rather than revolutions (as in the case of Sweden), or easily suppressed (as in the case of Geneva, Poland, and Saxony). Only one was progressive, revolutionary and successful by its own efforts—and that was the French.

The unique force of the French Revolution stemmed from the coincidence of two crises in the late 1780s. The first was political, precipitated by bankruptcy. On 20 August 1786, the French finance minister, Calonne, had presented Louis XVI with a bleak assessment: interest payments on the accumulated debt now absorbed more than half the annual revenue, much of the following year's income had been spent, and it was becoming increasingly difficult to raise loans, even at ruinous rates of interest. The attempt which followed to escape the abyss with a radical programme of reform only made the final plunge more certain. Neither consultation nor coercion could persuade the French élites to cooperate. Now that they had the monarch in their grasp, they were determined not to release him until a fundamental change in the way in which the country was governed had been agreed. After two years of squirming, Louis XVI finally ran up the white flag on 8 August 1788, when he announced that the Estates-General would meet at Versailles in the following May.

It is just possible—if unlikely—that the old regime might have kept this crisis confined to the world of high politics. What turned an aristocratic *fronde* into a revolution was the violence generated by the social crisis which now erupted. This had its origins in the inability of French agriculture to respond adequately to a growing population, which had increased by about 30 per cent since 1700 to reach *c*.28,000,000 in 1789. The adverse effects had been mitigated during the boom decades of mid-century by rapidly expanding manufacturing and commercial sectors, but in the 1770s the French economy entered a long recession. In the 1780s, a run of meteorological disasters reached a terrible climax in 1788 when the harvest failed in many parts of France. As the price of bread soared, demand for manufactured commodities collapsed, so the labouring poor were denied employment just when they needed it most.

These two crises were essentially separate but of course they interacted during the winter of 1788/9. They fused in the spring and early summer, the worst time for any regime with an agrarian economy, for it was then that the grain gathered by the old harvest was giving out but new supplies had not yet reached the markets. What made matters worse in 1789 was not just the scale of the price rise but the corrosive belief that a conspiracy was afoot, a *pacte de famine* between government ministers and grain racketeers to starve the French people into submission. All over France, violence erupted as people were mobilized by a potent combination of fear of starvation and hatred of their exploiters.

There had been plenty of bread riots in the past, notably in 1775, but never before had they coincided with a political crisis at the centre. For it was just now that the Estates-General at long last met at Versailles. At once they were deadlocked over the issue of whether they should sit and vote as three separate orders, which would allow the clergy (the first estate) and the nobility (the second estate) to dominate the commoners (the third estate) or whether they constituted a single body. Weeks passed in sterile wrangling until the deputies of the third estate cut the Gordian knot with three crucial decisions: on 10 June they announced that they would proceed unilaterally as if they were a single representative body and invited deputies from the other two estates to join them; on 17 June they adopted the title of 'National Assembly', and on 20 June they took the 'Tennis Court Oath' that they would not allow themselves to be dispersed until they had given France a new constitution.

Now the issue was well and truly joined. In effect, what the third estate did during these ten great days in June was to proclaim the principle of national sovereignty and to claim for themselves the right to exercise it. This was the true beginning of the French Revolution. Even the slow-burning Louis XVI could now grasp that the crunch had come. So he reached out for his weapon of last resort—the army, in one last desperate attempt to restore order in Paris and to return the Estates-General to obedience. As so often in the past, he contrived to have the worst of both worlds. On the one hand, his decision to call up troops made the Parisian crowds that much more afraid and that much more angry. On the other hand, it turned out that the 17,000-odd soldiers who reached Paris by the middle of July could not be used. They could not be used because the king became convinced that they would mutiny if ordered to take action against the revolutionary crowds. By deciding he could not use the army, Louis XVI also decided to resign himself to the revolution.

Meanwhile, the revolutionaries were creating their own army. They had grasped intuitively that at the heart of any regime is a monopoly of legitimate force. This is the true significance of the storming of the Bastille on 14 July 1789. It was attacked not because it was a symbol of old regime tyranny but because it was thought to contain the ammunition needed by the revolution's new paramilitary force—the National Guard. By subverting the old regime's army and creating its own, the French revolutionaries had succeeded where scores of insurgents had failed in the past—and were to fail again in the future. In this task they had received crucial assistance from all those inarticulate but violent French men and women who vented their fear and anger on tax collectors, châteaux-owners, grain merchants, and all the other representatives of the old regime. It was the belief that the country was out of control which frightened Louis XVI into accepting that sovereignty had passed from monarchy to nation.

His naturally feeble will had been softened further by the knowledge that what should have been the two stoutest props of the old order—the clergy and the nobility—were riddled with disaffection. It was not the rank and file of the army who first hoisted the flag of mutiny, but aristocratic officers alienated by the progressive collapse of French power and prestige since the glory days of Louis XIV. The last straw had been the failure to prevent the Prussian invasion of the Dutch Republic in the autumn of 1787, thus revealing French impotence in the most humiliating way possible. So the early leaders of the third estate were not bourgeois merchants or manufacturers but aristocratic army officers such as the marquis de Lafayette, the duc de La Rochefoucauld, the comte de Mirabeau, the comte de Lameth, or the vicomte de Noailles. In part, the French Revolution was a military putsch.

The Creation of a New France—and a New World

The victorious revolutionaries were now able to set about creating a new France from the bottom up. At a very early stage in their deliberations they took an axe to the most fundamental attribute of the old regime—privilege. During a very excited session of the National Assembly which lasted for most of the night of 4–5 August 1789, one privilege after another was cast aside in the name of liberty. Seigneurial dues and jurisdiction, hunting rights, the sale of offices, tithes, and all those special privileges which distinguished one man from another, one group from another, and one part of France from another, all made way for a new order based on uniformity, meritocracy, and standardization. In a word, the National Assembly introduced modernization. In fact, what was decided at Versailles was less important than was actually done by ordinary people at large. In one part of France after another, ordinary townspeople and peasants took the law into their own hands, presenting their legislators with a *fait accompli* to be rubber-stamped. They were driven not by a concern with rationalization but with a determination to make the shoe that presently pinched so cruelly fit more comfortably.

What the National Assembly was especially well qualified to do was the articulation of the principles which underlay the new France. As it included in its ranks some exceptionally gifted men of letters, it was no wonder that it generated manifestos of corresponding quality. The most eloquent and most important was the 'Declaration of the Rights of Man and the Citizen', promulgated on 26 August. That the legislature of a great power should proclaim that all men enjoyed certain inalienable rights by virtue of their very nature gave the French Revolution a unique universality. By declaring that 'Man'—and not just 'French Man'—had a natural right to liberty, property, security, equality of opportunity, fiscal equality, freedom from oppression and arbitrary arrest, equality before the law, religious tolera-

The National Assembly in session in the Salle des Menus Plaisirs. It was in this great room in the Palace of Versailles that the Estates General met on 5 May 1789. On 17 June the deputies of the Third Estate took the revolutionary step of proclaiming that they constituted the 'National Assembly', exercising sovereignty on behalf of the French people. Depicted here is the night-session of 4–5 August, during which the old regime's system of privilege was dismantled.

tion, and freedom of expression, association, and the press, the deputies threw down a challenge to all those regimes who denied their subjects some or all of these. By advertising the concept of citizenship, declaring that sovereignty resided in the nation and reserving to an elected assembly the right to legislate, tax, control the armed forces, and supervise ministers, they also established a liberal constitution against which not only patently despotic regimes such as Russia but also more benign polities such as Great Britain might be judged.

It was also the National Assembly which had to grapple with the issue which had destroyed the absolute monarchy—the national debt. The revolution had not solved the country's financial problems, on the contrary it had made revenue collection even more difficult. The obvious way out seemed to be a simple repudiation of obligations, but, quite apart from questions of probity, this escape route was blocked by the simple fact that many of the deputies were themselves creditors of the old regime. The answer was found in the rolling acres of the Catholic Church, covering on average some 10 per cent of the country's cultivable area. On 2 November

1789, the National Assembly voted by 510 to 346 that all ecclesiastical property was to be placed at the disposal of the nation. In return, the state would assume responsibility for paying the clergy and providing for the poor. Although 'only' 400,000,000 livres-worth were ordered to be sold initially, this sale of the century could only end with the total expropriation of what had been France's biggest landowner. In the process, a class of beneficiaries was created with the most deeply committed of stakes in the success of the revolution.

The fate of the Church under the Revolution exemplified the new order's concern with rational uniformity. In the past, there had been far too many dioceses in the south but not enough in the north. The National Assembly solved that by decreeing that in future there should be one bishop for each of the eighty-three departments into which the country was now divided. In similar vein, it also laid down that there should be one parish for every 6,000 souls, a rule which led to a drastic reduction of parishes in many towns. Many clergymen believed that these and the other innovations imposed by the Civil Constitution of the Clergy of 12 July 1790 were long overdue but few believed that the election of bishops should be entrusted to the laity, a regulation which allowed Jews, atheists, and even Protestants to choose the Catholic hierarchy. In the past, the Church had been truly the first estate, both the cultural centre and the great provider of social services in what was officially an exclusively Catholic country. After 1789 it was demoted and marginalized in the name of reason, toleration, and secularism—and the great beneficiary was the state.

Sub specie aeternitatis, that was the great irrevocable achievement of the French Revolution—the massive expansion of the competence and power of the state. With all the self-confidence which came from the conviction that nature was on their side, the revolutionaries reached down to touch every aspect of human life. Perhaps their most durable intervention—and arguably their most benign—was to decree that henceforth the basic unit of measurement would be exactly one ten-millionth of the distance from the North Pole to the equator, to be known as the 'metre'. During the first years of the revolution, this *dirigisme* was masked by its accompaniment by a political culture which stressed popular participation. From Rousseau the revolutionaries took the axiom that the power of the people cannot be alienated through representation. As direct democracy is impracticable in a country the size of France or even in a city the size of Paris, the essential task of the politician is to present himself and his cause in such a way as to personify popular sovereignty. This created a new form of political discourse, as politicians competed to claim legitimacy through all available media—press, pamphlets, theatres, clubs, songs, pageants, processions, and symbols of every conceivable kind. The language and ritual of political struggle were not just the external symptoms of some deeper social reality, they themselves were real. Together they established a new political benchmark. After 1789, no regime in France—or indeed in Europe—could rule without making some concessions to participatory politics.

The Failure of the Constitutional Monarchy

The National Assembly had laid down the fundamental principles of France's political future in the Declaration of the Rights of Man and the Citizen, but it was to be almost two years before they actually drafted a constitution. The delay was to prove fatal. In 1789 there was a broad consensus that the best way forward would lead via a modernized version of the British constitutional monarchy, but by the autumn of 1791 there were many determined to establish a republic. What had gone wrong?

Not the least of the National Assembly's problems stemmed from a change of venue. At Versailles, the deputies used the Salle des Menus Plaisirs, an elegant chamber conducive to orderly debate. While it certainly witnessed scenes of great excitement, most notably during the night of 4–5 August, here the deputies were in control. All that changed with the events of 5–6 October 1789, when a crowd which had marched from Paris mainly to protest against continuing bread shortages invaded the royal palace, took the king and queen prisoner and forced them to move to Paris. The National Assembly followed in their wake and moved into the only suitable building they could find. This was the Manège, a cavernous former riding school alongside the Tuileries Palace. The personnel of the Assembly remained the same but the working conditions were so different that it became a different kind of institution. The deputies were now exposed to the political culture of the capital, most directly in the shape of the several hundred Parisians who sat in the three huge public galleries. These were less spectators than participants, cheering their heroes and booing their villains. As a result, the National Assembly ceased to be a debating chamber similar to the American Congress or the British Parliament and became a kind of permanent political rally. It was certainly more open, transparent, and democratic than its Anglo-Saxon equivalents, but it was also much more demagogic, encouraging the promotion of simple answers to complex questions.

A second destabilizing force was the antics of the 'émigrés', those members of the privileged orders who could not stomach the prospect of any

Federation Day. On 14 July 1790, a great celebration was held on the Champs-de-Mars in Paris. More than a quarter of a million people took an oath 'To the Nation, to the Law, to the King'. It marked the climax of the honeymoon period of the Revolution when a peaceful transition from old regime to new still seemed possible. Symbolically, torrential rain fell throughout the ceremony.

concessions to the revolution. Only a few days after the fall of the Bastille, the younger of the king's two brothers, the comte d'Artois and several princes of the blood left for self-imposed exile. Once safely out of the country they agitated vigorously and publicly for military intervention by the rest of Europe to destroy the revolution and restore the old regime. This touched the rawest of nerves in what was naturally a hypersensitive revolutionary psychology. From their mentor Rousseau the revolutionaries had acquired the conviction that the general will was both infallible and indivisible. This 'terrible postulate of unanimity' created a Manichean world of absolute good and absolute evil, with a pure revolution opposed by the black treason of aristocratic conspiracy. By launching a counter-revolutionary campaign, Artois and his cohorts gave this paranoid scenario sufficient credibility to make it the central myth of revolutionary politics. That the other European powers had no interest whatsoever in intervening in France or that Louis XVI disapproved of the émigrés' activities mattered not one jot.

On every occasion that the revolution lurched to the left, there was a further surge of political emigration. Even so, only a tiny fraction of the French population was affected. If counter-revolution was ever to become more than a phantom conspiracy, it needed an issue which would mobilize mass support. This was the role of religion. An early indicator of its undimmed explosive power was provided by the violent reaction to the emancipation of the Protestants, especially in the south-east. However, it was the attempt by the National Assembly to enforce an oath of loyalty to the Civil Constitution on all clergymen wishing to retain their benefices by a decree of 27 November 1790 which launched a decade of civil strife. Especially in the west and in the non-French-speaking regions of the country (such as Breton-speaking Brittany or German-speaking Alsace), most priests refused to take the oath and were supported by their parishioners. Where the revolutionary state tried to enforce its will, violence erupted. The sweeping papal condemnation of the revolution and all its works in the spring of 1791 added to the revolutionaries' belief that they were threatened by a great international conspiracy.

It was confirmed by the knowledge that Louis XVI deeply disapproved of the revolution's ecclesiastical settlement and the suspicion that he disapproved of the revolution *tout court*. In the final analysis, it could be said that the constitutional monarchy failed in France because the king declined to play the role allotted to him. This was a personal failure, for on the rare occasions that he managed to speak his lines with conviction, he was almost overwhelmed with the great fund of goodwill towards him which persisted until remarkably late in the day. A serious handicap in his fumbling attempts to stay in control was the presence at his side of his formidable queen, 'the only man in the family', as Mirabeau called her. Marie Antoinette was deeply unpopular for her Austrian nationality, undoubted profligacy, and fabled bisexual promiscuity. In fact, the revolutionaries had every right to fear and hate her, for she was indeed busy seeking international military intervention to restore the old regime.

The Coming of War and the End of the Monarchy

A major milestone on the road which led from absolute monarchy to radical republic was reached on 20 June 1791 when Louis XVI and his family tried to escape from France. This advertised for all the world to see that the king was a prisoner in his own country and that his apparent cooperation with the new regime during the past two years had been insincere. This put republicanism squarely on the political agenda for the first time but it did not yet put an end to the monarchy. The soft centre of revolutionary politics was still numerous enough to prevent the radicals taking control. Republican demonstrations were suppressed, republican clubs were closed, and the new constitution was hurriedly brought to completion. As the new legislature—the 'Legislative Assembly'—met for the first time on 1 October 1791, most of its members hoped that the revolution was over.

It was not, not least because international events now impinged on the situation inside France. That they had not done so already was due to the preoccupation of the other European powers with their own quarrels. What have become known as 'the French Revolutionary wars' in fact began in August 1787, when Turkey declared war on Russia in an attempt to regain control of the Crimea. That conflict then spread rapidly to involve directly or indirectly all the other members of the European states system, with the significant exception of bankrupt and impotent France. But French isolation could not last for ever. Potentially the greatest power on the continent, its revival could only be a matter of time. The apparent completion of French domestic reconstruction in the summer of 1791 coincided with the ending of the war in the east. Now Frederick William II, king of Prussia, and Leopold II, Holy Roman Emperor and ruler of the Habsburg monarchy, could turn their attention to the west. The former was motivated primarily by the search for territorial gain, the latter more by a concern to come to the cause of monarchy in general and the cause of his sister, Marie Antoinette, in particular, although he too expected material reward.

Unwittingly, the two German sovereigns gave the republican campaign inside France a powerful boost by repeated attempts to intimidate the revolutionaries. In the Legislative Assembly the initiative was seized by Jacques-Pierre Brissot and a small number of republican deputies. What they lacked in numbers they made up for in eloquence and political acumen. At the heart of their strategy was the belief that if only France could be pushed into a foreign war, the king and his queen would be revealed for the traitors they undoubtedly were and the monarchy could be destroyed. In just six months during the winter of 1791–2 they succeeded in persuading virtually all their fellow-deputies that war was both desirable and inevitable. They did so by exploiting and intensifying revolutionary nationalism, Austrophobia, and paranoia and by promising that a war would be quick and easy. A revolutionary army would be invincible, they argued, for free men would be many times more effective than the hired mercenaries confronting them, who were more likely to desert than to resist. Moreover, the oppressed millions of old regime Europe only awaited the sounding of the revolutionary trump to rise in revolt against their despots and to welcome their liberators.

Whirled away by Brissotin rhetoric on a cloud of optimism, hatred, and fear, the Legislative Assembly declared war on Austria on 20 April 1792. Yet far from proving quick and easy, the war was a disaster. The first foray into Belgium was repulsed by the Austrians with risible ease, as the revolutionary soldiers simply ran away. This did not, however, create a sensible respect for the old regime armies, rather it intensified the belief in an enemy within and a determination to root it out before it could destroy the revolution. The last straw proved to be the notorious manifesto issued by the allied commander-in-chief, the duke of Brunswick, from his headquarters at Koblenz on 25 July. Among other things, he promised that if the Tuileries Palace were attacked or if Louis XVI and his family were harmed or insulted in any way, then Paris and its inhabitants would be put to the torch and the sword when he and his army reached the city. Of all the counterproductive declarations in history, this must surely take the palm, for it had exactly the opposite effect to that intended. Far from being intimidated, on 10 August the revolutionary crowd stormed the Tuileries, butchered the Swiss Guards defending it, took the royal family prisoner and forced the Legislative Assembly to decree the suspension of the monarchy. France formally became a republic on 22 September 1792.

Counter-revolution and the Terror

The revolution now suffered a prolonged agony. The creation of the republic put radicalism at a premium, as political groups competed to represent the cause of liberty, equality, and fraternity in a post-monarchist era. In this competition, Brissot and his associates were hopelessly outpointed by forces even further to their left, led on the streets of Paris by radical journalists such as Marat and in the more structured environment of the Jacobin Club by politicians such as Robespierre. So when the king was put on trial in January 1793, the Brissotins dithered while their opponents unequivocally called for the death sentence. The execution of Louis XVI on 21 January 1793 ensured that the revolution had a long way to go before it reached the limits of extremism.

What made a return to stability impossible was the war. After the early disasters, the revolutionary armies had done well. The allied invasion was checked at Valmy on 20 September 1792 and Belgium and the Rhineland were conquered during the autumn. During the winter of 1792–3, however, the situation deteriorated quickly as tens of thousands of volunteers streamed back from the front and the German powers began to take the war seriously. Moreover, the reckless declaration of war on Great Britain, the Dutch Republic, and Spain early in 1793 now meant that France was fighting virtually the whole of Europe, with the significant exception of Russia. To hold the line, the National Convention (which succeeded the Legislative Assembly in September 1792) decreed on 24 February the conscription of 300,000 men. The result was civil war. In the Vendée region of the west of France, this latest and most demanding intrusion of the revolutionary state turned long-standing passive resistance and sporadic violence into a general and sustained attempt to destroy the new regime by military force. By the middle of June the 'Catholic and Royal Army' was around 45,000 strong, controlled four departments, and was preparing to march on Paris. News from the front was also alarming, as the Austrians won a great victory at Neerwinden on 18 March, reconquered Belgium, and prepared to invade. Perhaps the nadir of revolutionary fortunes was reached on 29

The head of Louis XVI displayed to the crowd, 21 January 1793. The king died with dignity, which is more than can be said for the revolutionaries who rushed forward to taste his blood. His execution polarized opinion in France and horrified the rest of Europe. A fight to the death between the regicide French republic and the rest of Europe now began.

August when counter-revolutionaries surrendered the great port of Toulon and the French Mediterranean fleet to the British.

By that time, the patent failure of the Brissotins to win the war they had started with such blithe optimism had led to their fall at the end of May. They were replaced by a much more hard-headed group, prepared to do anything to pacify the country, win the war, and save the revolution. The new centre of power was the 'Committee of Public Safety', in theory only a supervisory committee of the National Convention but in reality the instrument of revolutionary dictatorship for the next twelve months. Among the torrent of radical measures which poured from the new regime, one stands out: on 23 August it was decreed that until peace was established, every man, woman, child, animal, and inanimate object in France was conscripted for the war effort. This is usually referred to as the 'levée en masse', but it is better seen as a declaration of total war, the first in European history but not alas the last. Its significance lay not so much in its actual provisions as in its terrible revelation that the revolutionary state was now prepared to abandon all restraints in the pursuit of total victory.

The effect was the mobilization of the largest army yet seen in Europe, perhaps as many as 800,000. This great horde proved sufficient to stop the allied invasion in the autumn of 1793 and go back on the offensive the following year, reconquering Belgium and western Germany, this time permanently. The Vendée was also subdued, but at a terrible price in human suffering. With the knowledge and approval of the central authorities, General Turreau sent what became known as 'columns of hell' through the insurgent territory, burning and killing as they went. No one will ever know how many people perished during the 'pacification' of the Vendée. The most authoritative estimate suggests a total of around 400,000 for both sides, which places the episode in the front rank of the atrocities of modern European history. Back in Paris, the regime was busy eliminating opponents on both right and left. Although its leaders, most notably Robespierre, presented their terrorist laws in the language of reason, humanity, and liberty, this was essentially a criminal exercise. Only when the rule of law had been suspended could psychopaths such as the public prosecutor Fouquier-Tinville or Robespierre's most glamorous and dangerous henchman, Saint-Just, emerge to inflict their dark fantasies on their fellow-human beings.

The Terror reached a climax in the summer of 1794, by which time it was becoming seriously dysfunctional. As the decisive victory over the Austrians at Fleurus on 26 June showed that the war had been won, a reaction against the blood-letting could not be long delayed. It came on 27 July ('9

Du 13 juillet 1793
Marie anne Charlotte
Corday au citoyen
Marat.
il suffit que je sois
bien Malheureux
pour avoir Droit
a votre bienveillance

À MARAT.
DAVID.

L'AN — DEUX

Thermidor' in the new revolutionary calendar) when the National Convention seized back the initiative and rushed off Robespierre and his supporters to the guillotine. The Terror was over but its effects were as long-lasting as they were momentous. The experience divided the population so sharply that every subsequent political crisis was influenced profoundly. Right across Europe, the horrors of this terrible year made even mildly progressive reform more difficult and made the political and social establishment both more secure and more conservative. So the revolution's political legacy was Janus-faced: on the one side benign libertarian ideology, on the other malignant state terrorism. It would be difficult to say which has proved the more influential.

Towards Military Dictatorship

The new regime in France renounced terror but it did not renounce the revolution. Too many of the leading political figures had burned their boats by voting for the execution of the king and too many had acquired ecclesiastical land to allow them to contemplate a return to the old regime. They were not helped by the utterly intransigent attitude displayed by 'Louis XVIII', as the comte de Provence styled himself after the death in prison of Louis XVI's only surviving son in 1795. Several times after Thermidor, a lurch to the left showed that the revolution still had a radical potential, most notably in 1797 when another coup—'Fructidor'—brought a surge of anti-clerical legislation. In 1795 a new constitution ushered in a new regime, called 'the Directory' after the five-man executive which now headed the government, but instability persisted. There was one important difference: whereas in the past it had been the revolutionary crowd which intruded from below to eject the legal government, it was now the government itself which intervened to annul elections when they yielded unwelcome results.

The result was that the revolution lost its legitimacy, in its own eyes as well as that of its opponents. The revolutionaries themselves had discarded any appeal to tradition as a source of authority right at the start, when they set out to create a brand new political order. Their claim to legality through representation of the general will was negated by the Terror and the Directory's electoral gerrymandering. So a vacuum of political legitimacy was

Jacques-Louis David, *À Marat*. The radical journalist Jean-Paul Marat was assassinated on 13 July 1793 by Charlotte Corday, a supporter of the Girondins, who gained admission by asking for help in the letter he is holding. Marat's friend, David, used the occasion to create this secular *pietà*, one of the greatest of all political works of art.

created into which sooner or later the only other kind of authority was bound to move: the charismatic leader.

His way was prepared by endless war. Victory in the west allowed the French to knock the Dutch, the Prussians, and the Spanish out of the war in 1795 but left the Austrians and the British still fighting. The conquest of Italy in 1796 by the 27-year-old General Napoleon Bonaparte brought peace to the continent by the treaty of Campo Formio in October 1797. This left the French the undisputed masters of western and southern Europe, with Belgium annexed, the Rhineland occupied, and the Dutch Republic and northern Italy organized as satellite states. Only the British remained unpacified, but that was enough to make the continental peace nothing more than a truce. Bonaparte's expedition to Egypt in 1798 brought Russia into the war for the first time and gave the British the opportunity to demonstrate the fragility of French power by destroying their Mediterranean fleet at the Battle of the Nile (1 August 1798). The result was the war of the Second Coalition which in 1799 brought the revolution to its knees.

That the revolution found it so difficult to maintain a firm grip on its conquests was due in large measure to the great gulf which had opened up between their rhetoric and their practice. They went to war with the slogan 'war to the châteaux, peace to the cottages', promising to liberate the oppressed peoples of Europe. They were unable to honour this commitment because they could not afford to do so. As the regime was bankrupt and any funds available had to be devoted to the urgent task of feeding the volatile citizens of Paris, the revolutionary armies were obliged to live off the land they liberated. So for the hapless Belgians, Germans, and Italians in their path, they brought not liberation but exploitation in the form of cash levies and the requisition of everything that could be consumed or moved. As the armies were both exceptionally large and exceptionally undisciplined, they also inflicted looting, murder, and rape on an unprecedented scale. Although attempts by the locals to resort to armed resistance were ruthlessly crushed, persistent passive resistance ensured that the revolution could maintain its conquests only by force.

It was a dismal experience for the revolutionaries. They had expected to be welcomed with open arms by a grateful humanity; so when they were rejected, they hardened their hearts and put France first. The rest of Europe had shown that they were still steeped in ignorance and prejudice, unworthy of liberation. Robespierre was not alone in thinking that the French people had outstripped the rest of the human race by two millennia and now constituted what amounted to a different species. This kind of arrogance, which also expressed itself in a rigorously Francophone policy towards the occupied territories, naturally provoked a strong reaction. If nationalism was not an invention of the French Revolution, it was certainly given a powerful impetus by revolutionary cultural and political imperialism.

Widespread anti-French revolts in 1799, the most spectacular of which was the reconquest of the kingdom of Naples by Cardinal Ruffo's *armata cristiana*, helped the allies to push the revolutionaries back to their own frontiers. Although final victory proved elusive, as the coalition was disabled by a misguided strategy and internal wrangling, the experience delivered the *coup de grâce* to the revolution's legitimacy. As in the past, the military disasters provoked a sharp swing to the left, giving rise to fears that a new terror was imminent. The key figure was now Sieyès, the veteran operator who had deftly negotiated the whirlpools of revolutionary politics with a pragmatism best summed up by his celebrated response to the inquiry about what he had done during the Terror: 'I survived'. Anxious not to have to repeat the experience but convinced that the Directory was now a dead duck, he was looking to the only alternative source of authority—the army.

That the revolution would end in military dictatorship had been predicted many years earlier by two observers at either end of the political spectrum—Edmund Burke and Robespierre. Their prophecy was eventually fulfilled because the interminable war naturally led to militarization. The mobilization of the entire population and the cult of the invincible citizen-in-arms promoted the glorification of military values, exemplified by the 'Marseillaise', the most militaristic and bloodthirsty of all the world's national anthems. During the early stages of the war, the government in Paris had kept a tight hold on its generals—indeed they were far more likely to perish on the guillotine than as a result of enemy action. It was only after Thermidor that the civilian grip relaxed and the generals began to be more assertive. Their power to intervene in domestic politics was demonstrated in October 1795, when troops commanded by General Bonaparte dispersed a royalist crowd 'with a whiff of grapeshot', and again in 1797 when the Directory carried out one of its *coups d'état* from above with the help of the army. As Bonaparte was incontestably the most successful of the republic's generals, he was also the best qualified to put an end to it. On his return from Egypt in October 1799 he at once got together with Sieyès to plot a *coup d'état*. They struck on 9 November (18 Brumaire). After two days of confusion, the Directory was overthrown and replaced by a 'Consulate'. That General Bonaparte was only one of three Consuls fooled no one—the man on horseback was patently the man in charge.

Reconstruction at Home

By this time, Bonaparte had discarded the youthful radicalism which once had given him the reputation of being a Jacobin. His experiences in Italy in 1796–7 had left him with a deep distrust of the politics of principle. Indeed, he was opposed to politics of any kind, looking instead for sound government with policy being decided at the centre by a single directing will and then being implemented by professional bureaucrats. This was a view shared by a country which for ten long years had been force-fed with an overdose of ideology. If wounds were still raw and nerves still stretched, only extremists at either end of the political spectrum wished to prolong the struggle between right and left *à l'outrance*.

At the heart of Bonaparte's success, therefore, was his ability to combine two apparently irreconcilable ideals: liberty and order. He managed this trick by giving the semblance of liberty but the reality of order. Behind the revolutionary rhetoric lay an autocratic will far stronger than anything an old regime monarch could boast. To perform this feat, he relied on plebiscites, ideally suited to his purpose for they allowed foregone conclusions to be presented as popular choices. Each step on the road to dictatorship—the Consulate of 1799, Bonaparte's appointment as 'Consul for Life' in 1802, and the creation of the empire in 1804—was given a democratic appearance by plebiscites. The reality was best summed up by the anecdote of the general who told his troops that they were free to vote for or against the new empire—but that the first soldier to register a negative vote would be taken out and shot. In similar vein, an imposing but empty structure of representative institutions was created at the centre. Purged of Bonaparte's critics in 1802, they were little more than docile rubber-stamps franking the First Consul's decisions.

The key figures in the new administration were the 'prefects', one for each of the departments, of which there were now ninety-eight thanks to the annexation of Belgium and other conquests. This new administration had many of the characteristics of a modern bureaucracy, being hierarchical, uniform, professional, salaried, and trained. It was something less than a meritocracy, however, for the emphasis on personal loyalty to Bonaparte when appointments or promotions were being decided made it look more like a feudal clientage-system. Those lucky enough to be chosen were certainly well rewarded, prefects taking home the generous salary of 20,000 francs per annum (about forty times the income of an average artisan). Their social composition demonstrated both Bonaparte's determination to put an end to the revolution's egalitarianism and his personal preference for men of property, for no fewer than 100 of the 281 prefects who served between 1800 and 1814 came from families which had enjoyed noble status under the old regime.

In spite of, or perhaps even because of this aristocratic flavour, the new system worked. It can safely be said that France had never been better governed, if quality is assessed in terms of effective obedience to orders issued by the centre. Almost everyone could be pleased by the dramatic improvement in public order which followed Bonaparte's seizure of power. The Vendée was pacified at long last by a judicious mixture of stick and carrot, the sectarian tit-for-tat killings in the Rhône valley were halted and everywhere banditry was suppressed. The prefects and their subordinates passed the acid test—the ability to enforce conscription—with flying colours, at least during the early years of the regime. Together with the repair of existing roads and the construction of new highways, physical communication enjoyed much-needed and long-overdue improvement. The other great failure of the successive revolutionary regimes—public finance—was also rectified. Building on preparatory work by the Directory and enjoying the benefit of a sustained recovery in the economy, Bonaparte established the Bank of France, stabilized the currency, improved revenue collection and brought the national debt under control. It should be noted, however, that although this certainly represented a significant improvement on the chaos of the 1790s, it was not good enough, for France was falling behind her arch-enemy in the struggle for war-sustaining revenue. At the height of the Napoleonic wars, Great Britain was collecting three times as much money per head of population.

In restoring order to a revolution-torn country and continent, Bonaparte was at his most statesman-like in his search for reconciliation. Proscribing only irreconcilable royalists and Jacobins, he encouraged the rest of the émigrés to return home and rally to the regime. This policy was an undoubted success, as the appearance of aristocratic names among the list of prefects shows. His greatest eirenic triumph, however, was making peace with the Catholic Church by the Concordat of 1802. At a stroke, he took from the counter-revolutionaries their most potent appeal. It was some measure of the catastrophe which had befallen the papacy since 1789 that Pius VII was prepared to accept the terms offered, including recognition of the expropriation of ecclesiastical property and the subordination of Church to state. Although Bonaparte's vaulting ambition eventually led to a new schism, in the short and medium term the Concordat greatly facilitated his hold not only on France but on all Catholic Europe.

His other great positive achievement at home was the promulgation of six legal codes, the Civil Code of 1804 being both the first and the most important. It was renamed the Napoleonic Code in 1806, a not unreasonable personification as it was he who took the chair at most of the sessions of the drafting committee and who gave the final document his own unmistakable stamp. As it was imported to many other parts of Europe, it became the most important single legal document of modern European history. It has often been criticized on the grounds that Bonaparte's personal conservatism was reflected in the provisions dealing with property, women, the family, and landed inheritance. No doubt these limitations would fall foul of some cosmic court of human rights, but compared with the chaos of the 400-odd legal codes of old regime France, the Napoleonic Code was a model of rationality and equity and was recognized as such by grateful recipients.

The Conquest of Europe

The French revolutionaries had conquered western Europe but had then got stuck. By 1795 it was clear that they had a firm hold on the Low Countries and the left bank of the Rhine but that that was the limit of their power, for every time they crossed into Germany they were thrown back again. It was General Bonaparte who decisively broke out of these 'natural frontiers' and expanded the French Empire into Italy with his victories of 1796–7. The fragility of his conquests was demonstrated in 1799 when a joint Austro-Russian force chased the revolutionary armies back to the French frontiers once more. So in 1799 the First Consul's top priority was the restoration of control of southern Europe. Everyone knew, not least himself, that his *coup d'état* could be legitimated only by military success. So his crushing defeat of the Austrians at Marengo on 14 June 1800 represented 'the baptism of Napoleon's personal power', as one contemporary noted.

Nothing if not dogged, the Austrians fought on, but after another defeat, at Hohenlinden on 3 December 1800, even they had to recognize the war was lost. Now deprived of continental allies, the British were also ready to come to terms. By the treaties of Lunéville (9 February 1801) and Amiens (27 March 1802) ten years of warfare were brought to an end. The settlement left France ruling the west and the south, Russia ruling the east, the British ruling the seas, and the centre of Europe balanced between two lesser powers, Prussia and Austria. This radical redistribution of territory and influence gave France a more dominant role than it had ever known before. It could have become permanent—if Bonaparte had been prepared to accept British and Russian hegemony in their own spheres of influence.

But he could not. The only relationship he ever accepted was that of master–servant.

In the short term, this led to even greater conquests, as he added the centre of Europe to the French portfolio. War resumed with the British within less than a year of Amiens, with the Austrians and Russians in 1805 and with the Prussians in 1806. The result was total defeat at sea, at the battle of Trafalgar on 21 October 1805, but equally total victory on land: over the Austrians at Ulm on 20 October 1805, over the Austrians and Russians at Austerlitz on 2 December 1805, over the Prussians at Jena and Auerstedt on 14 October 1806, and over the Russians at Friedland on 14 June 1807. By the time these conflicts were brought to an end by the treaty of Tilsit on 9 July 1807, Napoleon (as we should call him after his assumption of the imperial title in 1804) had all of continental Europe at his mercy.

This amazing feat, amazing in equal measure for its scale and its speed, was due in part to the errors of his enemies. Coalitions are always difficult to coordinate, but few can have shown such self-defeating mutual mistrust as those formed against Napoleonic France. It was due in part to the assets he inherited from the revolution, most notably a large, well-seasoned and well-trained army which was exceptionally well commanded at all levels. But ultimately it was Napoleon's personal achievement. Every account of his campaigns between 1796 and 1806 makes it clear that he was a true military genius, able to make all the difference between defeat and victory by his will power, his energy, and that priceless gift of insight—what Clausewitz called the *coup d'œil*—which allowed him to out-think the opposition.

When these two hectic years of warfare were over, the map of Europe had been redrawn and recoloured. In the process a great new dynasty had been created. The Netherlands had been changed into a kingdom, ruled by Napoleon's brother Louis. The Bourbons had been ejected from the kingdom of Naples, in favour of another Bonaparte brother, Joseph. In Germany, the Holy Roman Empire had been finally eliminated, its wonderful territorial diversity reduced to a couple of dozen principalities swollen by the addition of the smaller fry. Among the beneficiaries was yet another Bonaparte brother, Jerome, who became the ruler of the newly created kingdom of Westphalia. Another new creation, the grand duchy of Berg, was given to Joachim Murat, married to Napoleon's sister Caroline. Napoleon reserved northern Italy for himself, creating the 'kingdom of Italy' there and installing his stepson, Eugène de Beauharnais, as his viceroy. This proved to be by no means the limit of the Bonapartist dynasty. In 1808 Napoleon promoted his brother Joseph to be king of Spain, transferring

Murat to the vacancy thus created at Naples. In the same year he also gave Tuscany to his sister Élisa and her husband, Prince Bacciochi.

The major victims were the two German powers. The Habsburgs not only lost all their territory in Belgium, Italy, and Germany but also all the influence they had exerted over the Holy Roman Empire in their imperial capacity. The Hohenzollerns of Prussia suffered even more, losing half their territory and being subjected to a crippling burden of reparations. Prussia ceased to be a great power, indeed it was in danger of falling behind its old rival Saxony, for the king of Saxony was awarded the 'grand duchy of Warsaw', carved out of Prussia's share of the second and third partitions of Poland. This new satellite state extended Napoleon's influence to the very frontiers of Russia. It was taken even further by the creation of the 'Continental System', which was both an attempt to seal off the Continent from British goods and to establish French manufacturing and commercial hegemony. When Alexander I of Russia agreed to accept this system at Tilsit in 1807 he also in effect recognized Napoleonic hegemony. The greatest empire in the history of Europe had been created.

Decline and Fall

Napoleon's empire fell as fast as it had risen. Before he had time to finish the Arc de Triomphe, it was the allies who were holding a victory parade on the Champs Elysées. He himself liked to think that he had been the victim of bad luck (the early onset of the Russian winter in 1812, for example) and treachery (the desertion of his marshals in 1814), but with the advantage of hindsight we can see that his problems were more structural in nature. Perhaps the most intractable was demographic imbalance. As we have seen, the population of France had increased by about 30 per cent in the course of the eighteenth century, but this was a rate of growth eclipsed by the other countries of Europe. This relative decline was due less to any deficiency in virility or fecundity than to the simple fact that, by contemporary standards, France had been a densely populated country when the century began, so the population was soon banging its head against the demographic ceiling imposed by inelastic food supplies. By the time the revolutionary-Napoleonic wars began, the demographic dominance which had made Louis XIV so formidable was a thing of the past.

To conquer Europe from a base that was too narrow and shallow involved overexertion. The French were obliged to exert so much pressure on both their own population and that of occupied Europe that the law of diminishing returns soon began to operate. In the short term, the problem

Goya, *The Third of May 1808*. Goya's depiction of the brutal suppression by the French army of the popular rising in Madrid is an unsurpassed visual representation of ordinary Europeans' resistance to Napoleon's imperialism. The guerrilla war which followed made a major contribution to the decline and fall of his empire. The presence of the friar symbolizes the undimmed power of religion in a revolutionary age.

was dealt with by the establishment of the satellite state, an inspired invention which was to have a future as long as it was dishonourable. Wherever the French went in Europe, they found dissidents prepared to collaborate with the invaders to obtain support in dealing with their political enemies. If peace had ever been restored long enough to allow these new regimes to strike roots, this might have proved a permanent solution. In the event, the need to extract ever-increasing amounts or men, *matériel*, and money to feed the French war-machine made them reliant on force for their survival. As soon as the prop of the French army was removed, they collapsed in a heap. The same process of alienation occurred in Napoleon's satellite kingdoms. Even those German princes who were given royal titles and vast amounts of land began to wonder whether the game was worth the candle as the price escalated and their subjects became increasingly restive. The number of troops required by Napoleon from his German satraps rose from 63,000 in 1806 to 119,000 in 1809, finally reaching 190,000 with the invasion of Russia in 1812.

By that time, his empire was crumbling from within, as confidence and support were eroded further by failure in Spain after 1808, growing resistance to conscription, and a severe economic crisis which had begun in 1810. What was worse, Napoleon's enemies were beginning to put their own house in order. They had been prevented from mobilizing their full weight by three main failings: their preoccupation with eastern Europe, their mutual antipathies, and their reluctance to fight fire with fire. During the early stages of the revolutionary wars, the three great powers of eastern Europe were more concerned with Poland than with France. Indeed it is no exaggeration to say that Prussia and Austria went to war in 1792 with one eye on what was happening behind them and with one hand tied behind their backs, since they felt obliged to keep part of their army in the east. Catherine the Great of Russia stayed out of the war altogether, for the good reason that none of her vital interests were involved in the west. It was Napoleon's personal achievement to bring the western and eastern theatres of the war together. He provided a dress rehearsal of the final denouement in 1798 when his expedition to Egypt brought Russia into the war and nearly destroyed revolutionary France. The crucial moment, however, came in the autumn of 1806 after the battles of Jena and Auerstedt. By deciding to pursue the Prussians and their Russian allies, Napoleon also blundered into the morass of east European politics and was never able to extricate himself. In particular, his establishment of a Polish puppet-state ensured Russia's implacable hostility and made a resumption of the war inevitable.

Napoleon also dealt with the second handicap under which his enemies laboured—their mutual distrust. By treating them all so brutally during his glory years of 1805–7, he drummed into their thick skulls the message that they must sink their differences and unite against him. The lesson took some time to penetrate, for in 1809 the Austrians once again had to take the field alone, but eventually it was learnt. The result was the overwhelming victory at the 'Battle of the Nations' at Leipzig in October 1813 and the collapse of Napoleon's empire.

Similarly, it was also he who forced the old regime powers to adopt revolutionary methods to combat revolutionary force. It was not so much that they could not grasp what to do, rather that they could not face the terrible side effects. Certainly the French revolutionaries had constructed a state of colossal power but they appeared to have done so at the cost of killing their king and queen, expropriating their church, abolishing their nobility, instituting a reign of terror, plunging the country into civil war, unleashing galloping inflation, and so on and so forth. By 1808, however, Napoleon was busy rearranging the thrones of Europe. If he could depose the Bourbons in Spain and Naples, why not the Hohenzollerns and Habsburgs? Indeed, it was well known that he had toyed with just such an idea in 1807 and 1809 respectively. As it now seemed to be all or nothing, even radical reforms had to be risked in the search for survival. By 1812–13 it was the allies who were arming their peasants and mobilizing mass armies.

By then, it was also the allies who were using the rhetoric of liberation to mobilize support in Europe. In just twenty years there had occurred an astonishing reversal of roles. When the French revolutionaries went to war in 1792, they did so in the name of universal principles, with the intention of spreading liberty, equality, and fraternity to a suffering humanity. The war aims of the Austrians and Prussians, on the other hand, could not have been more self-seeking. Confronted with the reality of war and especially by the rejection of those they sought to liberate, the revolutionaries quickly moved to 'Revolution in one country' and to put France first. Napoleon then narrowed the focus still further to a single family, the Bonaparte dynasty. Yet even that was not the limit of the contraction, for by 1810 Napoleon found that his siblings were not sufficiently obedient and was clawing back what little independence they enjoyed. His brother Louis, for example, was obliged to abdicate as king of the Netherlands. In short, what had begun as a war for all mankind ended up as a war for just one man. Meanwhile, the allies were moving in the opposite direction towards a war for principle, presenting themselves convincingly as liberators combating Napoleonic tyranny.

In short, the higher Napoleon climbed, the more certain was his eventual fall. Just because his aims were unlimited, he was driven on and on until the weakness of his empire's foundations were exposed. In the event, it was the Russian invasion which pushed the imposing but top-heavy structure over. After Tilsit, Alexander I soon found that enforcing the Continental Blockade was simply incompatible with the economic interests of the Russian nobility, who relied on British markets for the sale of their agricultural produce. As both his father and grandfather had been assassinated in the course of palace revolutions, Alexander was sensibly sensitive to the landowning interests. When he decided in 1810 to suspend the blockade, he also made war inevitable, for by this time Napoleon's megalomania was such that he could brook no contradiction. Contrary to what he claimed, it was not the

The crossing of the Beresina at the end of November, 1812. Of all the terrible episodes suffered by Napoleon's Grand Army on its retreat from Moscow, this was probably the worst. Harassed by Cossacks and pounded by Russian artillery, at least 25,000 men, women, and children were blown apart, drowned, or crushed to death as they tried to cross on the two temporary bridges.

Russian winter which defeated him but distance—when the campaign was formally opened at Dresden in the summer of 1812, Napoleon and his Grand Army were closer to the west coast of Ireland than to Moscow.

It says a great deal for his will power, charisma, and sheer military skill that he lived to fight another day following the Russian disaster, in the course of which he had lost around 380,000 men in dead, prisoners of war, and deserters. It also says a great deal for the efficiency of the administrative system that it went on raising money and conscripting men, albeit in ever-diminishing and inadequate numbers. Their joint efforts could delay but not prevent the end. With the loss of the Spanish campaign, which had cost another 300,000 men, France was invaded on two fronts. After the allies entered Paris at the end of March 1814, Napoleon abdicated on 6 April. Any doubts as to the decisive nature of his defeat were then dispelled by the events of the 'Hundred Days' which began with Napoleon's return from exile on Elba in March 1815 and ended with the battle of Waterloo on

16 June. This time he was sent away for good, to the inhospitable island of St Helena in the south Atlantic, where he whiled away his last miserable years creating a Bonapartist legend. He died in 1821 at the age of 51.

The Legacy

Both to contemporaries and posterity, the revolutionary-Napoleonic era seemed a watershed, the divide between the old regime and the modern world. As we have seen, this view seems entirely plausible. So much happened so quickly in so many parts of Europe that it is natural to conclude that a radical change had occurred. Yet when the dust settled after 1815, many important things had changed very little or not at all. French society before 1789 had been dominated by a mixed élite of *notables*, some of whom were nobles and some of whom were commoners and all of whom were rich landowners. It was the same after 1815. For every aristocrat who had gone to the wall or the guillotine, there were many more who had sailed through unscathed. Catholic prelates had lost their position and civil servants had grown in number and prestige, but it has become something of a cliché to observe that the France of Louis XVIII resembled nothing more than the France of Louis XVI. What was true of France was doubly true of other parts of Europe. Indeed it would make more sense to argue that the revolutionary experience had consolidated and prolonged the landed aristocracy's hold on social and political power.

Nor had the economy been wrenched forwards into the modern world. Twenty-three years of virtually non-stop warfare had distorted but not modernized the French economy. Its most progressive and profitable sector before the revolution—overseas trade—had been destroyed by British command of the seas. Although manufacturing had flourished behind the tariff wall built by the continental blockade, most of the beneficiaries were artificial growths which could not survive the cold blast of British competition when peace returned. In 1789 there had been little to choose between British and French industrialization; by 1815 the gulf had become wide and unbridgeable. Indeed, it is difficult to avoid the conclusion that the revolution put the French economy into shackles from which it proved unable to escape until deep into the twentieth century. In the century after 1815, France fell behind the USA, Germany, Austria-Hungary, and Russia in terms of population; in terms of industrial production, France was outstripped by the USA, Germany, and the United Kingdom, and in terms of real income per capita by Switzerland, the Netherlands, Belgium, Scandinavia, and several parts of the British Empire as well.

What the French Revolution really did change was politics. With amazing speed the revolutionaries created a whole new political culture, quite different in theory and practice from even the most liberal polities of Europe. Underpinned by the principle of national sovereignty, it was an ideology with a short past but a great future, for it wrapped into one explosive package the three great abstractions of modern politics—the state, the nation, and the people. The impact was heightened by the accompanying emphasis on mass participation. Through electoral assemblies, demonstrations, marches, lynchings, clubs, pageants, and civic ceremonies of every kind, the French people announced its arrival as the main actor in the nation's political life. Moreover, the studied universality of the concepts and language employed ensured that the rest of Europe had to sit up and take notice too.

Much to the disappointment of the revolutionaries and the relief of the old regimes, emulation of the revolution outside France rarely went beyond declarations of solidarity by progressive intellectuals. The French Revolution was and remained *sui generis*. It was the war which brought it to the outside world, but it did so with shattering impact. So much force was unleashed by the revolutionary state that the old system of checks and balances which had kept Europe more or less intact for a millennium was destroyed. Both Spain and Portugal were so shaken by the depredations of war that, among other things, their great colonial empires fell apart. Although a version of the old regime was restored in Italy in 1815, the clock could not be turned back. The constant reshuffling of frontiers after 1796 and Napoleon's creation of a 'kingdom of Italy' meant that—*pace* Metternich—the country could no longer be treated as merely 'a geographical expression'. Similarly, the very various experiences of the Belgians ensured that they would not succumb meekly to rule by the Dutch after 1815, breaking away in 1830 to create their own nation state.

But the most momentous change was the destruction of the Holy Roman Empire, Europe's soft centre. Often threatened in the past by enemies within and without, it had always been saved by a self-balancing mechanism which prevented one power achieving sufficient power to destroy it. Aspiring hegemons such as Charles V, Ferdinand II, or Louis XIV had all eventually fallen back exhausted. It was the unprecedented power

François Rude, *Napoleon waking to immortality*. Of all Napoleon's accomplishments, the most durable proved to be the myth which he and his associates had created. As time passed, memories of the devastation he had inflicted on Europe faded. Not only did Bonapartism become one of the most potent ideologies of the nineteenth century; his 'republican monarchy' remains the system best suited for the government of France.

unleashed by the revolutionary armies, together with the ambition and folly of their political masters, which brought its final demise. This was not the sole responsibility of Napoleon, but he must shoulder most of it. His belief that a drastic reduction in the number of political units in German-speaking Europe would make the region easier to control was right in the short term, but in the long run could not have been more wrong. The humiliation and exploitation he heaped on the conquered Germans stored up a terrible revenge. Only partially exacted in 1813–15, its real day was to come in 1870–1. By that time it was also clear that his assault on German traditions had paved the way for the country to become the richest and most powerful in Europe, if not the world. As European history since the age of the French Revolution and Napoleon has been dominated by the 'German question', for this reason alone the period can be seen as forming the natural end to 'early modern Europe'.

FURTHER READING

Note that some works are appropriate to more than one chapter, as their titles indicate. Such works are only mentioned once in this section.

Prologue: Europe and the World Around

J. B. HARLEY and DAVID WOODWARD, *The History of Cartography*, 2 vols., continuing (Chicago, 1987–).

DONALD F. LACH, *Asia in the Making of Europe*, 2 vols. (Chicago, 1965).

FRIEDRICH MEINECKE, *Cosmopolitanism and the National State*, trans. Robert B. Kimber (Princeton, 1970).

ANTHONY PAGDEN, *European Encounters with the New World: From Renaissance to Romanticism* (New Haven, 1993).

ANTHONY PAGDEN, *Lords of All the Worlds: Ideologies of Empire in Spain, Britain and France c.1500–c.1850* (New Haven, 1995).

G. V. SCAMMELL, *The World Encompassed: The First European Maritime Empires, c.800– 1650* (London, 1981).

1. The Conditions of Life for the Masses

WILHELM ABEL, *Agricultural Fluctuations in Europe from the Thirteenth to the Twentieth Centuries*, trans. Olive Ordish (London, 1980).

PIERO CAMPORESI, *Bread of Dreams: Food and Fantasy in Early Modern Europe*, trans. David Gentilcore (Cambridge, 1989).

NATALIE ZEMON DAVIS, *The Return of Martin Guerre* (Harmondsworth, 1983).

MICHAEL FLINN, *The European Demographic System, 1500–1820* (Brighton, 1981).

CHRISTOPHER R. FRIEDRICHS, *The Early Modern City 1450–1750* (London, 1995).

BEATRICE GOTTLIEB, *The Family in the Western World from the Black Death to the Industrial Age* (Oxford, 1993).

ROBERT JÜTTE, *Poverty and Deviance in Early Modern Europe* (Cambridge, 1994).

EMMANUEL LE ROY LADURIE, *The French Peasantry 1450–1660*, trans. Alan Sheridan (Aldershot, 1986).

THOMAS ROBISHEAUX, *Rural Society and the Search for Order in Early Modern Germany* (Cambridge, 1989).

LYNDAL ROPER, *The Holy Household: Women and Morals in Reformation Augsburg* (Oxford, 1989).

PIETER SPIERENBURG, *The Broken Spell: A Cultural and Anthropological History of Pre-Industrial Europe* (London, 1991).

JOHN WALTER and ROGER SCHOFIELD (eds.), *Famine, Disease and the Social Order in Early Modern Society* (Cambridge, 1989).

MERRY E. WIESNER, *Women and Gender in Early Modern Europe* (Cambridge, 1993).

2. The Power of the Word: Renaissance and Reformation

EUAN CAMERON, *The European Reformation* (Oxford, 1991).

J. DELUMEAU, *Catholicism between Luther and Voltaire* (London, 1977).

ELIZABETH EISENSTEIN, *The Printing Revolution in Early Modern Europe* (Cambridge, 1993).

ANTHONY GOODMAN and A. MACKAY (eds.), *The Impact of Humanism on Western Europe* (London, 1990).

D. C. GOODMAN and C. A. RUSSELL (eds.), *The Rise of Scientific Europe 1500–1800* (London, 1991).

ANTHONY GRAFTON, *Defenders of the Text: The Traditions of Scholarship in an Age of Science, 1450–1800* (Cambridge, Mass., 1991).

M. LOWRY, *Nicholas Jenson and the Rise of Venetian Publishing in Renaissance Europe* (Oxford, 1991).

CHARLES G. NAUERT, *Humanism and the Culture of Renaissance Europe* (Cambridge, 1995).

FRANCIS OAKLEY, *The Western Church in the Later Middle Ages* (Ithaca, NY, and London, 1979).

ANDREW PETTEGREE (ed.), *The Early Reformation in Europe* (Cambridge, 1992).

ROY PORTER and MIKULÁŠ TEICH (eds.), *The Renaissance in National Context* (Cambridge, 1992).

ROY PORTER and MIKULÁŠ TEICH (eds.), *The Scientific Revolution in National Context* (Cambridge, 1992).

R. N. SWANSON, *Religion and Devotion in Europe, c.1215–c.1515* (Cambridge, 1995).

3. War, Religion, and the State

R. G. ASCH and A. M. BIRKE (eds.), *Princes, Patronage, and the Nobility: The Court at the Beginning of the Modern Age c.1450–1650* (Oxford, 1991).

R. BONNEY, *The European Dynastic States, 1494–1660* (Oxford, 1991).

A. CALABRIA, *The Cost of Empire: The Finances of the Kingdom of Naples in the Time of Spanish Rule* (Cambridge, 1991).

R. J. W. EVANS, *The Making of the Habsburg Monarchy, 1550–1700* (Oxford,1979).

J. R. HALE, *War and Society in Renaissance Europe* (London,1985).

R. J. KNECHT, *The Rise and Fall of Renaissance France* (London, 1996).

G. OESTREICH, *Neostoicism and the Early Modern State* (Cambridge,1982).

G. PARKER, *The Dutch Revolt* (London, 1977).

M.J. RODRÍGUEZ-SALGADO, *The Changing Face of Empire: Charles V, Philip II and Habsburg Authority, 1551–1559* (Cambridge, 1988).

G. R. STRAUSS, *Law, Resistance and the State: The Opposition to Roman Law in Reformation Germany* (Princeton, 1986).

R. STRONG, *Splendour at Court: Renaissance Spectacle and Illusion* (London, 1973).

I. A. A. THOMPSON, *War and Government in Habsburg Spain* (London, 1976).

P. ZAGORIN, *Rebels and Rulers, 1500–1650*, 2 vols. (Cambridge,1982).

4. Colonies, Enterprises, and Wealth: The Economies of Europe and the Wider World in the Seventeenth Century

FERNAND BRAUDEL, *The Structures of Everyday Life*, trans. Sian Reynolds (London, 1981).

FERNAND BRAUDEL, *The Wheels of Commerce*, trans. Sian Reynolds (London, 1982).

FERNAND BRAUDEL, *The Perspective of the World*, trans. Sian Reynolds (London, 1984).

JORDAN GOODMAN and KATRINA HONEYMAN, *Gainful Pursuits: The Making of Industrial Europe, 1600–1914* (London, 1988).

PIERRE GOUBERT, *The French Peasantry in the Seventeenth Century*, trans. Ian Patterson (Cambridge, 1986).

DAVID B. GRIGG, *Population Growth and Agrarian Change: An Historical Perspective* (Cambridge, 1980).

ROBERT A. HOUSTON, *The Population History of Britain and Ireland, 1500–1750* (Cambridge, 1995).

THOMAS MUNCK, *Seventeenth-Century Europe: State, Conflict and the Social Order in Europe 1598–1700* (London, 1990).

JAN DE VRIES, *The Economy of Europe in an Age of Crisis, 1600–1750* (Cambridge, 1976).

KEITH WRIGHTSON, *English Society, 1580–1680* (London, 1982).

5. Embattled Faiths: Religion and Natural Philosophy in the Seventeenth Century

J. BOSSY, *Christianity in the West, 1400–1700* (Oxford, 1985).

R. BRIGGS, *Communities of Belief: Cultural and Social Tensions in Early Modern France* (Oxford, 1989).

R. BRIGGS, *Witches and Neighbours: The Social and Cultural Context of European Witchcraft* (London, 1996).

J. H. BROOKE, *Science and Religion: Some Historical Perspectives* (Cambridge, 1991).

S. CLARK, *Thinking with Demons: The Idea of Witchcraft in Early Modern Europe* (Oxford, 1997).

P. COLLINSON, *The Religion of Protestants: The Church in English Society 1559–1625* (Oxford, 1982).

I. HACKING, *The Emergence of Probability* (Cambridge, 1975).

J. HENRY, *The Scientific Revolution and the Origins of Modern Science* (London, 1997).

M. HUNTER, *Science and Society in Restoration England* (Cambridge, 1981).

D. C. LINDBERG and R. S. WESTMAN (eds.), *Reappraisals of the Scientific Revolution* (Cambridge, 1990).

M. PRESTWICH (ed.), *International Calvinism, 1541–1715* (Oxford, 1985).

S. SHAPIN and S. SCHAFFER, *Leviathan and the Air Pump: Hobbes, Boyle and the Experimental Life* (Princeton, 1985).

K. V. THOMAS, *Religion and the Decline of Magic* (London, 1971).

B. VICKERS (ed.), *Occult and Scientific Mentalities in the Renaissance* (Cambridge, 1984).

C. WEBSTER, *The Great Instauration: Science, Medicine and Reform 1626–1660* (London, 1975).

R. S. WESTFALL, *Never at Rest: A Biography of Isaac Newton* (Cambridge, 1980).

6. Warfare, Crisis, and Absolutism

R. G. ASCH, *The Thirty Years War: The Holy Roman Empire and Europe, 1618–48* (London, 1997).

W. BEIK, *Absolutism and Society in Seventeenth-Century France: State Power and Provincial Aristocracy in Languedoc* (Cambridge, 1985).

J. M. BLACK, *Convergence or Divergence? Britain and the Continent* (London, 1994).

J. M. BLACK, *European Warfare 1660–1815* (London, 1994).

N. DAVIES, *God's Playground: A History of Poland*, vol. i, *The Origins to 1795* (Oxford, 1981).

P. DUKES, *The Making of Russian Absolutism, 1613–1801* (London, 1982).

J. H. ELLIOTT, *Richelieu and Olivares* (Cambridge, 1984).

R. J. W. EVANS, *The Making of the Habsburg Monarchy 1550–1700* (Oxford, 1979).

N. HENSHALL, *The Myth of Absolutism: Change and Continuity in Early Modern European Monarchy* (London, 1992).

J. A. LYNN, *Giant of the Grand Siècle: The French Army 1610–1715* (Cambridge, 1997).

M. ROBERTS, *The Swedish Imperial Experience, 1560–1718* (Cambridge, 1979).

S. J. SHAW, *History of the Ottoman Empire and Modern Turkey*, vol. i (Cambridge, 1976).

D. STURDY, *Louis XIV* (Basingstoke, 1998).

7. A Widening Market in Consumer Goods

DEREK H. ALDCROFT and RICHARD RODGER, *Bibliography of European Economic and Social History*, 2nd edn (Manchester, 1993).

JOHN BREWER, *The Sinews of Power: War, Money, and the English State, 1688–1783* (New York, 1989).

JOHN BREWER and ROY PORTER (eds.), *Consumption and the World of Goods* (London, 1993).

ARLETTE FARGE, *Fragile Lives: Violence, Power and Solidarity in Eighteenth-Century Paris*, trans. Carol Shelton (Cambridge, 1993).

GAY L. GULLICKSON, *Spinners and Weavers of Auffay: Rural Industry and the Sexual Division of Labour in a French Village, 1750–1850* (Cambridge, 1986).

BRIDGET HILL, *Women, Work, and Sexual Politics in Eighteenth-Century England* (Oxford, 1989).

MASSIMO LIVI BACCI, *Population and Nutrition: An Essay on European Demographic History*, trans. Tania Croft-Murray (Cambridge, 1991).

JOEL MOKYR, *The Lever of Riches: Technological Creativity and Economic Progress* (New York, 1990).

DANIEL ROCHE, *The Culture of Clothing: Dress and Fashion in the 'ancien régime'*, trans. Jean Birrell (Cambridge, 1994).

JAN DE VRIES, *European Urbanization, 1500–1800* (Cambridge, Mass., 1984).

JAN DE VRIES, 'The Industrial Revolution and the Industrious Revolution', in *Journal of Economic History* 54 (1994), 249–70.

CHARLES WILSON and GEOFFREY PARKER (eds.), *An Introduction to the Sources of European Economic History, 1500–1800* (Ithaca, NY, 1977).

8. The Enlightenment

K. M. BAKER (ed.), *The Political Culture of the Ancien Régime* (Oxford, 1987).

C. L. BECKER, *The Heavenly City of the Eighteenth-Century Philosophers* (New Haven, 1959).

E. CASSIRER, *The Philosophy of the Enlightenment* (Princeton, 1979).

W. DOYLE, *The Old European Order 1660–1800*, 2nd edn (Oxford, 1992).

P. GAY, *The Enlightenment: An Interpretation*, 2 vols. (New York, 1966-9).

D. GORDON, *Citizens without Sovereignty* (Princeton, 1994).

R. L. MEEK, *Social Science and the Ignoble Savage* (Cambridge, 1976).

D. MORNET, *Les Origines intellectuelle de la révolution française* (Paris, 1967).

R. MORTIER, *Le Coeur et la raison* (Oxford, 1990).

H. C. PAYNE, *The Philosophes and the People* (New Haven, 1976).

ROY PORTER and MIKULÁŠ TEICH (eds.), *The Enlightenment in National Context* (Cambridge, 1981).

F. VENTURI, *The End of the Old Regime in Europe* (Princeton, 1989).

9. Europe Turns East: Political Developments in the Eighteenth Century

M. S. ANDERSON, *Europe in the Eighteenth Century 1713–1783*, 3rd edn (London, 1987).

M. S. ANDERSON, *Peter the Great*, 2nd edn (London, 1995).

T. C. W. BLANNING, *Joseph II* (London, 1994).

JOHN HARDMAN, *Louis XVI* (London, 1993).

R. H. HATTON, *Charles XII of Sweden* (London, 1968).

WALTER HUBATSCH, *Frederick the Great: Absolutism and Administration* (London, 1975).

PAUL LANGFORD, *A Polite and Commercial People: England, 1727–1783* (Oxford, 1989).

J. T. LUTOWSKI, *Liberty's Folly: The Polish-Lithuanian Commonwealth in the Eighteenth Century* (London, 1991).

JOHN LYNCH, *Bourbon Spain, 1700–1808* (Oxford, 1989).

DEREK MCKAY and H. M. SCOTT, *The Rise of the Great Powers 1648–1815* (London, 1983).

ISABEL DE MADARIAGA, *Catherine the Great: A Short History* (New Haven, 1990).

KENNETH MAXWELL, *Pombal: Paradox of the Enlightenment* (Cambridge, 1995).

H. M. SCOTT (ed.), *Enlightened Absolutism: Reform and Reformers in Later Eighteenth-Century Europe* (London, 1990).

H. M. SCOTT (ed.), *The European Nobilities in the Seventeenth and Eighteenth Centuries*, 2 vols. (London, 1995).

DENNIS E. SHOWALTER, *The Wars of Frederick the Great* (London, 1995).

GEOFFREY SYMCOX, *Victor Amedeus II: Absolutism in the Savoyard State, 1675–1730* (London, 1983).

Franz A. J. Szabo, *Kaunitz and Enlightened Absolutism 1753–1780* (Cambridge, 1994).

Epilogue: The Old Order Transformed 1789-1815

T. C. W. Blanning, *The French Revolutionary Wars 1787–1802* (London, 1996).

T. C. W. Blanning (ed.), *The Rise and Fall of the French Revolution* (Chicago, 1996).

T. C. W. Blanning, *The French Revolution: Class War or Culture Clash?* (London, 1997).

M. R. Broers, *Europe under Napoleon 1799–1815* (London, 1996).

William Doyle, *The Oxford History of the French Revolution* (Oxford, 1989).

Charles J. Esdaile, *The Wars of Napoleon* (London, 1995).

Geoffrey Ellis, *The Napoleonic Empire* (London, 1991).

Colin Lucas (ed.), *Rewriting the French Revolution* (Oxford, 1991).

Simon Schama, *Citizens: A Chronicle of the French Revolution* (London, 1989).

Paul Schroeder, *The Transformation of European Politics, 1763–1848* (Oxford, 1994).

Jean Tulard, *Napoleon: The Myth of the Saviour* (London, 1984).

INDEX

decoration, household 153, 245
deism 270–4, 285, 289
Delft 261
Delmenhorst 325
demesne states 114
democracy 285–6, 288
demography *see* population
Denmark 36, 80, 93, 102–3, 111, 114, 163, 211,
    215, 221, 229, 304, 313, 324–5, 335
Desargues 201
Descartes, René 194–7, 267
design, argument from 274
Dessau, battle of 211
Detwang 34
Devil, beliefs about 187–9
Devolution, War of 222–3
d'Holbach, Paul, baron 270, 273–4, 281, 286
diaries, spiritual 182, 187
Diderot 19, 21, 274, 279, 286, 288, 291–2
diet:
    peasant 53–4, 243
    social differentiation 234
Diggers 181
Dioscorides 77
Directory, French Revolutionary 359, 361, 363
discipline, religious 100, 174–5, 182
disease 40, 112, 120, 142, 199
    explanations for 234
    see also plague
Dissenters, English 181
Dithmarschen 103
divination xx
Donatus, Aelius 68
Dordrecht *see* Dort
Dorp, Maarten 74
Dort, Synod of 180–1
Dover, Secret Treaty of 222
dowries 38, 57
dragonnades 178
drainage *see* land reclamation
Drake, Francis 130
Dresden 370
Dublin 152, 324
Dunes, battle of the 217
Dunkirk 217–18
Dürer, Albrecht 33
Dutch language 165
Dutch Reformed Church 180–1
Dutch Republic
    colonies 207–8
    Descartes in 195
    economic policies 157–60, 169–70,
    international influence xxx, 304
    manufacturing in 246
    political structures 130, 208, 345, 372
    privateers 138
    religious policies 176
    social and economic conditions 49–50, 237,

247, 260–1, 371
    state funding 114, 204, 307
    warfare 132–3, 178, 210–11, 222–4, 303–4,
        348, 356, 360
    see also Holland; Low Countries; Netherlands
Dutch revolt *see* Netherlands, Revolt of the
Dutch War (1672–5) 222
    see also Dutch Republic; Low Countries;
        Netherlands
dykes 271
dysentery 40, 234

East, trade with 138, 170, 208
Easter customs 84
East India Company, Dutch 165
East India Company, English 161
East Indies 138, 165, 239
Eck, Johann 127
economics 296
economy 31–62 *passim*, 137–70 *passim*,
    developed xvii–xviii
    Enlightenment and 276–80
    expansion of xxi–xxii
    state management of 120, 277
    traditional xx
Edict of Restitution 177
Edinburgh 143, 156, 161, 324
education 291
    control of 126, 172, 255, 282, 288, 335–6
    theories of 72, 92, 101, 292–4
Edward VI, king of England 103, 113
Egypt 105, 282, 360, 361, 368
Elam 27
Elba 370
Elbe 46–7, 140, 154, 169, 215, 333
Elizabeth I, queen of England 106, 111, 116,
    119, 126
Elizabeth, queen of Bohemia 133
émigrés 351–3, 363
Empire, French 362–71
employment *see* work
enclaves 325
enclosure 51, 145
Encyclopédie 21, 288, 290
energy, sources of 147
England 102–3, 106, 124, 130, 137, 218–19,
    222–4
    agriculture xxi, 36–7, 51–3, 144–5, 242, 250
    Arminianism in 181
    Church of 93, 126, 181
    colonies 157, 170
    economy 49–50, 144, 151, 237, 261
    Exchequer 151
    exports 138, 144, 168
    government xxvi, 282, 329
    industrialization in 246–7
    inheritance customs 34–5
    interest rates 150

Moses 288
movable type *see* printing
Mozambique 207
Mozart, W. A. 273
Mühlberg, battle of 125
Muller, Adam 25
Müller, Heinrich 53
Munich 213
Münster:
  city of 104–5, 127
  Treaty of 215
Münster, Sebastian 18, 20–1
Murat, Joachim 365–6
Muratori, Ludovico Antonio 337
Murray, Sir Robert 161
Muscovy 103, 114–15, 131
  see also Russia
musket xxviii, 109, 207, 307
Muslims *see* Islam, Ottoman Empire
Mustafa I, Ottoman Sultan 105
mutual societies 258
mysticism 185

nails 248–50
Namur 143, 221
Nantes 25, 148, 167
  Edict of, and its Revocation 128–9, 178–9,
    184, 221
Naples 96, 107, 110, 112, 114, 123, 215, 225, 361,
    365–6, 369
Napoleon xxviii, 10, 14, 27, 255, 294, 303,
    365–71, 372–4
  see also Bonaparte
Napoleonic Code 363–4
Napoleonic Wars 23, 296, 364–71
Narva, battle of 229, 311
Naseby, battle of 218
Nassau, Maurice of 130
National Assembly, French 347–9, 351–3
National Convention, French 294, 356, 359
National Guard, French 347
nationalism 288, 299, 361, 372
Nations, Battle of the 368
nation-states 137
  see also under individual countries
natural philosophy 75–81, 171–4, 191–205 *passim*
  see also science
nature, attitudes to 265–7, 270–1, 273–5, 277–8,
    281, 289, 297
Navarre 103
navies 111–12, 206, 307
Navigation Acts, English 157
navigation techniques 198, 203
Necker, Jacques 279
Neerwinden, battle of 356
Neoplatonist philosophy 70, 73, 78, 80, 172
Netherlands xxi, xxvii, 92–3, 95–6, 103, 105,

106, 110, 112, 120, 144–5, 150–1, 165, 169,
    291–2, 371
  Austrian 294, 303, 324, 345
  kingdom of 365, 369
  Revolt of the 49, 95–6, 129–30, 158, 178, 219
  Spanish 210, 215, 223–4, 225, 303
  see also Dutch Republic
Neumann, Balthasar 19
New Amsterdam 208
Newcastle upon Tyne 154
New England 164
Newfoundland 225
'New Palace', Potsdam 318–20
news, gathering of 152
newspapers 258, 291
Newton, Isaac xxiv, 192–3, 197–200, 203, 205,
    267–8, 274, 279
New World *see* Americas
New York 208
Niemen 314
Nietzsche, F. 27–8
Nijmegen, Treaty of 223–4
Niklashausen 43
Nile, battle of the 360
nitrogen-fixing crops 242
Noah 2
Noailles, vicomte de 348
nobility 115–17, 120–3, 131, 161, 220, 280, 299,
    313, 330–3, 335, 371
  Prussian *see* Junkers
Nogari, Giuseppe 248–9
Nordic countries *see* Scandinavia
Nördlingen, battle of 214
Norfolk system 242
Normandy 35, 103, 128
Norris, Sir John 112
North Sea 156
Northampton 153
Northern War, Great (1700–21) 206, 228–9,
    304–5, 306, 311, 314
Norway 48, 102, 235, 325
Nova Scotia 225
Novalis 25
novel, the modern 260
Novgorod 115
nunneries 335
Nuremberg 55–7, 59, 61, 65, 93, 103, 167
Nystad, Peace of 229, 305

observatories 198
'occult philosophy' 173–4
Ochakov crisis 13–14
Oder 215
Odessa 339
Okeley 160
Okhotsk 207
Oldenburg 325
Olivares, count-duke of 177, 214